RANMA 1/2

VOL. 28
Action Edition

Story and Art by
RUMIKO TAKAHASHI

English Adaptation/Gerard Jones
Translation/ Kaori Inoue
Touch-Up Art & Lettering/Bill Schuch
Cover and Interior Design & Graphics/Yuki Ameda
Editor/Avery Gotoh
Supervising Editor/Michelle Pangilinan

Managing Editor/Annette Roman
Director of Production/Noboru Watanabe
Editorial Director/Alvin Lu
Sr. Dir. of Licensing & Acquisitions/Rika Inouye
VP of Sales & Marketing/Liza Coppola
Executive Vice President/Hyoe Narita
Publisher/Seiji Horibuchi

For the purposes of publication in English, the artwork in this publication is printed in reverse from the original Japanese version.

Printed in Canada.

Published by VIZ, LLC
P.O. Box 77010
San Francisco, CA 94107

Action Edition
10 9 8 7 6 5 4 3 2 1
First Printing, October 2004

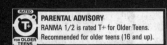

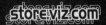

Ranma ½

VOL. 28 — Action Edition

STORY & ART BY

RUMIKO TAKAHASHI

STORY THUS FAR

The Tendos are an average, run-of-the-mill Japanese family—on the surface, that is. Soun Tendo is the owner and proprietor of the Tendo Dojo, where "Anything-Goes Martial Arts" is practiced. Like the name says, anything goes, and usually does.

When Soun's old friend Genma Saotome comes to visit, Soun's three lovely young daughters—Akane, Nabiki, and Kasumi—are told that it's time for one of them to become the fiancée of Genma's teenaged son, as per an agreement made between the two fathers years ago. Youngest daughter Akane—who says she hates boys—is quickly nominated for bridal duty by her sisters.

Unfortunately, Ranma and his father have suffered a strange accident. While training in China, both plunged into one of many "cursed" springs at the legendary martial arts training ground of Jusenkyo. These springs transform the unlucky dunkee into whoever—or whatever—drowned there hundreds of years ago.

From then on, a splash of cold water turns Ranma's father into a giant panda, and Ranma becomes a beautiful, busty young woman. Hot water reverses the effect... but only until next time. As it turns out, Ranma and Genma aren't the only ones who have taken the Jusenkyo plunge—and it isn't long before they meet several other members of the Jusenkyo "cursed."

Although their parents are still determined to see Ranma and Akane marry and carry on the training hall, Ranma seems to have a strange talent for accumulating surplus fiancées... and Akane has a few stubbornly determined suitors of her own. Will the two ever work out their differences, get rid of all these "extra" people, or will they just call the whole thing off? What's a half-boy, half-girl (not to mention all-girl, *angry* girl) to do...?

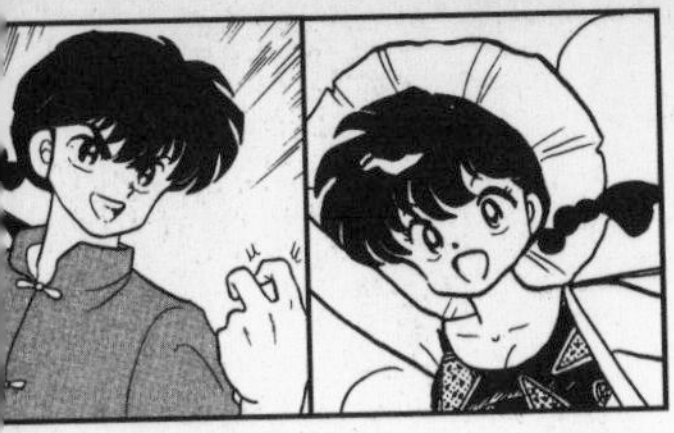

RYOGA HIBIKI
Melancholy martial artist with no sense of direction, a hopeless crush on Akane, and a stubborn grudge against Ranma. Changes into a small, black pig Akane's named "P-chan."

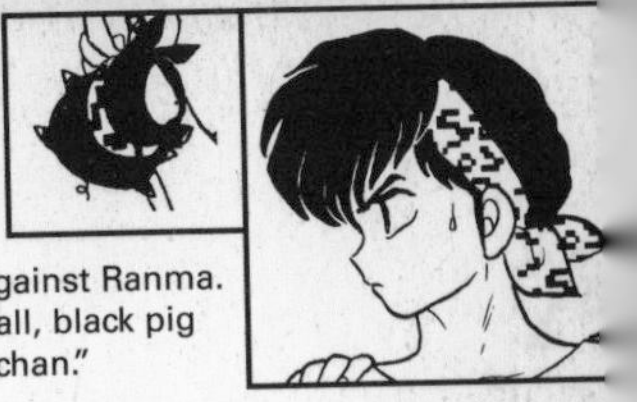

ANMA SAOTOME
artial artist with far too many fiancées and an o that won't let him take defeat. Changes to a girl when splashed with cold water.

SHAMPOO
Chinese-Amazon warrior who's gone from wanting to kill Ranma to wanting to marry him. Changes into a cute kitty-cat when splashed.

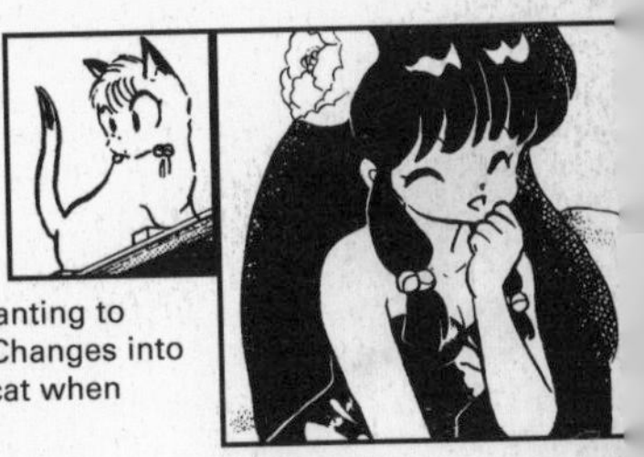

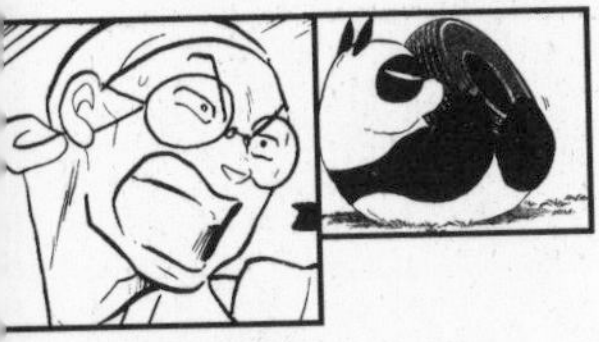

ENMA SAOTOME
anma's lazy father, who left his wife and home ears ago with his young son (Ranma) to train in ne martial arts. Changes into a panda.

COLOGNE
Shampoo's great-grandmother, a martial artist and matchmaker.

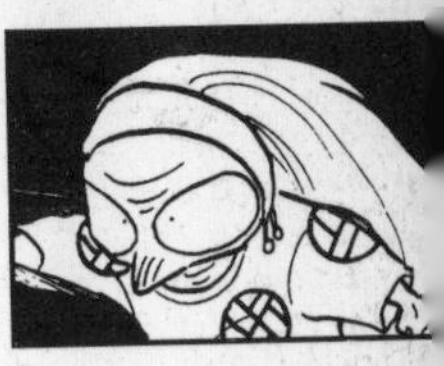

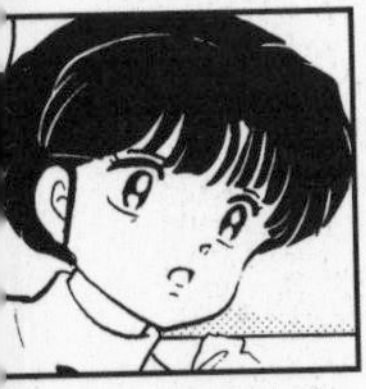

AKANE TENDO
Martial artist, tomboy, and Ranma's reluctant fiancée. Has no clue how much Ryoga likes her, or what relation he might have to her pet black pig, P-chan.

HAPPOSAI
Martial arts master who trained both Genma and Soun. Also a world-class pervert.

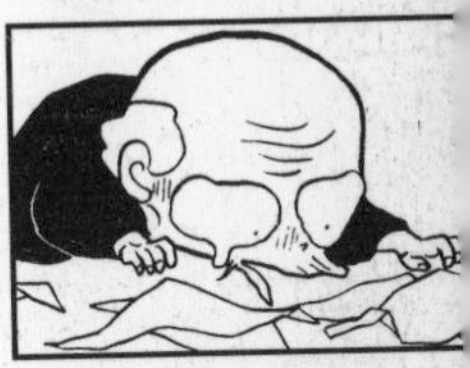

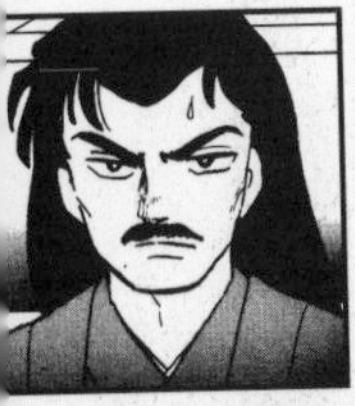

SOUN TENDO
Head of the Tendo household and owner of the Tendo Dojo.

TATEWAKI KUNO
Blustering upperclassman with a love of the ancient Japanese arts, Akane Tendo, and the mysterious "pig-tailed girl," who he has no idea is really girl-type Ranma.

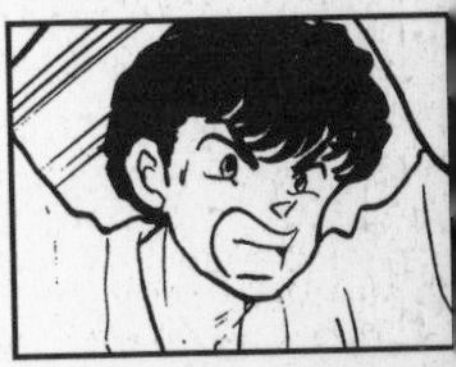

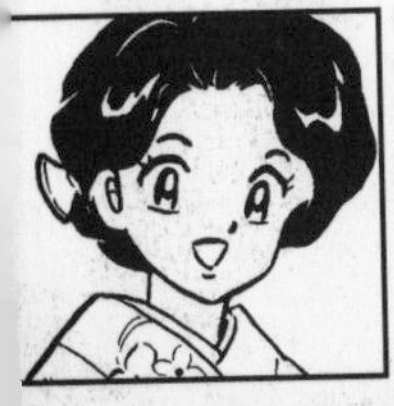

NODOKA SAOTOME
Ranma's mother and Genma's wife...only, she doesn't know Ranma is sometimes a girl, and her husband sometimes a panda. Has previously vowed to assist the *seppuku* of them both should Ranma turn out anything less than "manly."

AKARI UNRYÛ
Breeder of championship sumo-wrestling pigs and (possible?) new love interest for Ryoga.

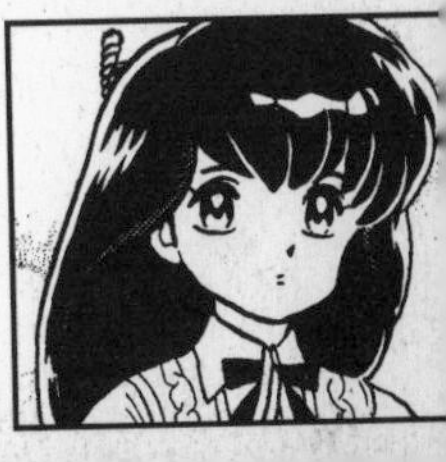

CONTENTS

PART 1

SPRING COMES TO RYOGA

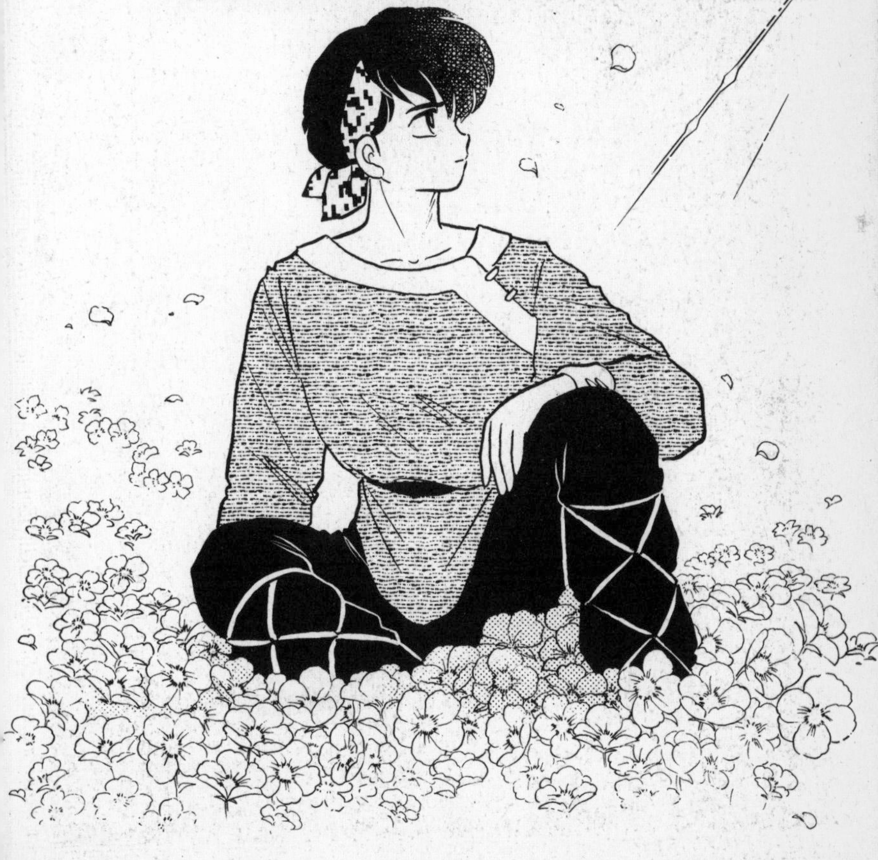

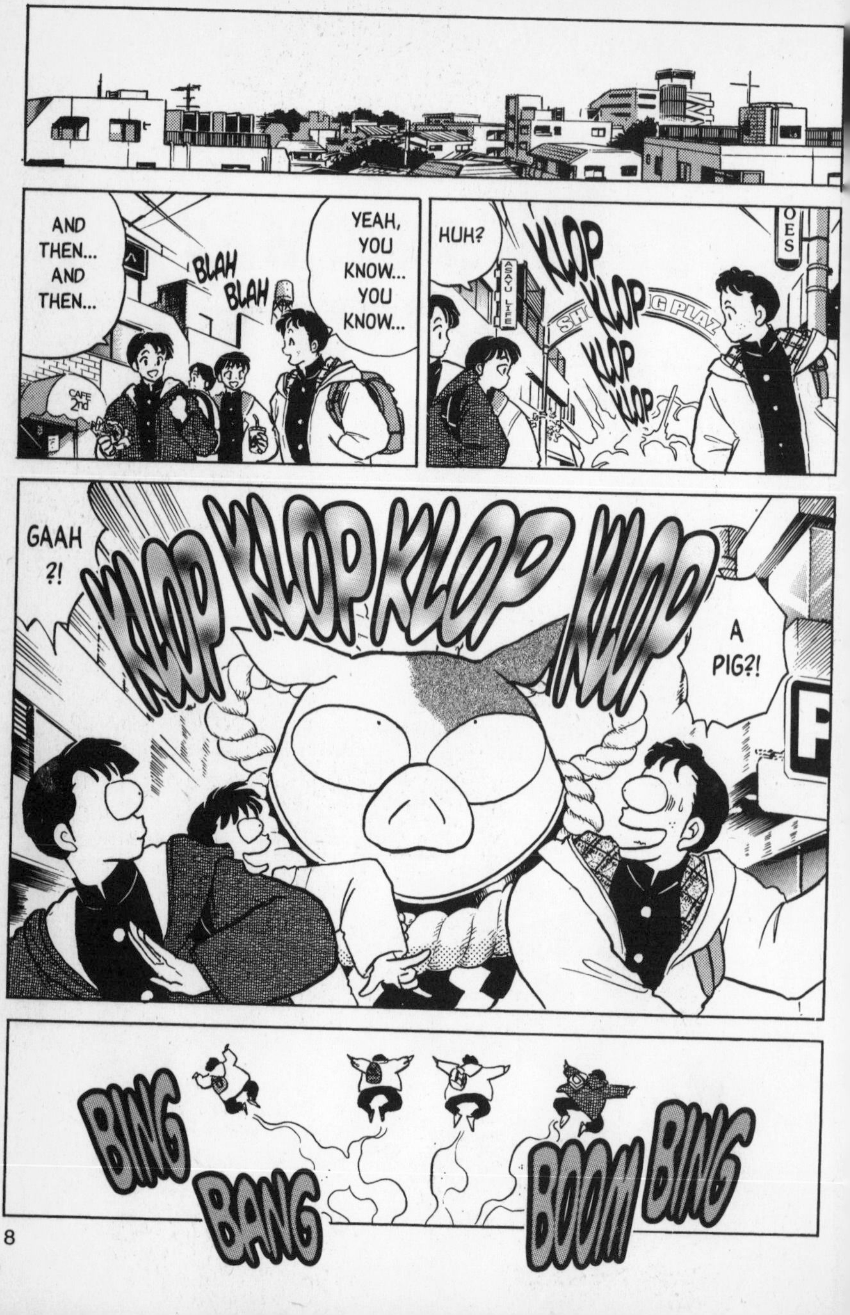
AND THEN... AND THEN... AND THEN...
BLAH BLAH
YEAH, YOU KNOW... YOU KNOW...
CAFE 2nd
HUH?
KLOP KLOP KLOP KLOP
ASAYU LIFE
OES
GAAH ?!
KLOP KLOP KLOP KLOP
A PIG?!
BING BANG BOOM BING

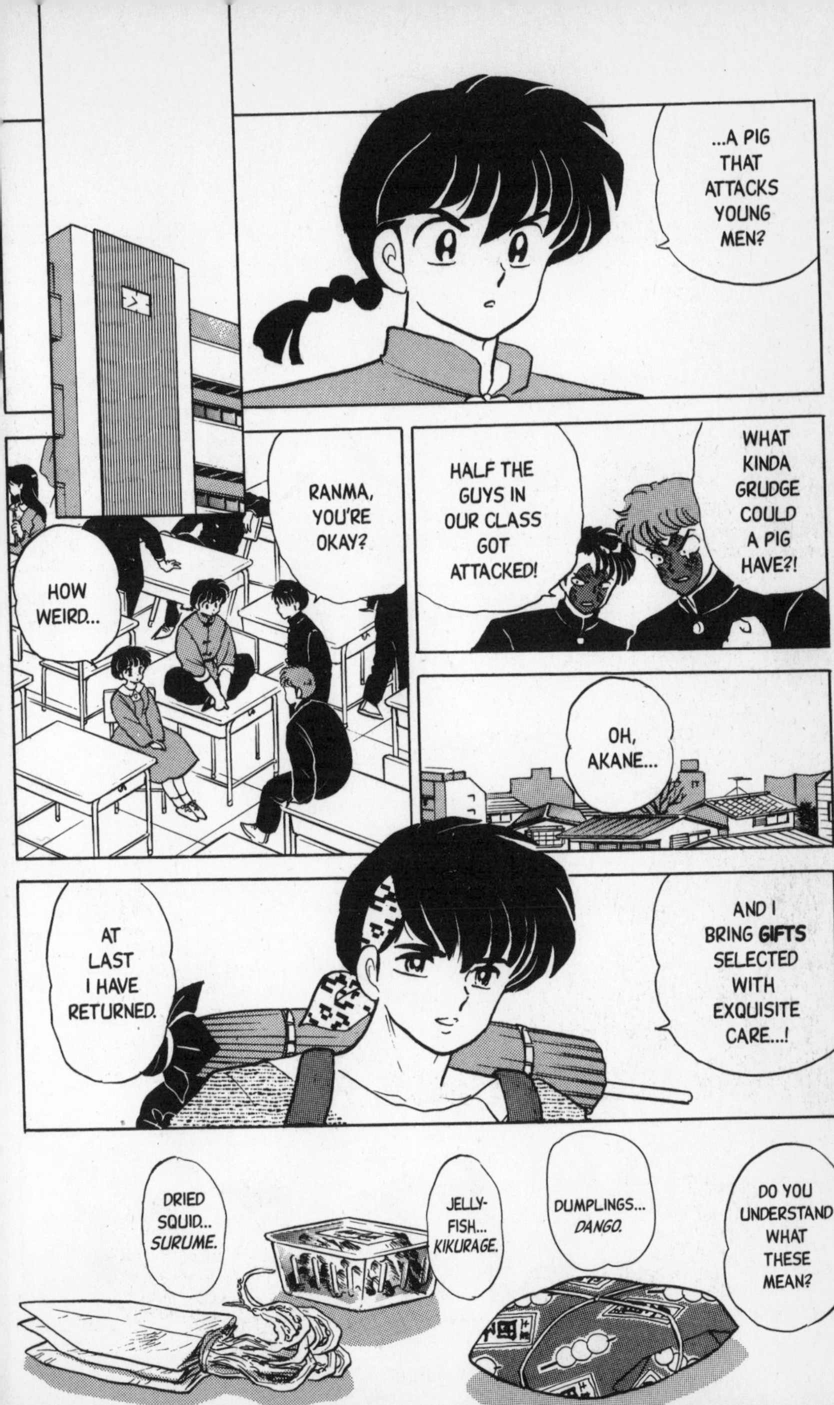

...A PIG THAT ATTACKS YOUNG MEN?
HOW WEIRD...
RANMA, YOU'RE OKAY?
HALF THE GUYS IN OUR CLASS GOT ATTACKED!
WHAT KINDA GRUDGE COULD A PIG HAVE?!
OH, AKANE...
AT LAST I HAVE RETURNED.
AND I BRING **GIFTS** SELECTED WITH EXQUISITE CARE...!
DRIED SQUID... *SURUME.*
JELLY-FISH... *KIKURAGE.*
DUMPLINGS... *DANGO.*
DO YOU UNDERSTAND WHAT THESE MEAN?

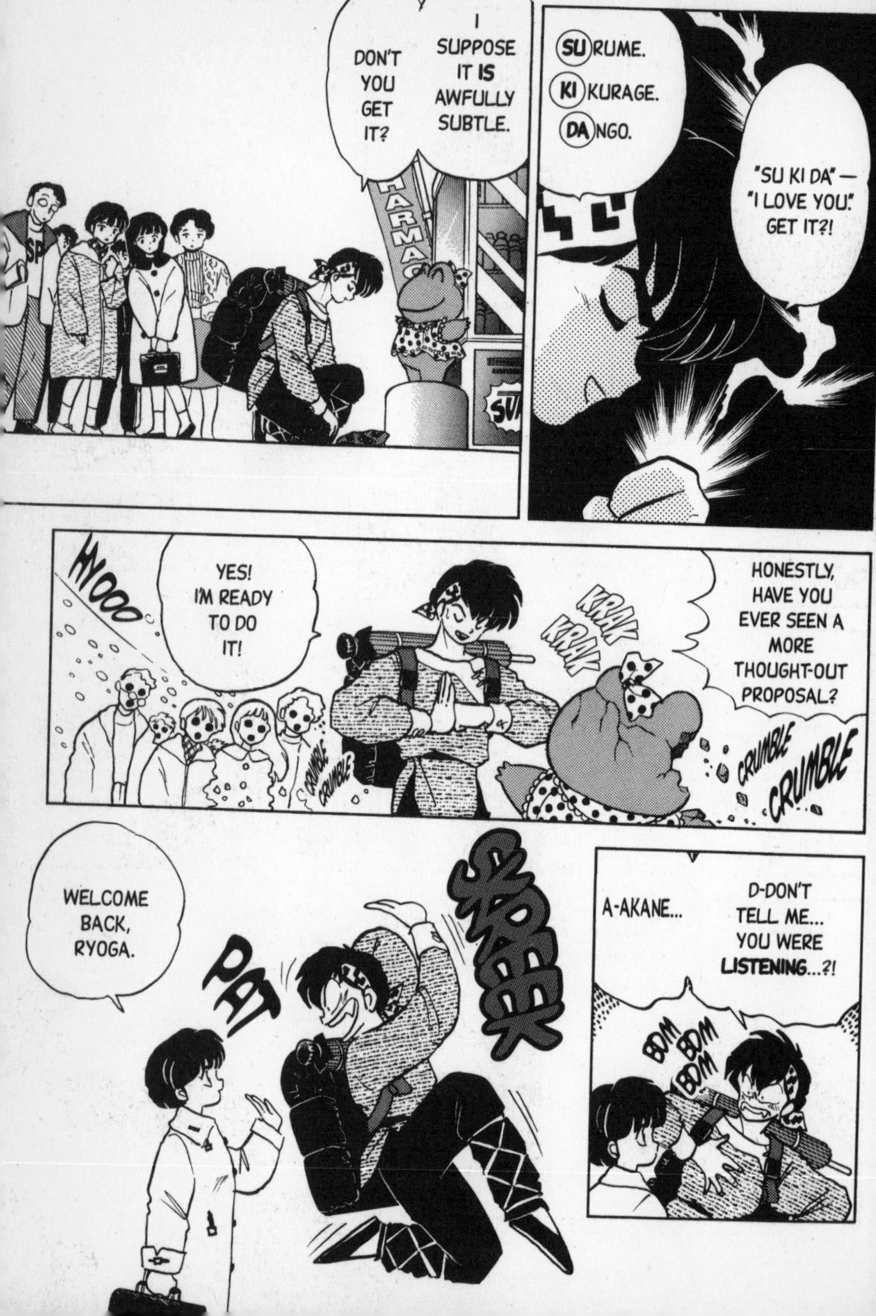
DON'T YOU GET IT?
I SUPPOSE IT IS AWFULLY SUBTLE.
SURUME. KIKURAGE. DANGO.
"SU KI DA"— "I LOVE YOU." GET IT?!
HYOOO
YES! I'M READY TO DO IT!
CRUMBLE CRUMBLE
KRAK KRAK
HONESTLY, HAVE YOU EVER SEEN A MORE THOUGHT-OUT PROPOSAL?
CRUMBLE CRUMBLE
WELCOME BACK, RYOGA.
PAT
SKREEK
A-AKANE...
D-DON'T TELL ME... YOU WERE LISTENING...?!
BDM BDM BDM

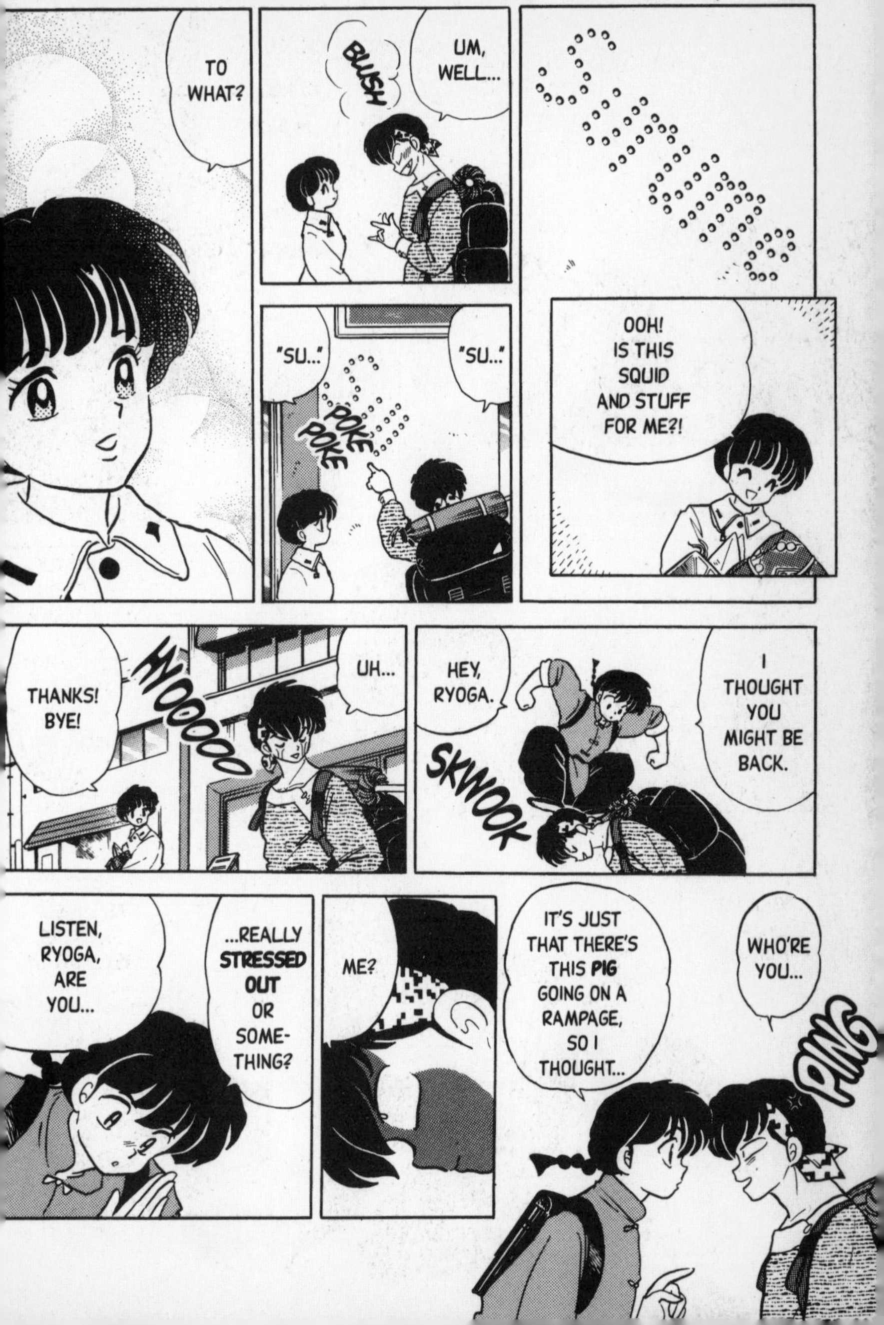
TO WHAT?
BLUSH
UM, WELL...
"SU..."
"SU..."
POKE POKE
OOH! IS THIS SQUID AND STUFF FOR ME?!
THANKS! BYE!
HYOOOOOO
UH...
HEY, RYOGA.
SKWOOK
I THOUGHT YOU MIGHT BE BACK.
LISTEN, RYOGA, ARE YOU...
...REALLY **STRESSED OUT** OR SOME-THING?
ME?
IT'S JUST THAT THERE'S THIS **PIG** GOING ON A RAMPAGE, SO I THOUGHT...
WHO'RE YOU...
PING

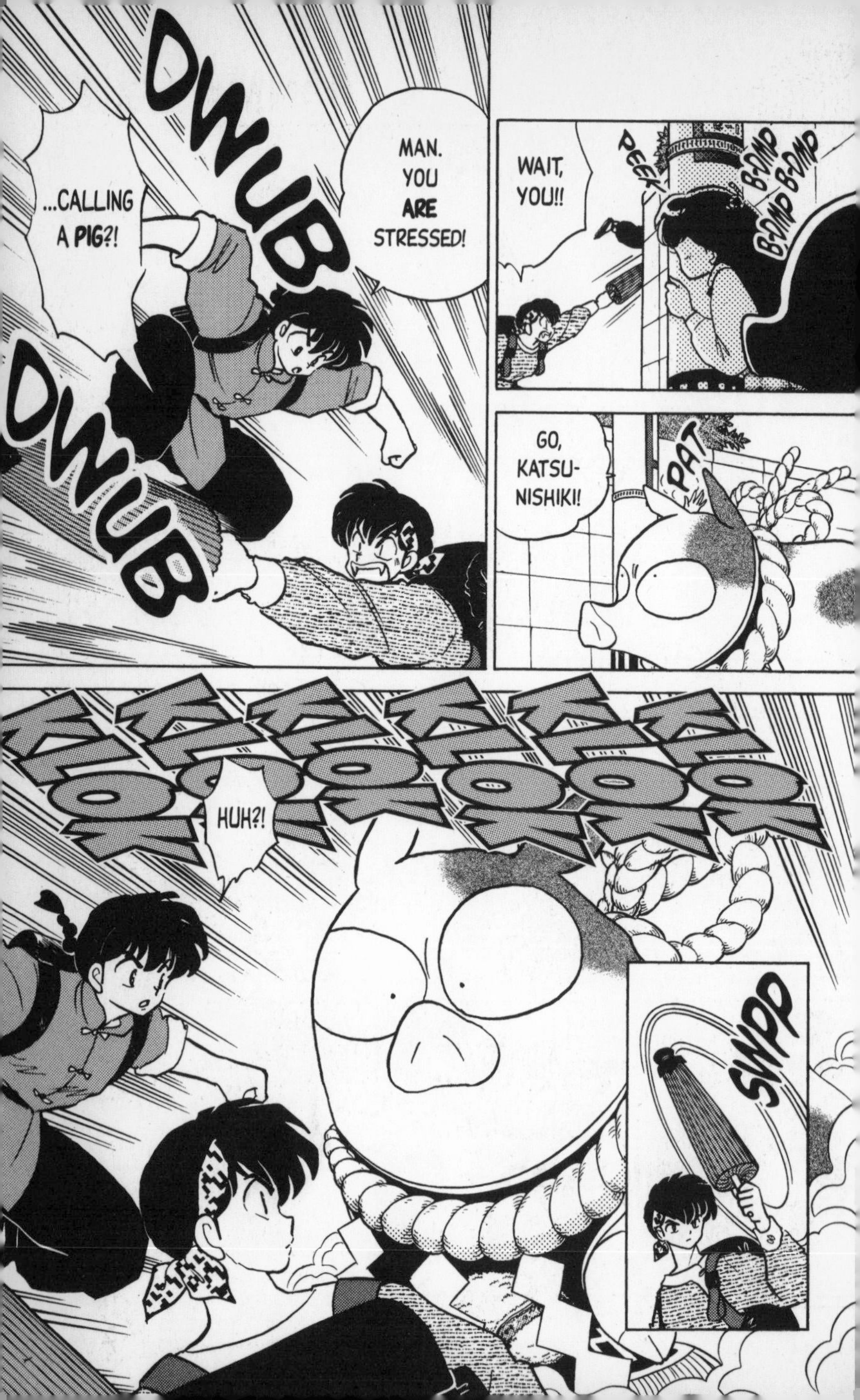
DWUB
...CALLING A PIG?!
MAN. YOU ARE STRESSED!
DWUB
WAIT, YOU!!
PEEK
B-DMP B-DMP B-DMP B-DMP
GO, KATSU-NISHIKI!
PAT
KLOK KLOK KLOK KLOK KLOK KLOK
HUH?!
SWPP

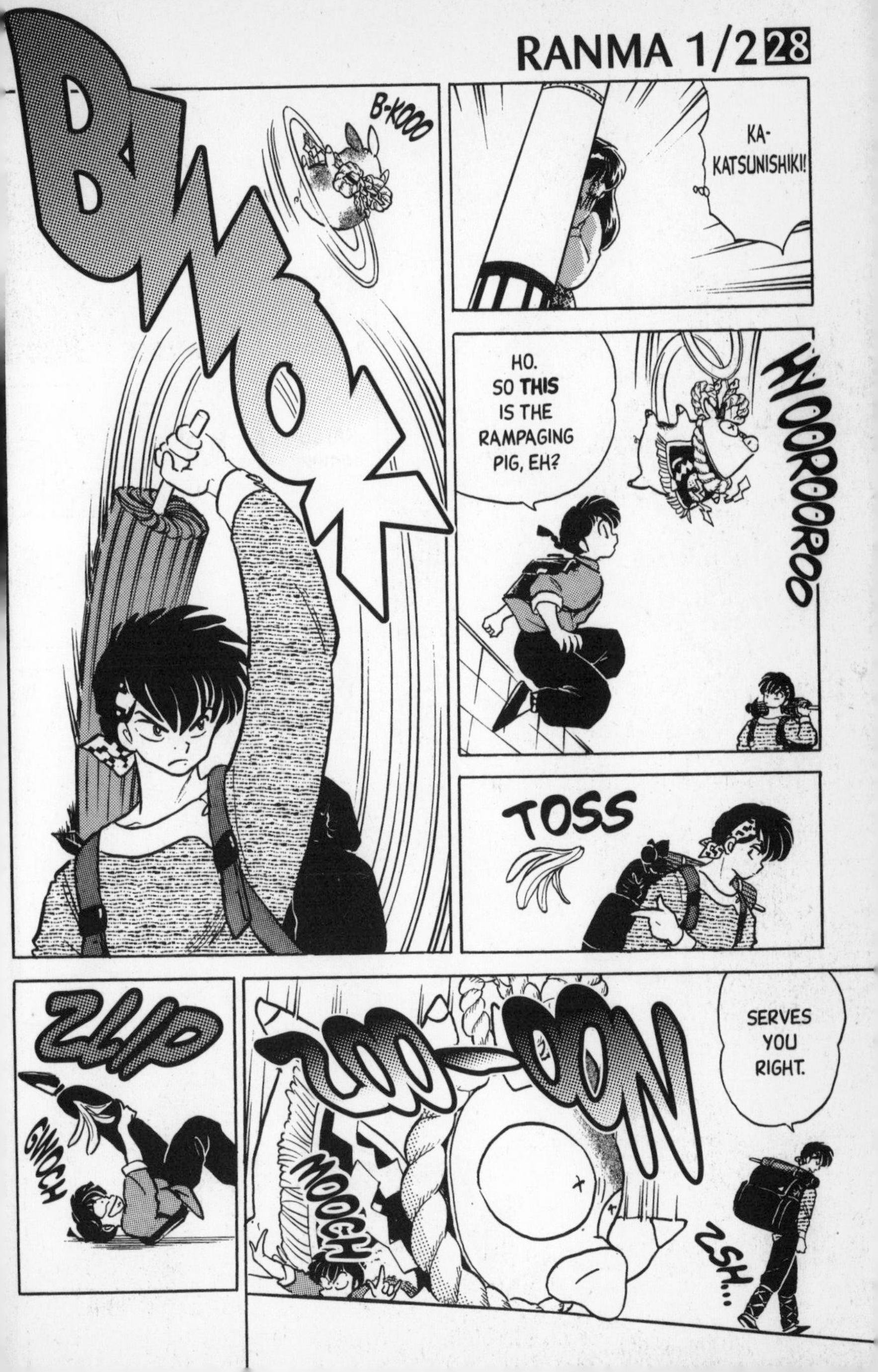
BWOK
B-KOOO
KA-
KATSUNISHIKI!!
HO.
SO **THIS**
IS THE
RAMPAGING
PIG, EH?
HOOROOROOROO
TOSS
ZLIP
GWOCH
ZOO-DON
MOOCH
SERVES
YOU
RIGHT.
ZSH...

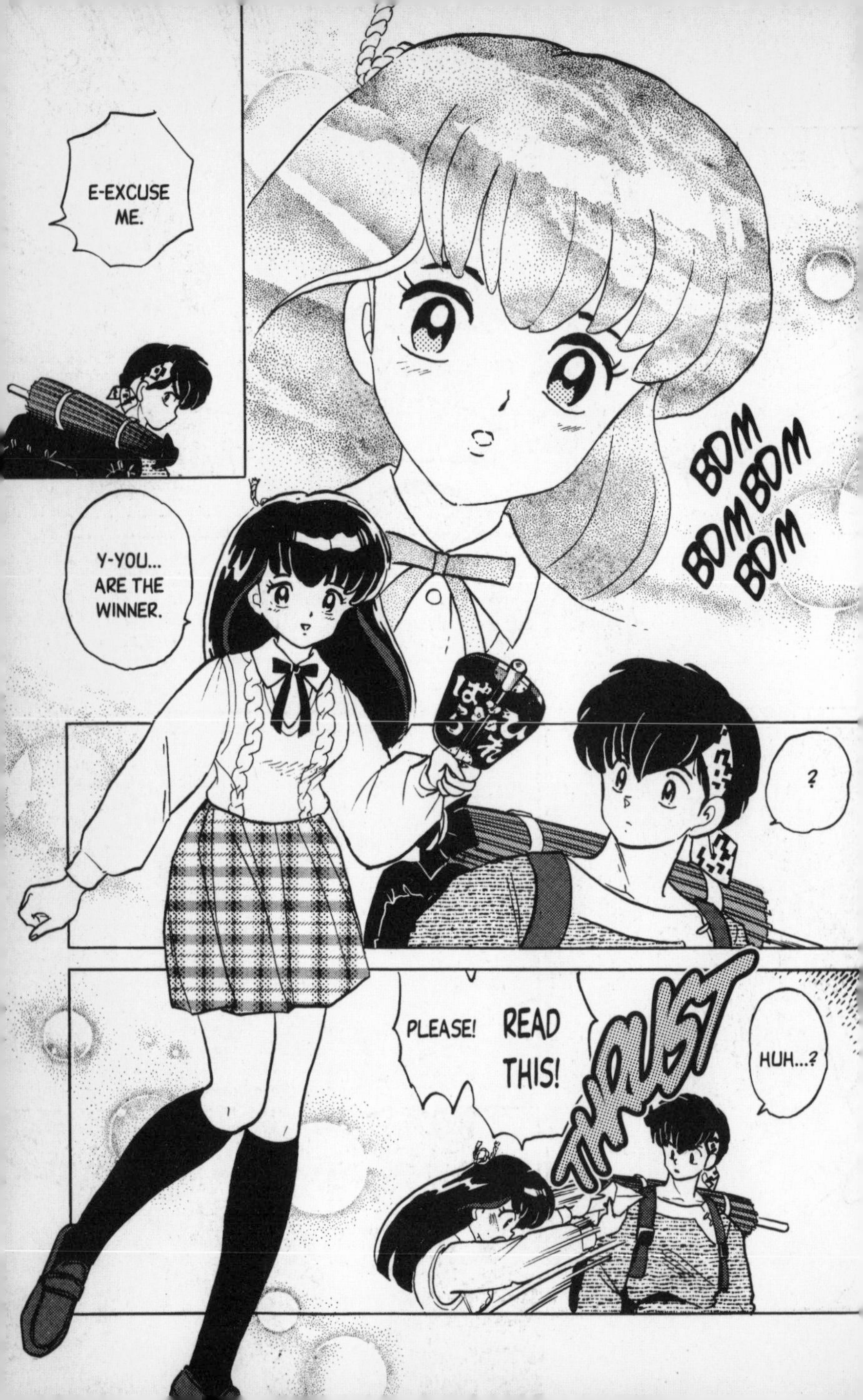
E-EXCUSE ME.
BDM BDM BDM BDM
Y-YOU... ARE THE WINNER.
?
PLEASE!
READ THIS!
THRUST
HUH...?

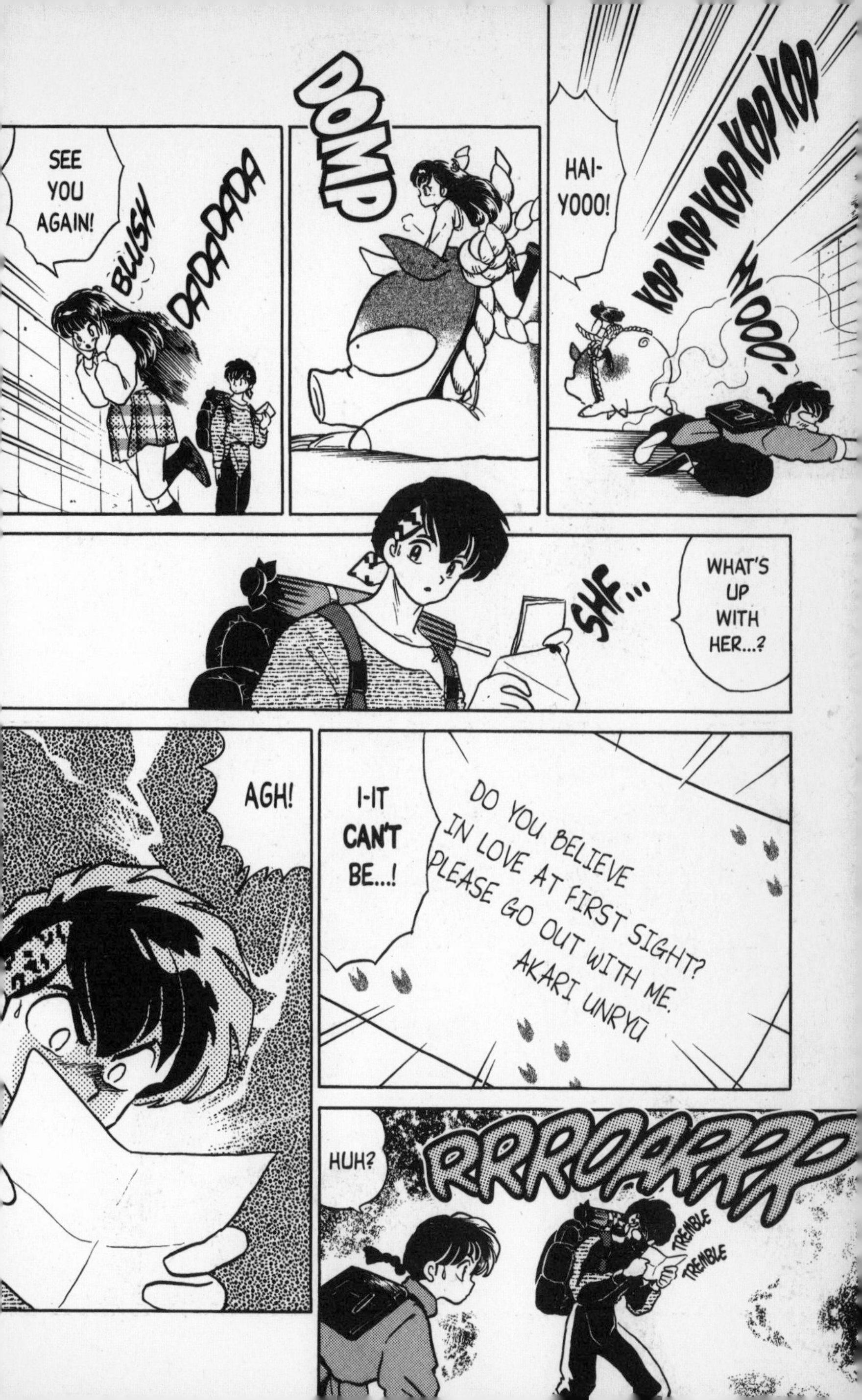
SEE YOU AGAIN!
BLUSH
DADADADA
DOMP
HAI-YOOO!
KOP KOP KOP KOP KOP KOP
MYOOO
SHF...
WHAT'S UP WITH HER...?
AGH!
I-IT CAN'T BE...!
DO YOU BELIEVE IN LOVE AT FIRST SIGHT?
PLEASE GO OUT WITH ME.
AKARI UNRYŪ
HUH?
RRROARRR
TREMBLE
TREMBLE

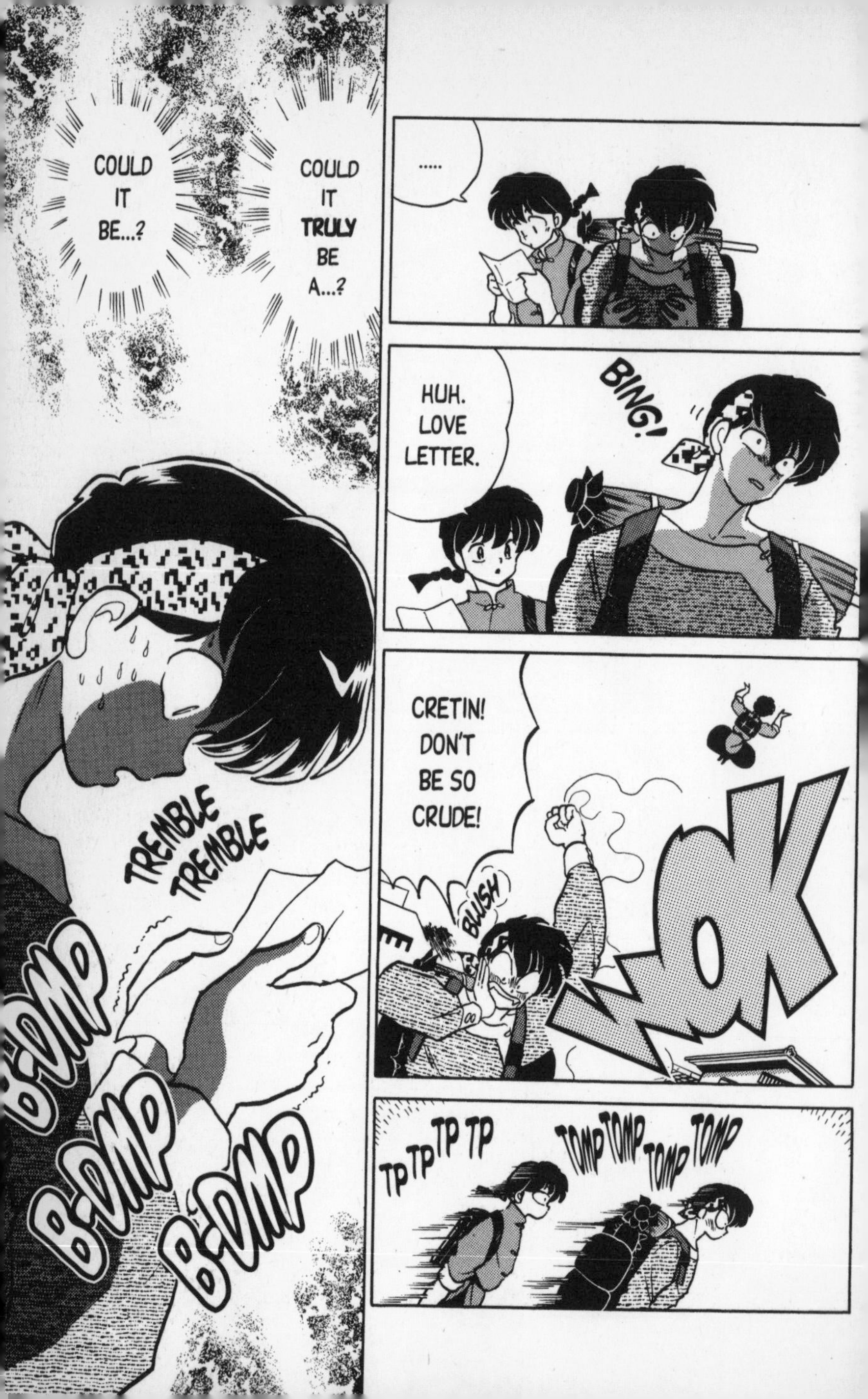
COULD IT BE...?
COULD IT TRULY BE A...?
TREMBLE TREMBLE
B-DMP
B-DMP
B-DMP
.....
HUH. LOVE LETTER.
BING!
CRETIN! DON'T BE SO CRUDE!
BLUSH
WOK
TP TP TP TP
TOMP TOMP TOMP TOMP

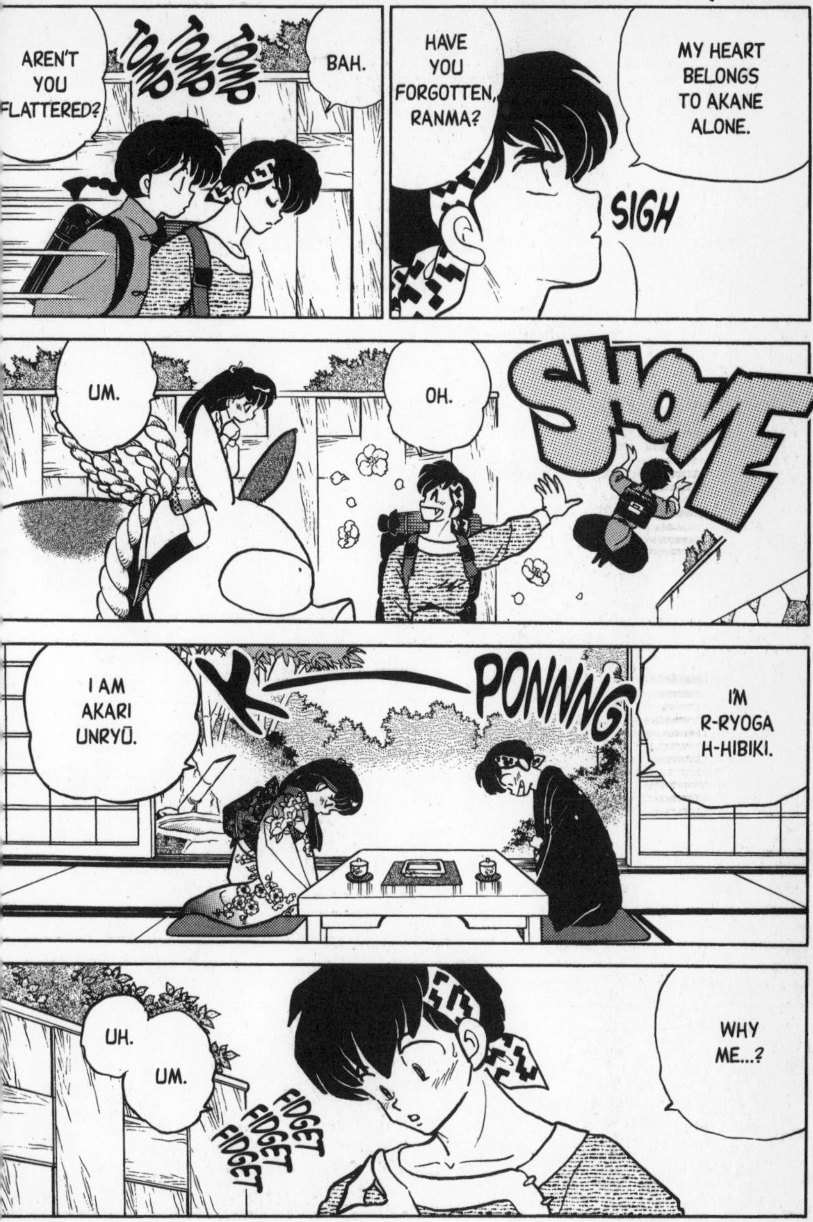
AREN'T YOU FLATTERED?
TOMP TOMP TOMP
BAH.
HAVE YOU FORGOTTEN, RANMA?
MY HEART BELONGS TO AKANE ALONE.
SIGH
UM.
OH.
SHOVE
I AM AKARI UNRYŪ.
K—PONNNG
I'M R-RYOGA H-HIBIKI.
UH.
UM.
FIDGET FIDGET FIDGET
WHY ME...?

FOR GENERATIONS MY FAMILY HAS RAISED CHAMPION SUMO WRESTLING PIGS.

THIS IS KATSUNISHIKI, 14TH YOKOZUNA OF PIGDOM.

SHOVE SHOVE

LEAVE POLE BE

BEFORE HE DIED, MY FATHER SAID...

SNIF

AKARI... FIND YOURSELF A STRONG MAN...

ZEE-HEE ZEE-HEE

I WILL NOT ALLOW YOU TO CONSIDER **ANY** MAN UNTIL HE HAS DEFEATED THE YOKOZUNA, KATSUNISHIKI.

HIS DYING WORDS.

ZEE-HEE ZEE-HEE

AND HE'S STILL AROUND TO SAY 'EM.

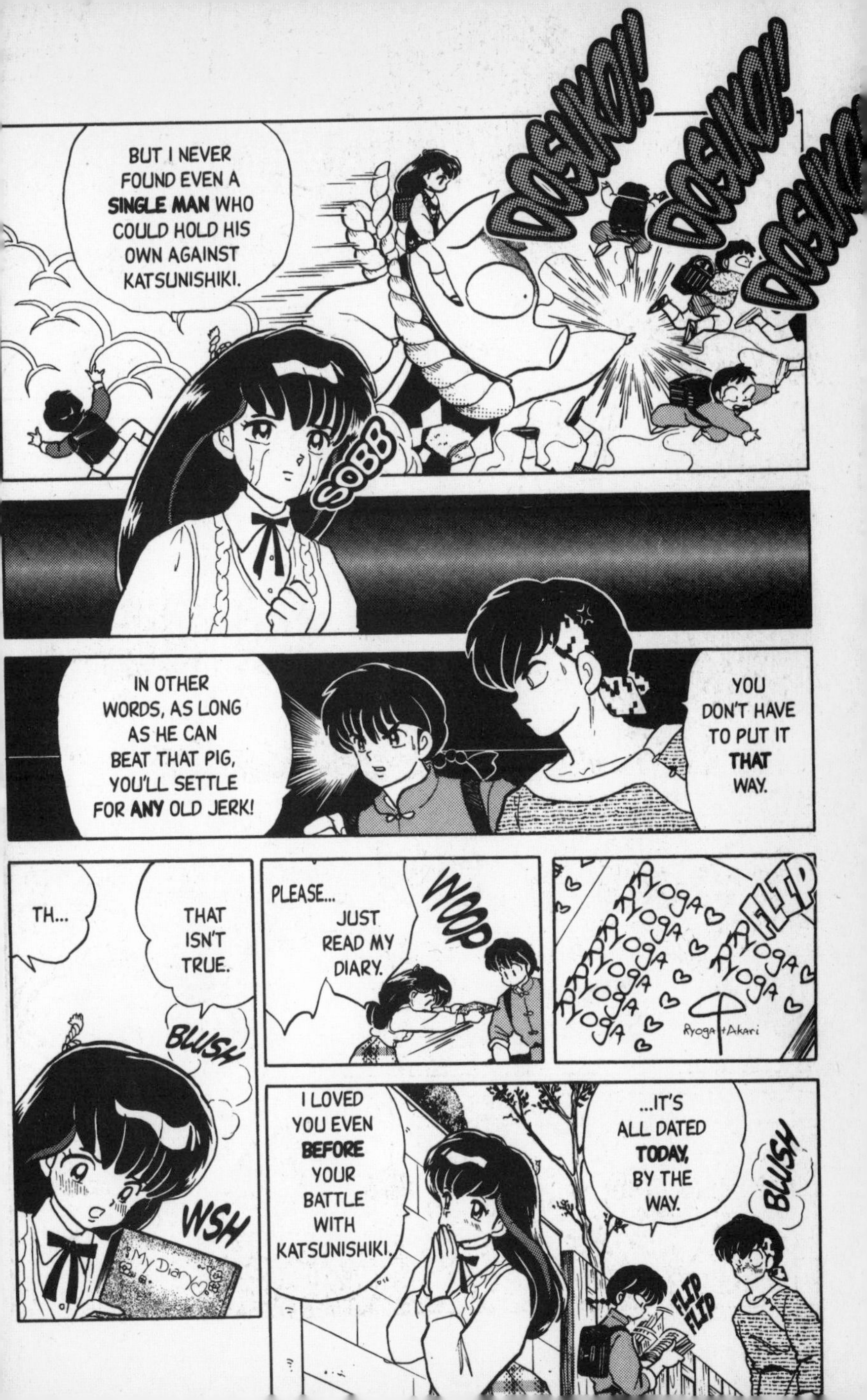
BUT I NEVER FOUND EVEN A **SINGLE MAN** WHO COULD HOLD HIS OWN AGAINST KATSUNISHIKI.
DOSUKOI!
DOSUKOI!
DOSUKOI!
SOBB
IN OTHER WORDS, AS LONG AS HE CAN BEAT THAT PIG, YOU'LL SETTLE FOR **ANY** OLD JERK!
YOU DON'T HAVE TO PUT IT **THAT** WAY.
TH...
THAT ISN'T TRUE.
BLUSH
WSH
My Diary
PLEASE... JUST READ MY DIARY.
WOOP
FLIP
Ryoga+Akari
I LOVED YOU EVEN **BEFORE** YOUR BATTLE WITH KATSUNISHIKI.
...IT'S ALL DATED **TODAY,** BY THE WAY.
BLUSH
FLIP FLIP

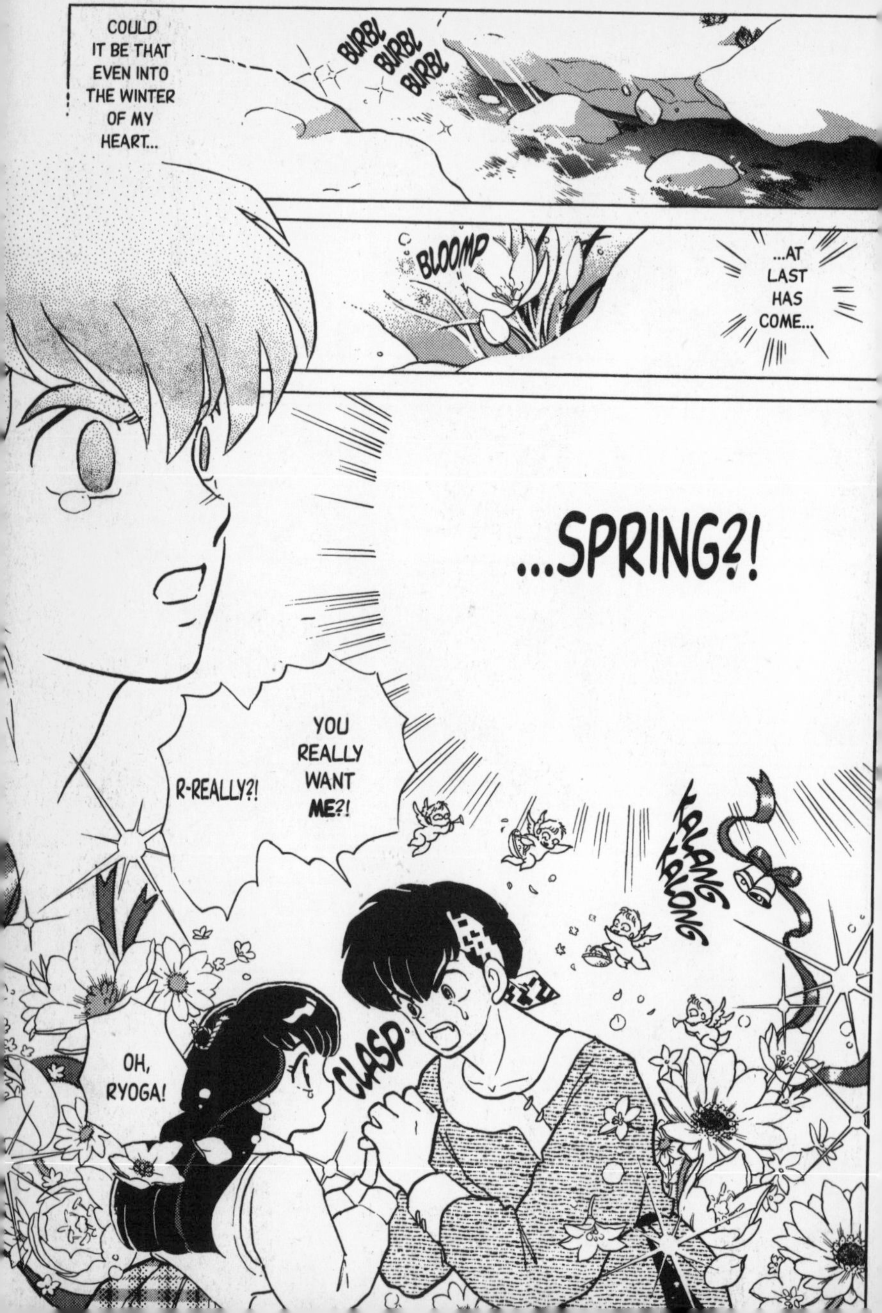
COULD IT BE THAT EVEN INTO THE WINTER OF MY HEART...
BURBL BURBL BURBL
BLOOMP
...AT LAST HAS COME...
...SPRING?!
R-REALLY?!
YOU REALLY WANT ME?!
KALONG KALONG
OH, RYOGA!
CLASP

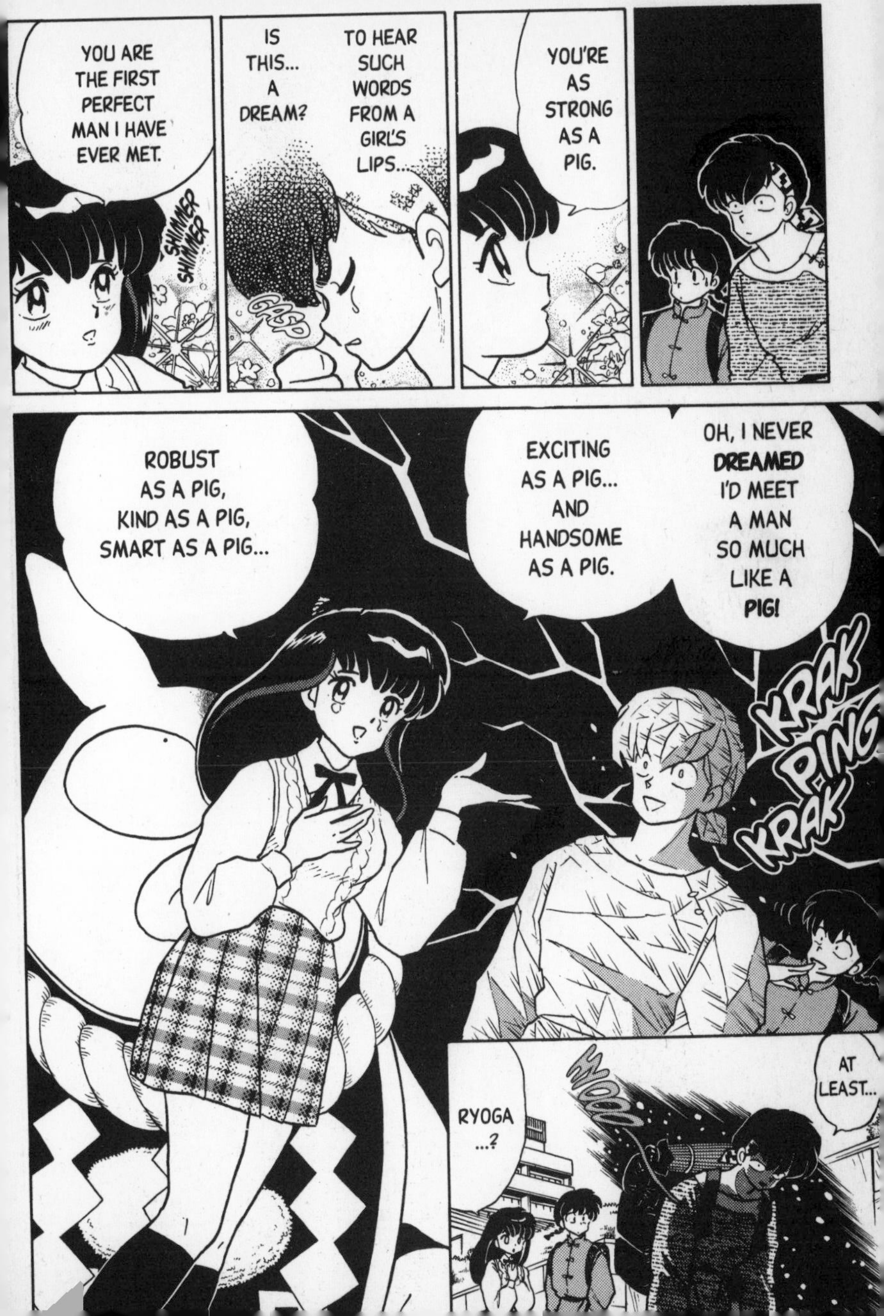
YOU ARE THE FIRST PERFECT MAN I HAVE EVER MET.
SHIMMER SHIMMER
IS THIS... A DREAM?
TO HEAR SUCH WORDS FROM A GIRL'S LIPS...
GASP
YOU'RE AS STRONG AS A PIG.
ROBUST AS A PIG, KIND AS A PIG, SMART AS A PIG...
EXCITING AS A PIG... AND HANDSOME AS A PIG.
OH, I NEVER DREAMED I'D MEET A MAN SO MUCH LIKE A PIG!
KRAK PING KRAK
RYOGA ...?
WOOO
AT LEAST...

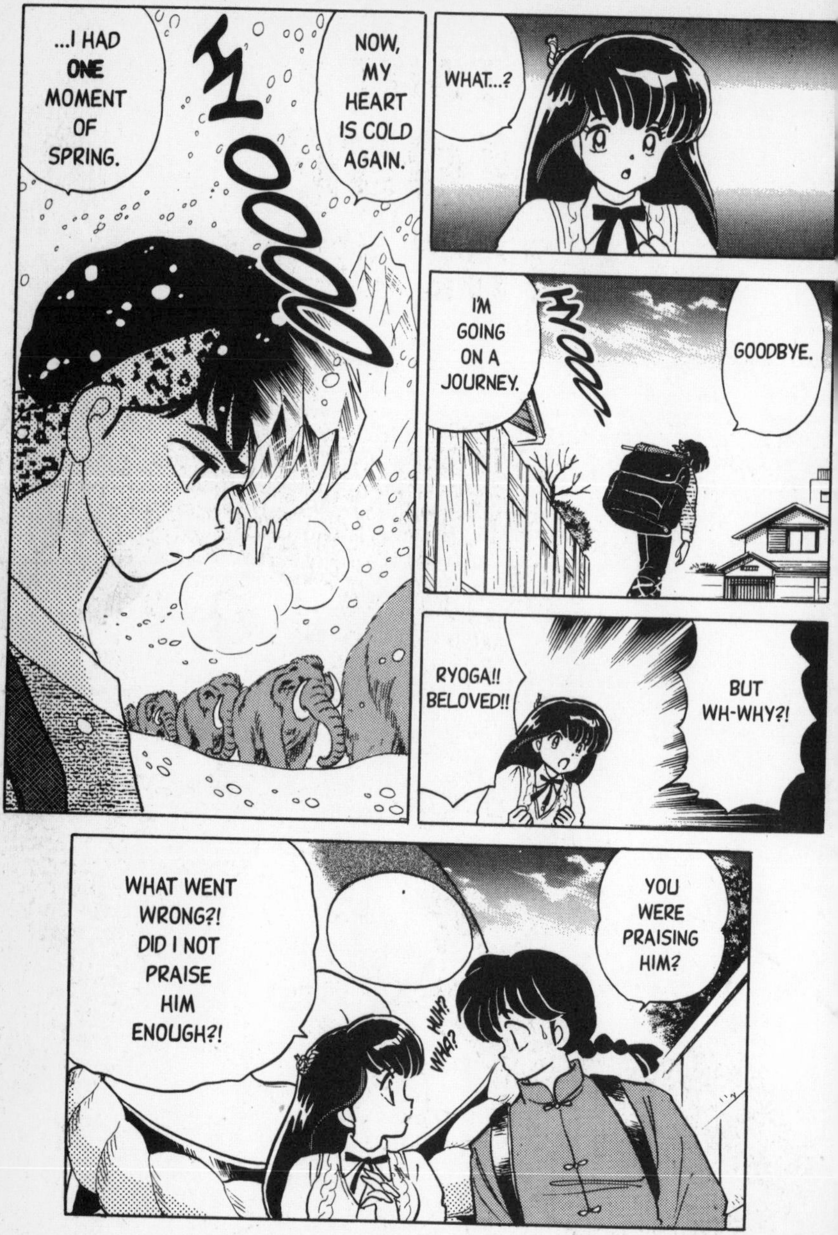

...I HAD ONE MOMENT OF SPRING.
HYOOOO
NOW, MY HEART IS COLD AGAIN.
WHAT...?
I'M GOING ON A JOURNEY.
HYOOO
GOODBYE.
RYOGA!! BELOVED!!
BUT WH-WHY?!
WHAT WENT WRONG?! DID I NOT PRAISE HIM ENOUGH?!
HUH? WHA?
YOU WERE PRAISING HIM?

PART 2
LOVE THE PIG!

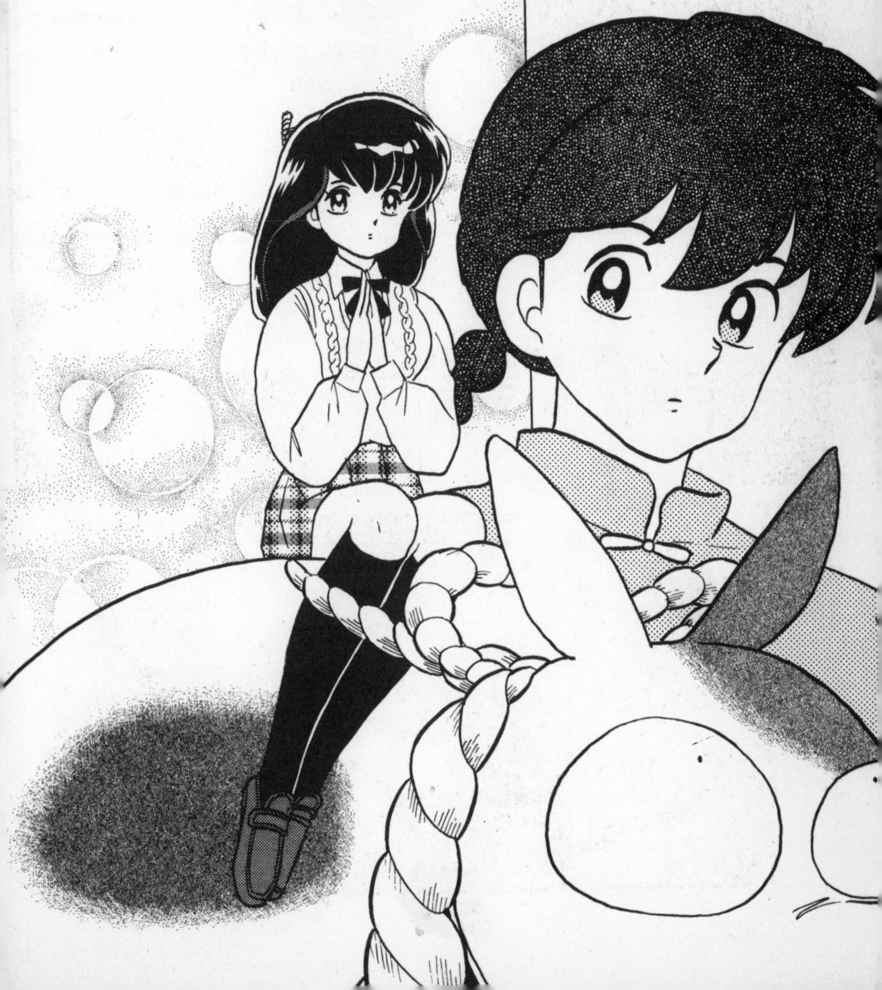

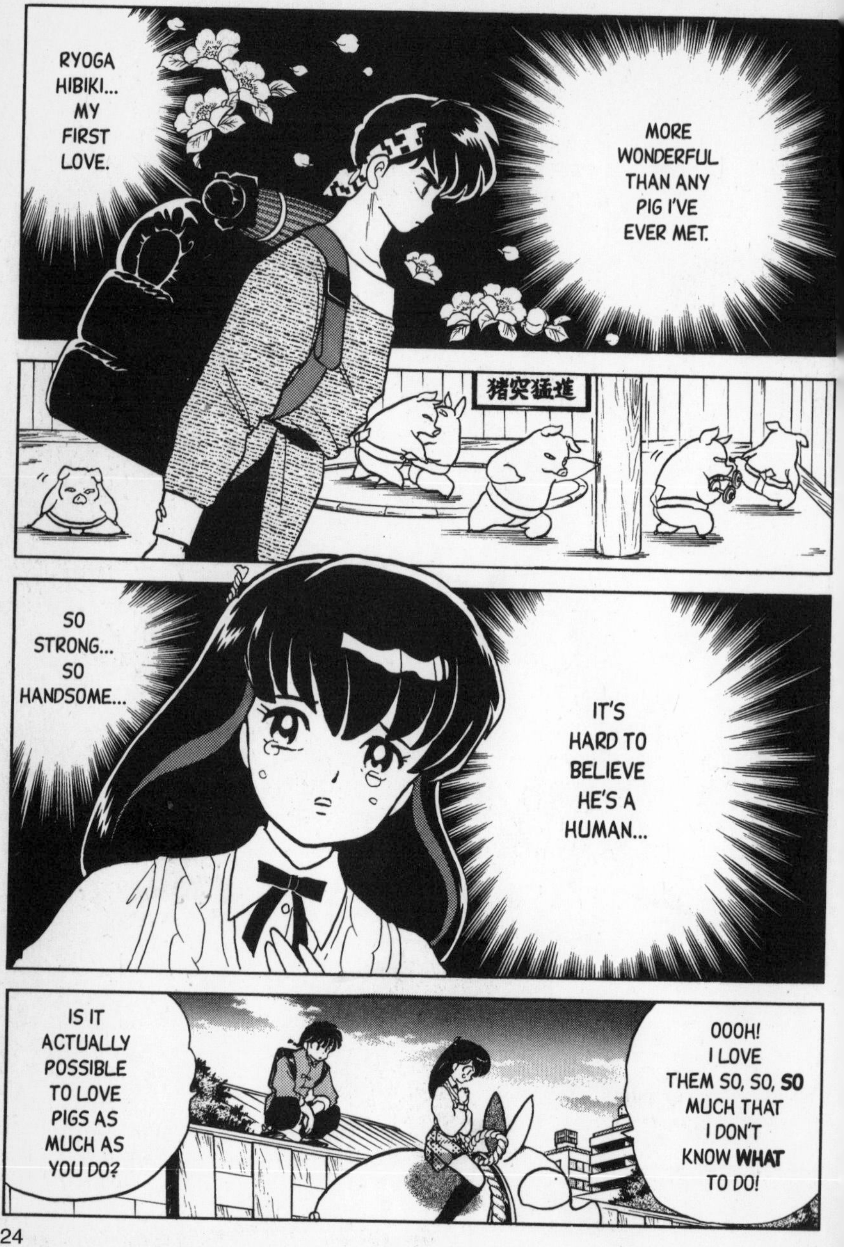
RYOGA HIBIKI... MY FIRST LOVE.
MORE WONDERFUL THAN ANY PIG I'VE EVER MET.
猪突猛進
SO STRONG... SO HANDSOME...
IT'S HARD TO BELIEVE HE'S A HUMAN...
IS IT ACTUALLY POSSIBLE TO LOVE PIGS AS MUCH AS YOU DO?
OOOH! I LOVE THEM SO, SO, **SO** MUCH THAT I DON'T KNOW **WHAT** TO DO!

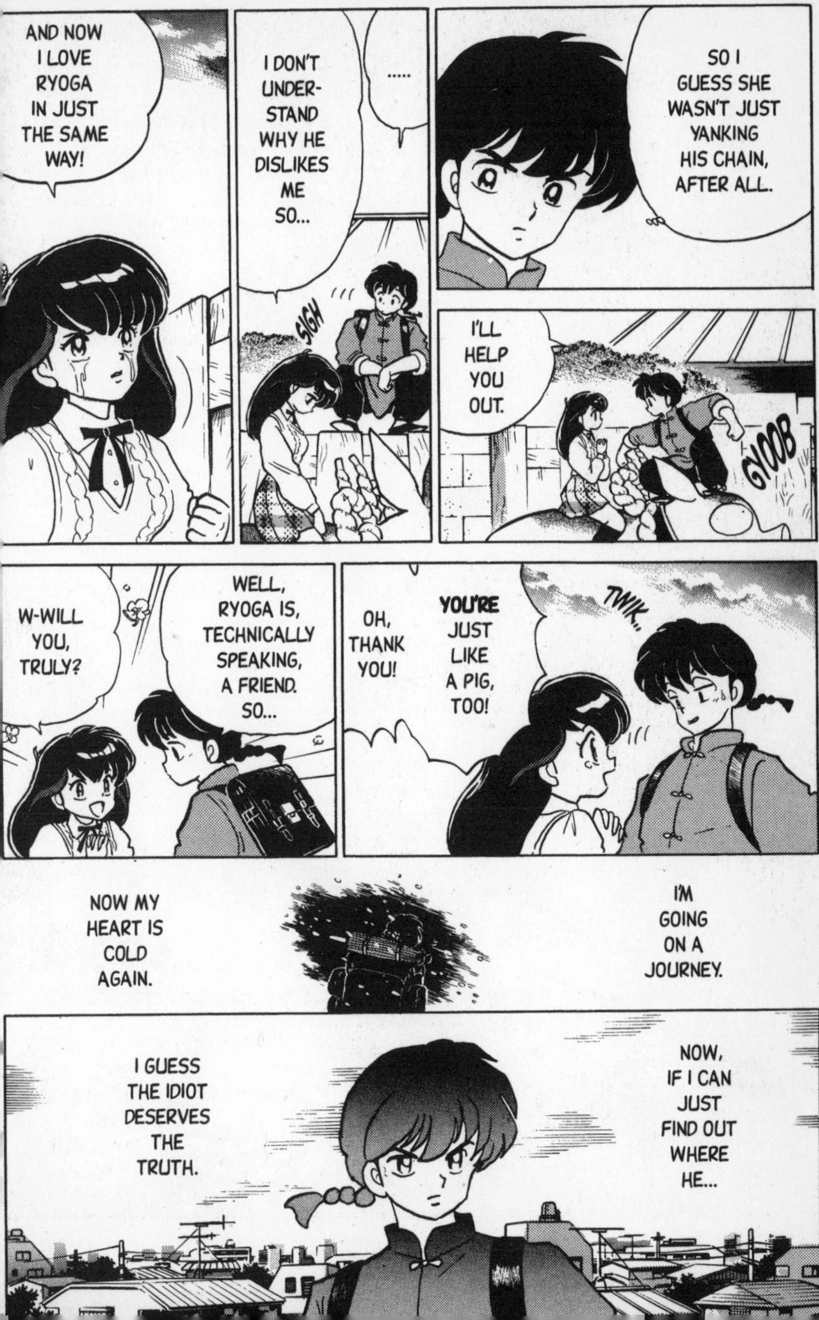
AND NOW I LOVE RYOGA IN JUST THE SAME WAY!
I DON'T UNDER-STAND WHY HE DISLIKES ME SO...
.....
SIGH
SO I GUESS SHE WASN'T JUST YANKING HIS CHAIN, AFTER ALL.
I'LL HELP YOU OUT.
GYOOB
W-WILL YOU, TRULY?
WELL, RYOGA IS, TECHNICALLY SPEAKING, A FRIEND. SO...
OH, THANK YOU!
YOU'RE JUST LIKE A PIG, TOO!
TWIK
NOW MY HEART IS COLD AGAIN.
I'M GOING ON A JOURNEY.
I GUESS THE IDIOT DESERVES THE TRUTH.
NOW, IF I CAN JUST FIND OUT WHERE HE...

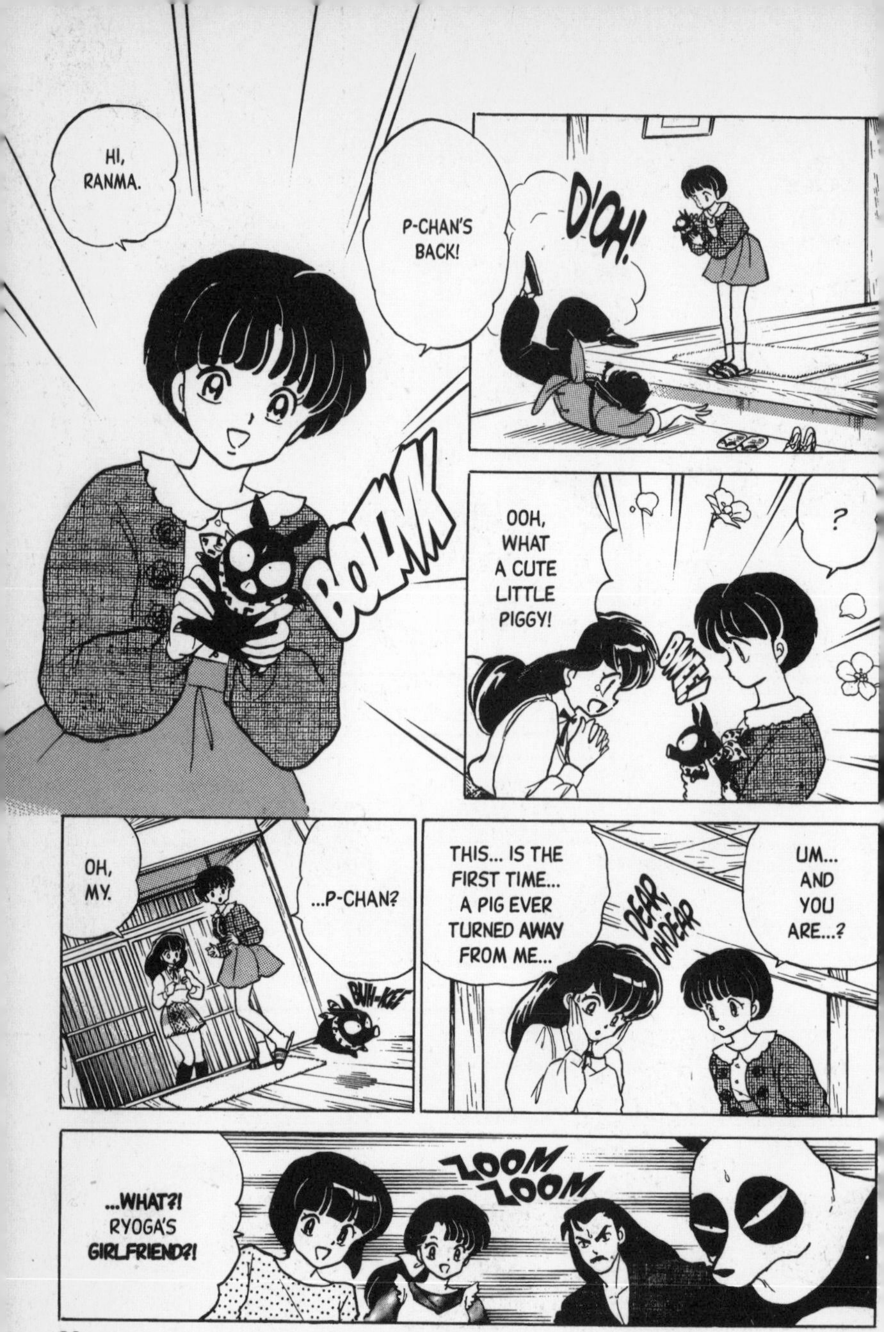
HI, RANMA.
P-CHAN'S BACK!
BOIINK
D'OH!
OOH, WHAT A CUTE LITTLE PIGGY!
BWEE
?
OH, MY.
...P-CHAN?
BUH-KEE
THIS... IS THE FIRST TIME... A PIG EVER TURNED AWAY FROM ME...
DEAR, OH DEAR
UM... AND YOU ARE...?
...WHAT?! RYOGA'S GIRLFRIEND?!
ZOOM ZOOM

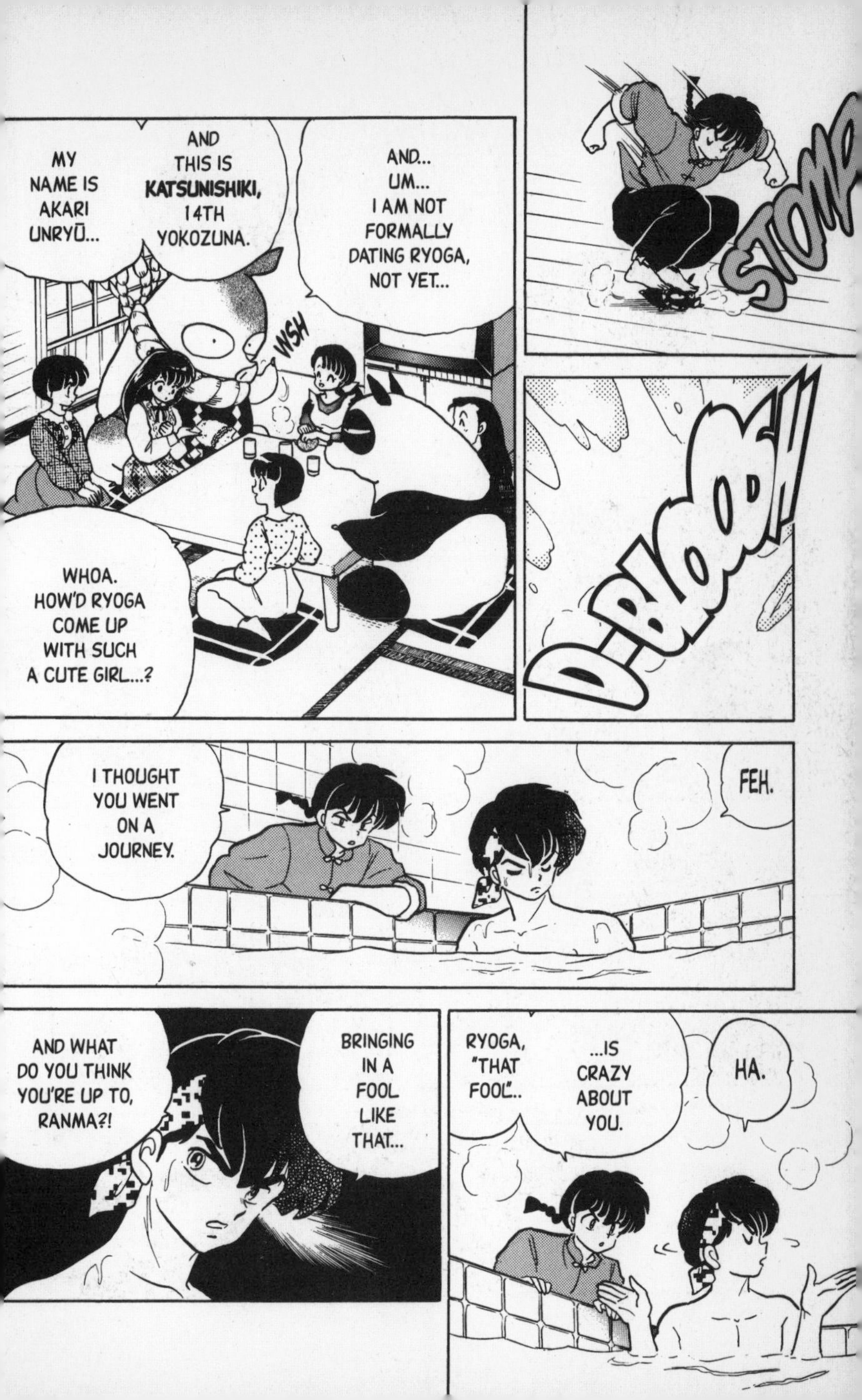
MY NAME IS AKARI UNRYŪ...
AND THIS IS **KATSUNISHIKI,** 14TH YOKOZUNA.
AND... UM... I AM NOT FORMALLY DATING RYOGA, NOT YET...
WSH
WHOA. HOW'D RYOGA COME UP WITH SUCH A CUTE GIRL...?
STOMP
D-BLOOOSH
I THOUGHT YOU WENT ON A JOURNEY.
FEH.
AND WHAT DO YOU THINK YOU'RE UP TO, RANMA?!
BRINGING IN A FOOL LIKE THAT...
RYOGA, "THAT FOOL"..
...IS CRAZY ABOUT YOU.
HA.

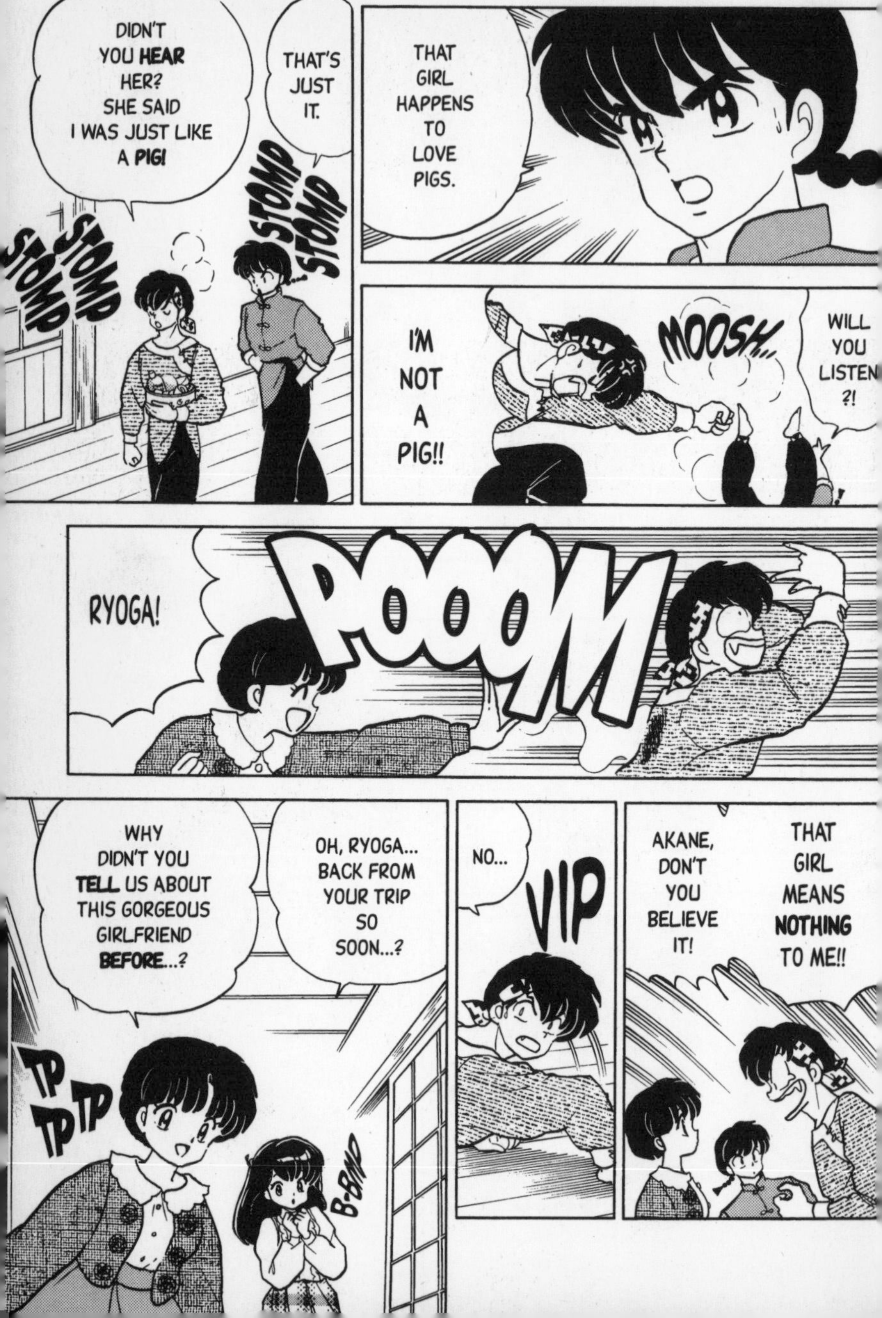
DIDN'T YOU HEAR HER? SHE SAID I WAS JUST LIKE A PIG!
THAT'S JUST IT.
STOMP STOMP
STOMP STOMP
THAT GIRL HAPPENS TO LOVE PIGS.
I'M NOT A PIG!!
MOOSH...
WILL YOU LISTEN?!
RYOGA!
POOOM
WHY DIDN'T YOU TELL US ABOUT THIS GORGEOUS GIRLFRIEND BEFORE...?
OH, RYOGA... BACK FROM YOUR TRIP SO SOON...?
TP TP TP
B-BMP
NO...
VIP
AKANE, DON'T YOU BELIEVE IT!
THAT GIRL MEANS NOTHING TO ME!!

AWW, DON'T BE SHY ABOUT IT...!

I'M REALLY **HAPPY** THAT YOU FINALLY HAVE A GIRLFRIEND!

YOU ALWAYS SEEMED SO LONELY. I WAS WORRIED ABOUT YOU...

...AS A FRIEND!

SEE?

JUST DON'T PRETEND YOU DIDN'T HEAR THAT.

DUHHH

FLUTTA FLUTTA FLUT

PAT

ZP...

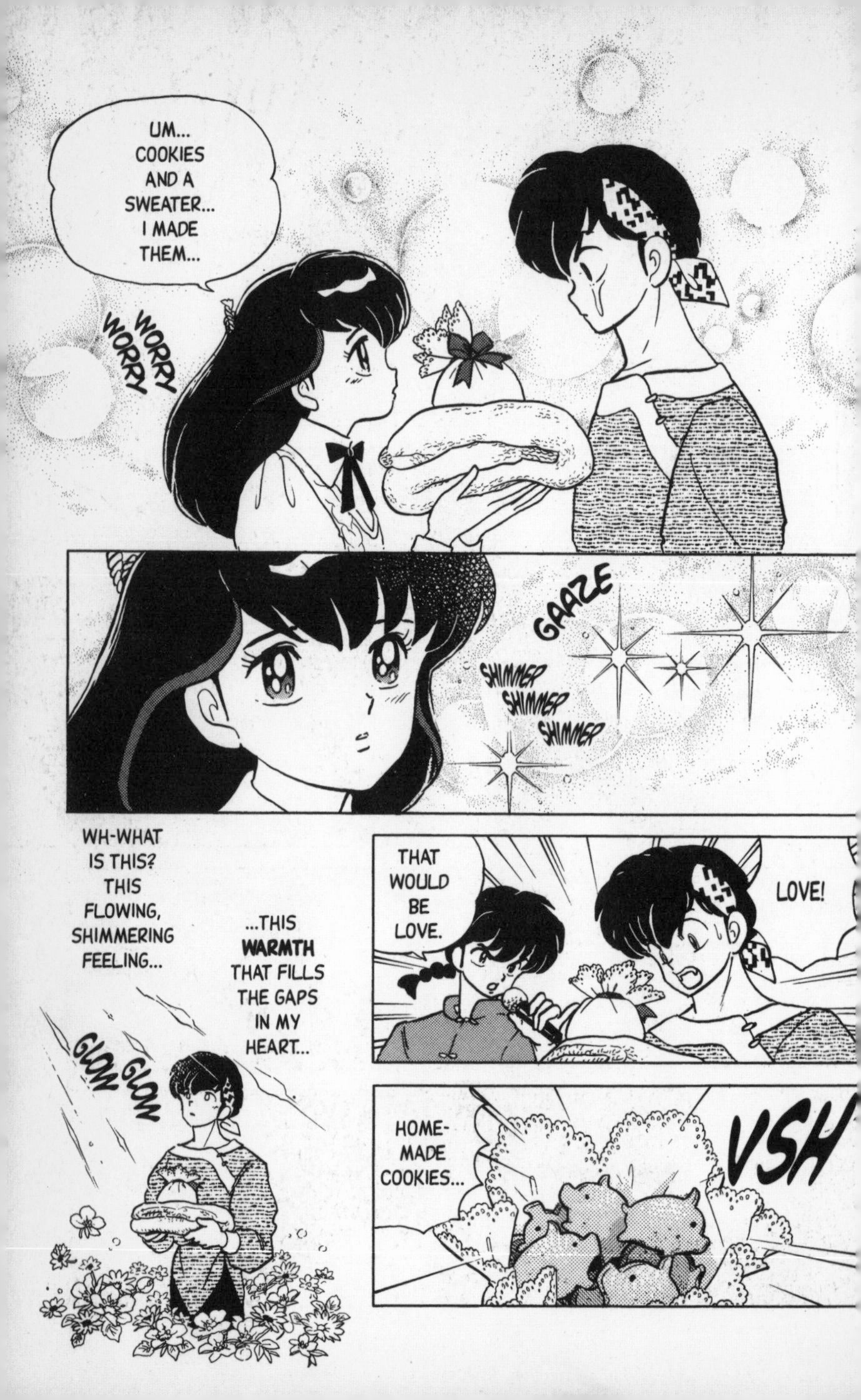
UM... COOKIES AND A SWEATER... I MADE THEM...
WORRY WORRY
GAAZE
SHIMMER SHIMMER SHIMMER
WH-WHAT IS THIS? THIS FLOWING, SHIMMERING FEELING...
...THIS WARMTH THAT FILLS THE GAPS IN MY HEART...
GLOW GLOW
THAT WOULD BE LOVE.
LOVE!
HOME-MADE COOKIES...
VSH

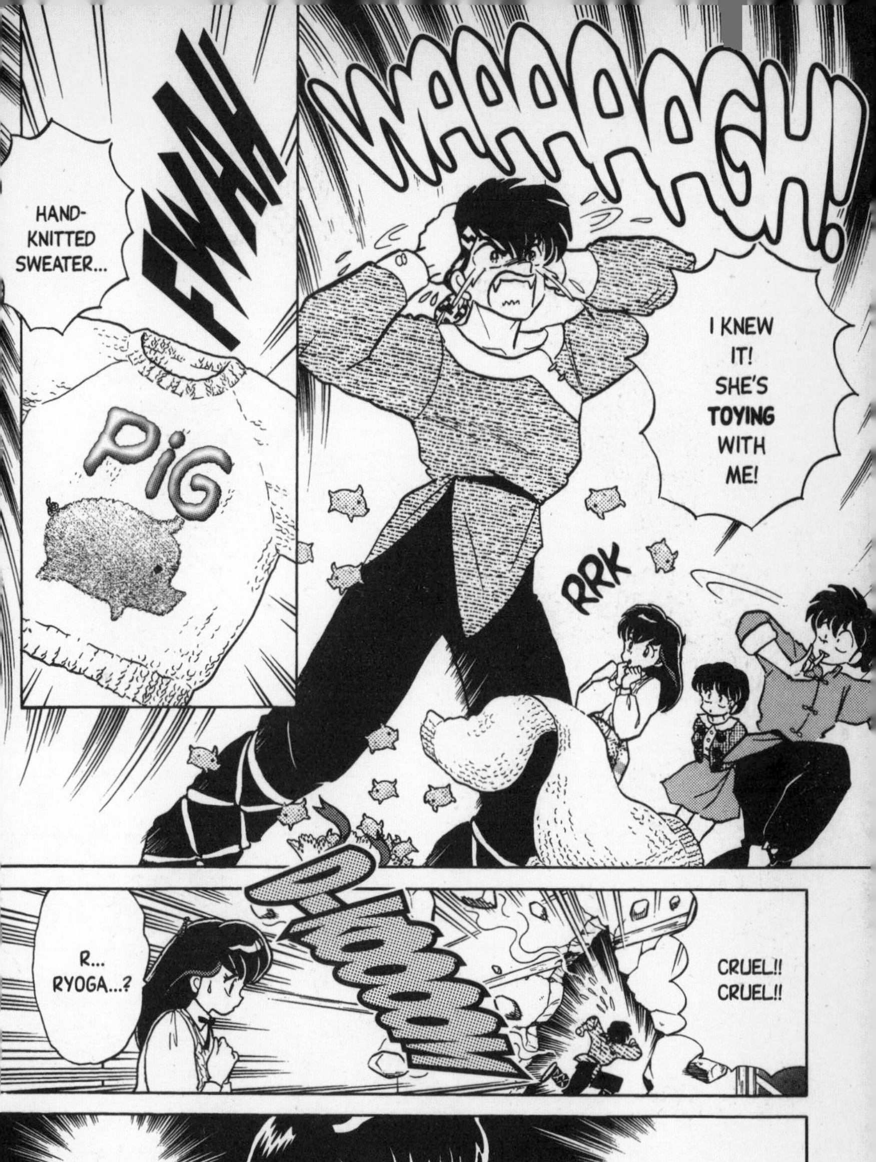
HAND-KNITTED SWEATER...
FWAH
PIG
WAAAAAGH!
I KNEW IT! SHE'S **TOYING** WITH ME!
RRK
R... RYOGA...?
CRUEL!! CRUEL!!
GASP..!
C... COULD IT BE...?

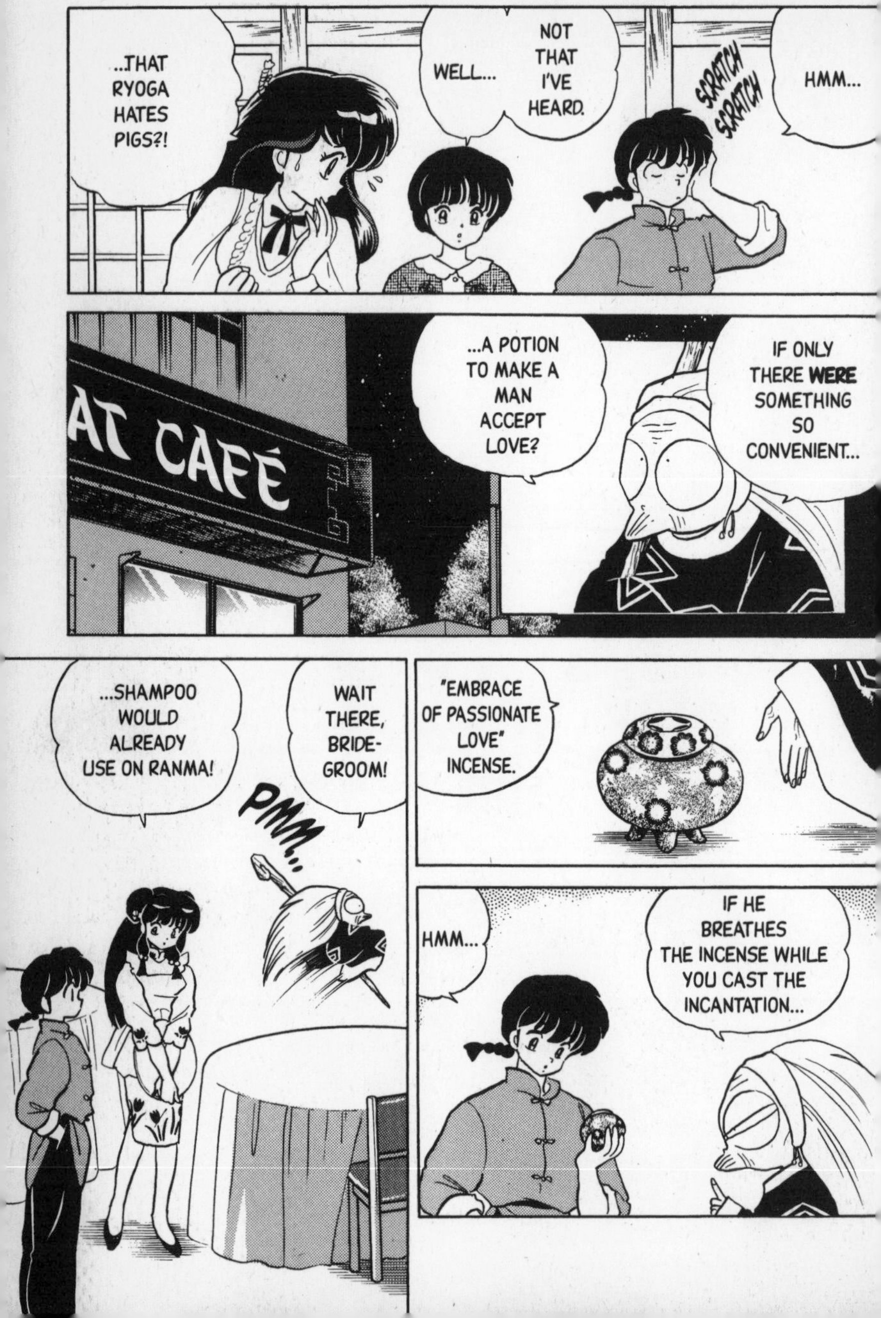

...THAT RYOGA HATES PIGS?!
WELL...
NOT THAT I'VE HEARD.
SCRATCH SCRATCH
HMM...
AT CAFÉ
...A POTION TO MAKE A MAN ACCEPT LOVE?
IF ONLY THERE **WERE** SOMETHING SO CONVENIENT...
...SHAMPOO WOULD ALREADY USE ON RANMA!
WAIT THERE, BRIDE-GROOM!
PMM...
"EMBRACE OF PASSIONATE LOVE" INCENSE.
HMM...
IF HE BREATHES THE INCENSE WHILE YOU CAST THE INCANTATION...

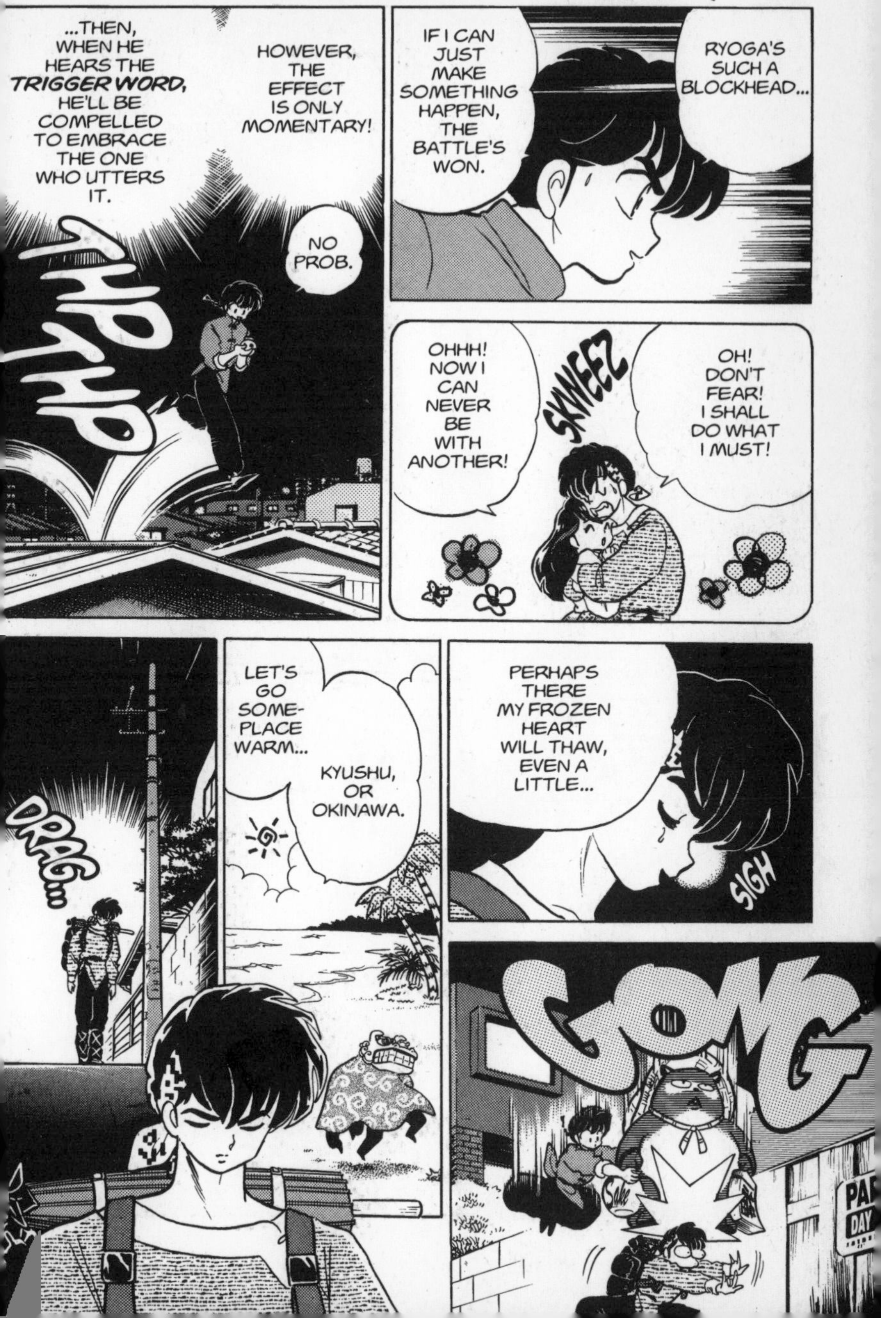
...THEN, WHEN HE HEARS THE *TRIGGER WORD,* HE'LL BE COMPELLED TO EMBRACE THE ONE WHO UTTERS IT.
HOWEVER, THE EFFECT IS ONLY MOMENTARY!
NO PROB.
THPTHP
IF I CAN JUST MAKE SOMETHING HAPPEN, THE BATTLE'S WON.
RYOGA'S SUCH A BLOCKHEAD...
OHHH! NOW I CAN NEVER BE WITH ANOTHER!
SKWEEZ
OH! DON'T FEAR! I SHALL DO WHAT I MUST!
DRAG...
LET'S GO SOME-PLACE WARM...
KYUSHU, OR OKINAWA.
PERHAPS THERE MY FROZEN HEART WILL THAW, EVEN A LITTLE...
SIGH
GONG

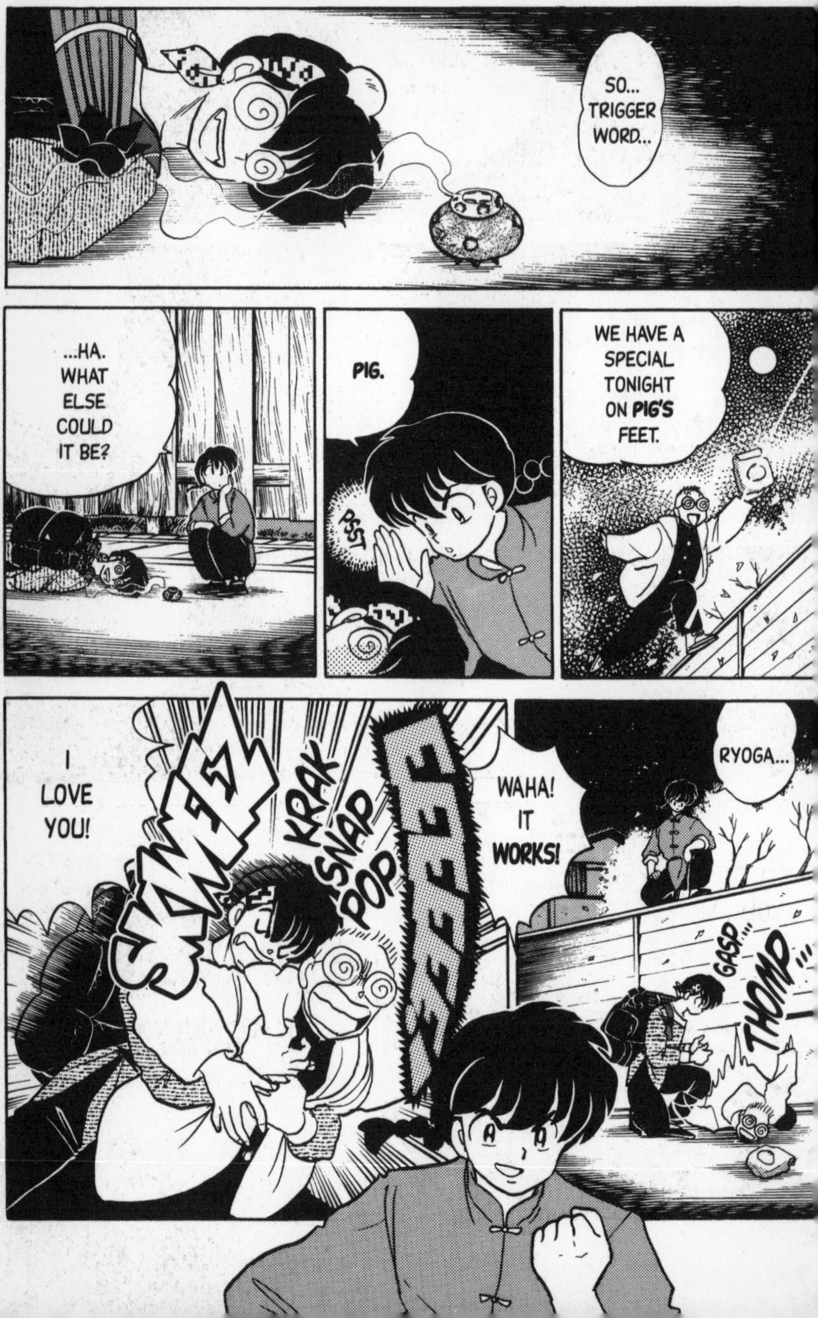
SO... TRIGGER WORD...
...HA. WHAT ELSE COULD IT BE?
PSST
PIG.
WE HAVE A SPECIAL TONIGHT ON PIG'S FEET.
I LOVE YOU!
KRAK SNAP POP
WAHA! IT WORKS!
RYOGA...
GASP...
THOMP!!

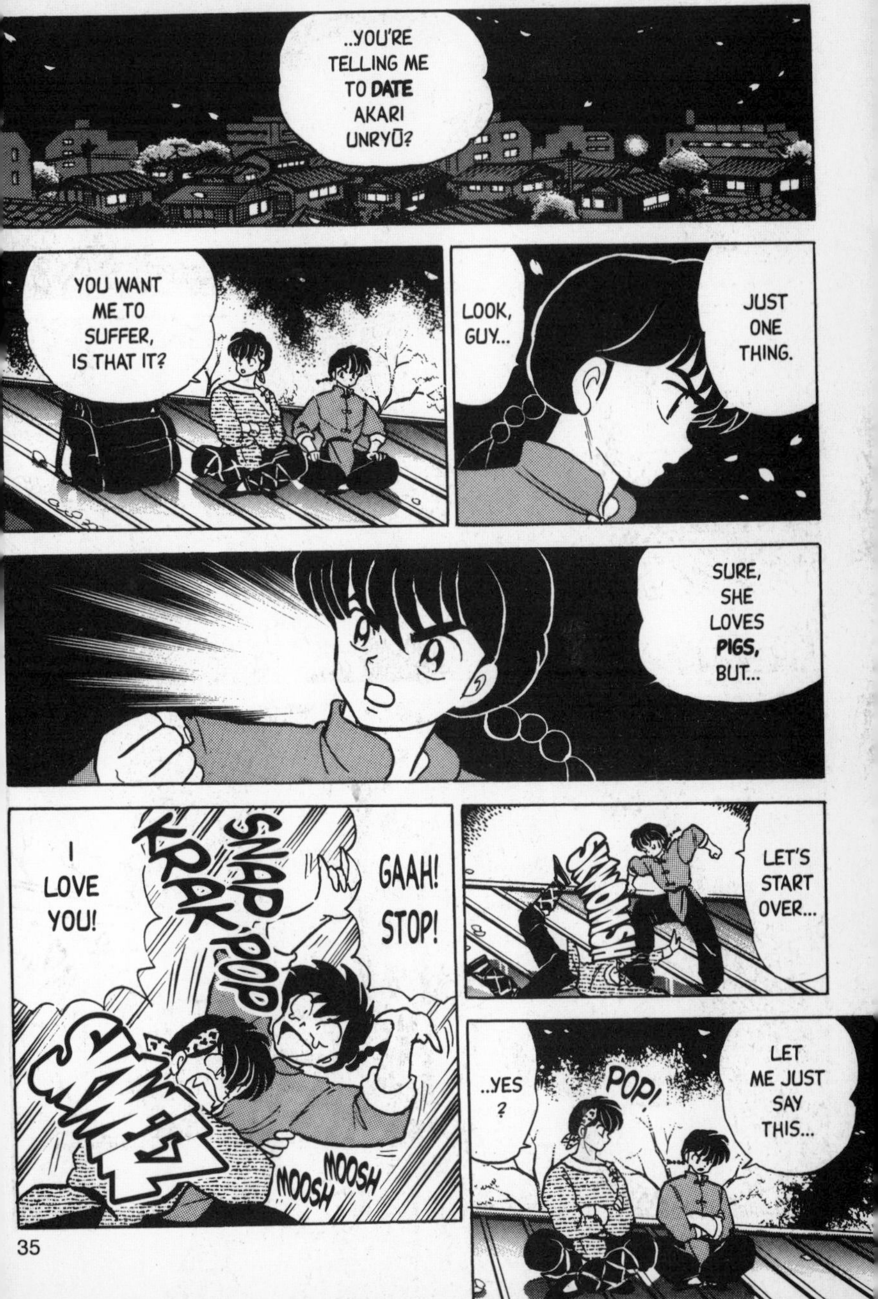
...YOU'RE TELLING ME TO **DATE** AKARI UNRYŪ?
YOU WANT ME TO SUFFER, IS THAT IT?
LOOK, GUY...
JUST ONE THING.
SURE, SHE LOVES **PIGS,** BUT...
I LOVE YOU!
SNAP
KRAK
POP
GAAH! STOP!
SKWEE
MOOSH
MOOSH
SKWOMSH
LET'S START OVER...
...YES ?
POP!
LET ME JUST SAY THIS...

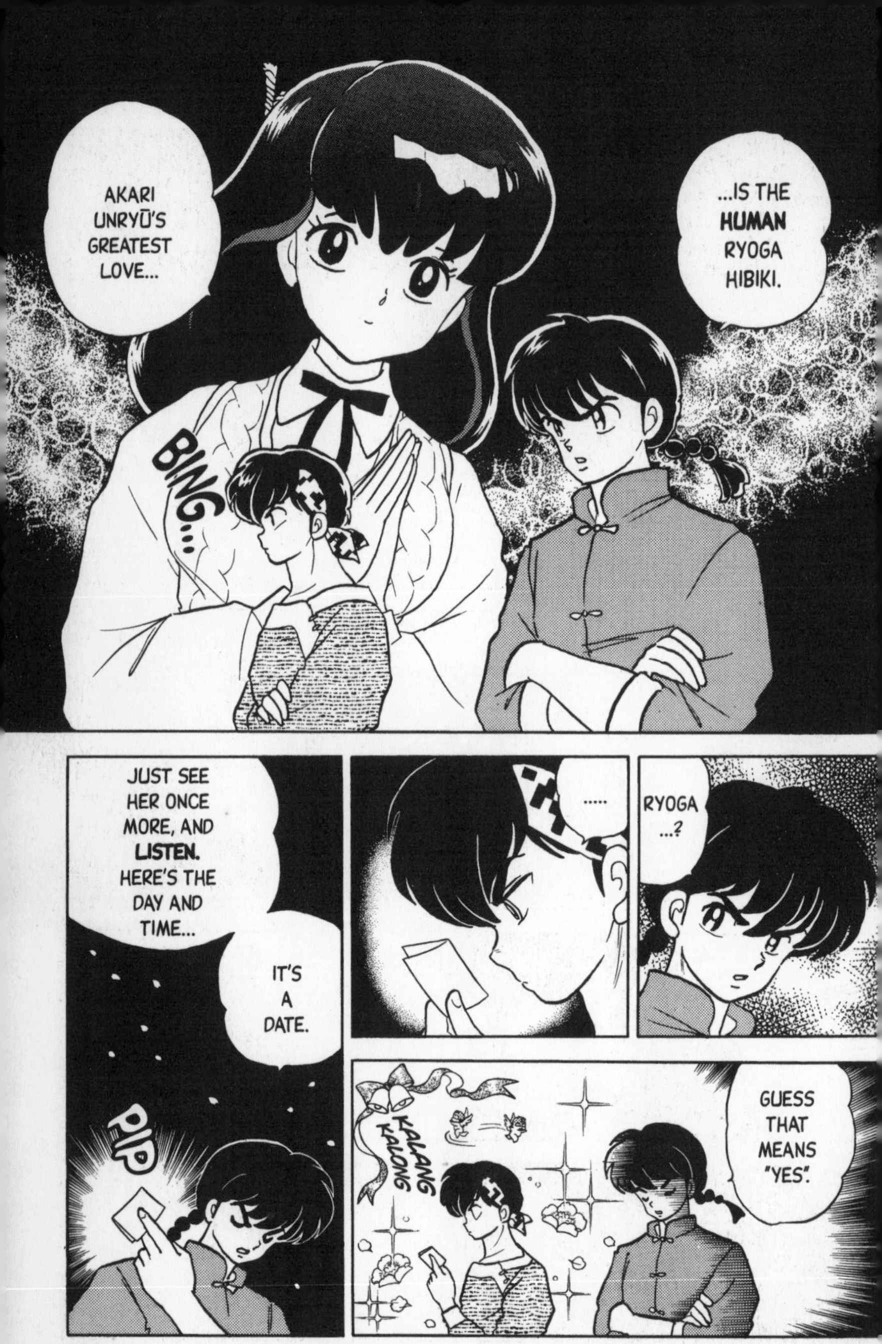
AKARI UNRYŪ'S GREATEST LOVE...
BING...
...IS THE **HUMAN** RYOGA HIBIKI.
JUST SEE HER ONCE MORE, AND **LISTEN.** HERE'S THE DAY AND TIME...
IT'S A DATE.
PIP
.....
RYOGA ...?
KALANG KALONG
GUESS THAT MEANS "YES".

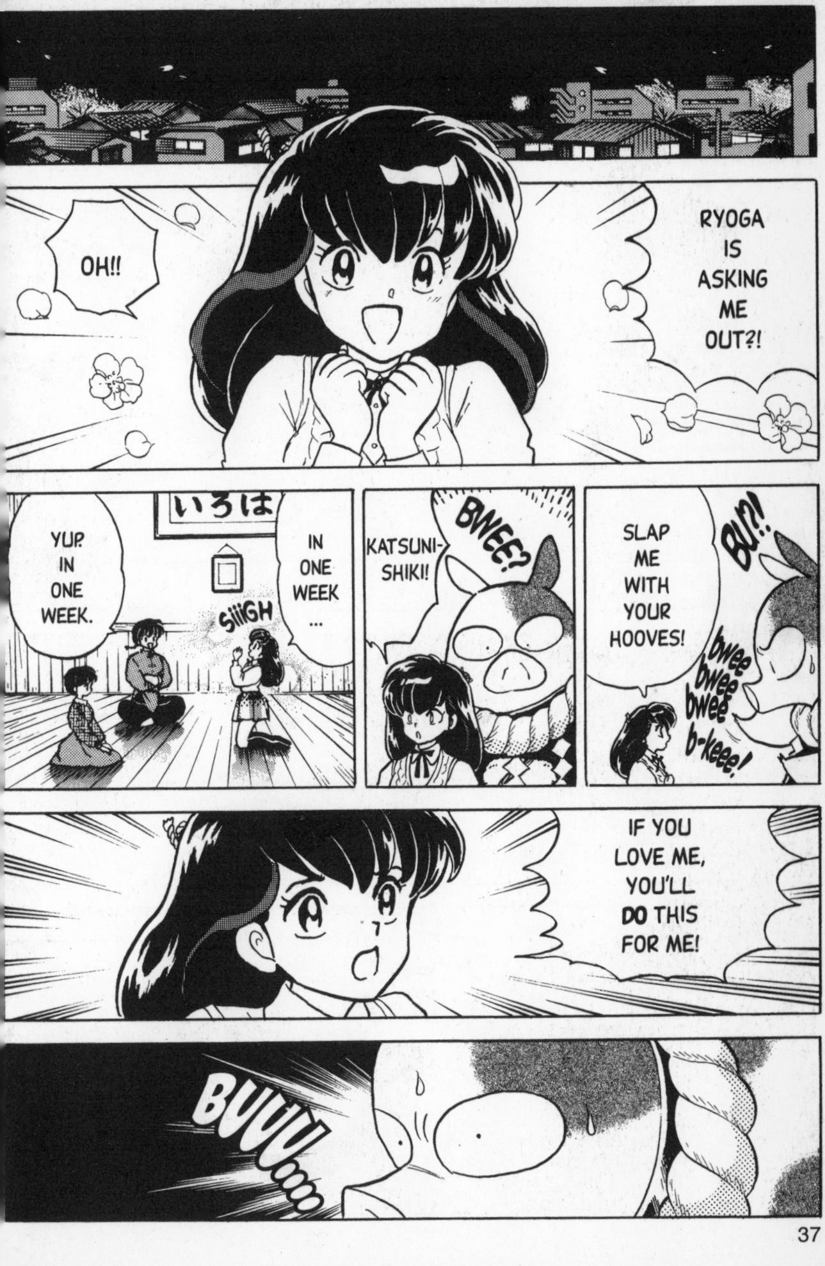
OH!!
RYOGA IS ASKING ME OUT?!
YUP. IN ONE WEEK.
SIIIGH
IN ONE WEEK ...
KATSUNI-SHIKI!
BWEE?
SLAP ME WITH YOUR HOOVES!
BU?!
bwee bwee bwee b-keee!
IF YOU LOVE ME, YOU'LL DO THIS FOR ME!
BUUU....

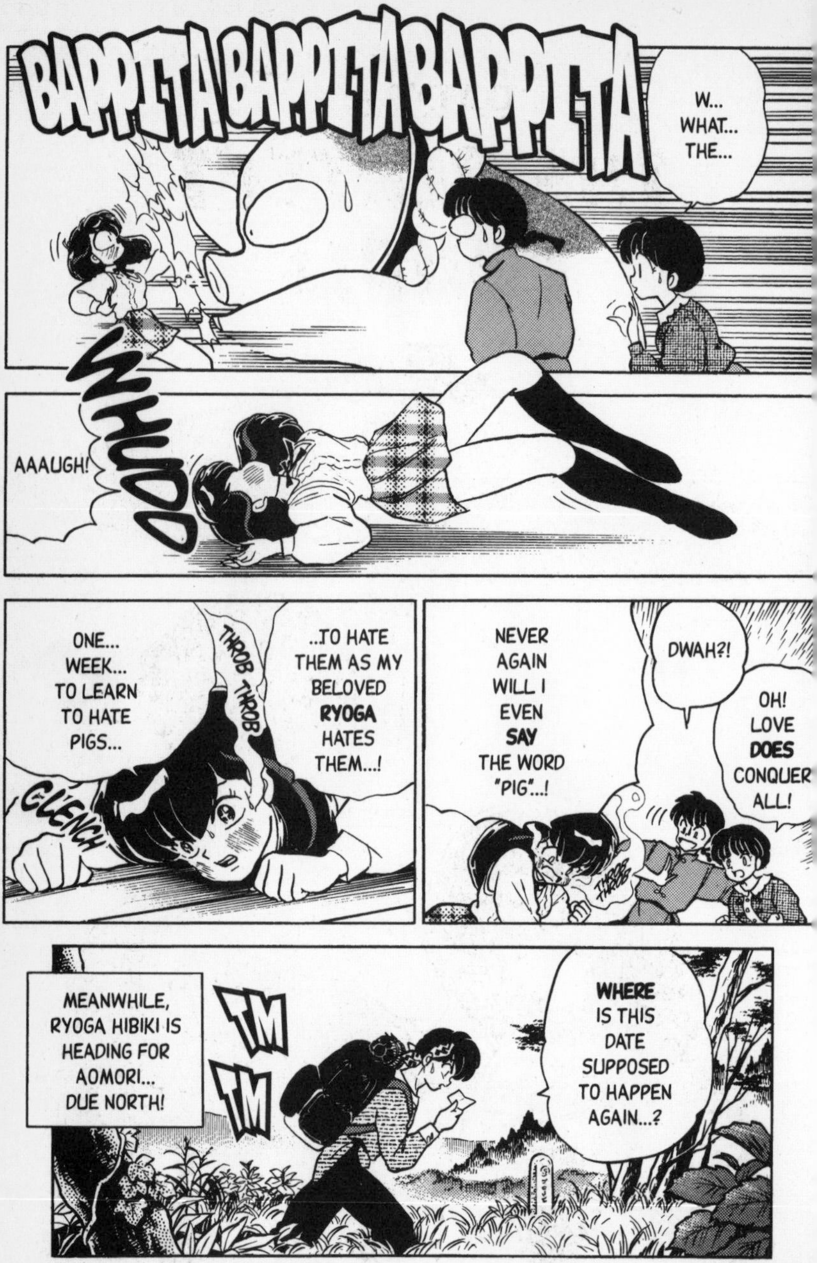
BAPPITA BAPPITA BAPPITA
W... WHAT... THE...
WHUDD
AAAUGH!
ONE... WEEK... TO LEARN TO HATE PIGS...
THROB THROB
...TO HATE THEM AS MY BELOVED RYOGA HATES THEM...!
CLENCH
NEVER AGAIN WILL I EVEN SAY THE WORD "PIG"...!
DWAH?!
OH! LOVE DOES CONQUER ALL!
MEANWHILE, RYOGA HIBIKI IS HEADING FOR AOMORI... DUE NORTH!
TM TM
WHERE IS THIS DATE SUPPOSED TO HAPPEN AGAIN...?

PART 3

THE PERFECT COUPLE

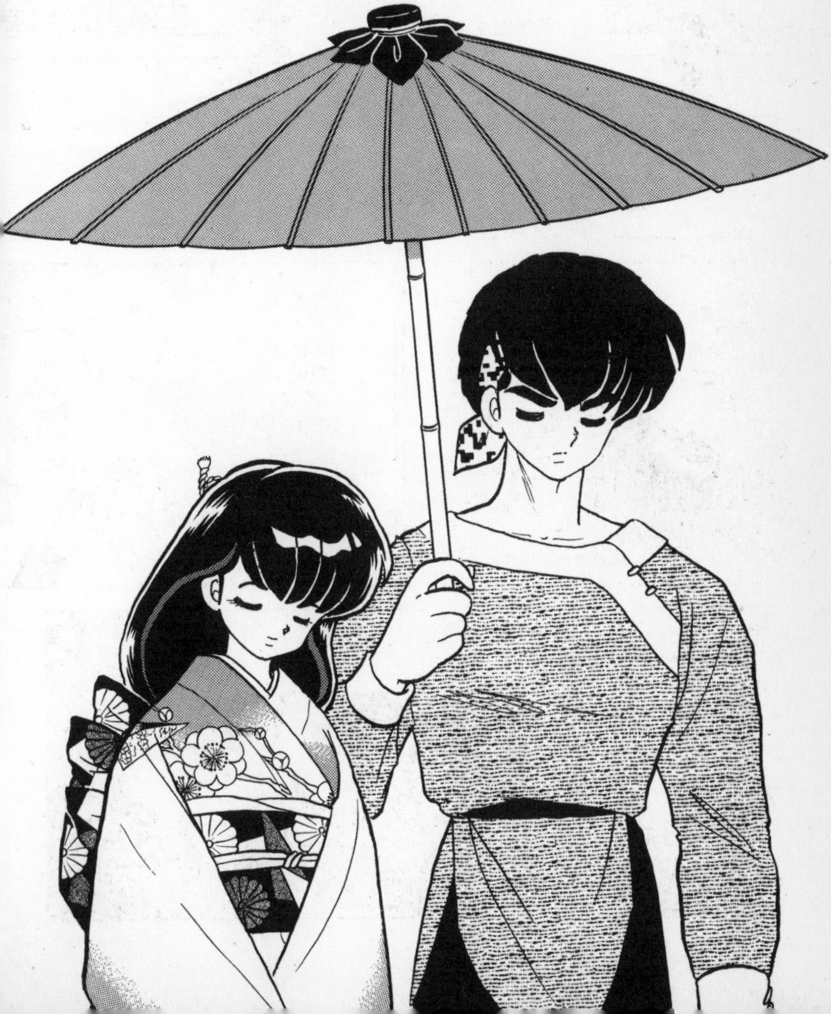

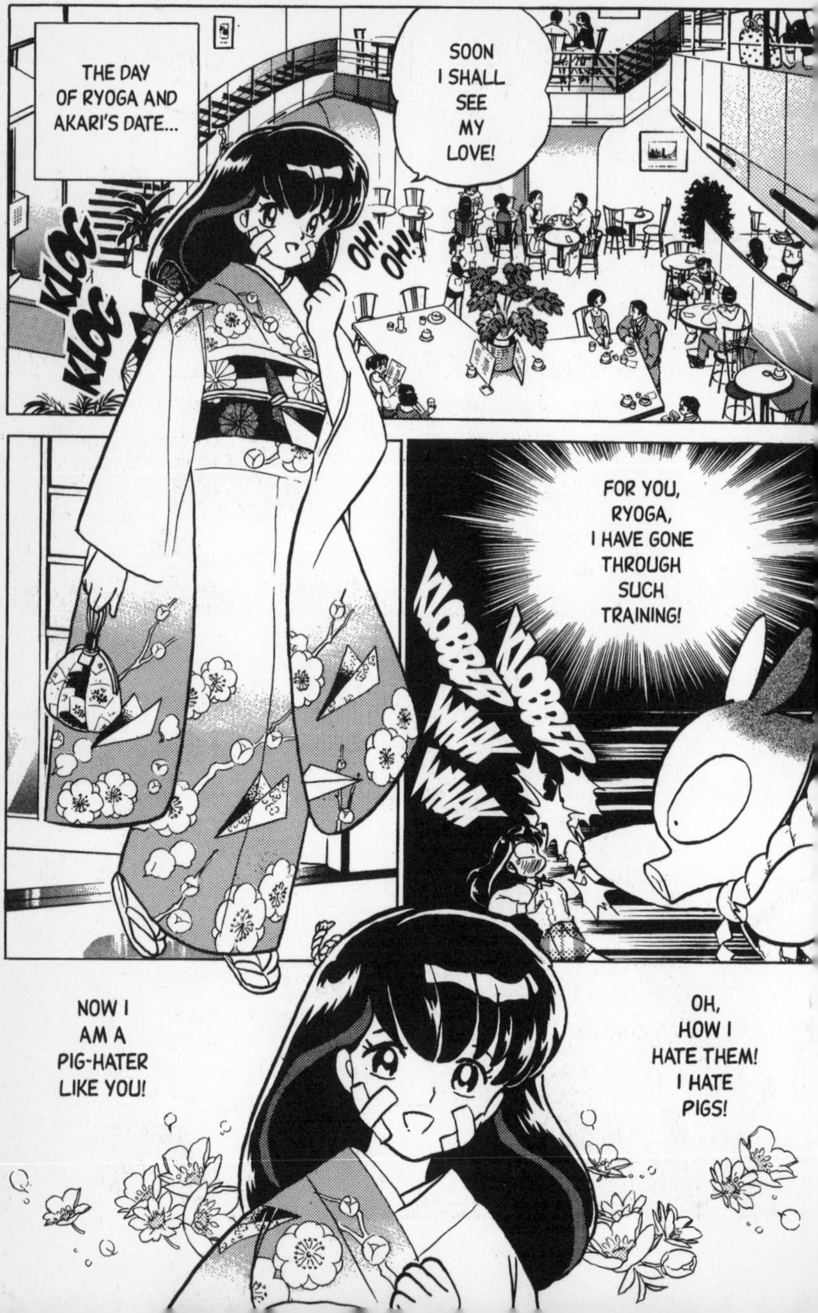
THE DAY OF RYOGA AND AKARI'S DATE...
SOON I SHALL SEE MY LOVE!
OH! OH!
KLOG KLOG
FOR YOU, RYOGA, I HAVE GONE THROUGH SUCH TRAINING!
KLOBBER KLOBBER WHAK WHAK
NOW I AM A PIG-HATER LIKE YOU!
OH, HOW I HATE THEM! I HATE PIGS!

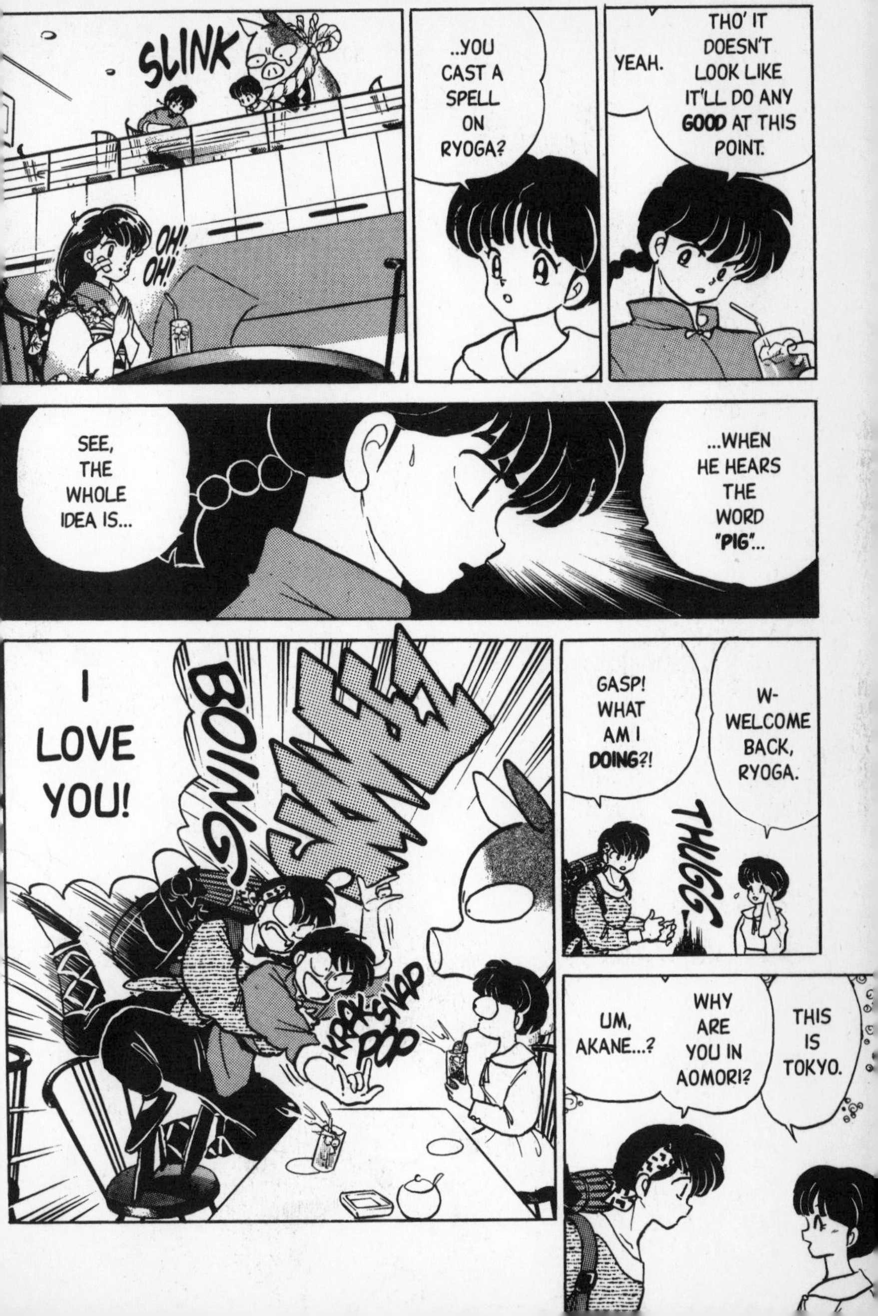
SLINK
OH! OH!
...YOU CAST A SPELL ON RYOGA?
YEAH.
THO' IT DOESN'T LOOK LIKE IT'LL DO ANY GOOD AT THIS POINT.
SEE, THE WHOLE IDEA IS...
...WHEN HE HEARS THE WORD "PIG"...
I LOVE YOU!
BOING
KRAK SNAP POP
GASP! WHAT AM I DOING?!
W-WELCOME BACK, RYOGA.
THUGG
UM, AKANE...?
WHY ARE YOU IN AOMORI?
THIS IS TOKYO.

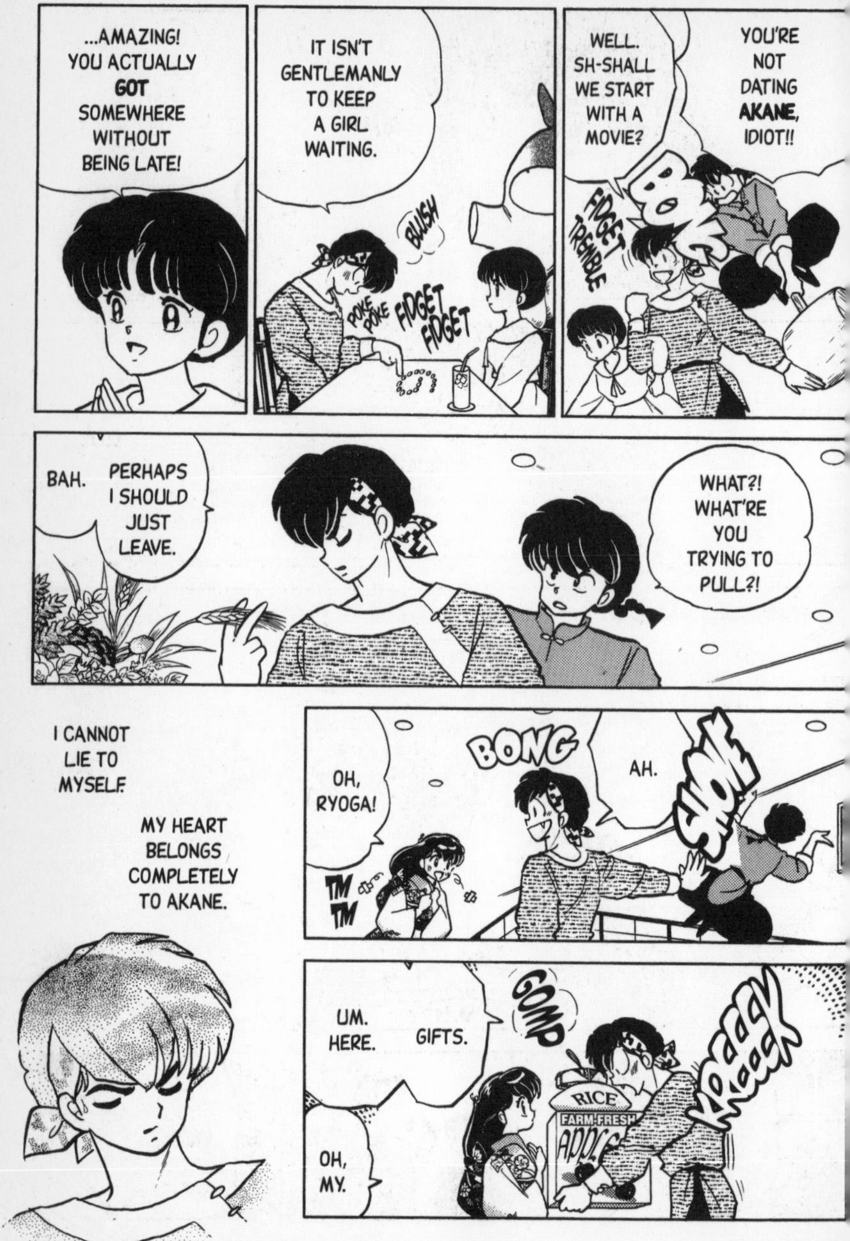
...AMAZING! YOU ACTUALLY GOT SOMEWHERE WITHOUT BEING LATE!
IT ISN'T GENTLEMANLY TO KEEP A GIRL WAITING.
BLUSH
POKE POKE
FIDGET FIDGET
WELL. SH-SHALL WE START WITH A MOVIE?
FIDGET TREMBLE
YOU'RE NOT DATING AKANE, IDIOT!!
BAH.
PERHAPS I SHOULD JUST LEAVE.
WHAT?! WHAT'RE YOU TRYING TO PULL?!
I CANNOT LIE TO MYSELF.
MY HEART BELONGS COMPLETELY TO AKANE.
OH, RYOGA!
TM TM
BONG
AH.
SHOVE
UM. HERE.
GIFTS.
GOMP
RICE
FARM-FRESH
OH, MY.

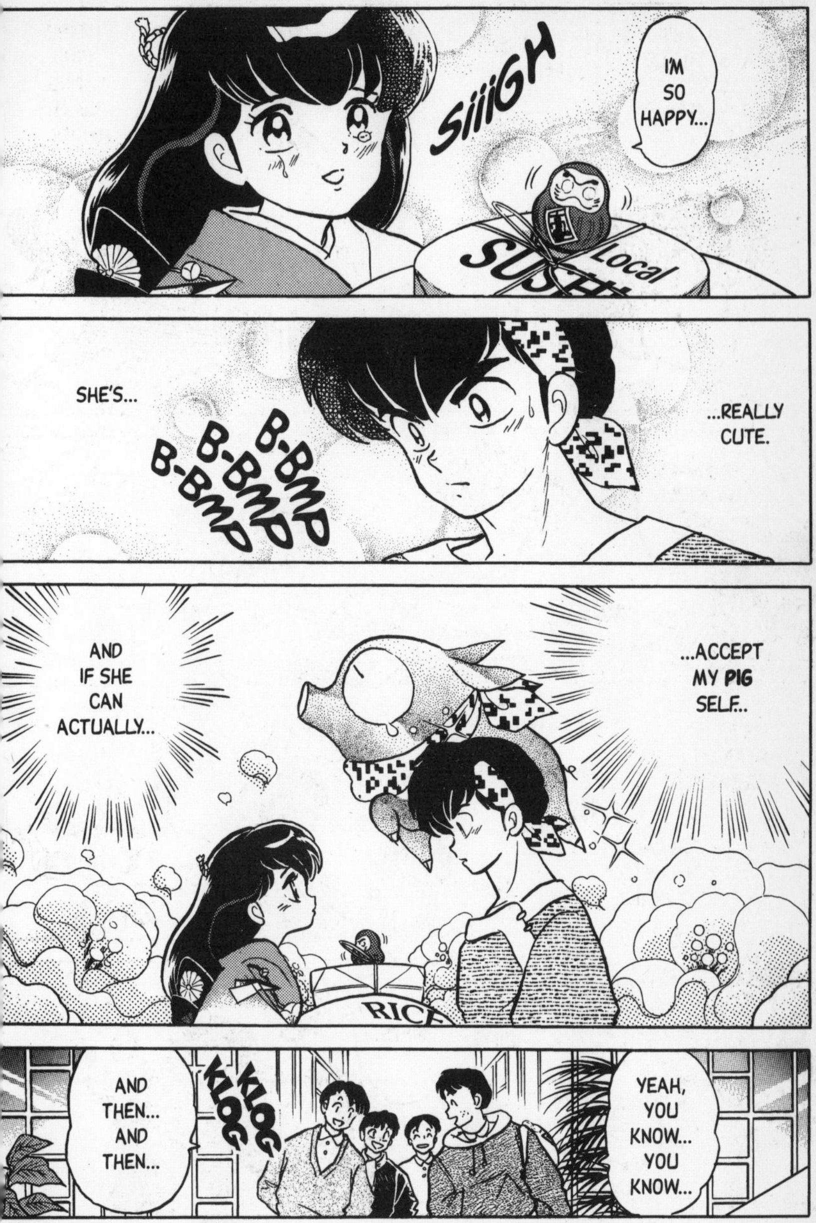
SiiiGH
I'M SO HAPPY...
Local
SHE'S...
B-BMP B-BMP B-BMP
...REALLY CUTE.
AND IF SHE CAN ACTUALLY...
...ACCEPT MY PIG SELF...
RICE
AND THEN... AND THEN...
KLOG KLOG
YEAH, YOU KNOW... YOU KNOW...

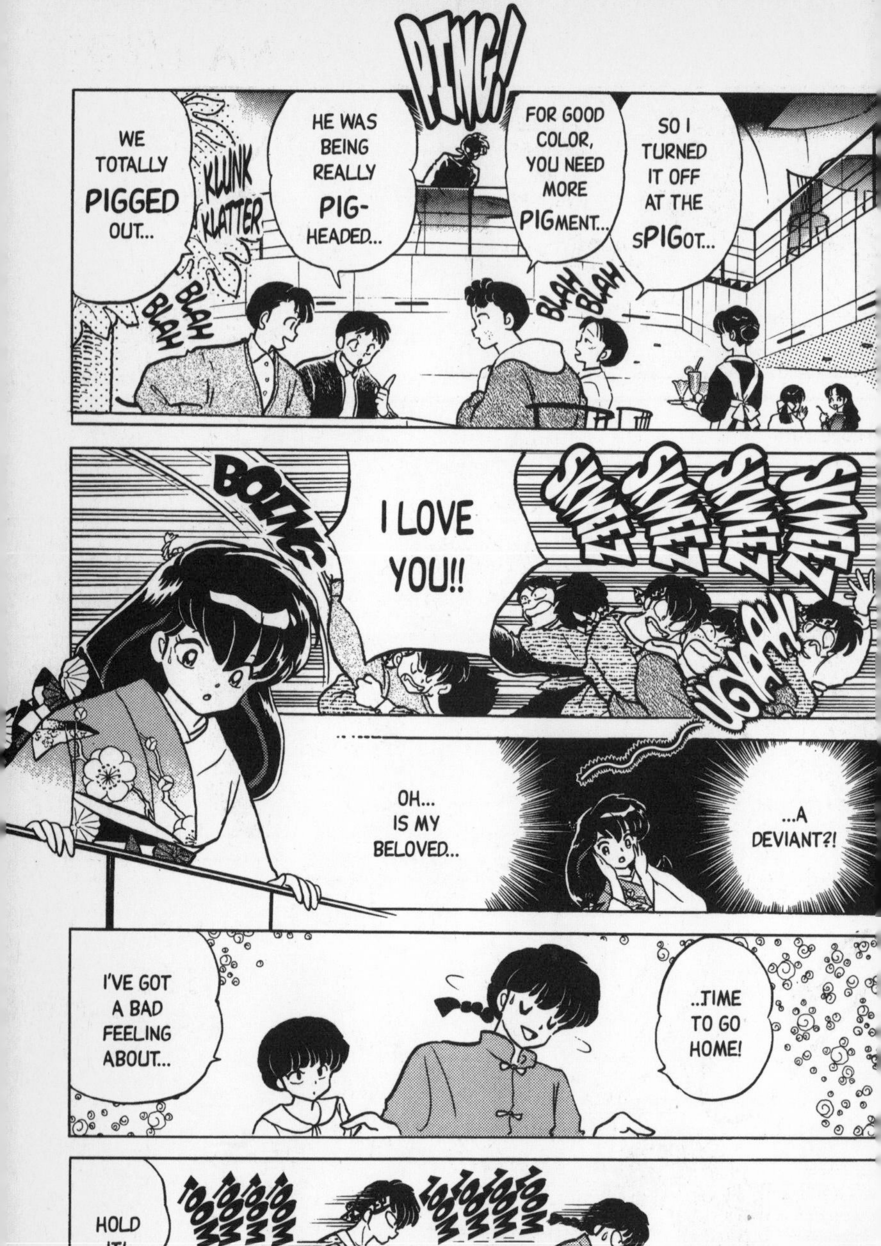
PING!
WE TOTALLY PIGGED OUT...
KLUNK KLATTER
BLAH BLAH
HE WAS BEING REALLY PIG-HEADED...
FOR GOOD COLOR, YOU NEED MORE PIGMENT...
BLAH BLAH
SO I TURNED IT OFF AT THE sPIGot...
BOING
I LOVE YOU!!
SKWEEZ SKWEEZ SKWEEZ SKWEEZ
UGYAH!
OH... IS MY BELOVED...
...A DEVIANT?!
I'VE GOT A BAD FEELING ABOUT...
..TIME TO GO HOME!
HOLD IT!
TOOM TOOM TOOM TOOM
ZOOM ZOOM ZOOM ZOOM

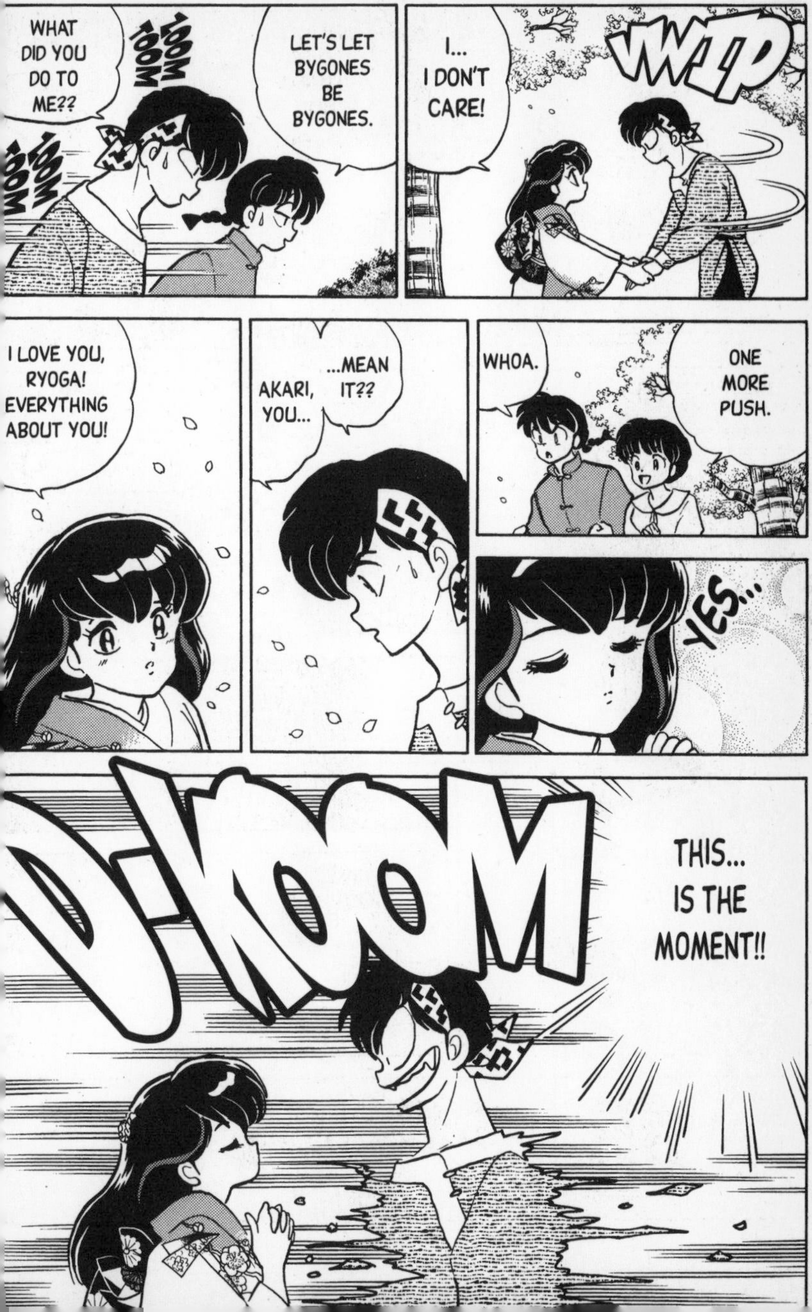
WHAT DID YOU DO TO ME??
TOOM TOOM
TOOM TOOM
LET'S LET BYGONES BE BYGONES.
I... I DON'T CARE!
VWIP
I LOVE YOU, RYOGA! EVERYTHING ABOUT YOU!
AKARI, YOU...
...MEAN IT??
WHOA.
ONE MORE PUSH.
YES...
D-KOOM
THIS... IS THE MOMENT!!

B-DMP B-DMP B-DMP B-DMP B-DMP

B-DMP B-DMP B-DMP B-DMP

CRUNCH CRUNCH CRUNCH

...AUGH!! I CAN'T CONCENTRATE!!

BO OB

LET'S GO HOME, RANMA. EVERYTHING'S FINE NOW.

YEAH.

WOOSH...

SSHH...

AFTER PASSING THROUGH THE LONG, DARK, COLD TUNNEL OF YOUTH...

THIS PRECIOUS MOMENT OF JOY...

SOB...

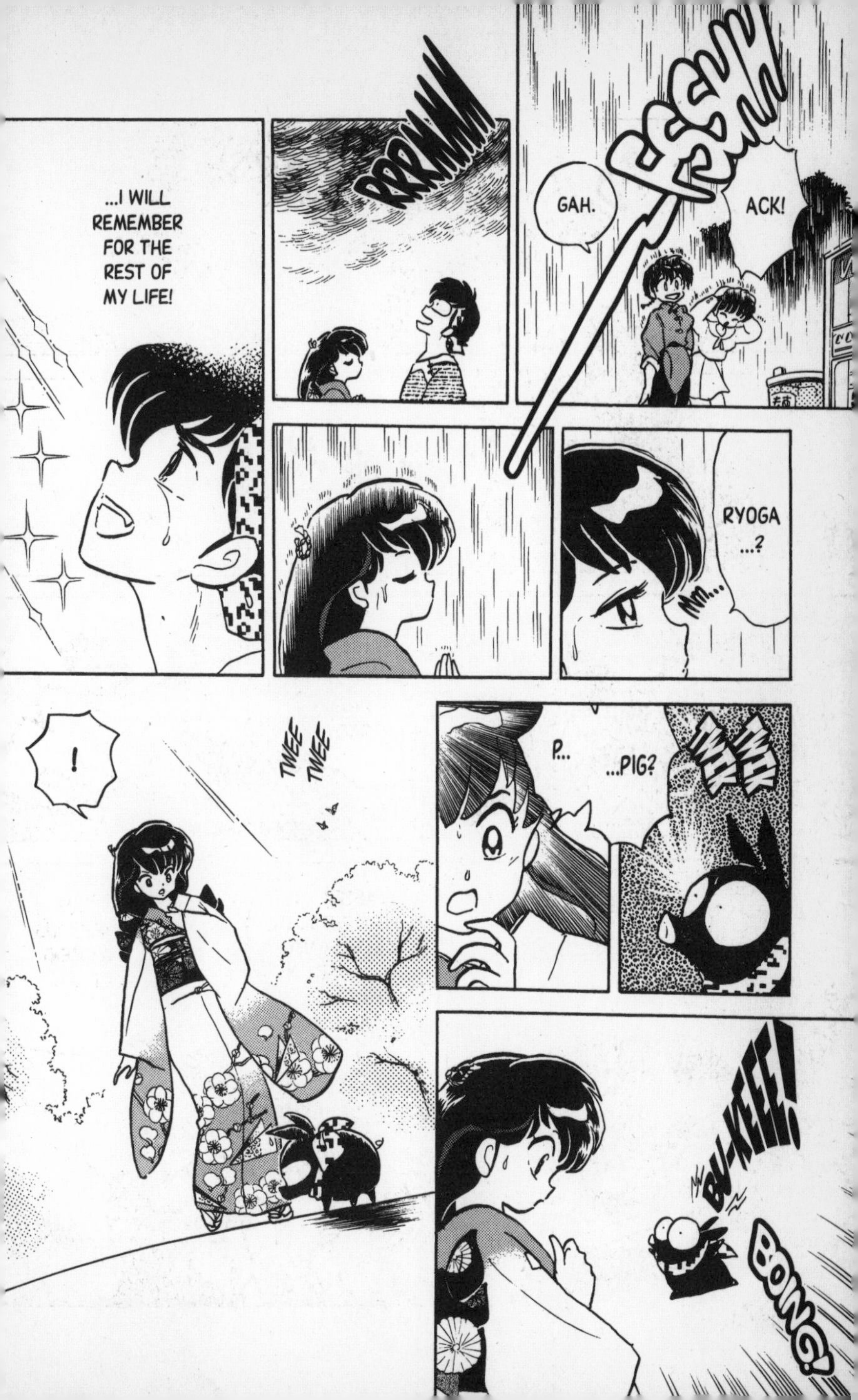
...I WILL REMEMBER FOR THE REST OF MY LIFE!
BRRMMM
GAH.
ACK!
RYOGA ...?
Mm...
!
TWEE TWEE
P...
...PIG?
TWIK TWIK
BU-KEEE!
BOING!

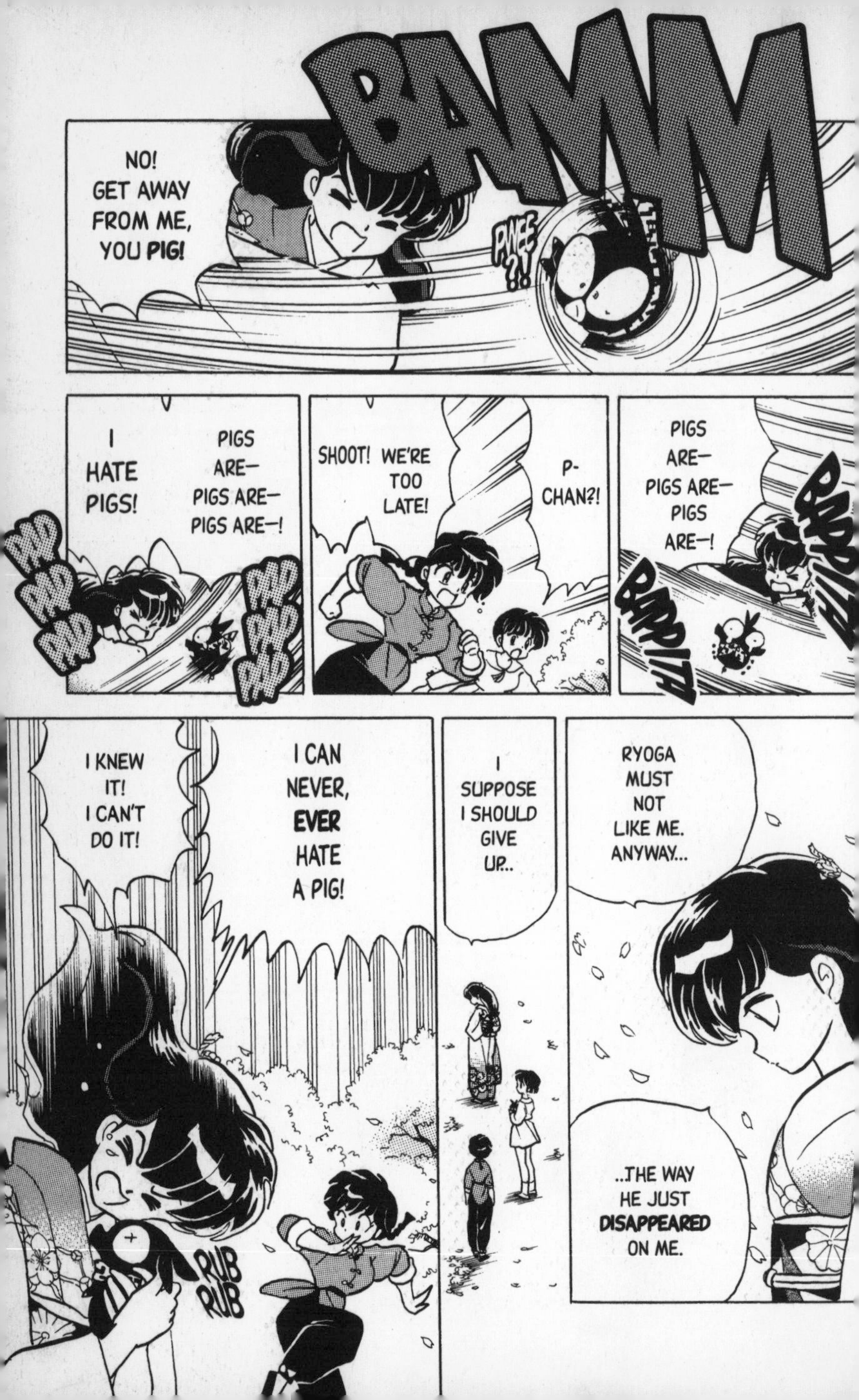
BAMM
NO! GET AWAY FROM ME, YOU **PIG!**
PWEE ?!
I HATE PIGS!
PIGS ARE— PIGS ARE— PIGS ARE—!
SHOOT! WE'RE TOO LATE!
P-CHAN?!
PIGS ARE— PIGS ARE— PIGS ARE—!
BADDITA
BADDITA
I KNEW IT! I CAN'T DO IT!
I CAN NEVER, **EVER** HATE A PIG!
RUB RUB
I SUPPOSE I SHOULD GIVE UP...
RYOGA MUST NOT LIKE ME. ANYWAY...
...THE WAY HE JUST **DISAPPEARED** ON ME.

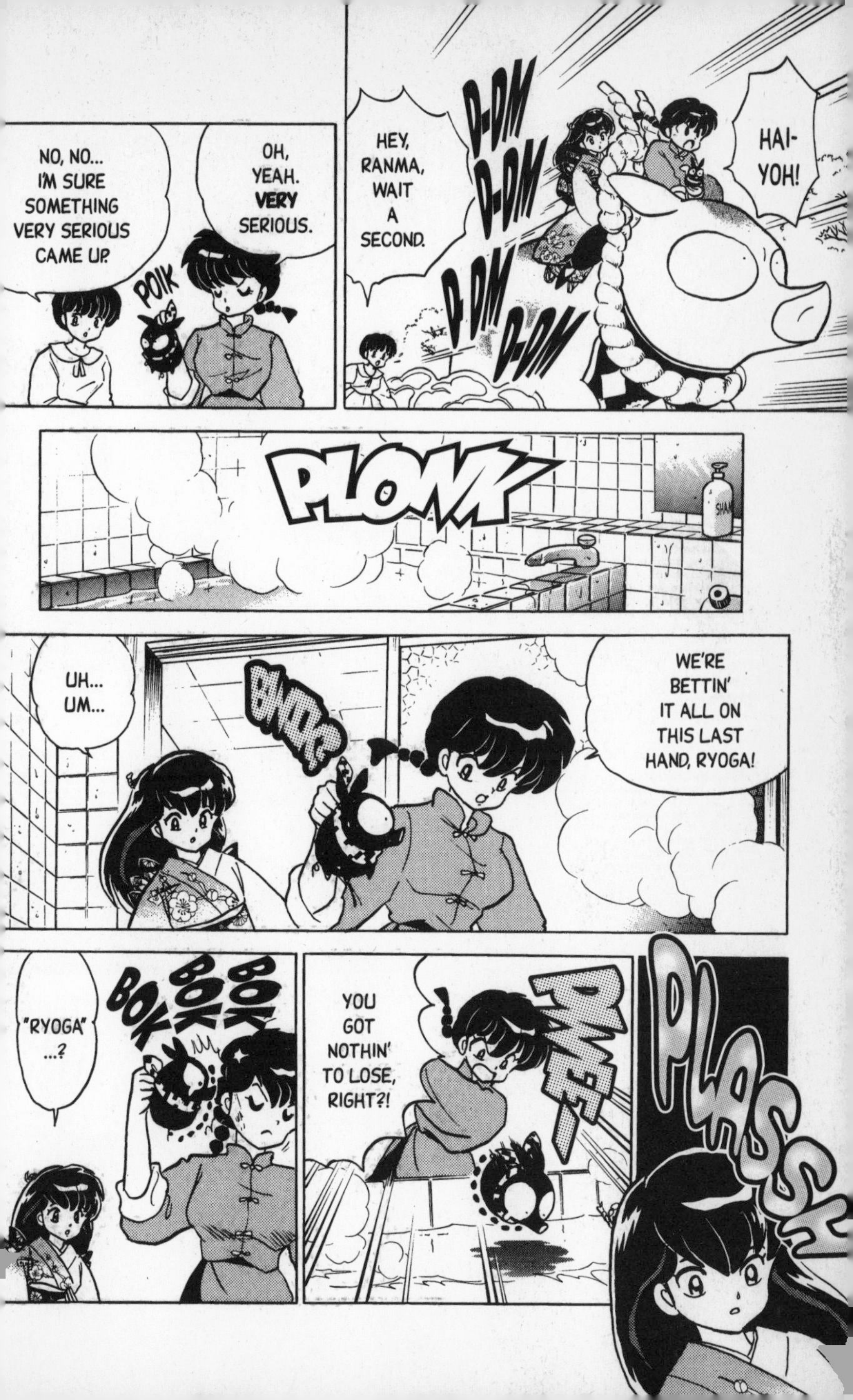
NO, NO... I'M SURE SOMETHING VERY SERIOUS CAME UP.
OH, YEAH. **VERY** SERIOUS.
POIK
HEY, RANMA, WAIT A SECOND.
D-DM D-DM D-DM D-DM
HAI-YOH!
PLONK
UH... UM...
WE'RE BETTIN' IT ALL ON THIS LAST HAND, RYOGA!
"RYOGA" ...?
BOK BOK BOK
YOU GOT NOTHIN' TO LOSE, RIGHT?!
PLASSH

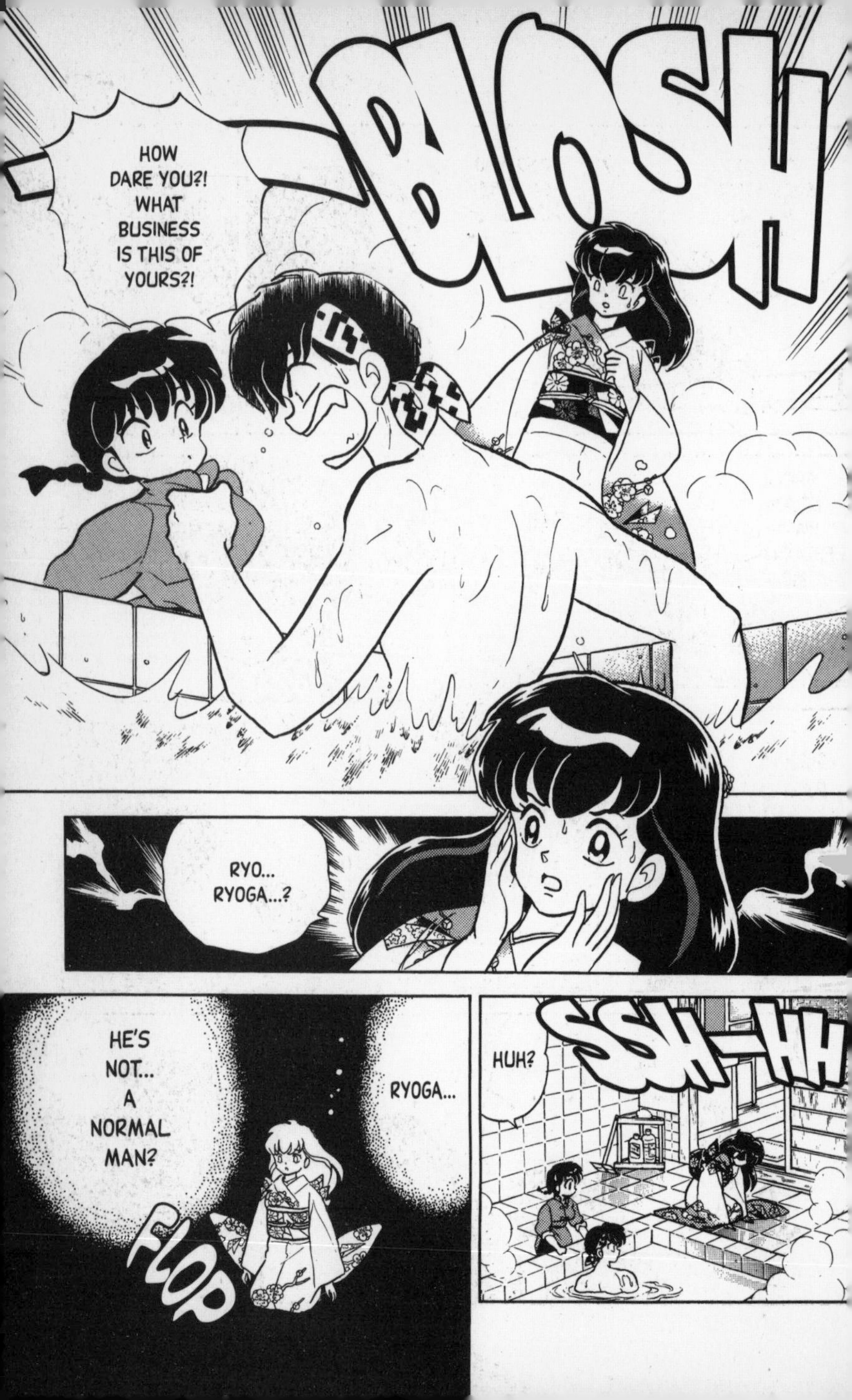
BASH
HOW DARE YOU?! WHAT BUSINESS IS THIS OF YOURS?!
RYO... RYOGA...?
HE'S NOT... A NORMAL MAN?
RYOGA...
FLOP
SSH-HH
HUH?

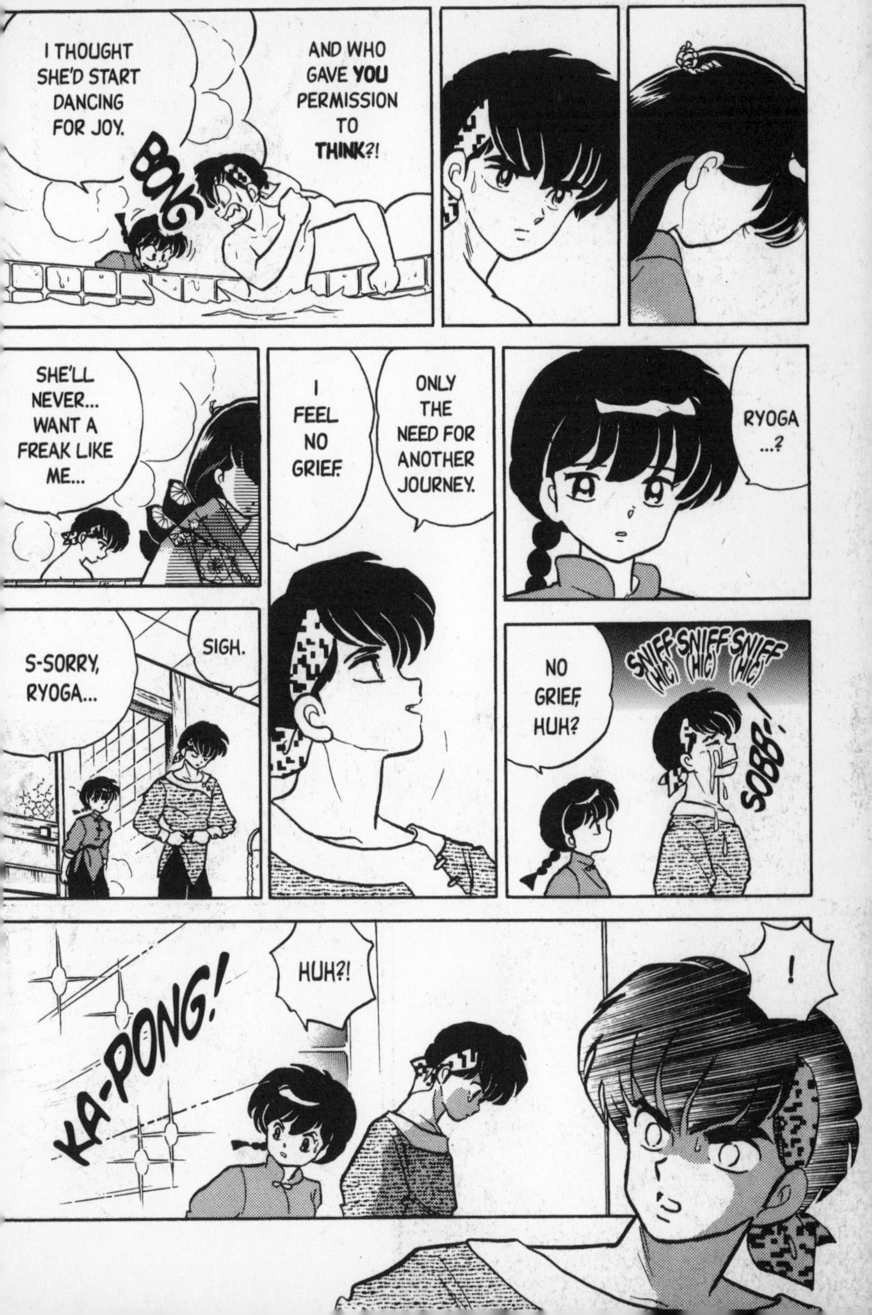
I THOUGHT SHE'D START DANCING FOR JOY.
AND WHO GAVE **YOU** PERMISSION TO **THINK?!**
BONG
SHE'LL NEVER... WANT A FREAK LIKE ME...
S-SORRY, RYOGA...
SIGH.
I FEEL NO GRIEF.
ONLY THE NEED FOR ANOTHER JOURNEY.
RYOGA ...?
NO GRIEF, HUH?
SNIFF SNIFF SNIFF
(HIC) (HIC) (HIC)
SOBB-!
KA-PONG!
HUH?!
!

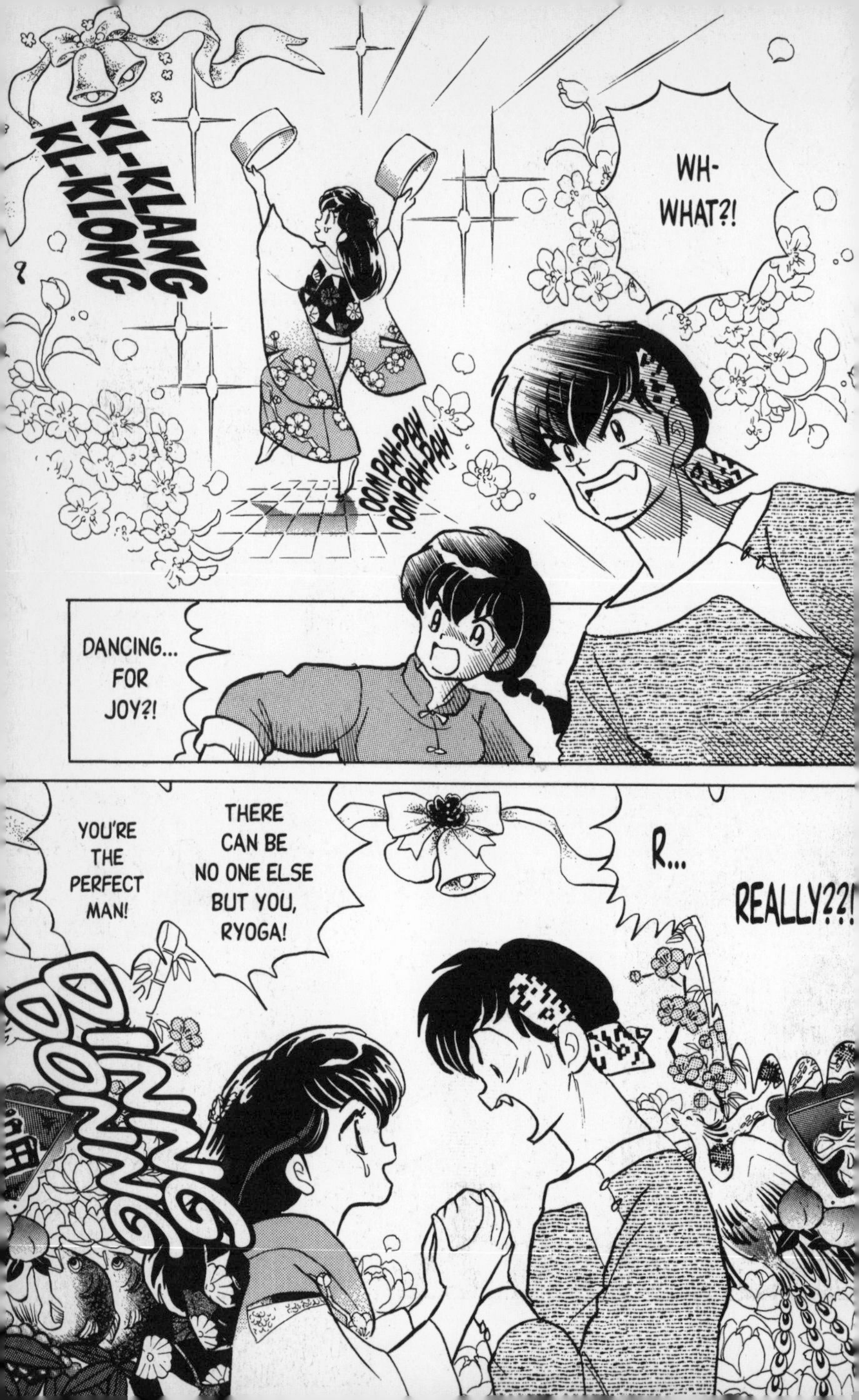
KL-KLANG KL-KLONG
OOM PAH-PAH OOM PAH-PAH
WH- WHAT?!
DANCING... FOR JOY?!
YOU'RE THE PERFECT MAN!
THERE CAN BE NO ONE ELSE BUT YOU, RYOGA!
DING DONG
R... REALLY??!

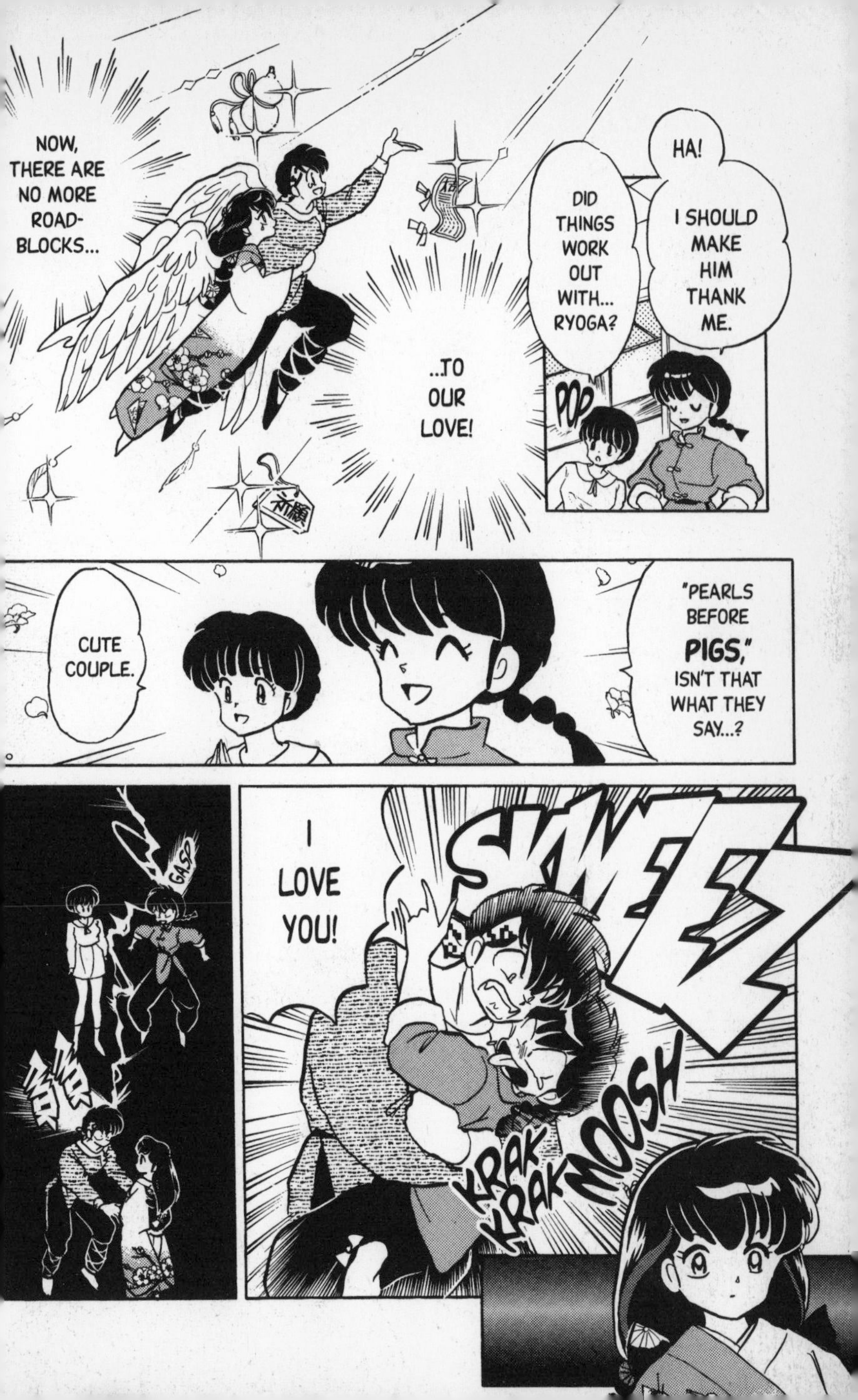
NOW, THERE ARE NO MORE ROAD-BLOCKS...
...TO OUR LOVE!
DID THINGS WORK OUT WITH... RYOGA?
HA!
I SHOULD MAKE HIM THANK ME.
POP
CUTE COUPLE.
"PEARLS BEFORE PIGS," ISN'T THAT WHAT THEY SAY...?
GASP
I LOVE YOU!
KRAK KRAK MOOSH

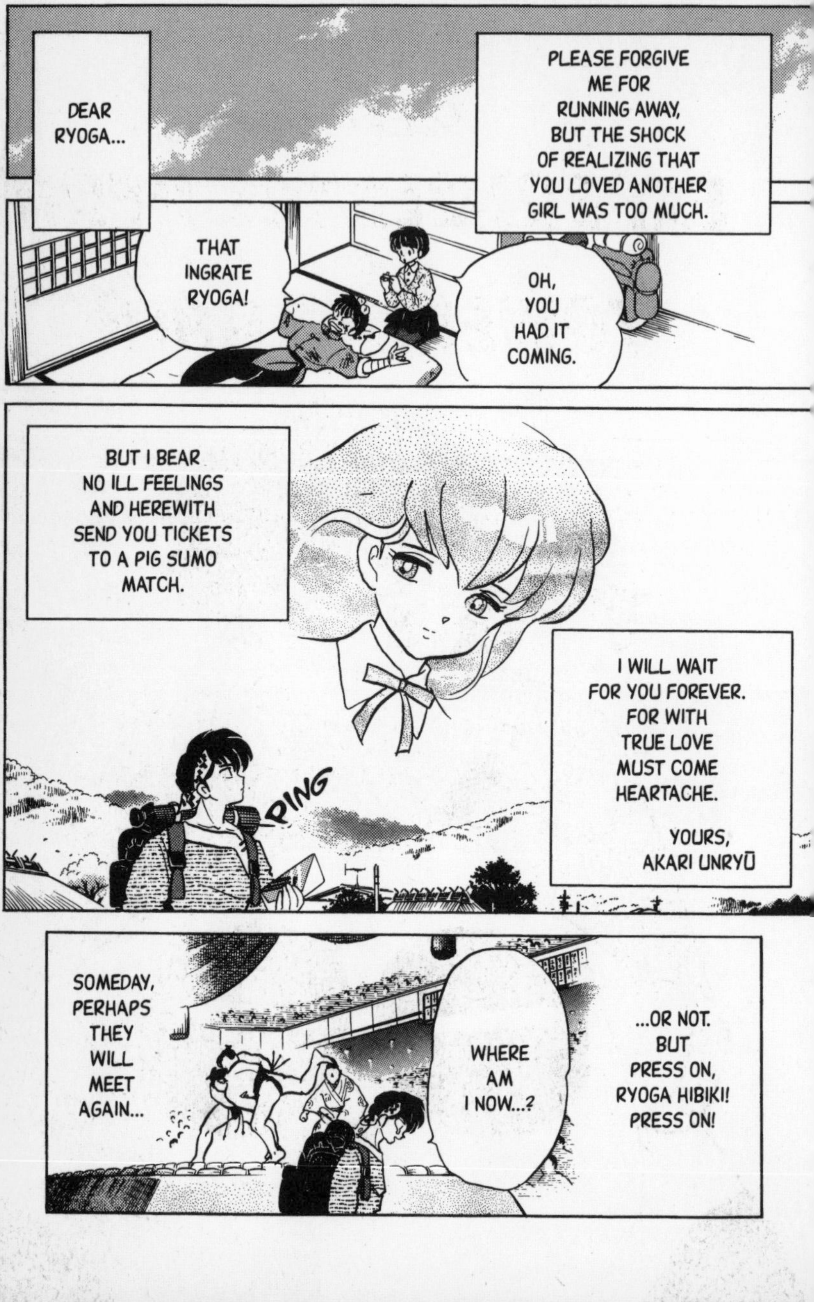
DEAR RYOGA...
PLEASE FORGIVE ME FOR RUNNING AWAY, BUT THE SHOCK OF REALIZING THAT YOU LOVED ANOTHER GIRL WAS TOO MUCH.
THAT INGRATE RYOGA!
OH, YOU HAD IT COMING.
BUT I BEAR NO ILL FEELINGS AND HEREWITH SEND YOU TICKETS TO A PIG SUMO MATCH.
I WILL WAIT FOR YOU FOREVER. FOR WITH TRUE LOVE MUST COME HEARTACHE.
YOURS, AKARI UNRYŪ
PING
SOMEDAY, PERHAPS THEY WILL MEET AGAIN...
WHERE AM I NOW...?
...OR NOT. BUT PRESS ON, RYOGA HIBIKI! PRESS ON!

PART 4
EXPERIMENTAL HERB • TOWERING HAIR

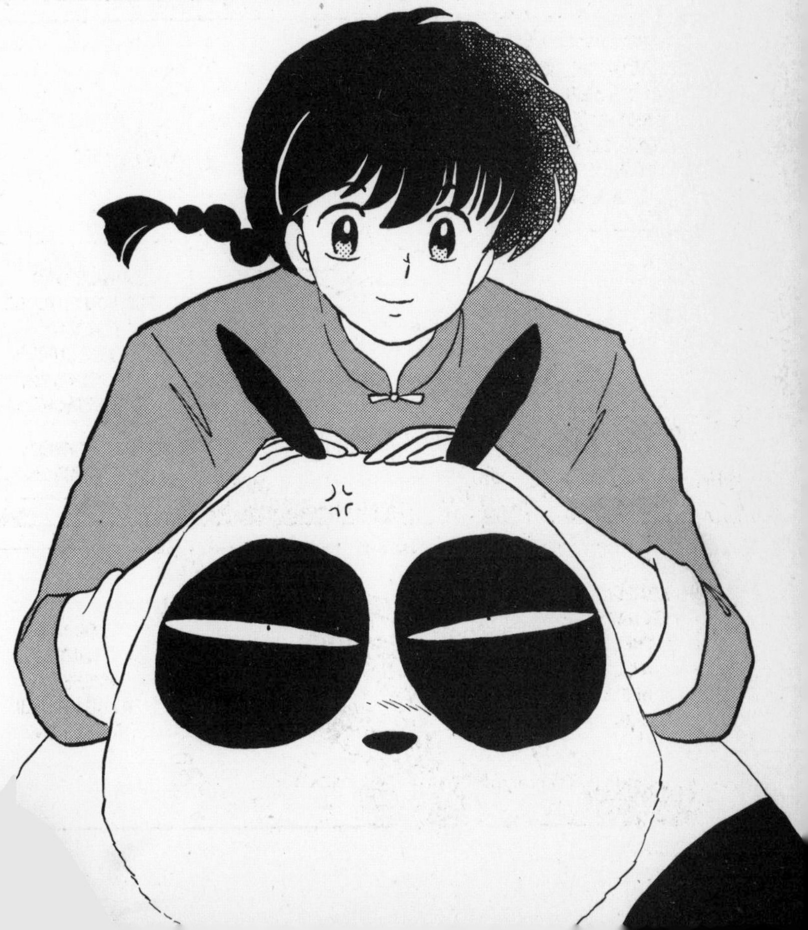

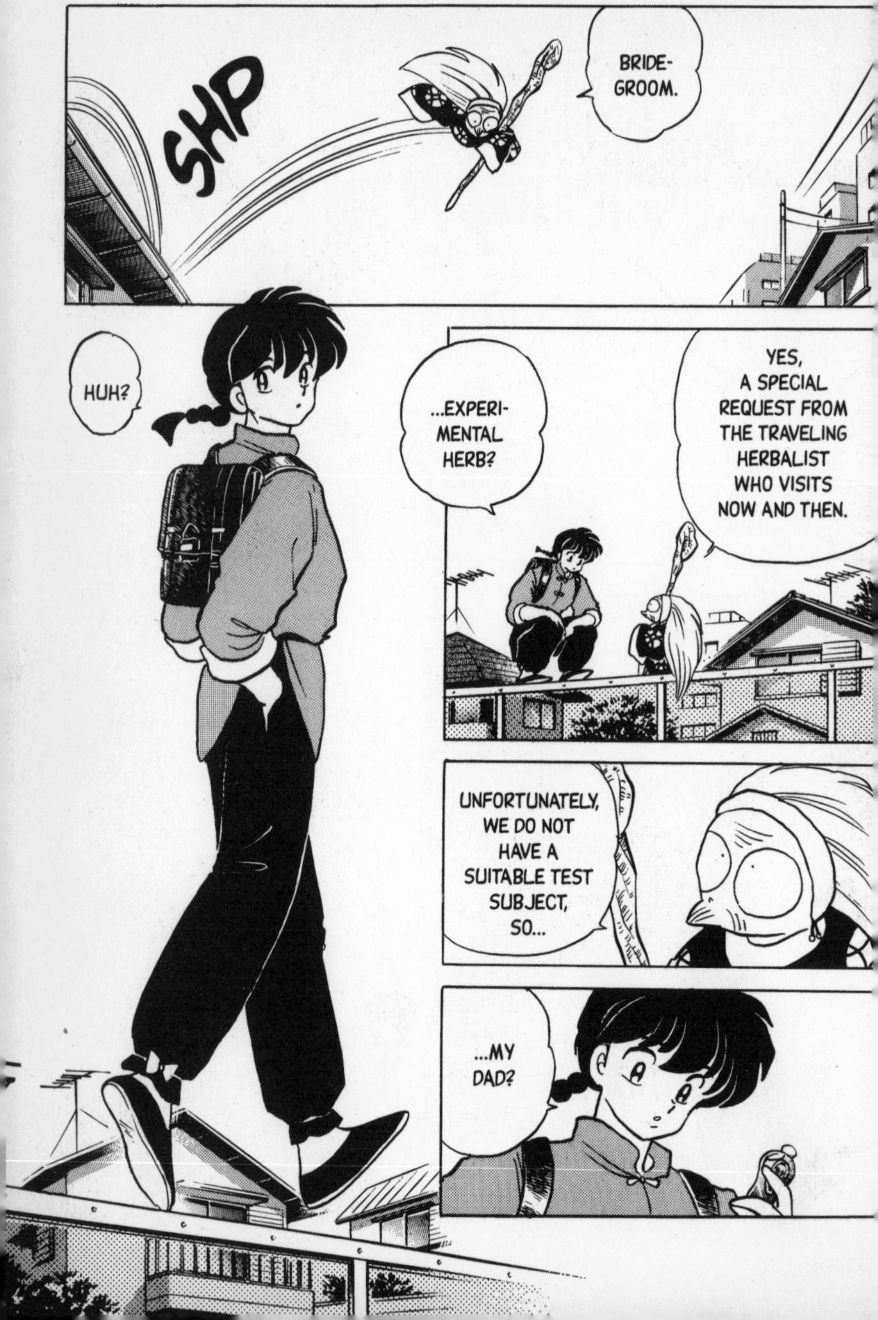
SHP
BRIDE-GROOM.
HUH?
...EXPERI-MENTAL HERB?
YES, A SPECIAL REQUEST FROM THE TRAVELING HERBALIST WHO VISITS NOW AND THEN.
UNFORTUNATELY, WE DO NOT HAVE A SUITABLE TEST SUBJECT, SO...
...MY DAD?

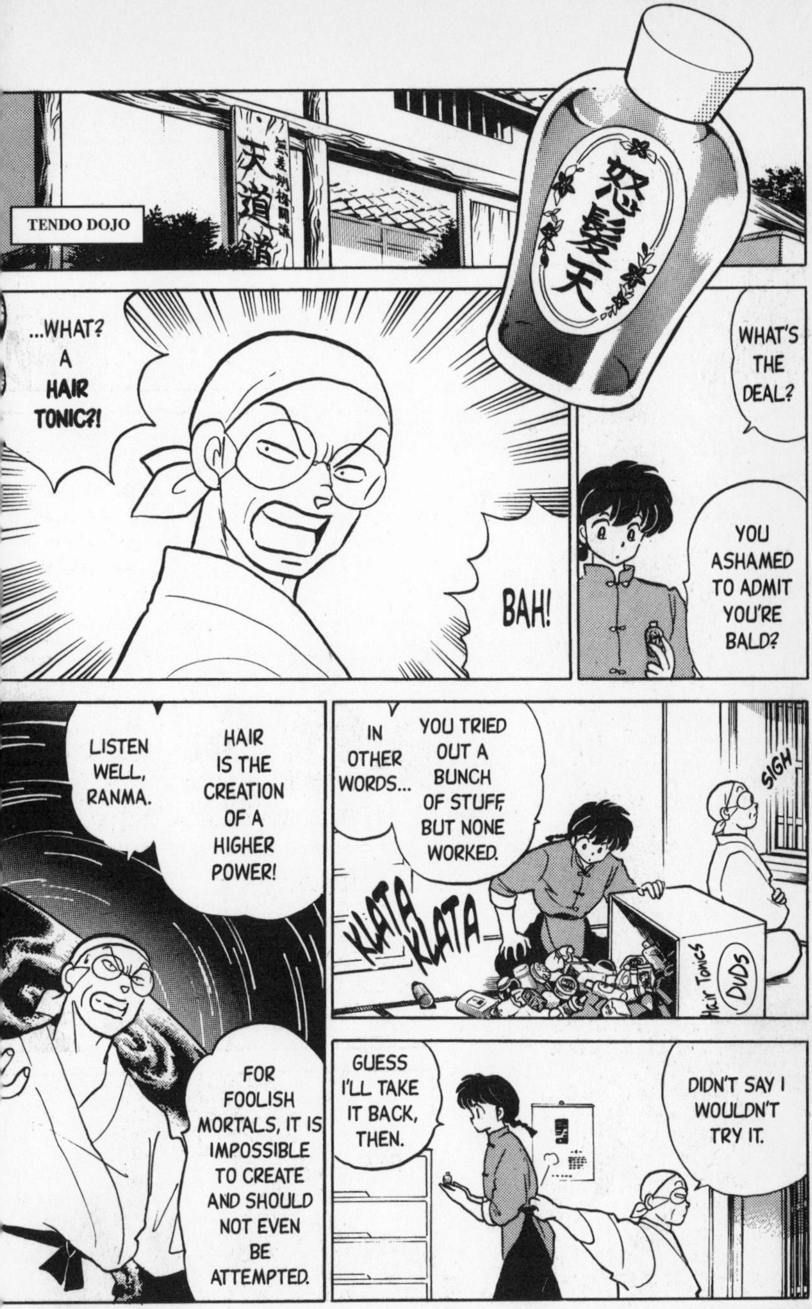
TENDO DOJO
怒髪天
...WHAT? A HAIR TONIC?!
BAH!
WHAT'S THE DEAL?
YOU ASHAMED TO ADMIT YOU'RE BALD?
LISTEN WELL, RANMA.
HAIR IS THE CREATION OF A HIGHER POWER!
FOR FOOLISH MORTALS, IT IS IMPOSSIBLE TO CREATE AND SHOULD NOT EVEN BE ATTEMPTED.
IN OTHER WORDS...
YOU TRIED OUT A BUNCH OF STUFF, BUT NONE WORKED.
SIGH
KLATA KLATA
Hair Tonics
DUDS
GUESS I'LL TAKE IT BACK, THEN.
DIDN'T SAY I WOULDN'T TRY IT.

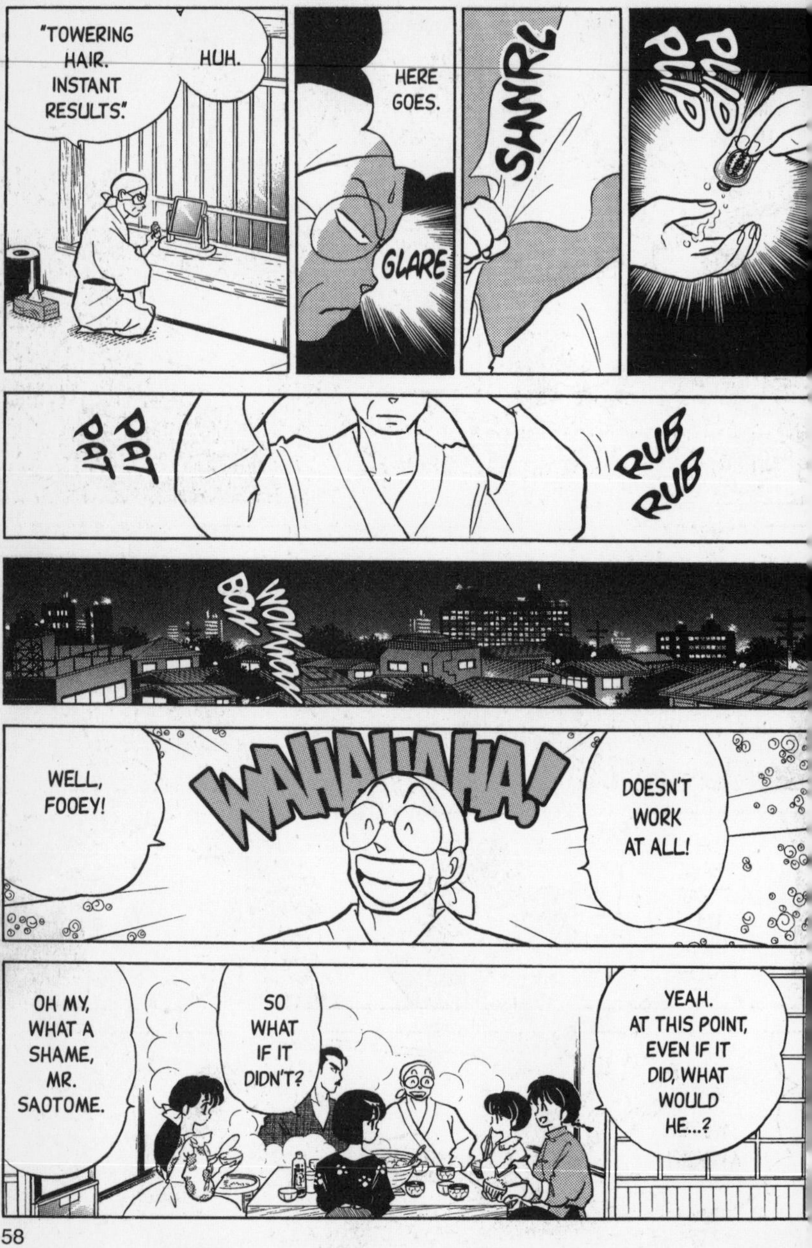

"TOWERING HAIR. INSTANT RESULTS."
HUH.
HERE GOES.
GLARE
SHWRL
PLIP PLIP
PAT PAT
RUB RUB
WOWWOW BOW
WELL, FOOEY!
WAHAHAHA!
DOESN'T WORK AT ALL!
OH MY, WHAT A SHAME, MR. SAOTOME.
SO WHAT IF IT DIDN'T?
YEAH. AT THIS POINT, EVEN IF IT DID, WHAT WOULD HE...?

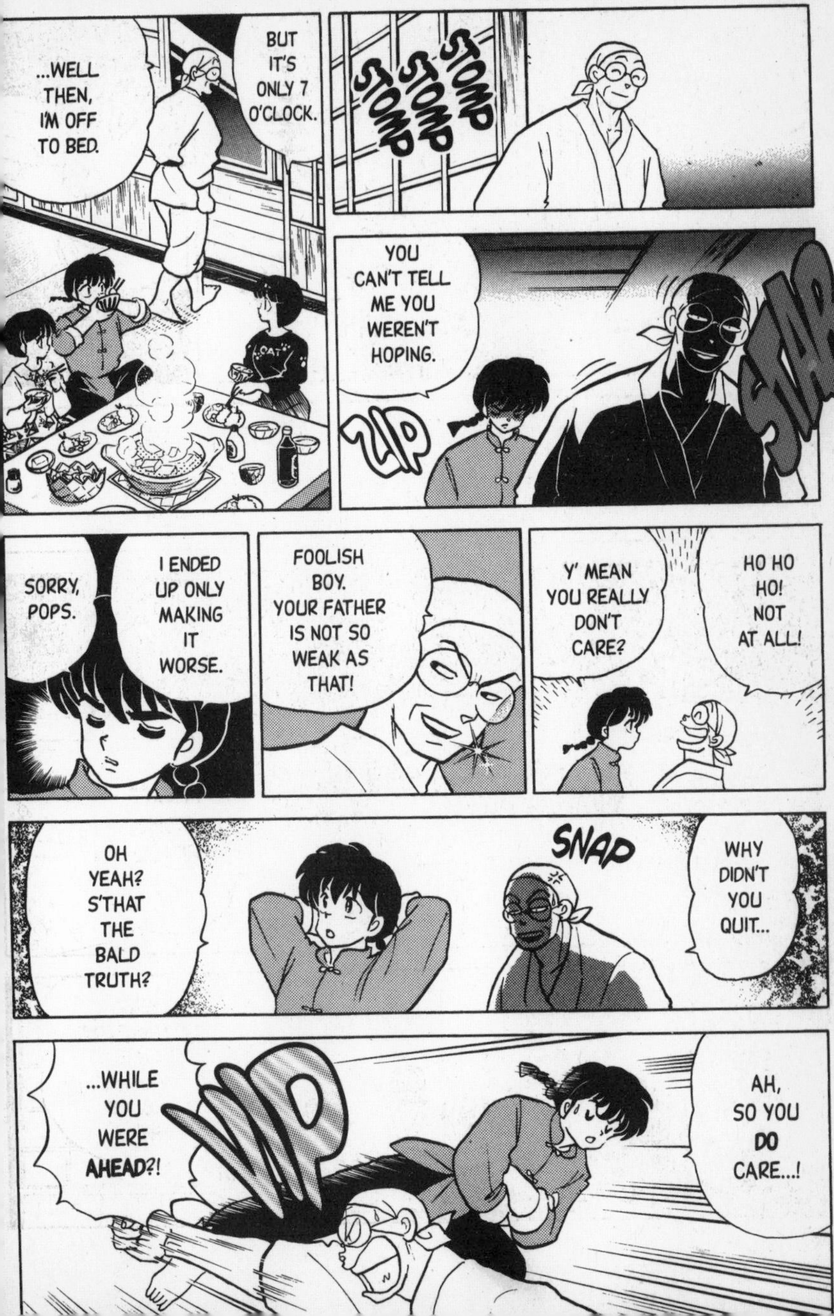
...WELL THEN, I'M OFF TO BED.
BUT IT'S ONLY 7 O'CLOCK.
STOMP STOMP STOMP
YOU CAN'T TELL ME YOU WEREN'T HOPING.
ZIP
STAB
SORRY, POPS.
I ENDED UP ONLY MAKING IT WORSE.
FOOLISH BOY. YOUR FATHER IS NOT SO WEAK AS THAT!
Y' MEAN YOU REALLY DON'T CARE?
HO HO HO! NOT AT ALL!
OH YEAH? S'THAT THE BALD TRUTH?
SNAP
WHY DIDN'T YOU QUIT...
...WHILE YOU WERE **AHEAD**?!
WHIP
AH, SO YOU **DO** CARE...!

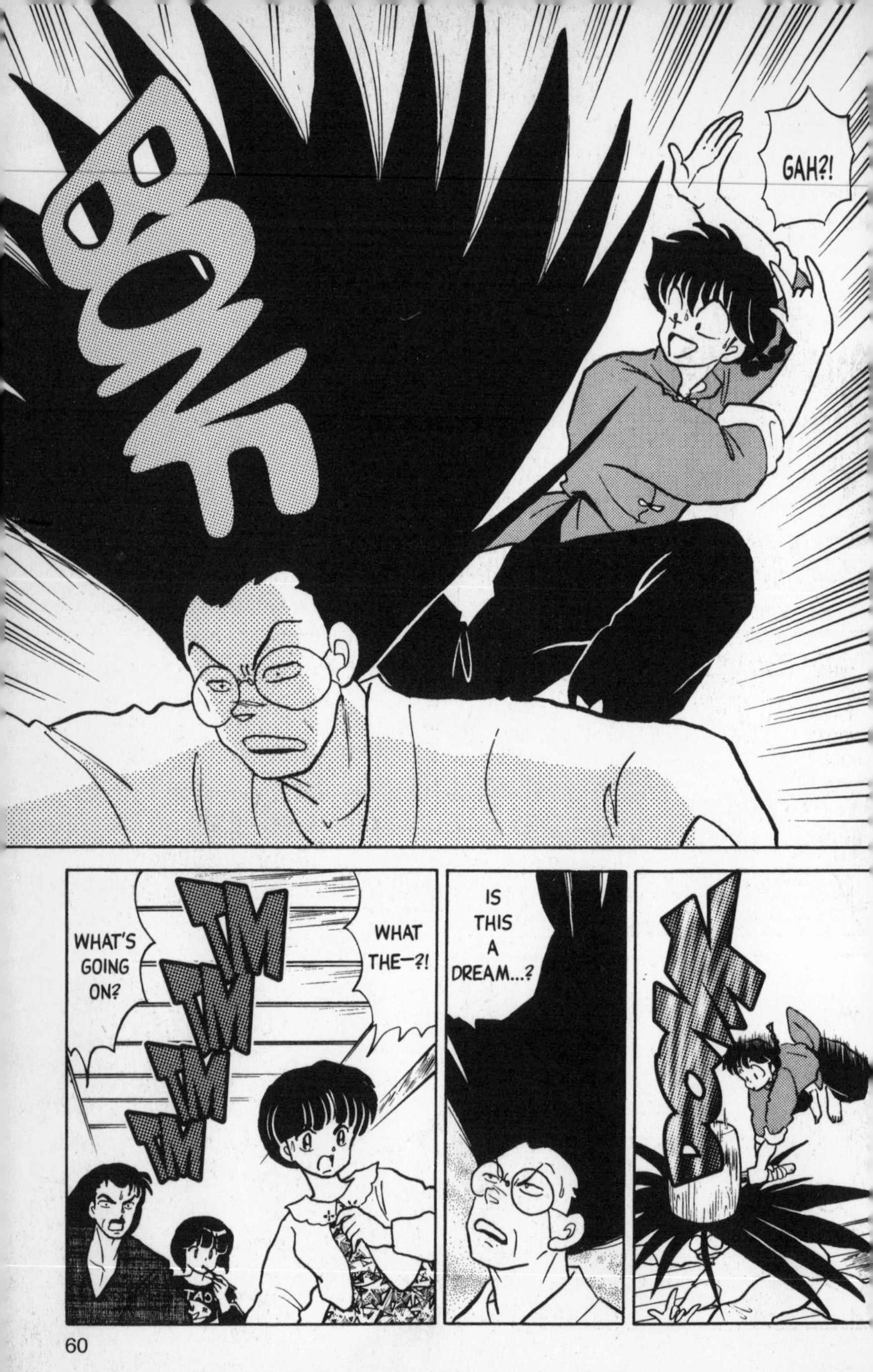
BONK
GAH?!
WHAT'S GOING ON?
WHAT THE—?!
IS THIS A DREAM...?

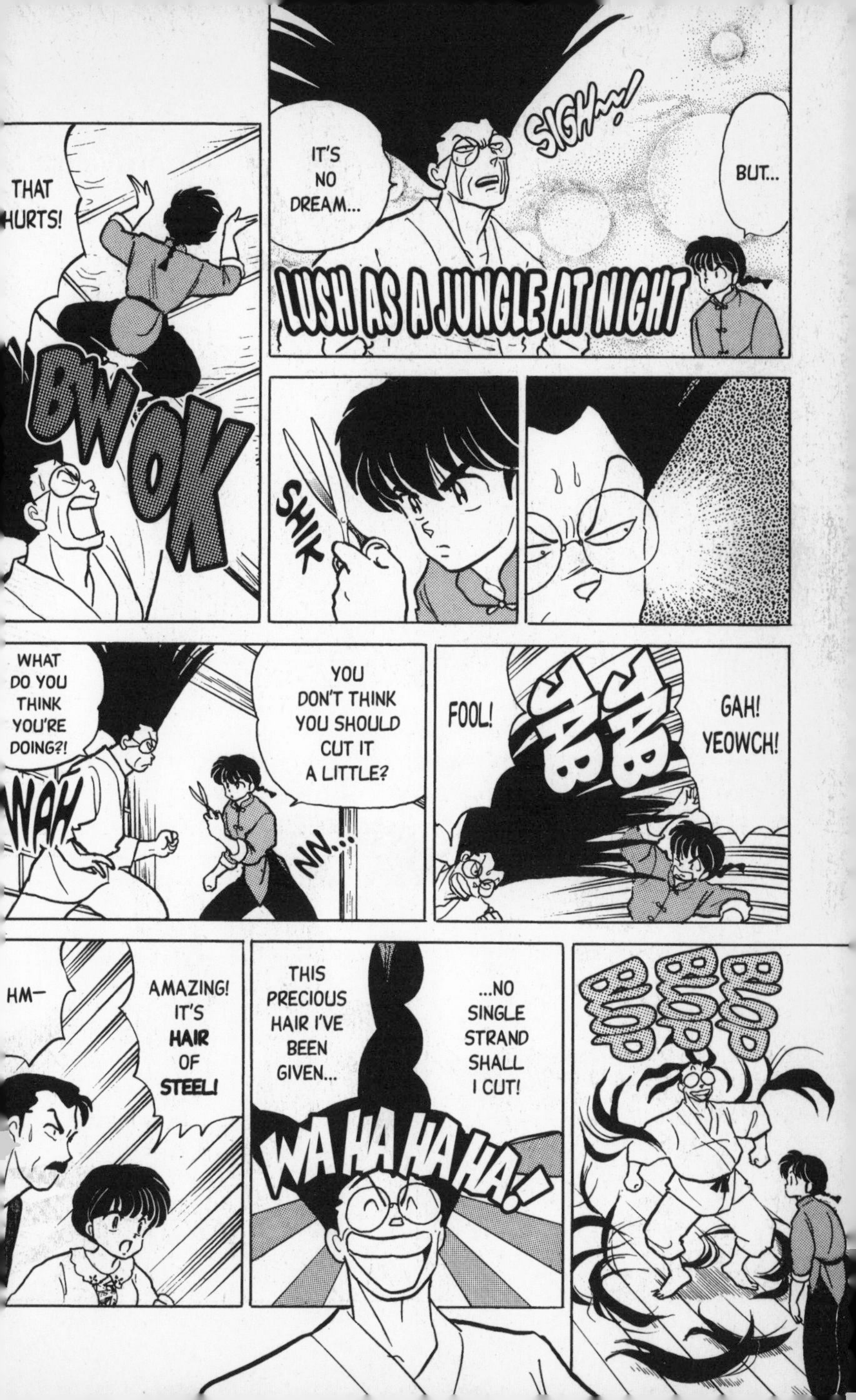
THAT HURTS!
BWOK
IT'S NO DREAM...
SIGH~~!
BUT...
LUSH AS A JUNGLE AT NIGHT
SHIK
WHAT DO YOU THINK YOU'RE DOING?!
WAH
YOU DON'T THINK YOU SHOULD CUT IT A LITTLE?
NN...
FOOL!
JAB JAB
GAH! YEOWCH!
HM—
AMAZING! IT'S HAIR OF STEEL!
THIS PRECIOUS HAIR I'VE BEEN GIVEN...
...NO SINGLE STRAND SHALL I CUT!
WA HA HA HA HA!
BLOOP BLOOP BLOOP

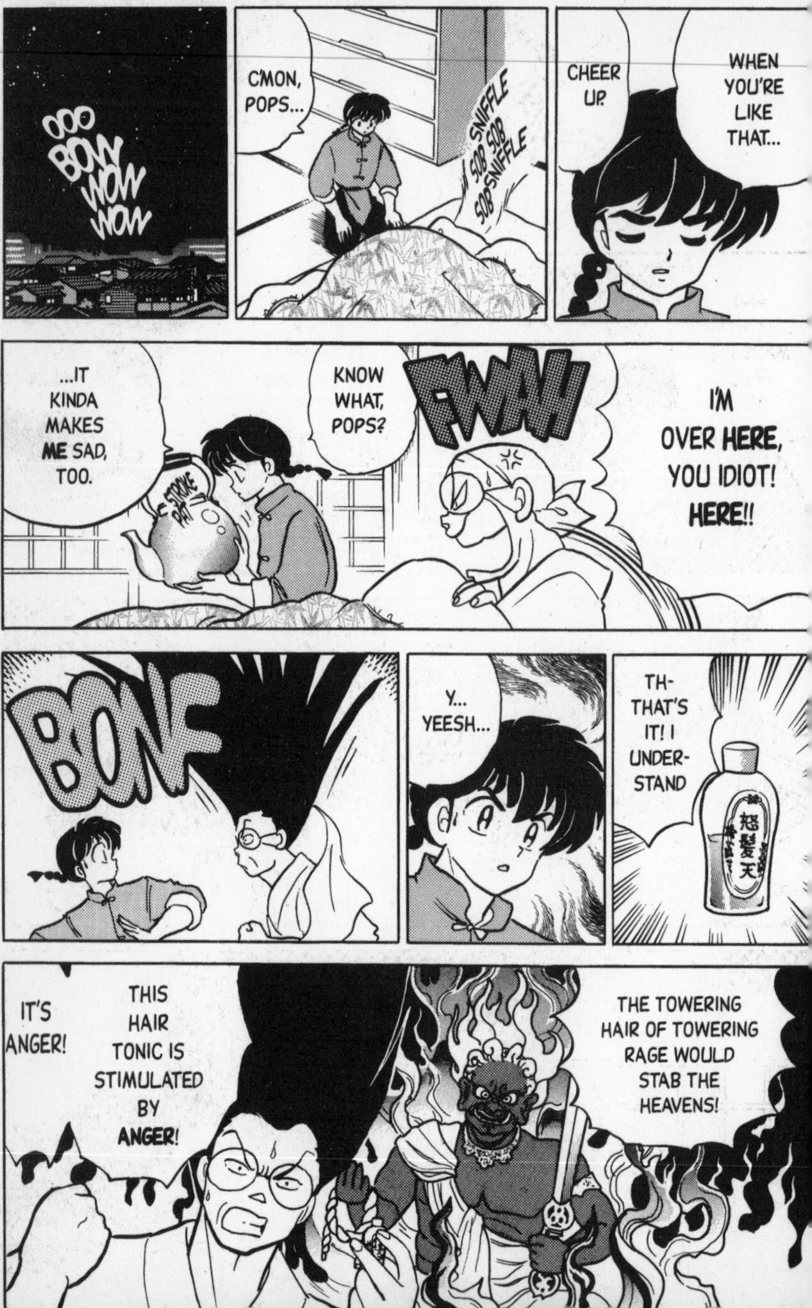

OOO BOW WOW WOW
C'MON, POPS...
SNIFFLE SOB SOB SOB SNIFFLE
CHEER UP.
WHEN YOU'RE LIKE THAT...
...IT KINDA MAKES ME SAD, TOO.
STROKE PAT
KNOW WHAT, POPS?
FWAH
I'M OVER HERE, YOU IDIOT! HERE!!
BONF
Y... YEESH...
TH-THAT'S IT! I UNDER-STAND
怒髪天
IT'S ANGER!
THIS HAIR TONIC IS STIMULATED BY ANGER!
THE TOWERING HAIR OF TOWERING RAGE WOULD STAB THE HEAVENS!

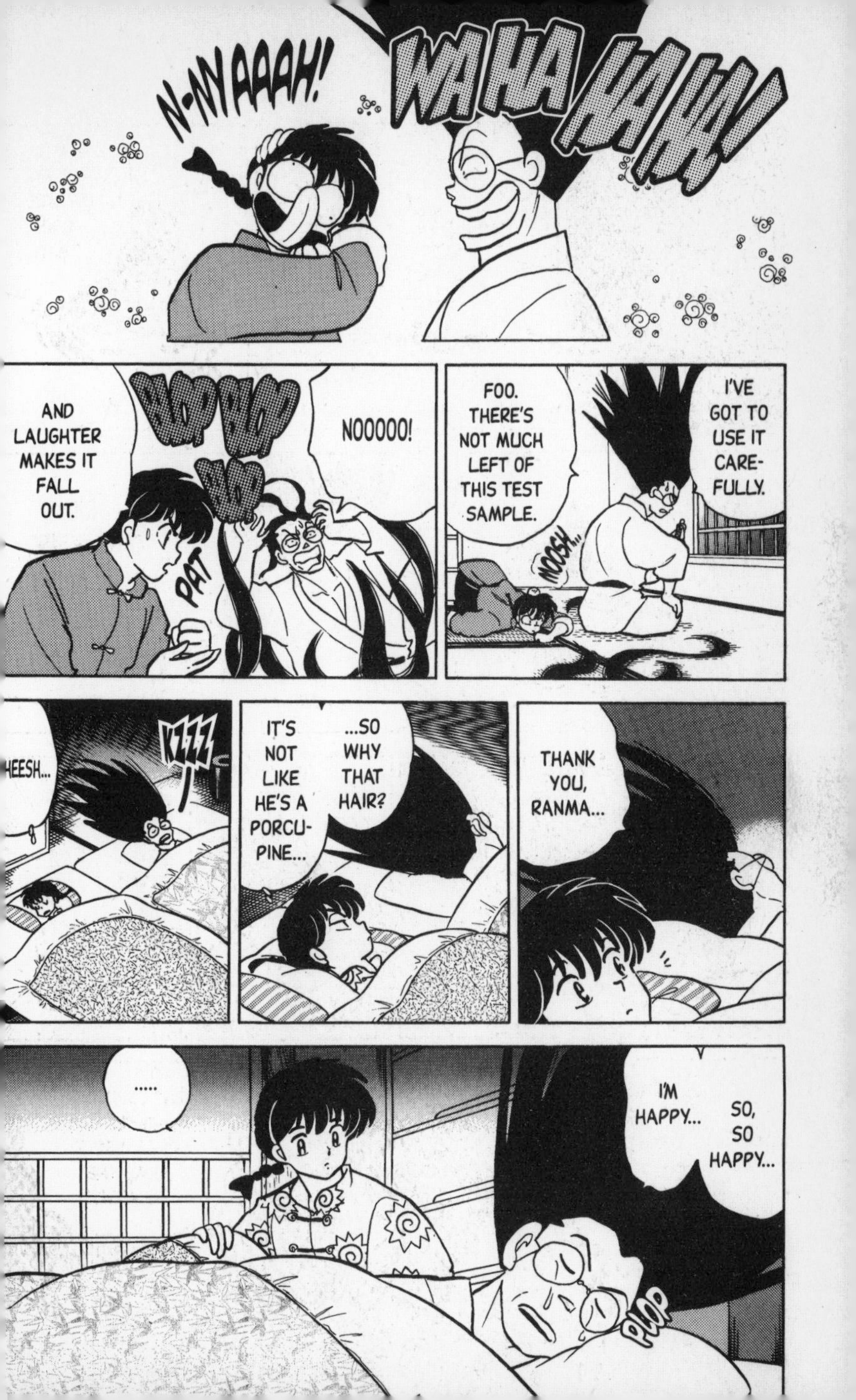
N-NYAAAH!
WA HA HA HA!
AND LAUGHTER MAKES IT FALL OUT.
PAT
NOOOOO!
FOO. THERE'S NOT MUCH LEFT OF THIS TEST SAMPLE.
WOOSH...
I'VE GOT TO USE IT CAREFULLY.
HEESH...
IT'S NOT LIKE HE'S A PORCUPINE...
...SO WHY THAT HAIR?
THANK YOU, RANMA...
......
I'M HAPPY...
SO, SO HAPPY...
PLOP

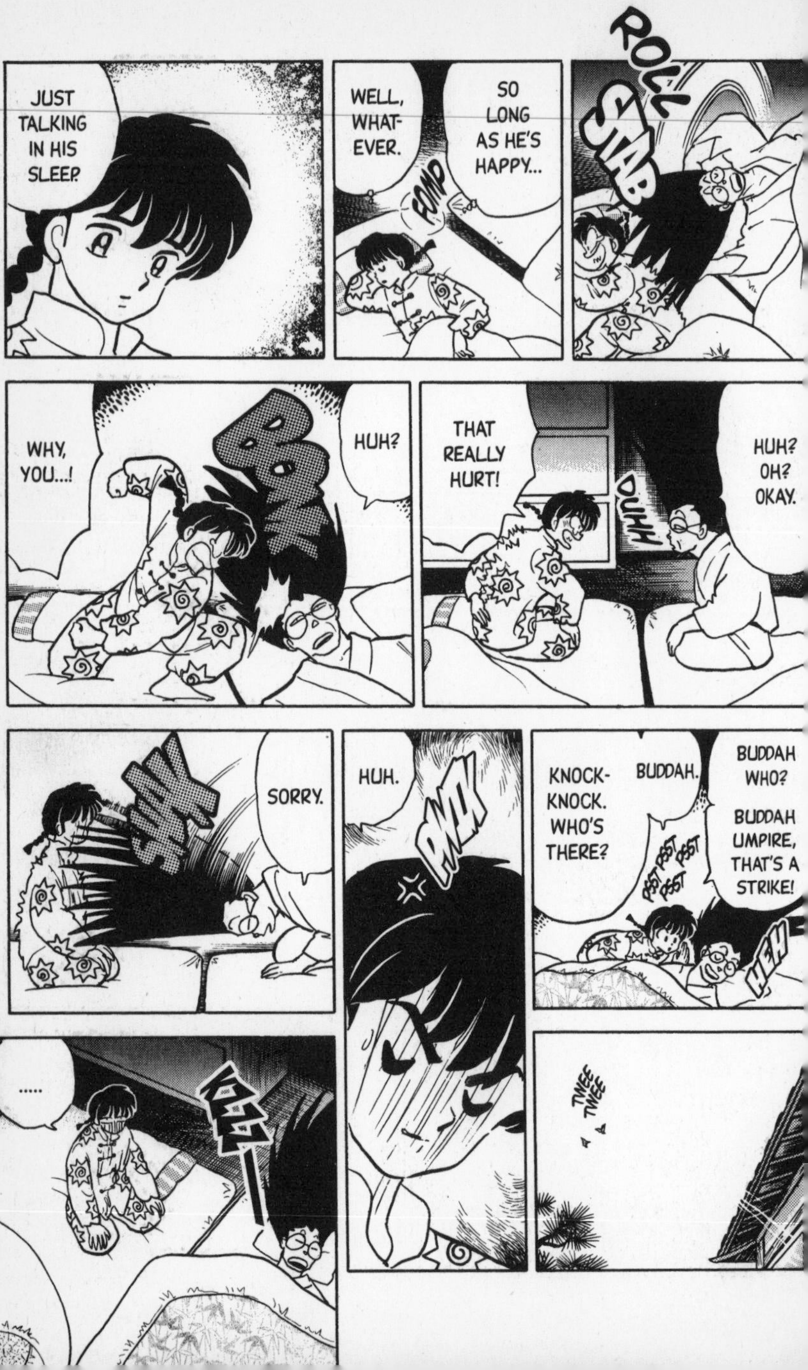

JUST TALKING IN HIS SLEEP.
WELL, WHAT-EVER.
SO LONG AS HE'S HAPPY...
FOMP
ROLL
STAB
WHY, YOU...!
HUH?
THAT REALLY HURT!
DUHH
HUH? OH? OKAY.
SORRY.
HUH.
KNOCK-KNOCK. WHO'S THERE?
BUDDAH.
BUDDAH WHO?
BUDDAH UMPIRE, THAT'S A STRIKE!
PSST PSST PSST PSST
HEH
.....
TWEE TWEE

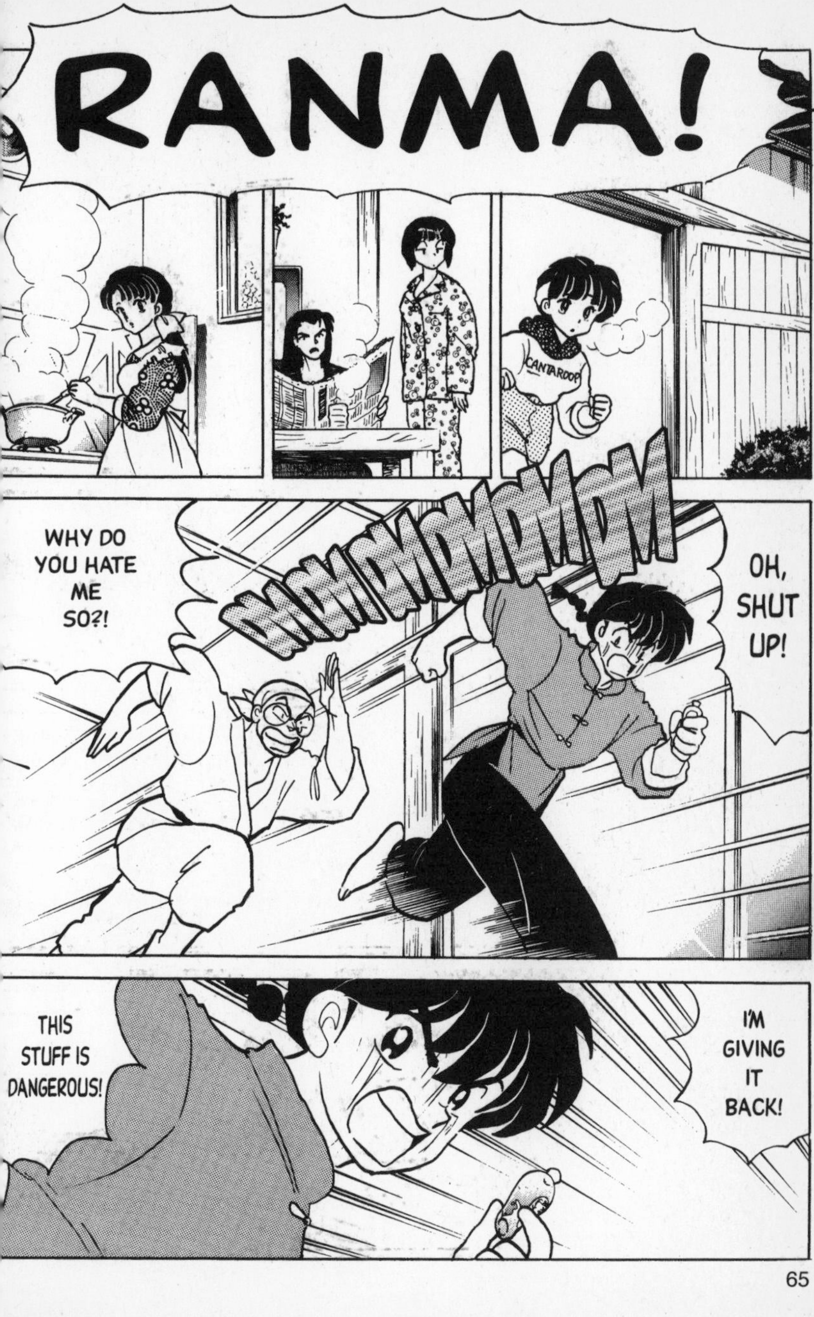
RANMA!
CANTAROOP
WHY DO YOU HATE ME SO?!
OH, SHUT UP!
THIS STUFF IS DANGEROUS!
I'M GIVING IT BACK!

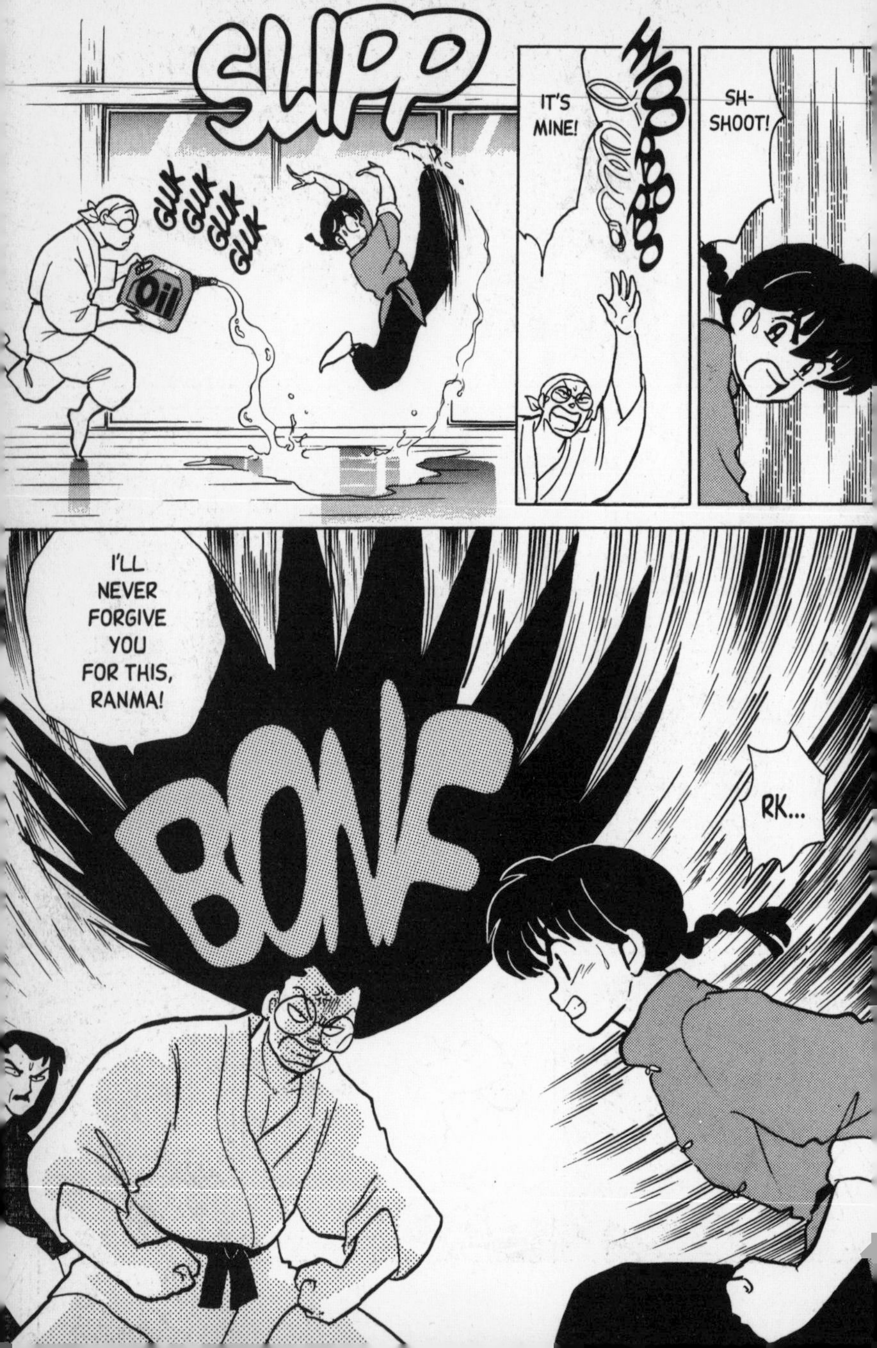
SLIPP
GLUK GLUK GLUK GLUK
Oil
IT'S MINE!
WHOOOOOOOOOO
SH- SHOOT!
I'LL NEVER FORGIVE YOU FOR THIS, RANMA!
BONK
RK...

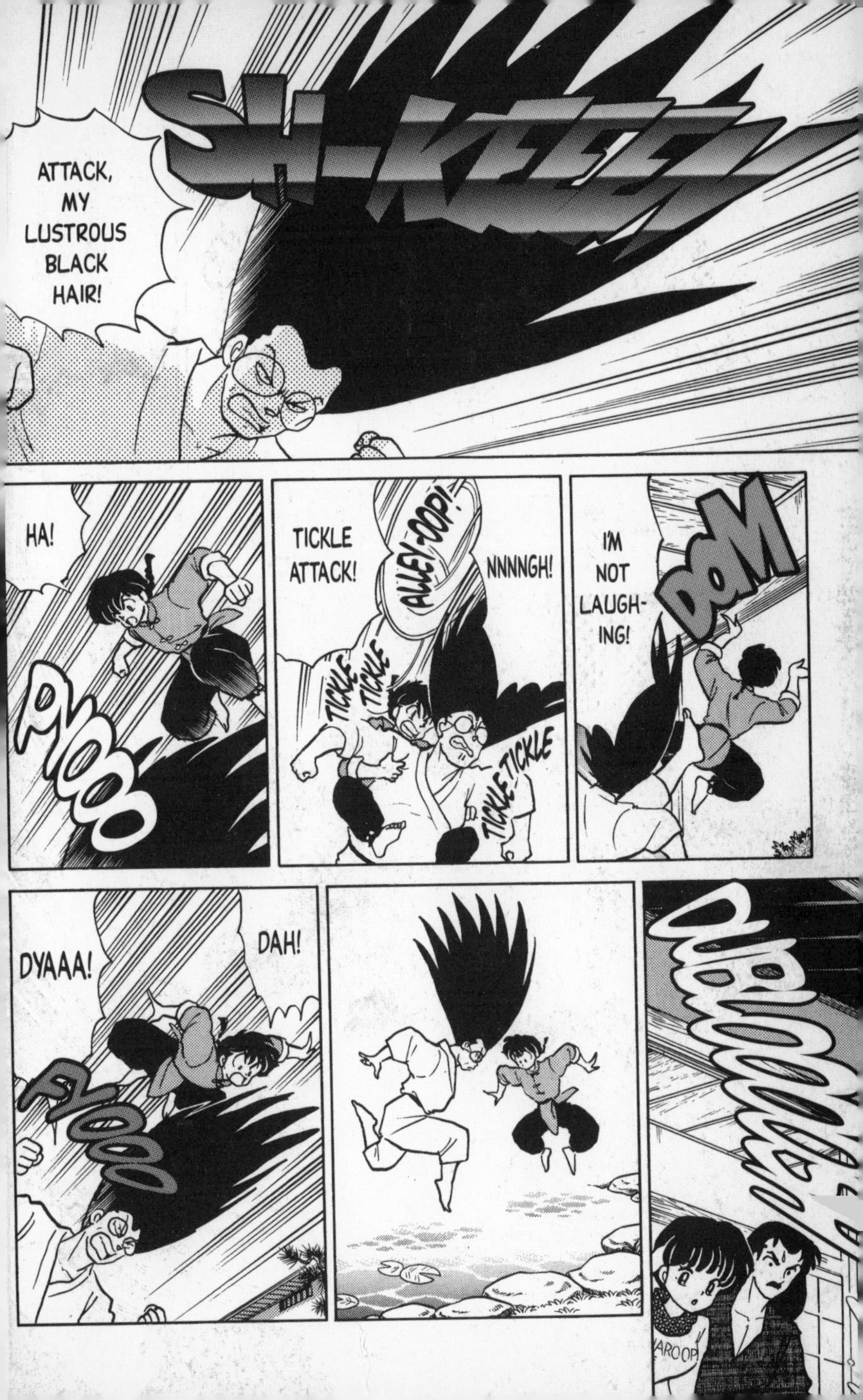
SH-KEESH
ATTACK, MY LUSTROUS BLACK HAIR!
HA!
PYOOO
TICKLE ATTACK!
ALLEY-OOP!
NNNNGH!
TICKLE TICKLE
TICKLE TICKLE
I'M NOT LAUGH-ING!
BOM
DYAAA!
DAH!
PYOOO
AROOP

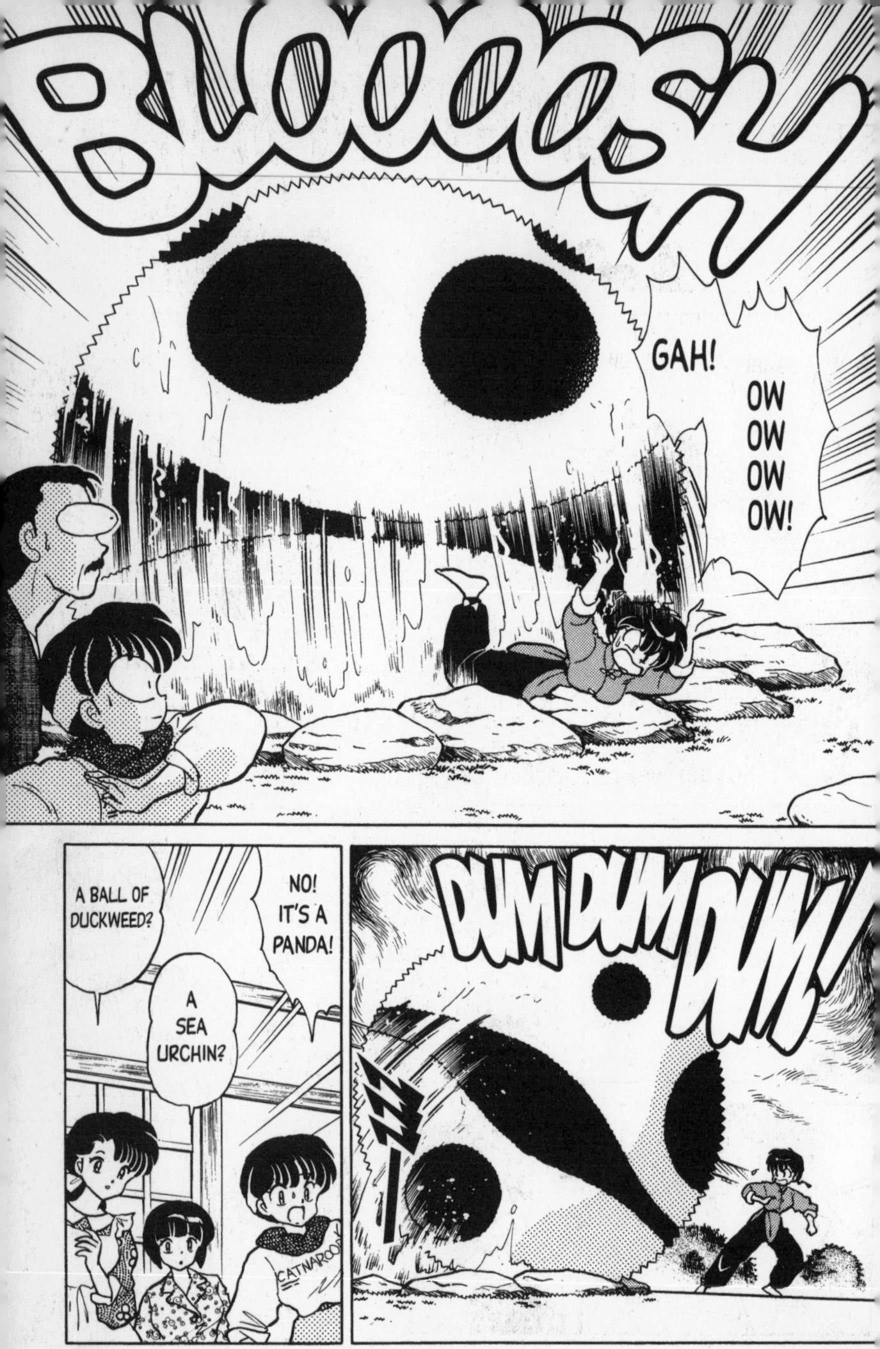
BLOOOSH
GAH!
OW OW OW OW!
A BALL OF DUCKWEED?
NO! IT'S A PANDA!
A SEA URCHIN?
CATNAROO
DUM DUM DUM!

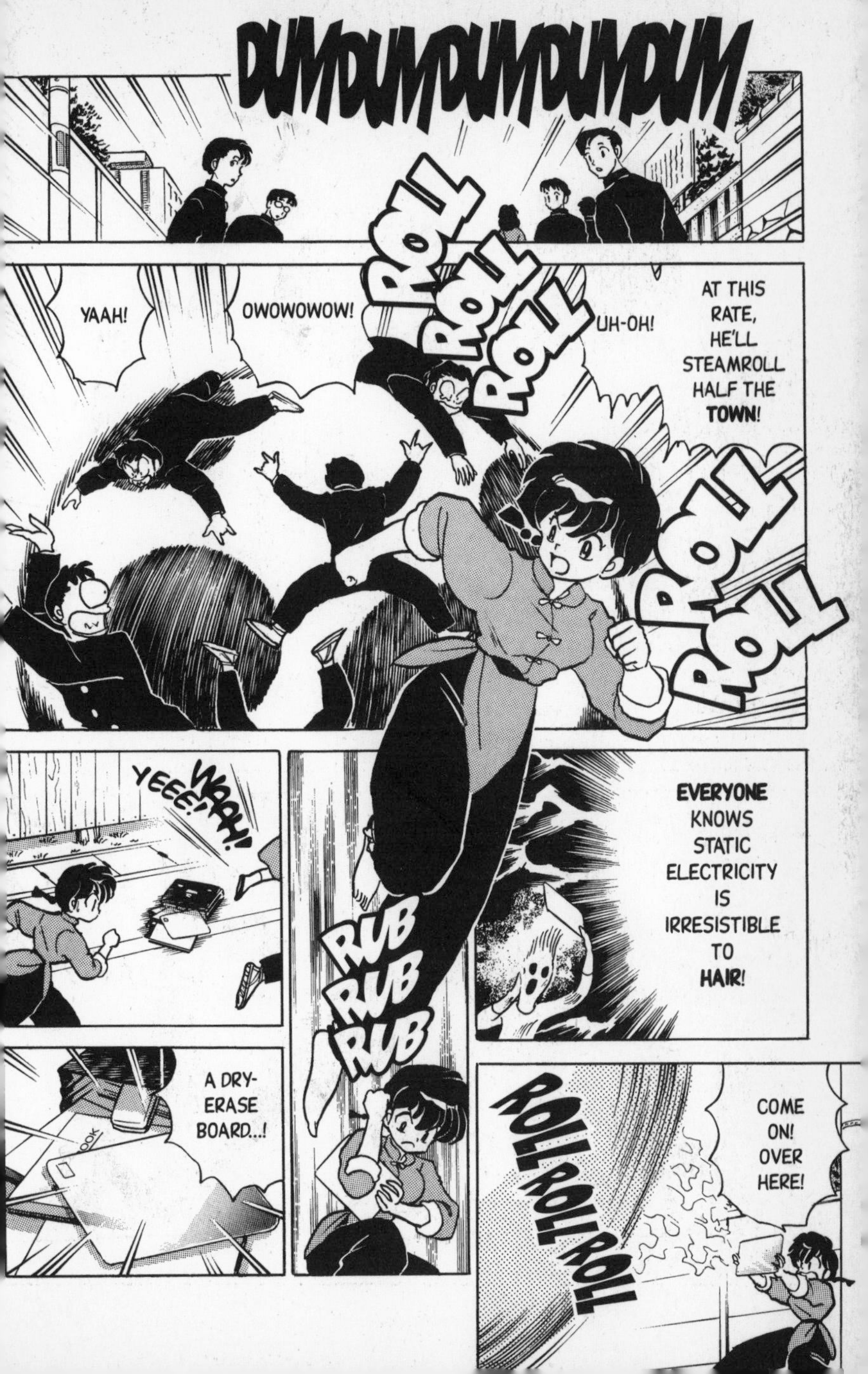
DUMDUMDUMDUMDUM
ROLL ROLL ROLL
YAAH!
OWOWOWOW!
UH-OH!
AT THIS RATE, HE'LL STEAMROLL HALF THE TOWN!
ROLL ROLL
WAAAH! YEEE!
RUB RUB RUB
EVERYONE KNOWS STATIC ELECTRICITY IS IRRESISTIBLE TO HAIR!
A DRY-ERASE BOARD...!
ROLLROLLROLL
COME ON! OVER HERE!

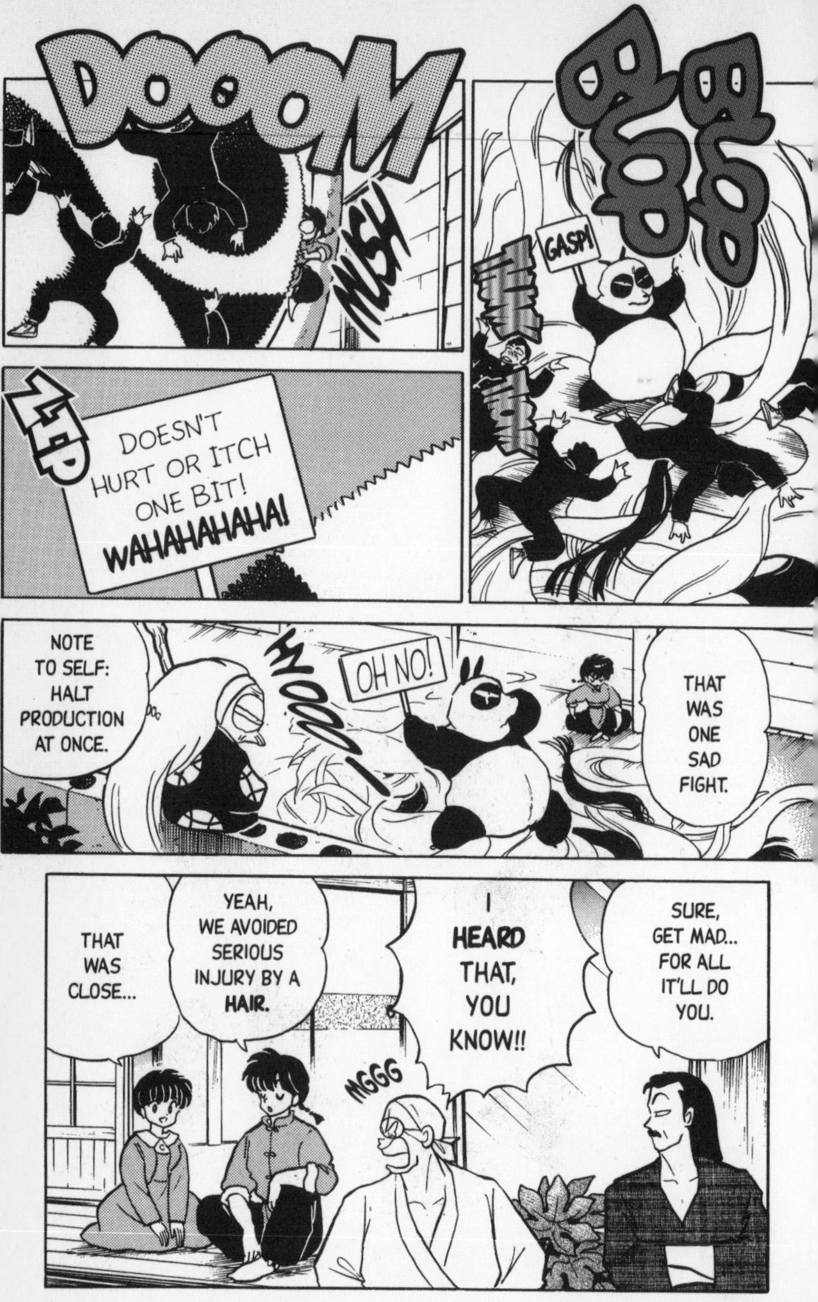
DOOOM
WUSH
GASP!
ZIP
DOESN'T HURT OR ITCH ONE BIT! WAHAHAHAHA!
NOTE TO SELF: HALT PRODUCTION AT ONCE.
WOOO...!
OH NO!
THAT WAS ONE SAD FIGHT.
THAT WAS CLOSE...
YEAH, WE AVOIDED SERIOUS INJURY BY A HAIR.
MGGG
I HEARD THAT, YOU KNOW!!
SURE, GET MAD... FOR ALL IT'LL DO YOU.

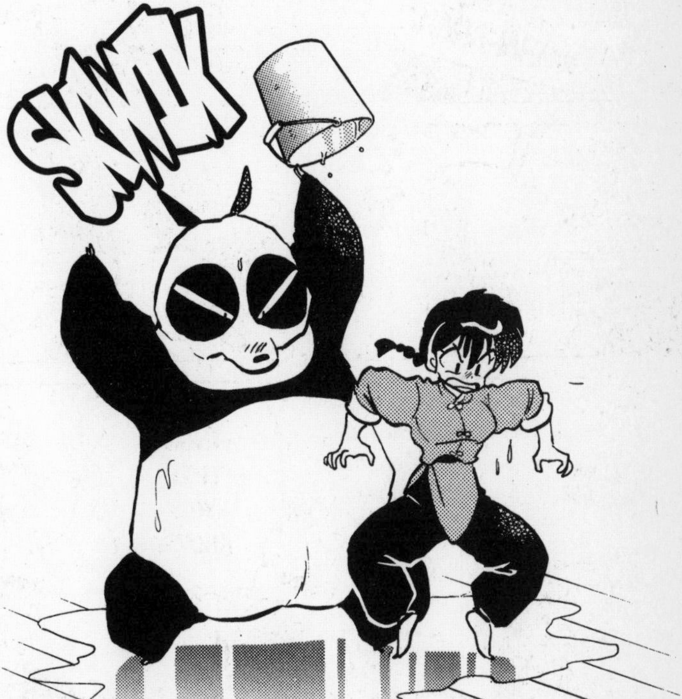
SWISH

PART 5

INFINITE BATTLE "KI"

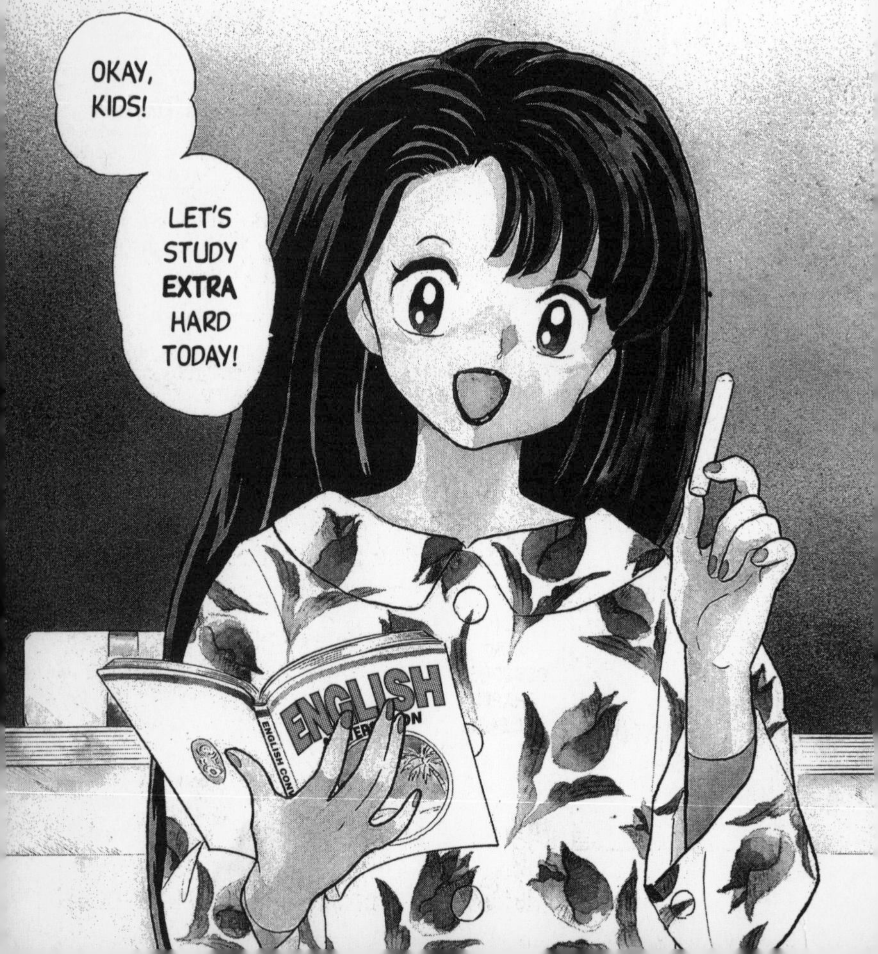
OKAY, KIDS!
LET'S STUDY **EXTRA** HARD TODAY!
ENGLISH

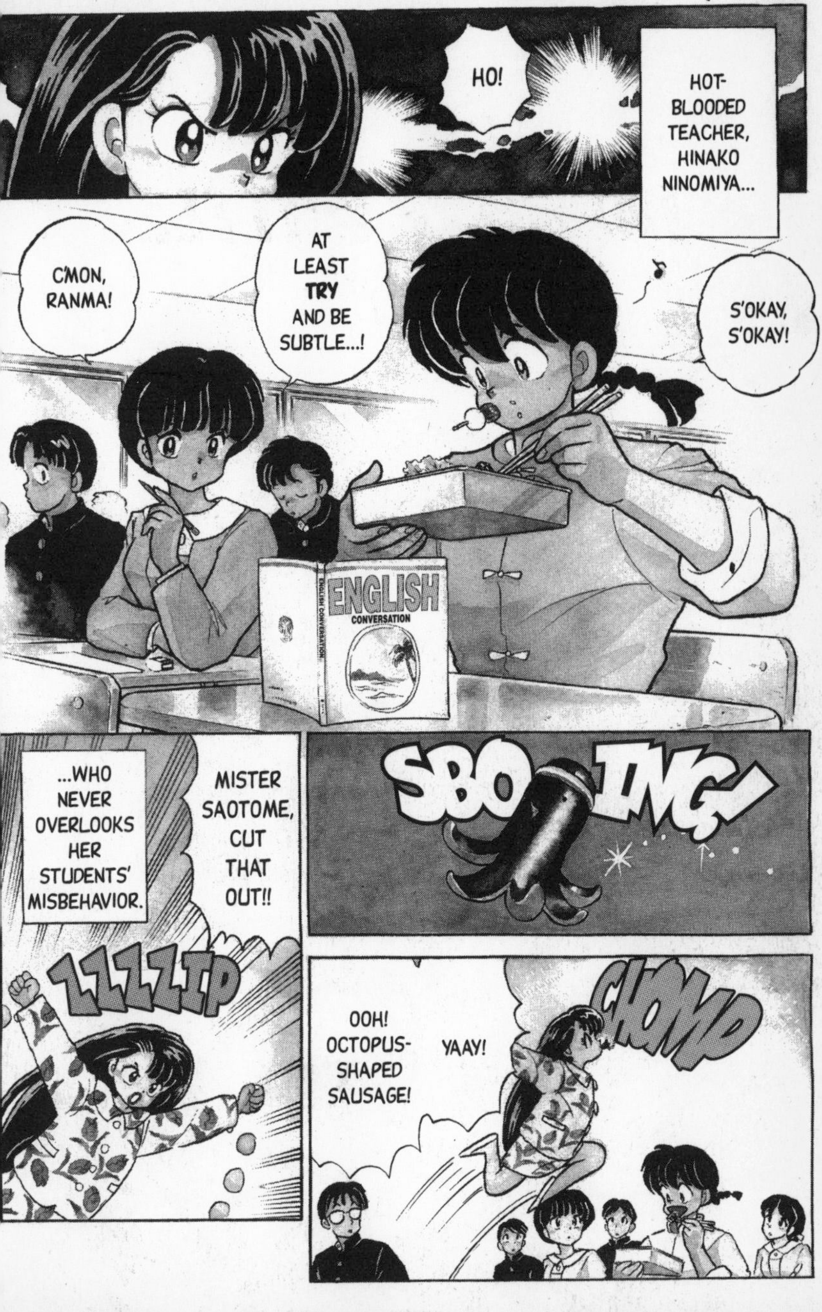
HO!
HOT-BLOODED TEACHER, HINAKO NINOMIYA...
C'MON, RANMA!
AT LEAST **TRY** AND BE SUBTLE...!
S'OKAY, S'OKAY!
ENGLISH CONVERSATION
...WHO NEVER OVERLOOKS HER STUDENTS' MISBEHAVIOR.
MISTER SAOTOME, CUT THAT OUT!!
SBOING!
ZZZZZIP
CHOMP
OOH! OCTOPUS-SHAPED SAUSAGE!
YAAY!

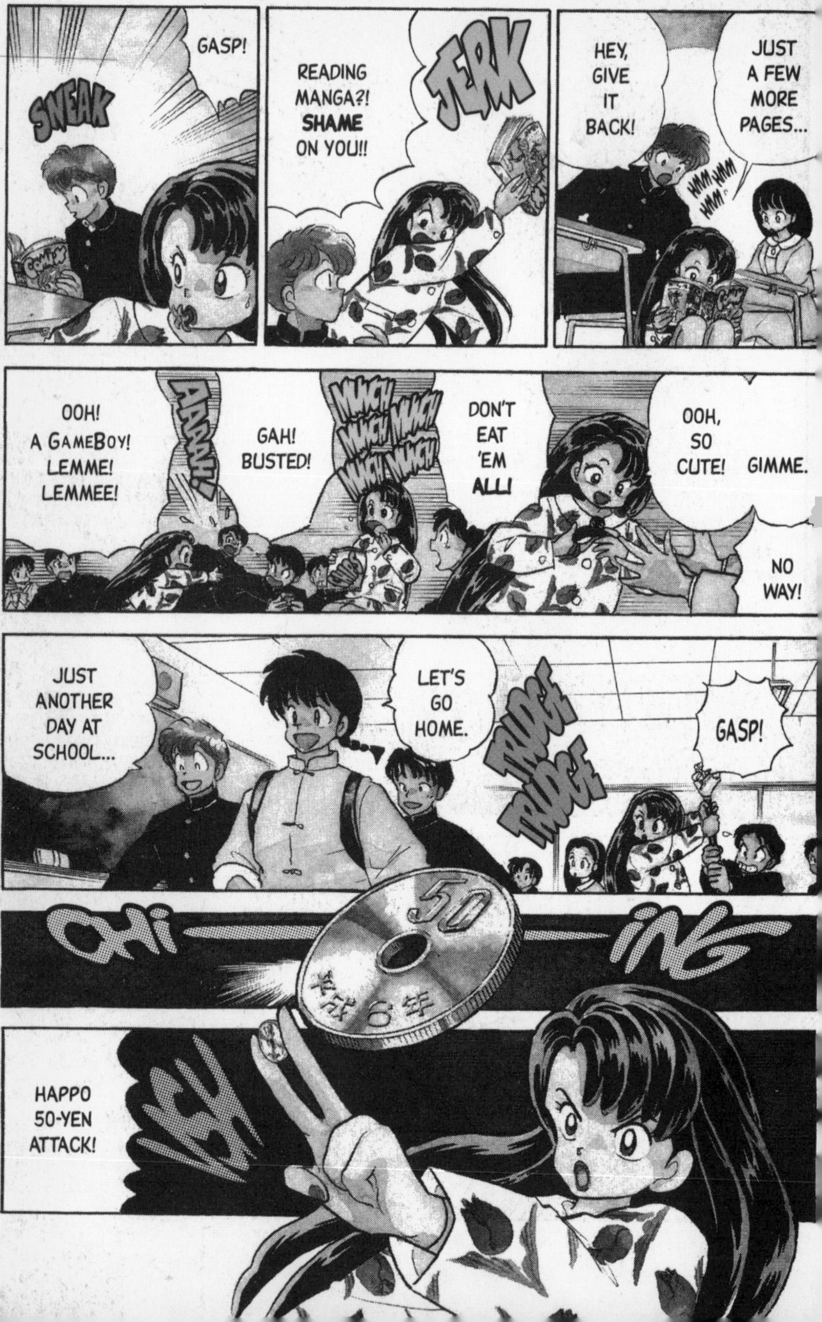
GASP!
SNEAK
READING MANGA?! SHAME ON YOU!!
JERK
HEY, GIVE IT BACK!
JUST A FEW MORE PAGES...
HMM HMM HMM HMM
OOH! A GAMEBOY! LEMME! LEMMEE!
AAAAH!
GAH! BUSTED!
MUNCH MUNCH MUNCH MUNCH MUNCH
DON'T EAT 'EM ALL!
OOH, SO CUTE!
GIMME.
NO WAY!
JUST ANOTHER DAY AT SCHOOL...
LET'S GO HOME.
TRUDGE TRUDGE
GASP!
CHI-
ING
50
HAPPO 50-YEN ATTACK!

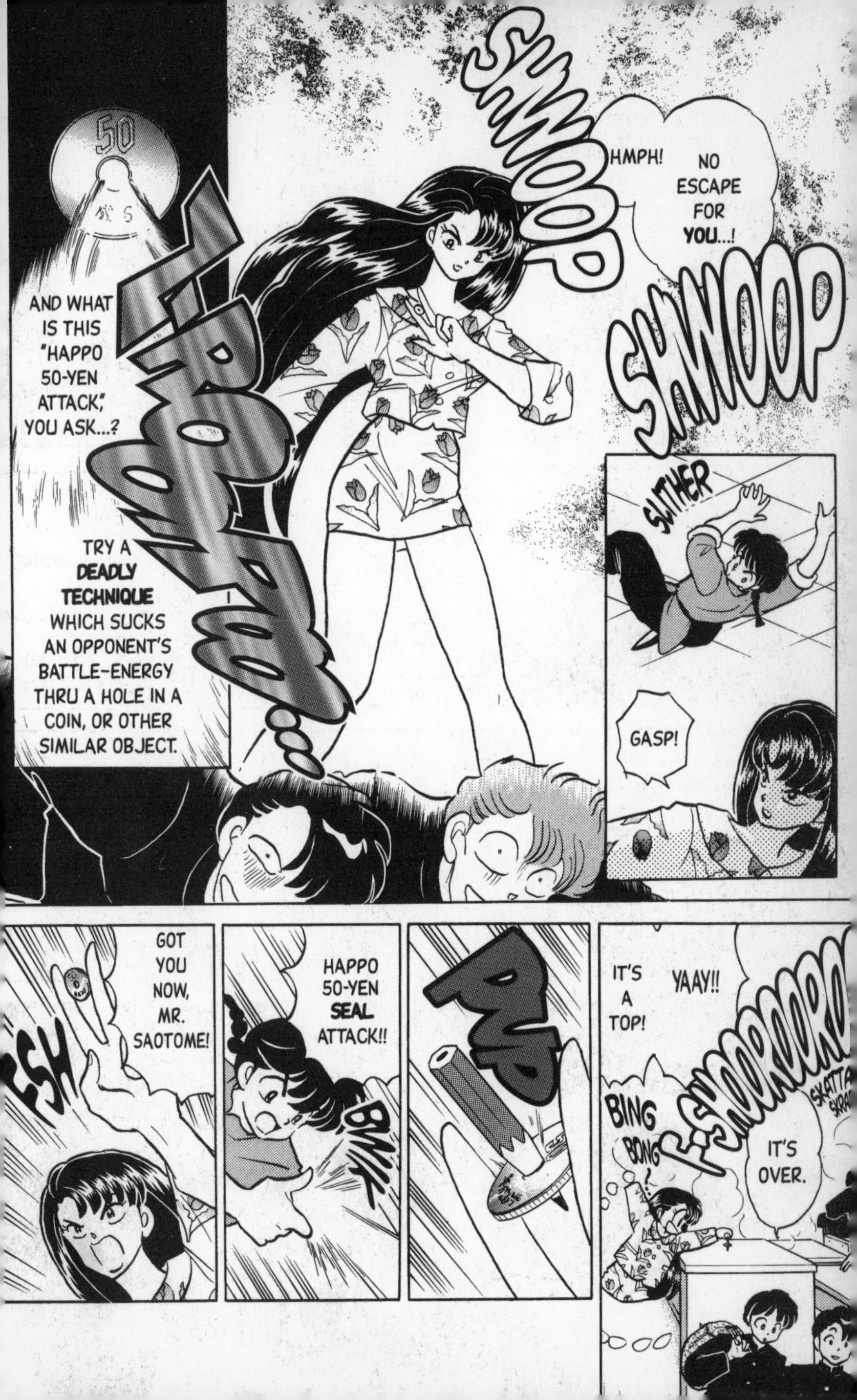

SHWOOP
HMPH!
NO ESCAPE FOR YOU...!
SHWOOP
AND WHAT IS THIS "HAPPO 50-YEN ATTACK," YOU ASK...?
TRY A DEADLY TECHNIQUE WHICH SUCKS AN OPPONENT'S BATTLE-ENERGY THRU A HOLE IN A COIN, OR OTHER SIMILAR OBJECT.
SLITHER
GASP!
GOT YOU NOW, MR. SAOTOME!
HAPPO 50-YEN SEAL ATTACK!!
IT'S A TOP!
YAAY!!
BING BONG
IT'S OVER.

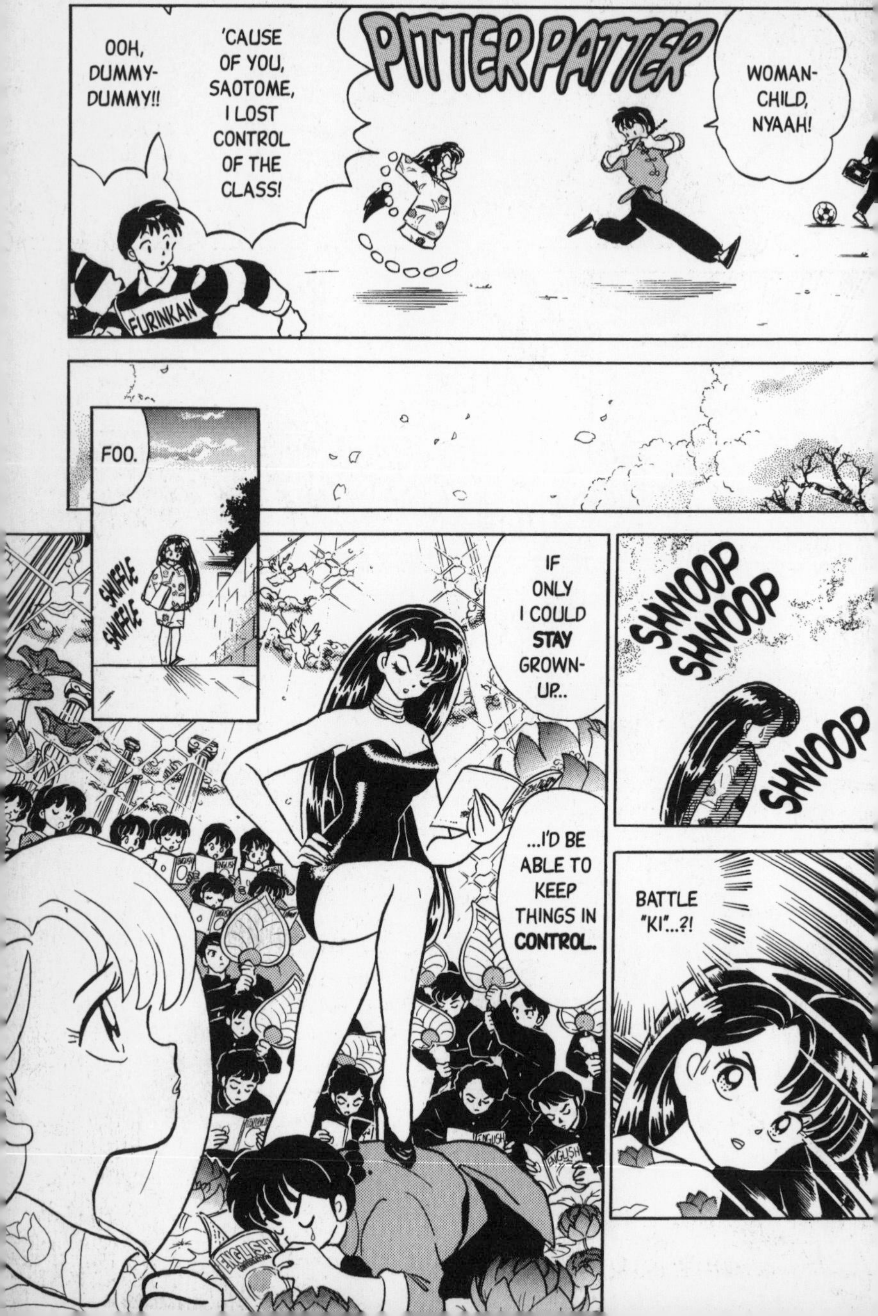
OOH, DUMMY-DUMMY!!
'CAUSE OF YOU, SAOTOME, I LOST CONTROL OF THE CLASS!
FURINKAN
PITTER PATTER
WOMAN-CHILD, NYAAH!
FOO.
SHUFFLE SHUFFLE
IF ONLY I COULD STAY GROWN-UP...
...I'D BE ABLE TO KEEP THINGS IN CONTROL.
ENGLISH
SHWOOP SHWOOP
SHWOOP
BATTLE "KI"...?!

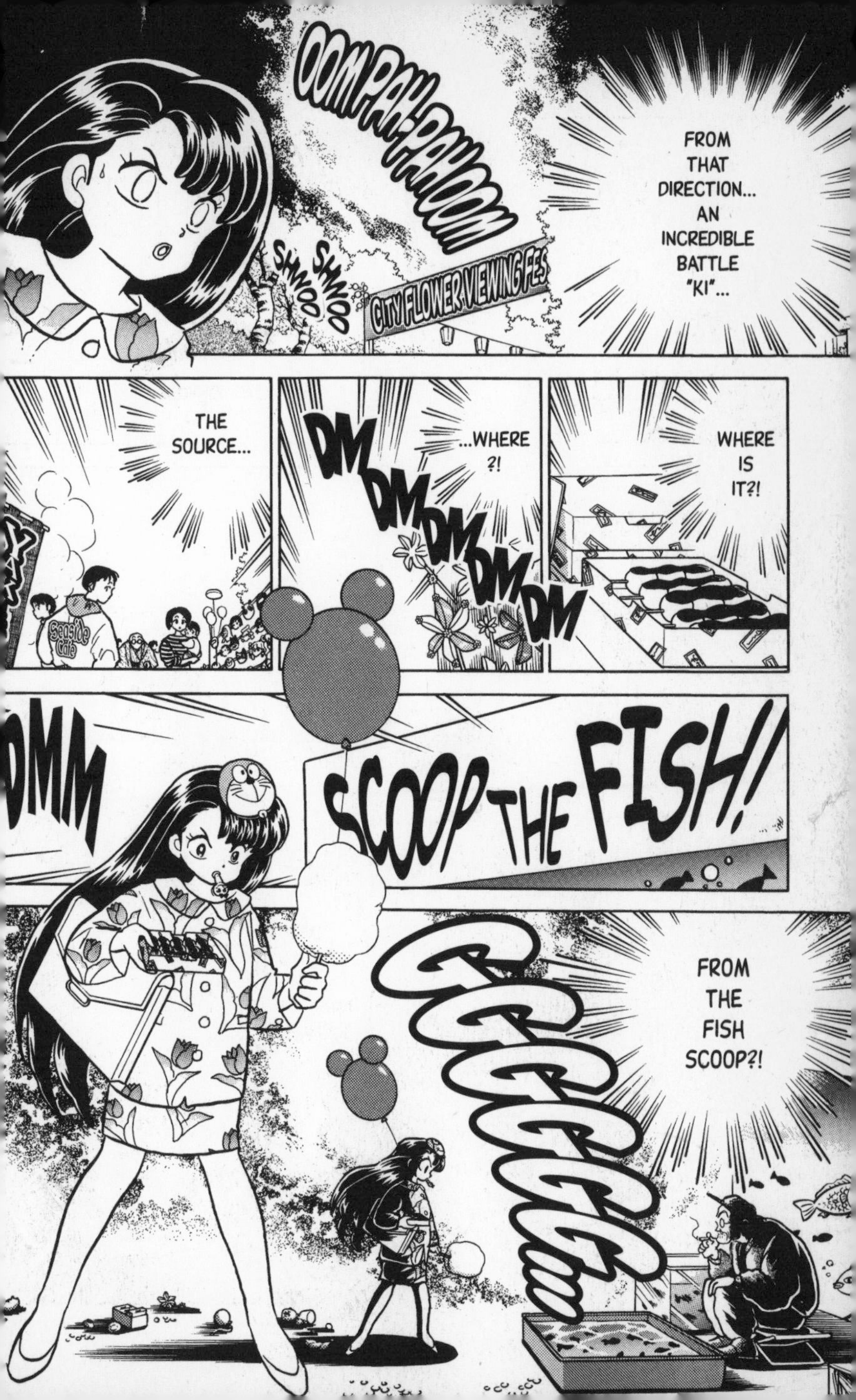
OOMPAH-PAHOOM
SHWOO
SHWOO
CITY FLOWER VIEWING FES
FROM THAT DIRECTION... AN INCREDIBLE BATTLE "KI"...
THE SOURCE...
Seaside Cafe
DM DM DM DM DM DM
...WHERE ?!
WHERE IS IT?!
DMM
SCOOP THE FISH!
FROM THE FISH SCOOP?!

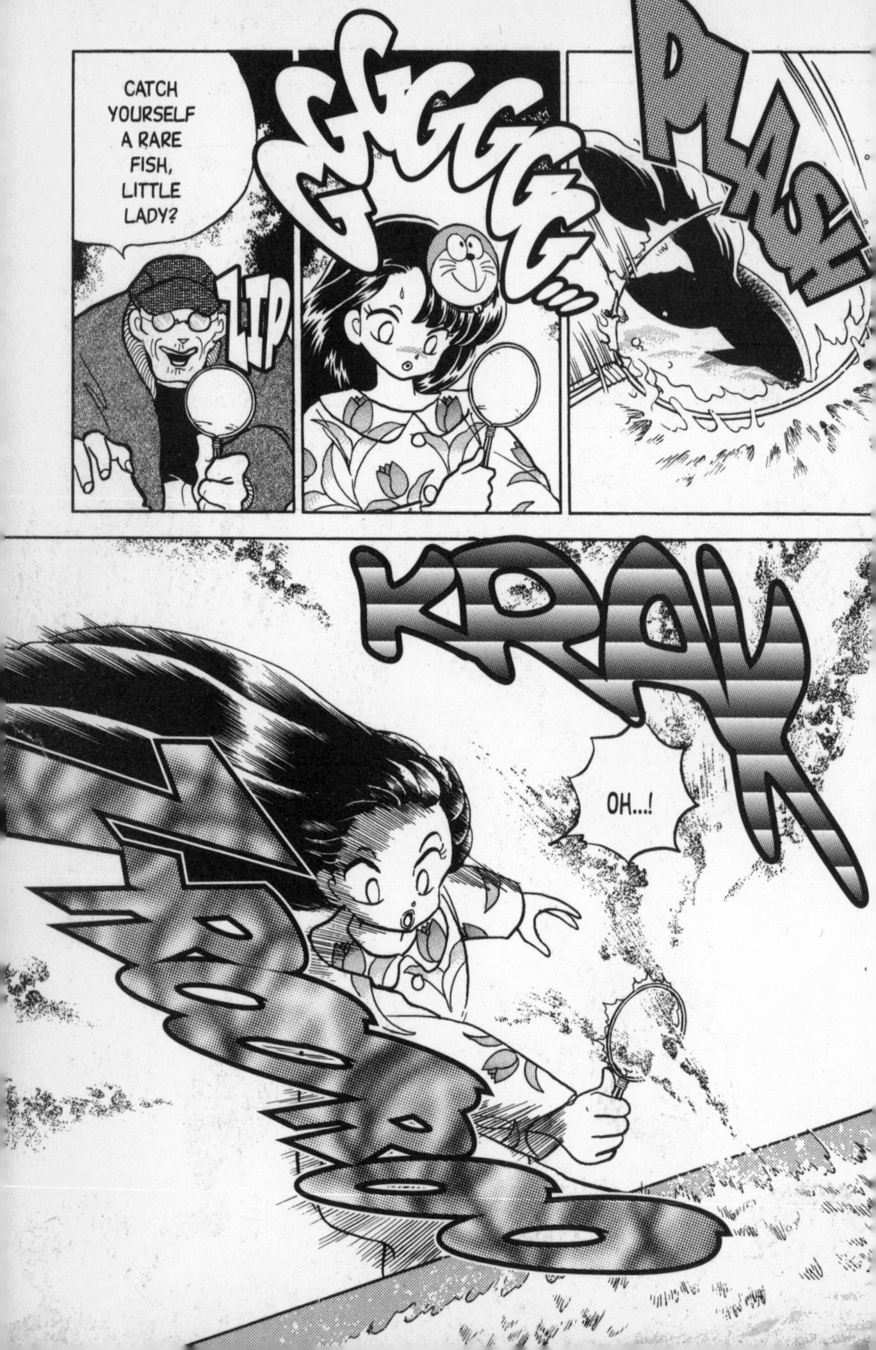
CATCH YOURSELF A RARE FISH, LITTLE LADY?
ZIP
PLASH!
OH...!

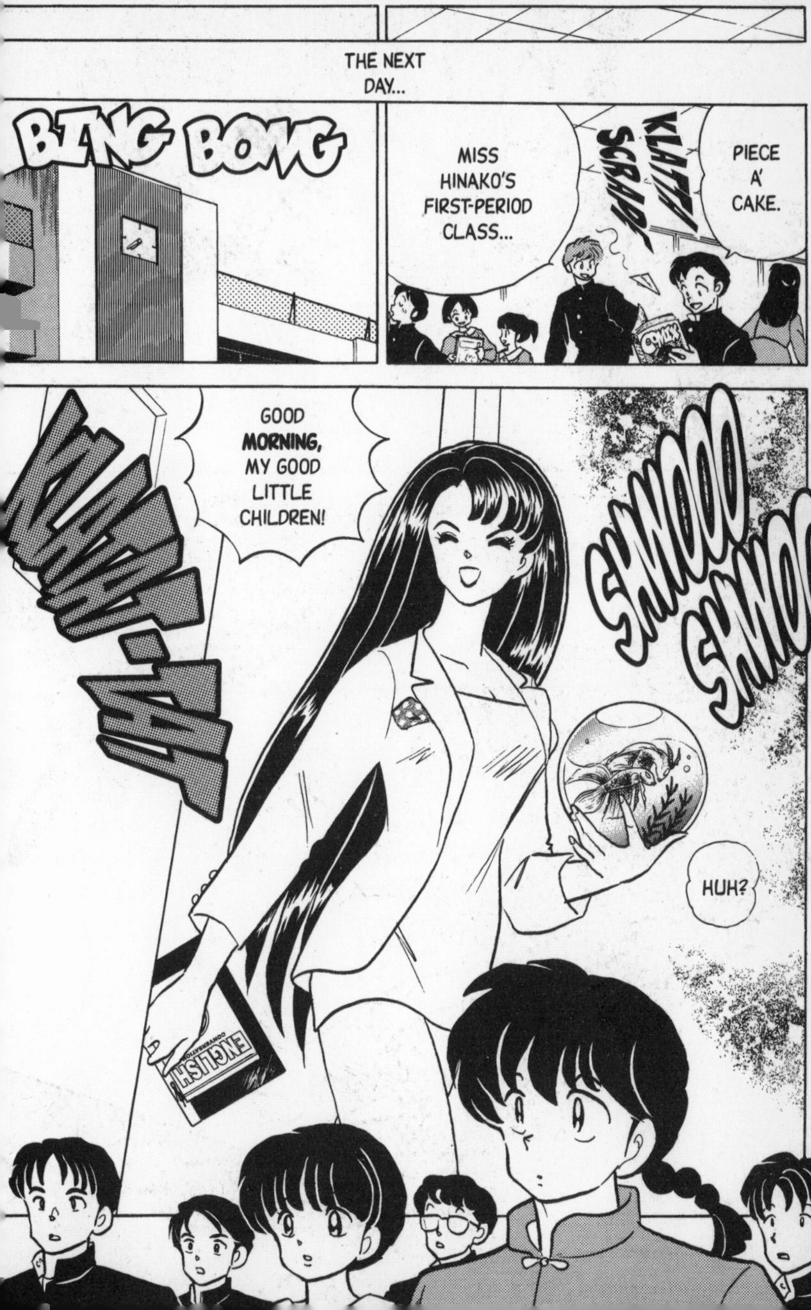
THE NEXT DAY...
BING BONG
MISS HINAKO'S FIRST-PERIOD CLASS...
KLATTA SCRAPE
PIECE A' CAKE.
GOOD MORNING, MY GOOD LITTLE CHILDREN!
SHWOOO SHWOOO
HUH?

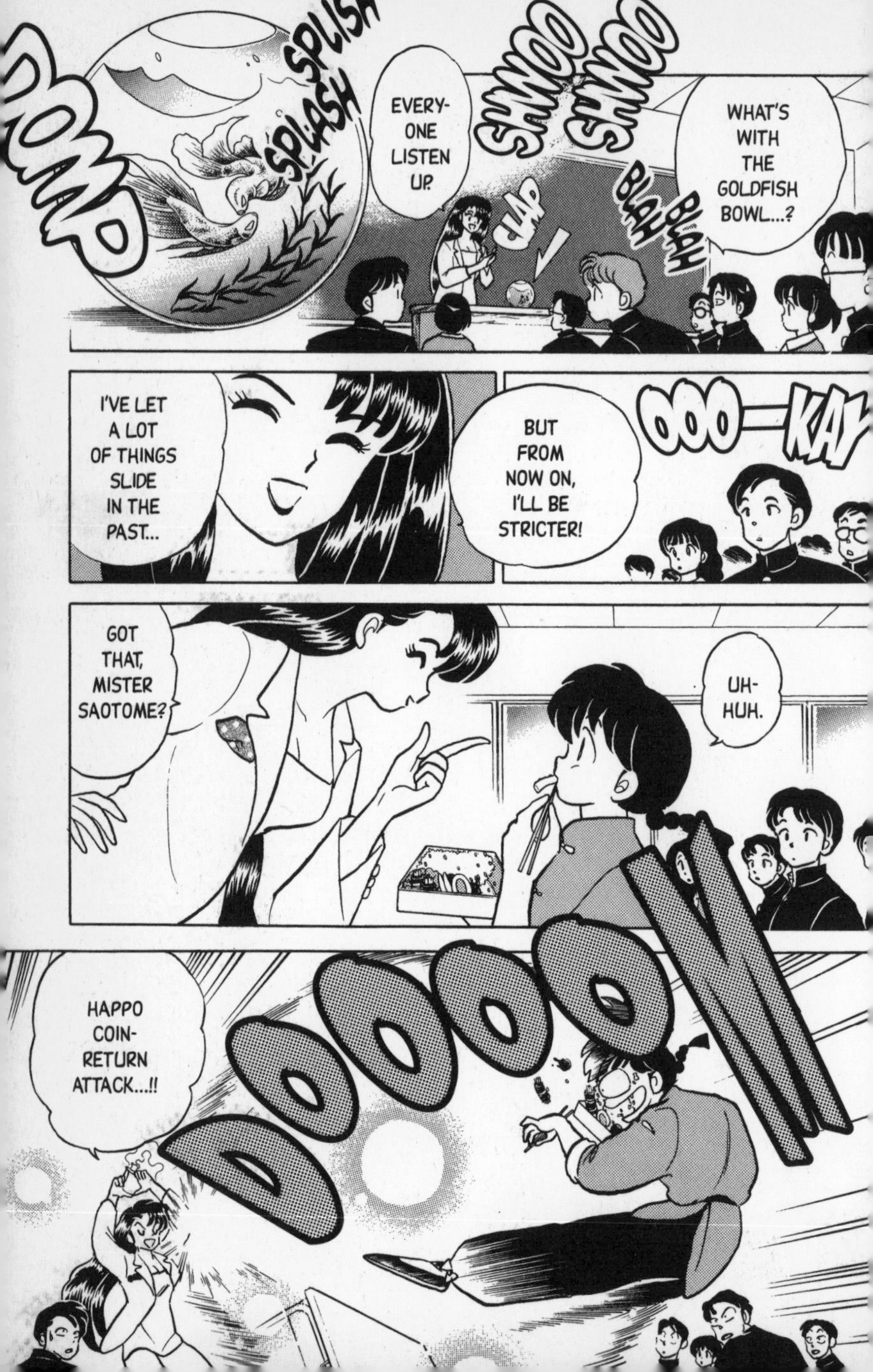
DOMP
SPLISH SPLASH
EVERY-ONE LISTEN UP.
SHWOO SHWOO
CLAP
BLAH BLAH
WHAT'S WITH THE GOLDFISH BOWL...?
I'VE LET A LOT OF THINGS SLIDE IN THE PAST...
BUT FROM NOW ON, I'LL BE STRICTER!
OOO—KAY
GOT THAT, MISTER SAOTOME?
UH-HUH.
HAPPO COIN-RETURN ATTACK...!!
DOOOON

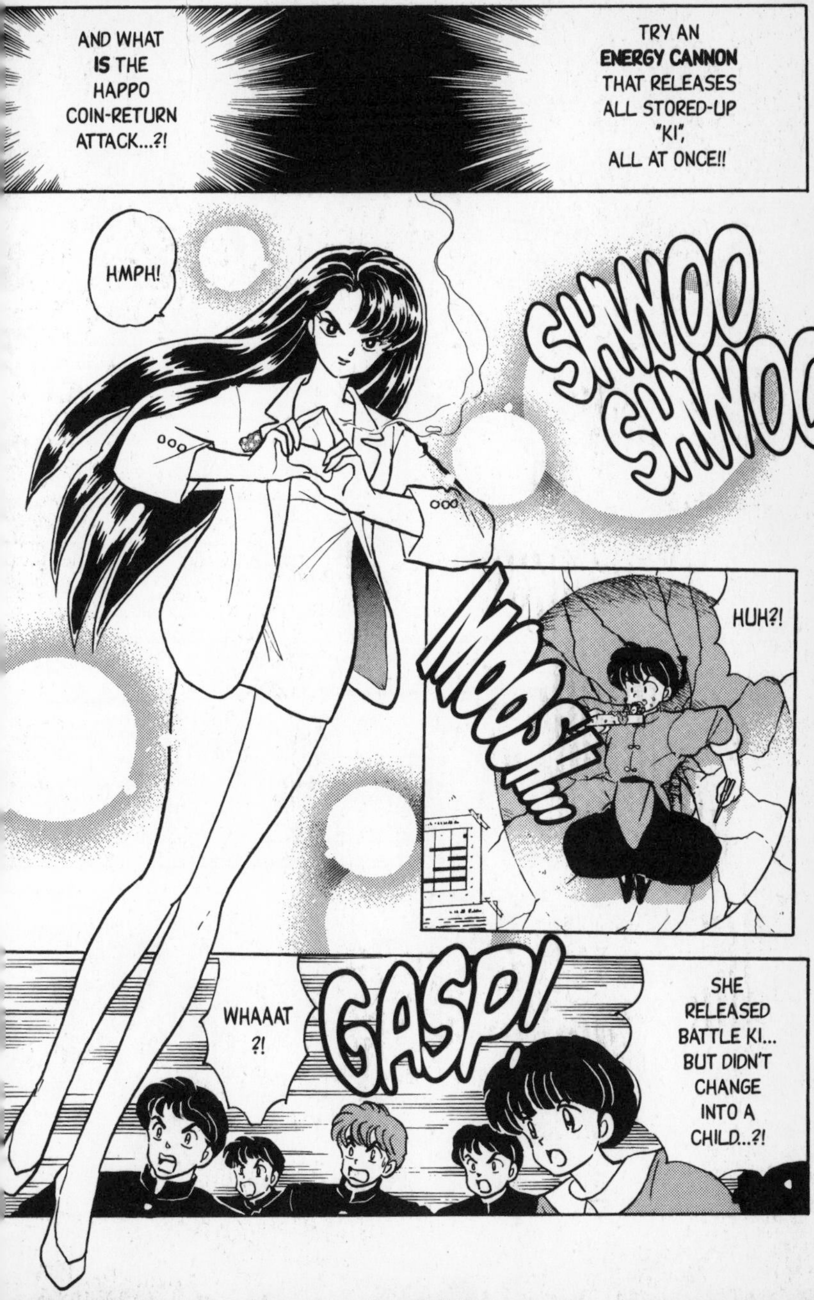
AND WHAT IS THE HAPPO COIN-RETURN ATTACK...?!
TRY AN ENERGY CANNON THAT RELEASES ALL STORED-UP "KI", ALL AT ONCE!!
HMPH!
SHWOO SHWOO
MOOSH...
HUH?!
WHAAAT ?!
GASP!
SHE RELEASED BATTLE KI... BUT DIDN'T CHANGE INTO A CHILD...?!

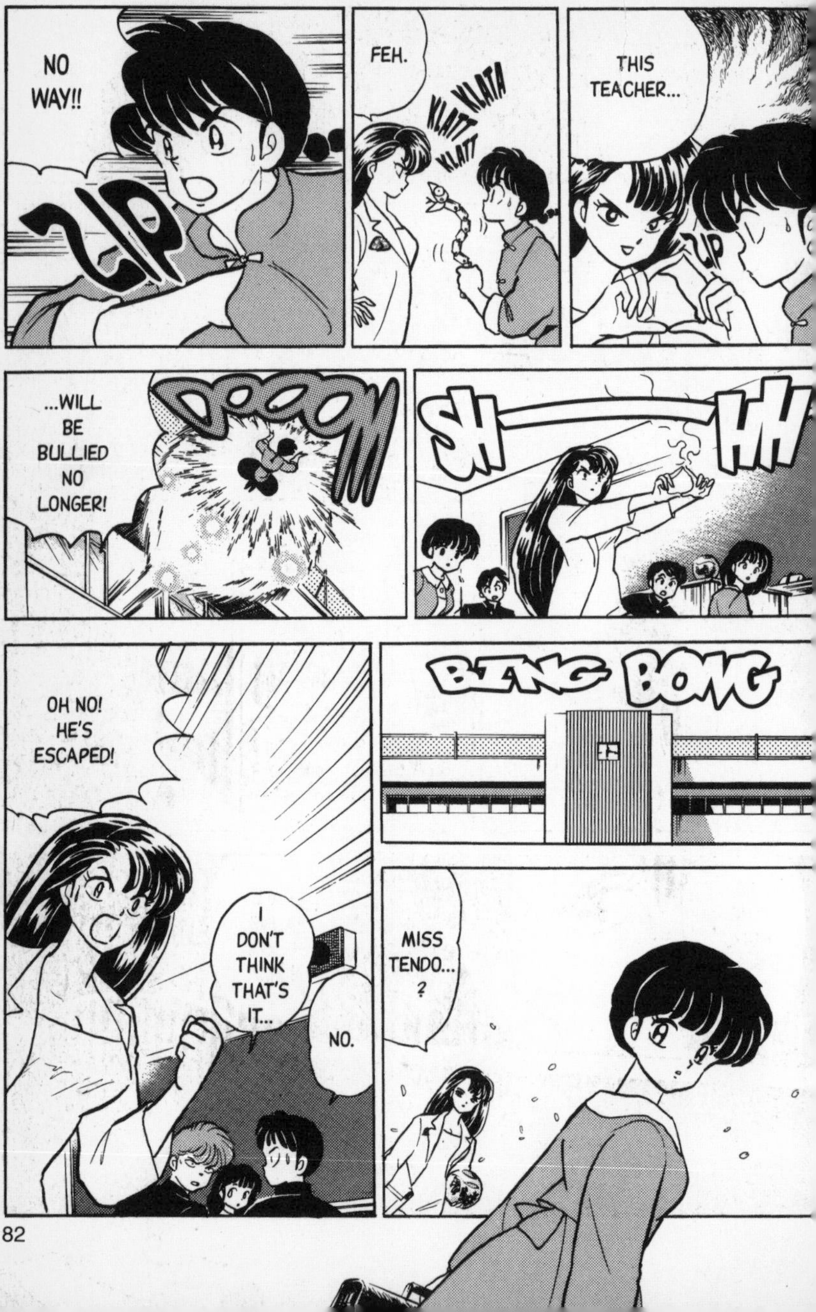
NO WAY!!
ZIP
FEH.
KLATT KLATA
KLATT
THIS TEACHER...
ZIP
...WILL BE BULLIED NO LONGER!
DOOOM
SH
HH
OH NO! HE'S ESCAPED!
I DON'T THINK THAT'S IT...
NO.
BING BONG
MISS TENDO...?

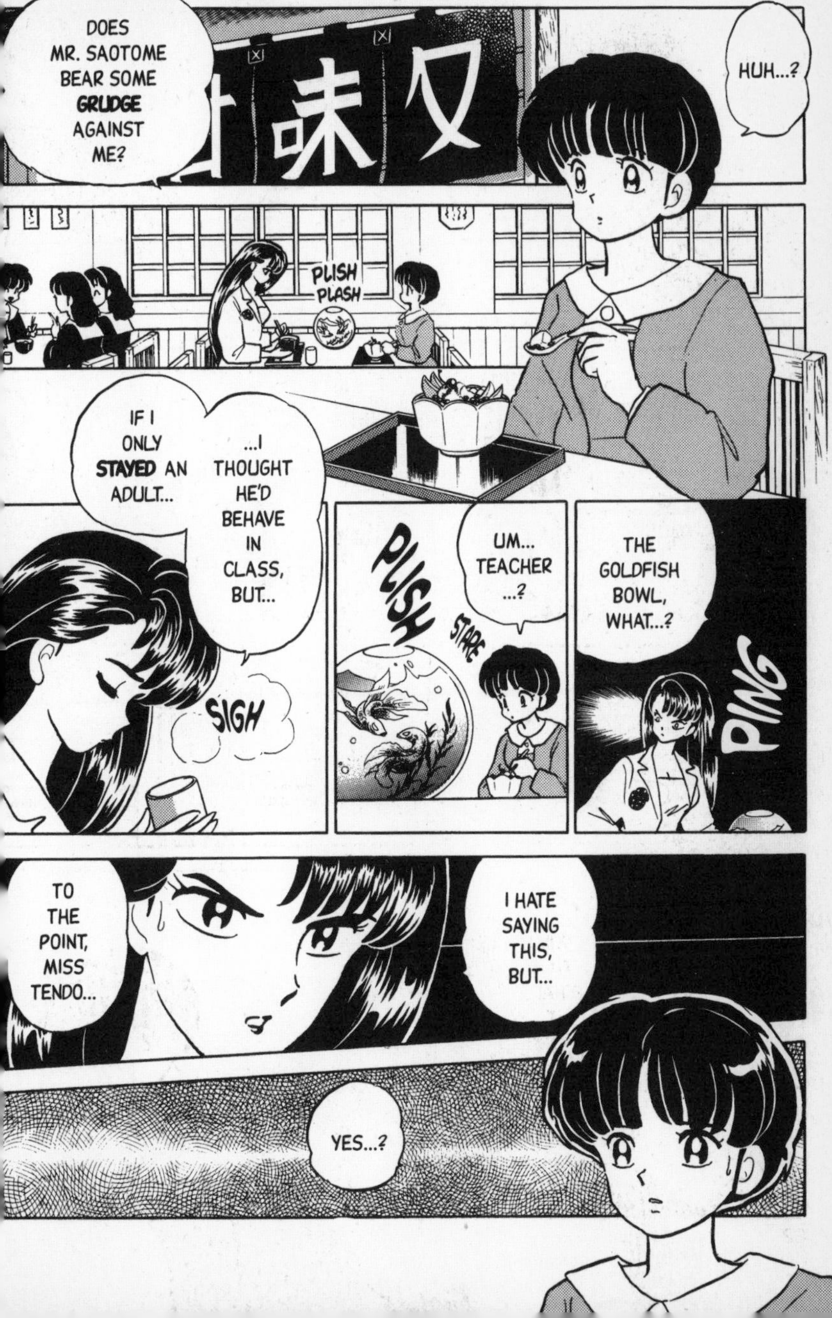
DOES MR. SAOTOME BEAR SOME GRUDGE AGAINST ME?
HUH...?
PLISH PLASH
IF I ONLY STAYED AN ADULT...
...I THOUGHT HE'D BEHAVE IN CLASS, BUT...
SIGH
PLISH
STARE
UM... TEACHER ...?
THE GOLDFISH BOWL, WHAT...?
PING
TO THE POINT, MISS TENDO...
I HATE SAYING THIS, BUT...
YES...?

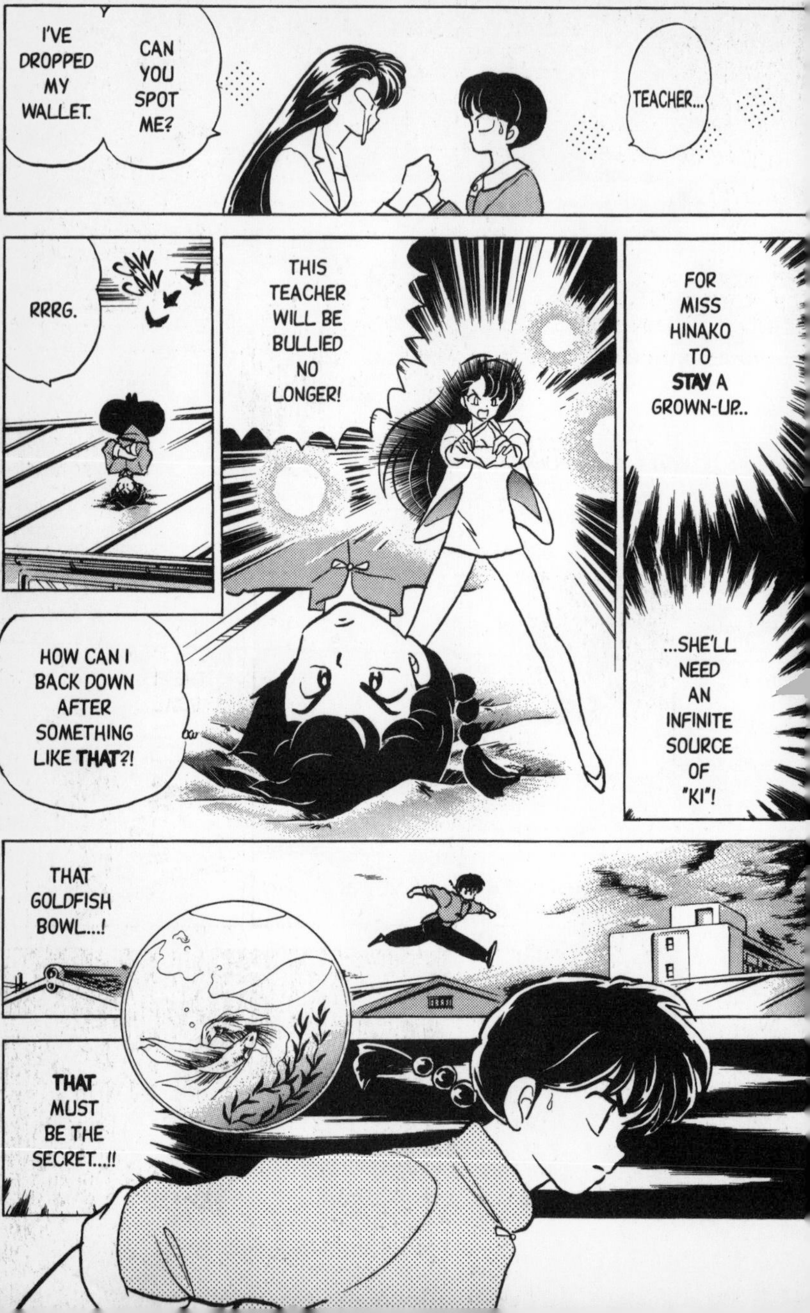
I'VE DROPPED MY WALLET.
CAN YOU SPOT ME?
TEACHER...
RRRG.
CAW CAW
THIS TEACHER WILL BE BULLIED NO LONGER!
FOR MISS HINAKO TO STAY A GROWN-UP..
...SHE'LL NEED AN INFINITE SOURCE OF "KI"!
HOW CAN I BACK DOWN AFTER SOMETHING LIKE THAT?!
THAT GOLDFISH BOWL...!
THAT MUST BE THE SECRET...!!

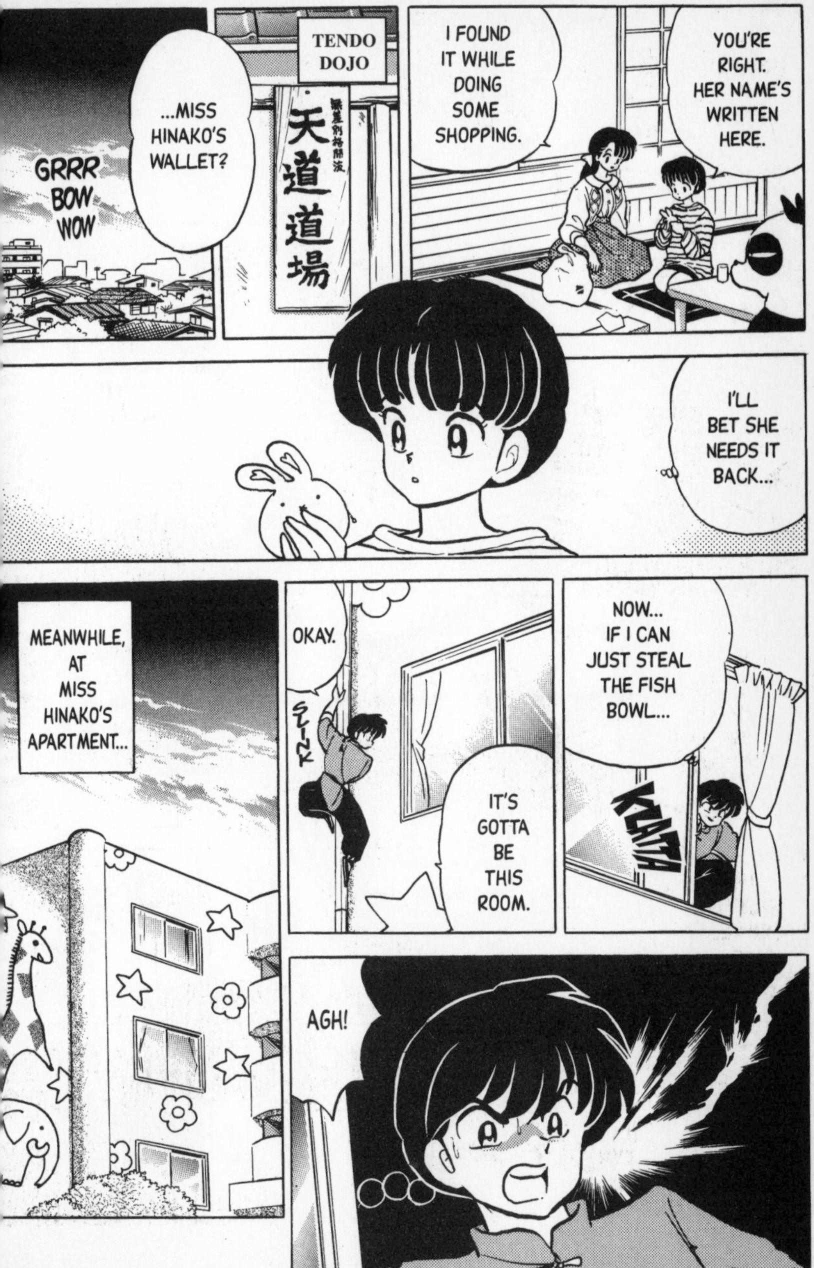
...MISS HINAKO'S WALLET?
GRRR BOW WOW
TENDO DOJO
天道道場
I FOUND IT WHILE DOING SOME SHOPPING.
YOU'RE RIGHT. HER NAME'S WRITTEN HERE.
I'LL BET SHE NEEDS IT BACK...
MEANWHILE, AT MISS HINAKO'S APARTMENT...
OKAY.
SLINK
IT'S GOTTA BE THIS ROOM.
NOW... IF I CAN JUST STEAL THE FISH BOWL...
KLATTA
AGH!

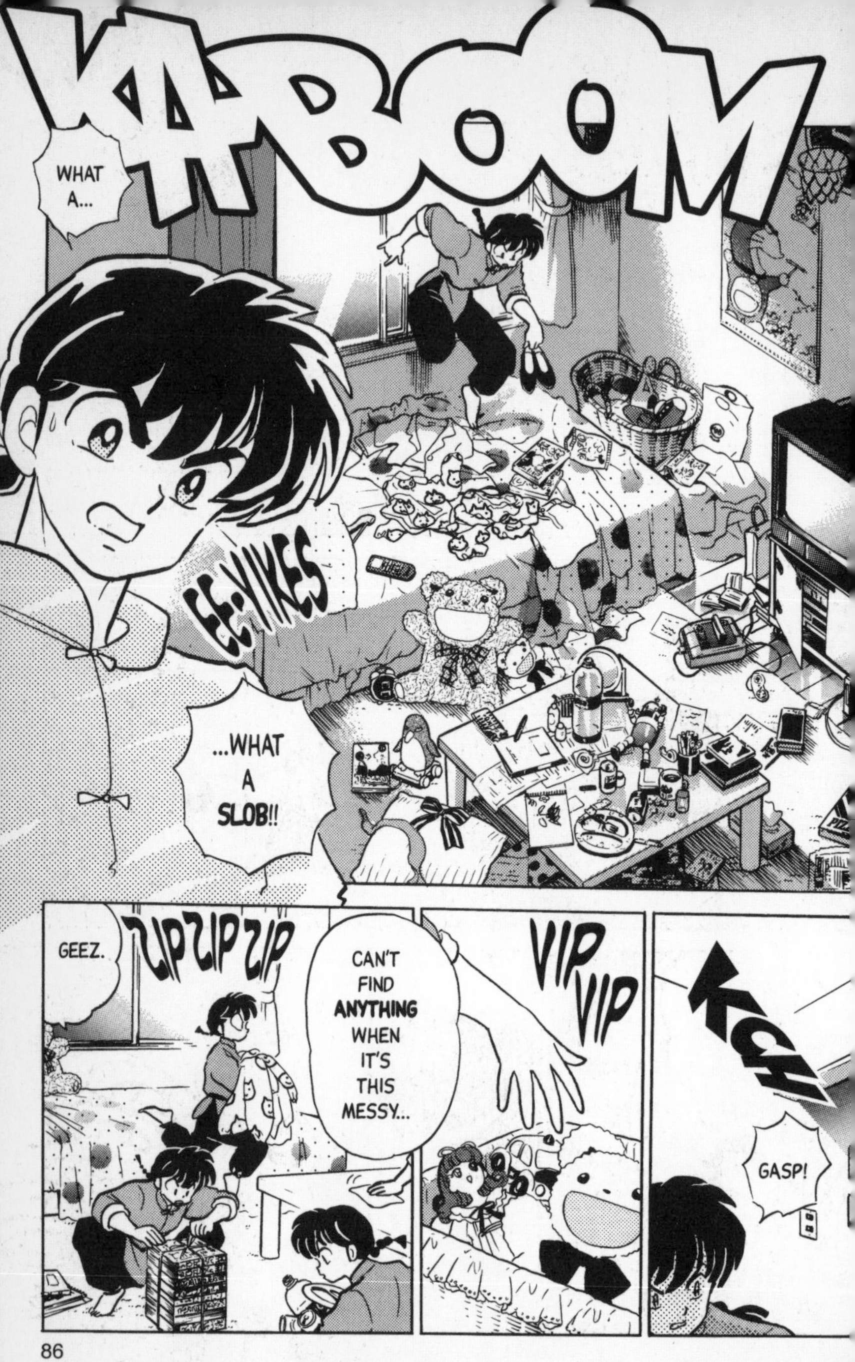
KABOOM
WHAT A...
EE-YIKES
...WHAT A SLOB!!
GEEZ.
ZIP ZIP ZIP
CAN'T FIND ANYTHING WHEN IT'S THIS MESSY...
VIP VIP
KCH
GASP!

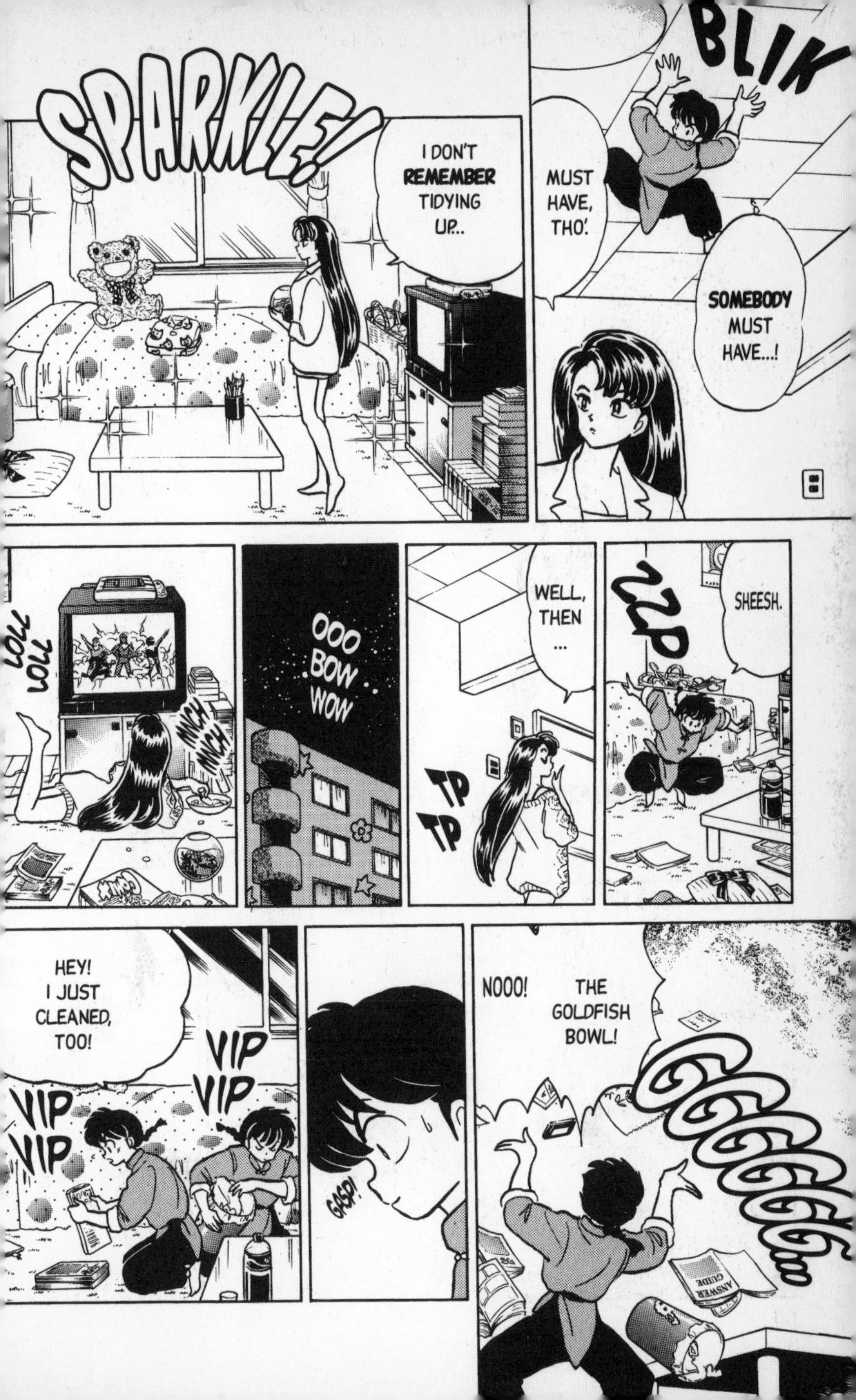
SPARKLE!
I DON'T REMEMBER TIDYING UP..
BLIK
MUST HAVE, THO'.
SOMEBODY MUST HAVE...!
LOLL LOLL
MNCH MNCH
OOO BOW WOW
WELL, THEN ...
TP TP
ZZP
SHEESH.
HEY! I JUST CLEANED, TOO!
VIP VIP
VIP VIP
GASP!
NOOO!
THE GOLDFISH BOWL!
GGGGGGoo
ANSWER GUIDE

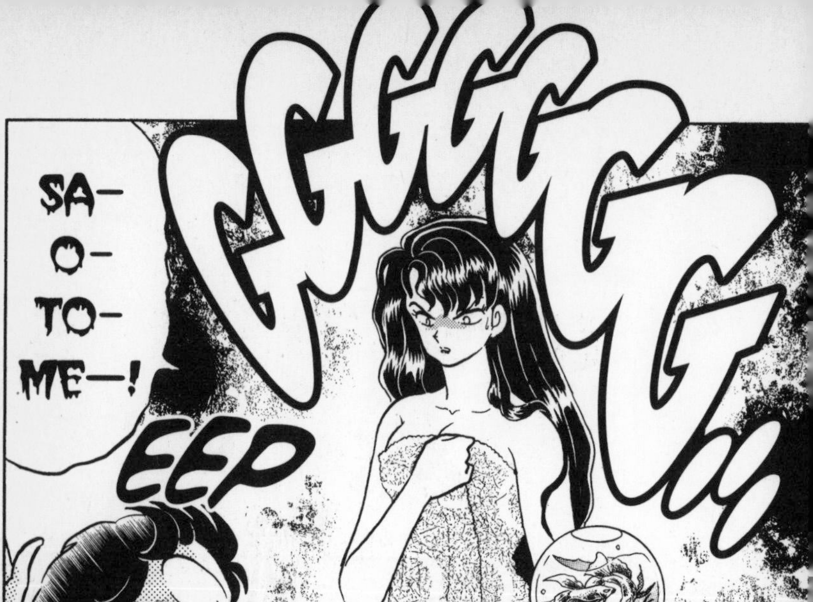
SA—
O—
TO—
ME—!
EEP

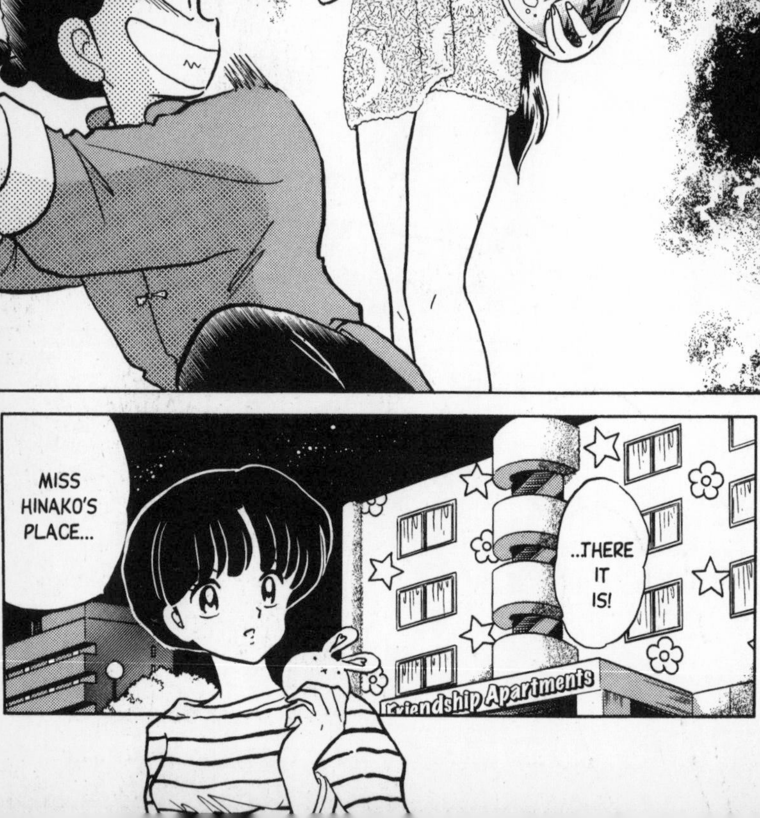
MISS HINAKO'S PLACE...
...THERE IT IS!
Friendship Apartments

PART 6
LET'S STUDY!

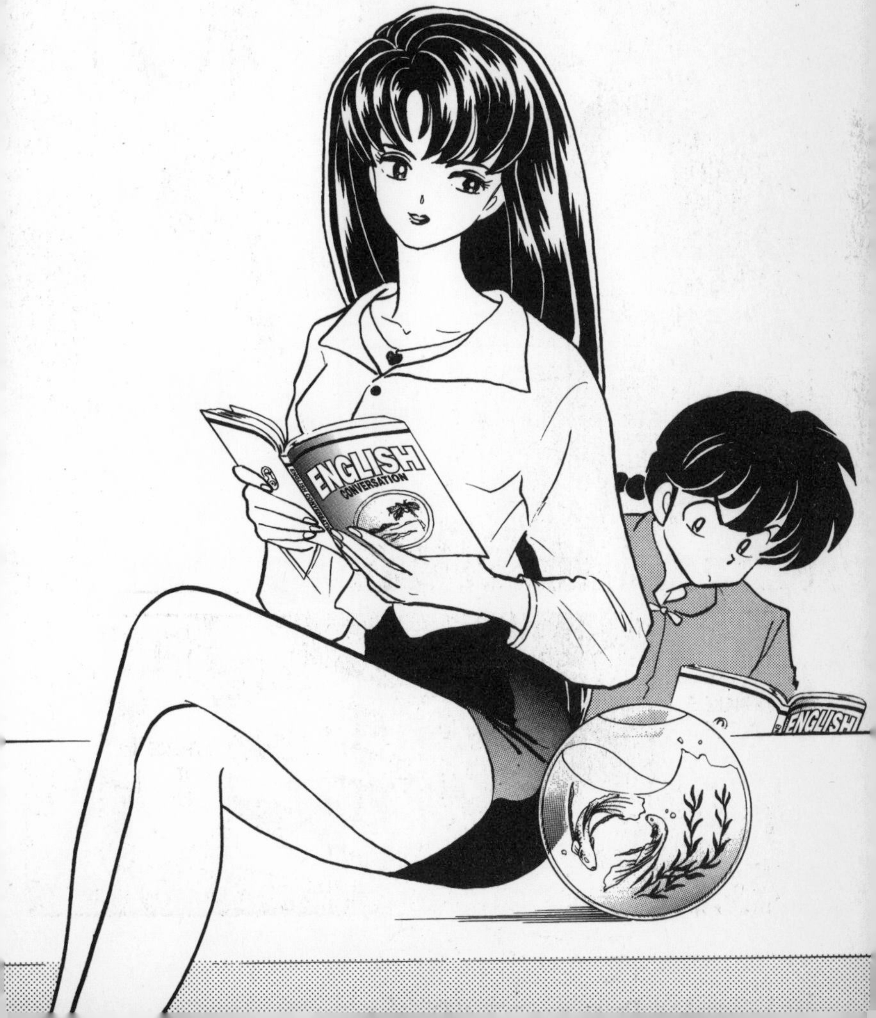
ENGLISH
CONVERSATION
ENGLISH

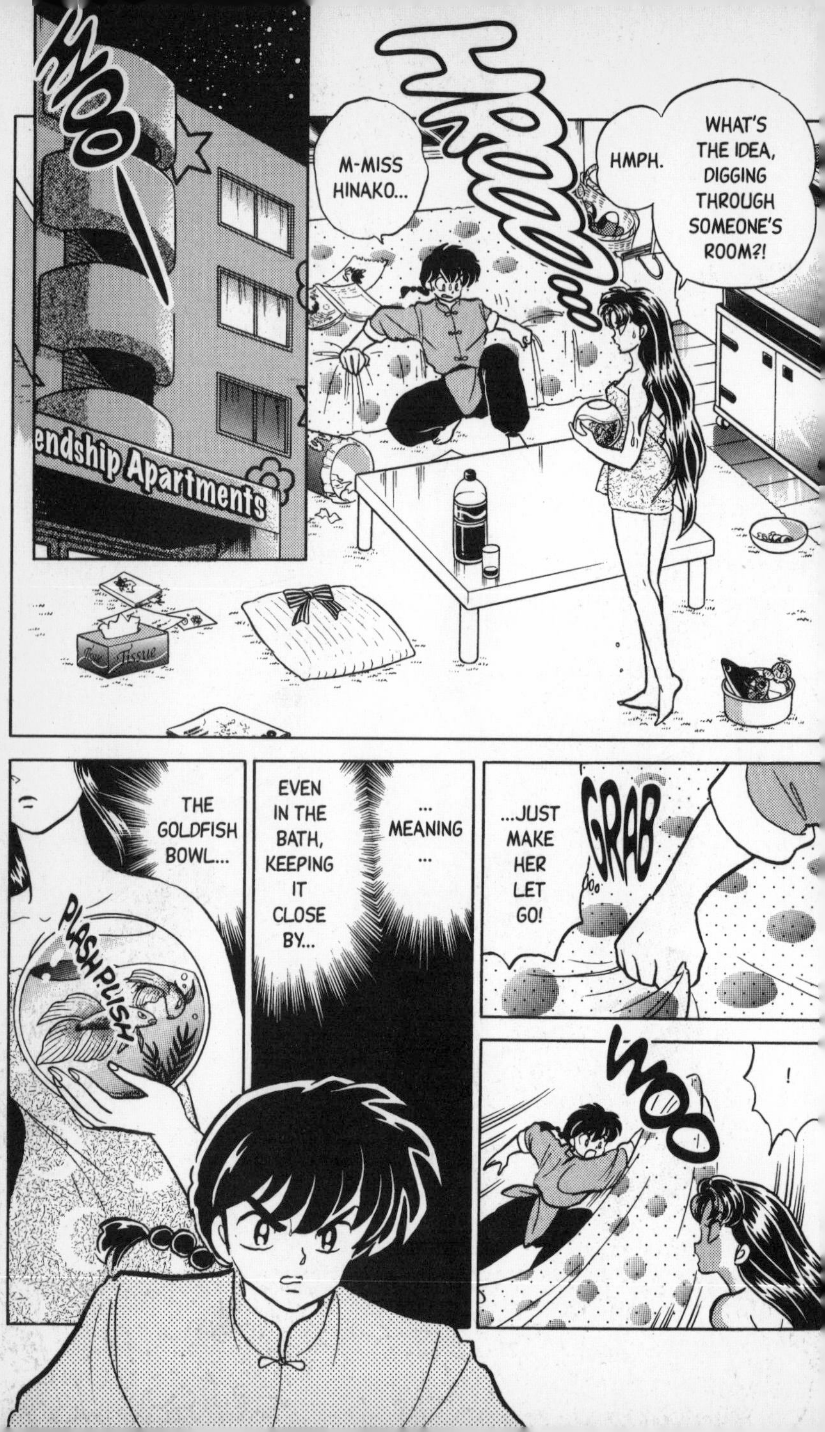
HWOO
endship Apartments
HWOOOO
M-MISS HINAKO...
HMPH.
WHAT'S THE IDEA, DIGGING THROUGH SOMEONE'S ROOM?!
Tissue
PLASH PLISH
THE GOLDFISH BOWL...
EVEN IN THE BATH, KEEPING IT CLOSE BY...
...MEANING...
...JUST MAKE HER LET GO!
GRAB
WOO
!

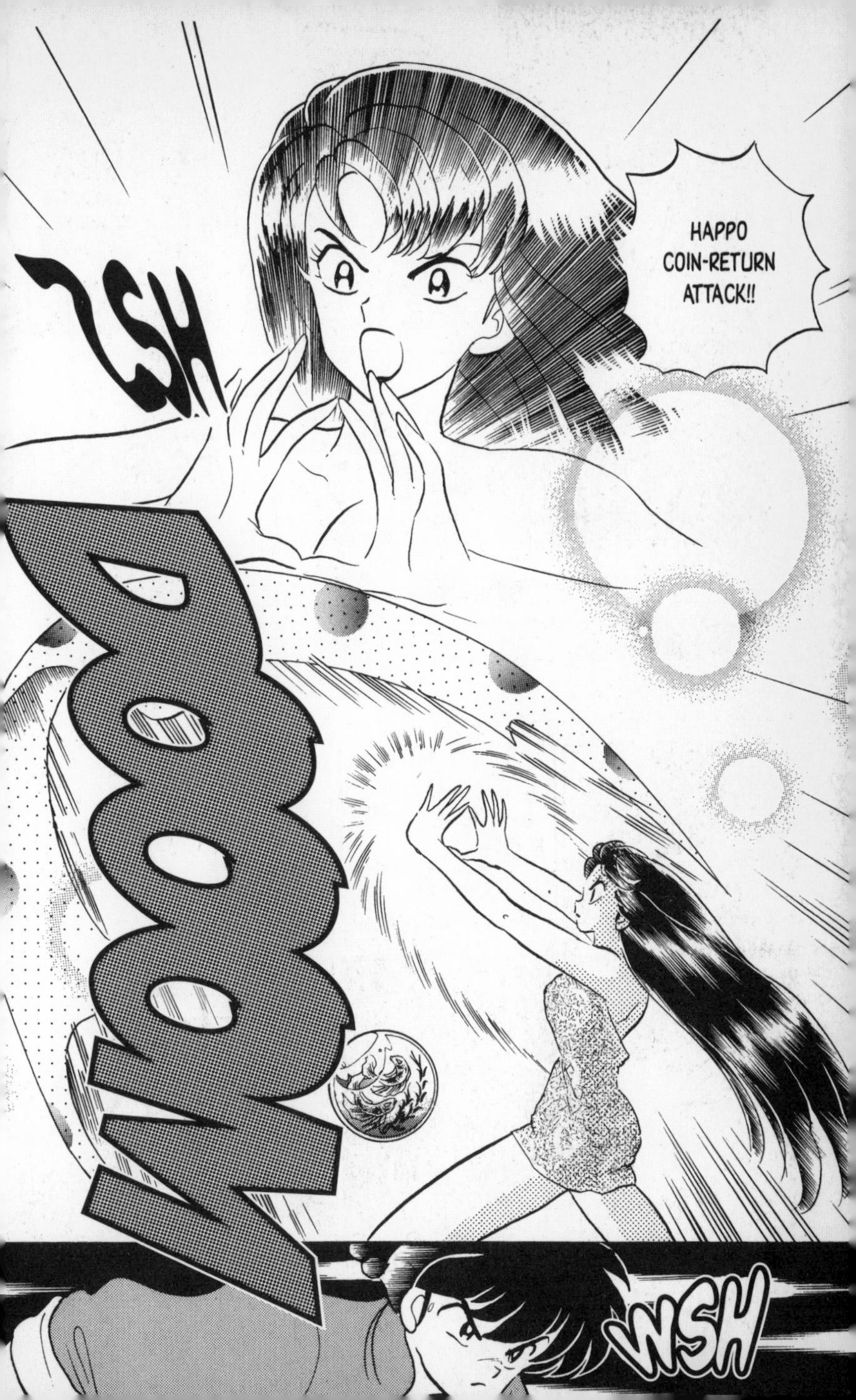
ZSH
HAPPO COIN-RETURN ATTACK!!
VOOOOM
WSH

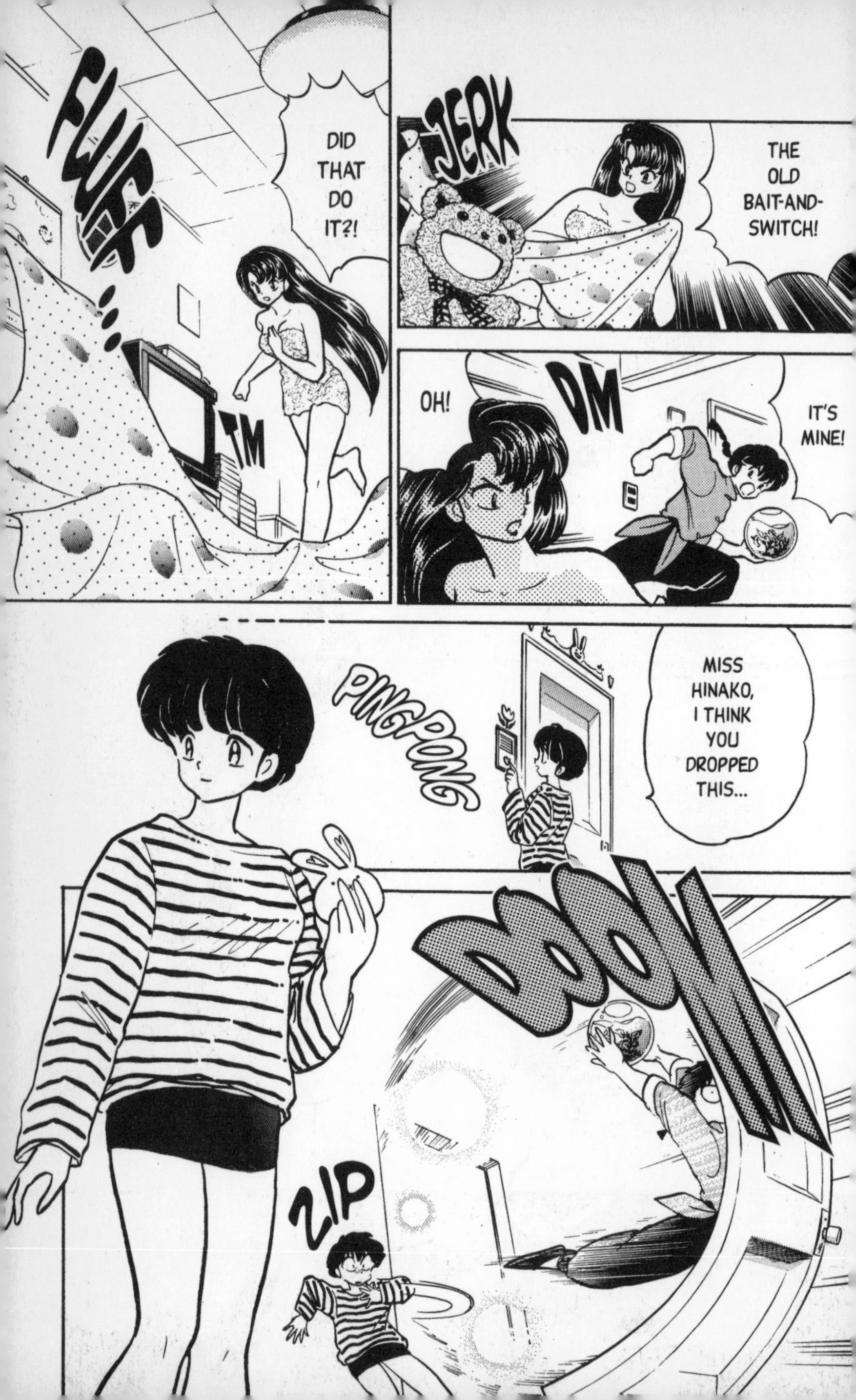
FLUFF...
DID THAT DO IT?!
TM
JERK
THE OLD BAIT-AND-SWITCH!
OH!
DM
IT'S MINE!
PINGPONG
MISS HINAKO, I THINK YOU DROPPED THIS...
BOOM
ZIP

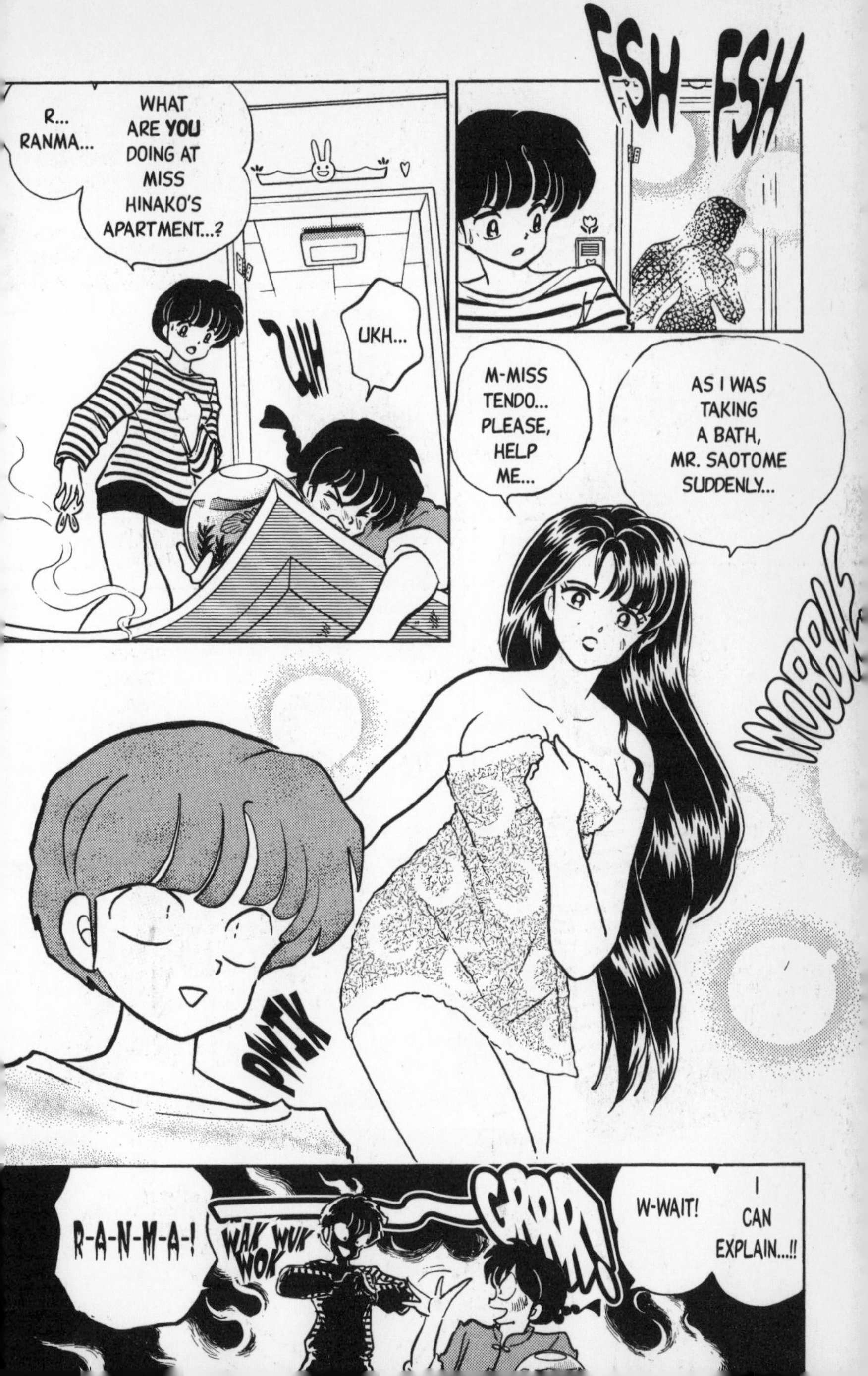
R... RANMA...
WHAT ARE YOU DOING AT MISS HINAKO'S APARTMENT...?
UKH...
FSH FSH
M-MISS TENDO... PLEASE, HELP ME...
AS I WAS TAKING A BATH, MR. SAOTOME SUDDENLY...
WOBBLE
PWIK
R-A-N-M-A-!
WAK WUK WOK
GRRR
W-WAIT!
I CAN EXPLAIN...!!

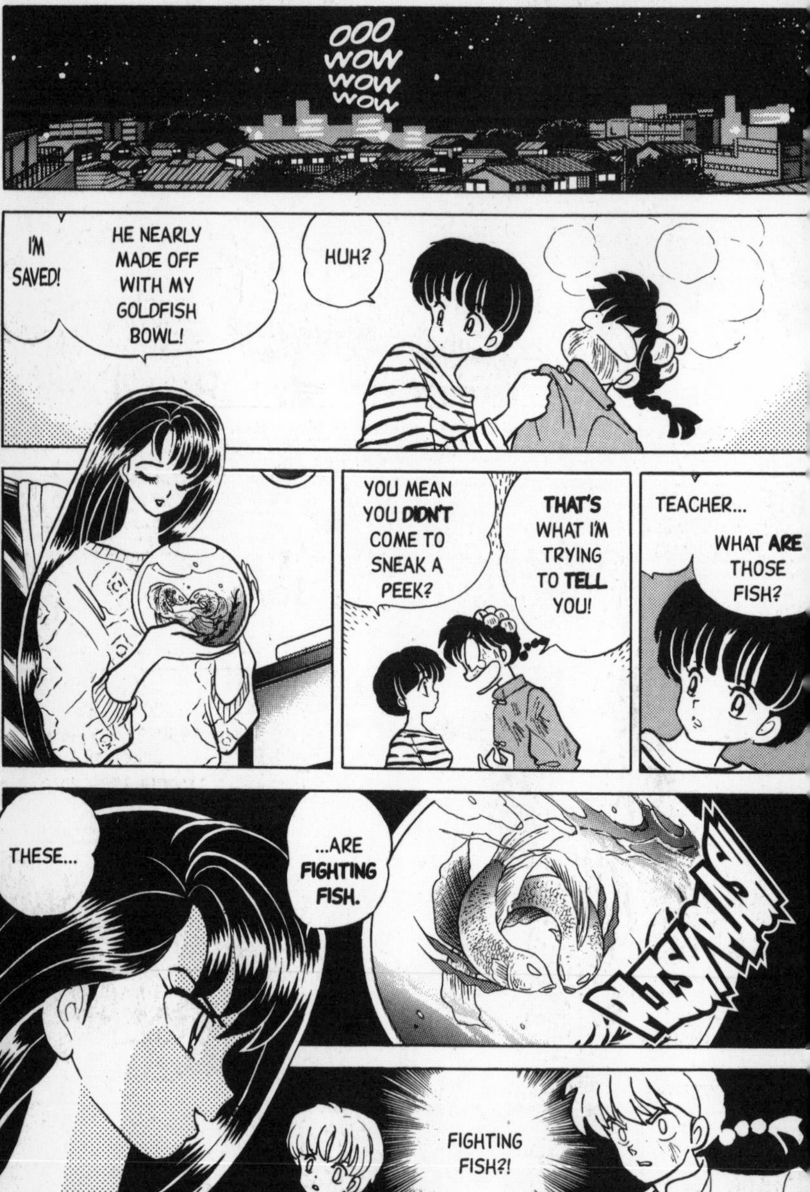
OOO WOW WOW WOW
I'M SAVED!
HE NEARLY MADE OFF WITH MY GOLDFISH BOWL!
HUH?
YOU MEAN YOU **DIDN'T** COME TO SNEAK A PEEK?
THAT'S WHAT I'M TRYING TO **TELL** YOU!
TEACHER...
WHAT **ARE** THOSE FISH?
THESE...
...ARE **FIGHTING FISH.**
PASHASH!
FIGHTING FISH?!

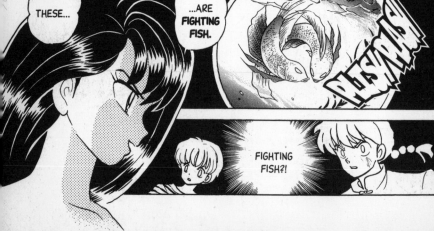

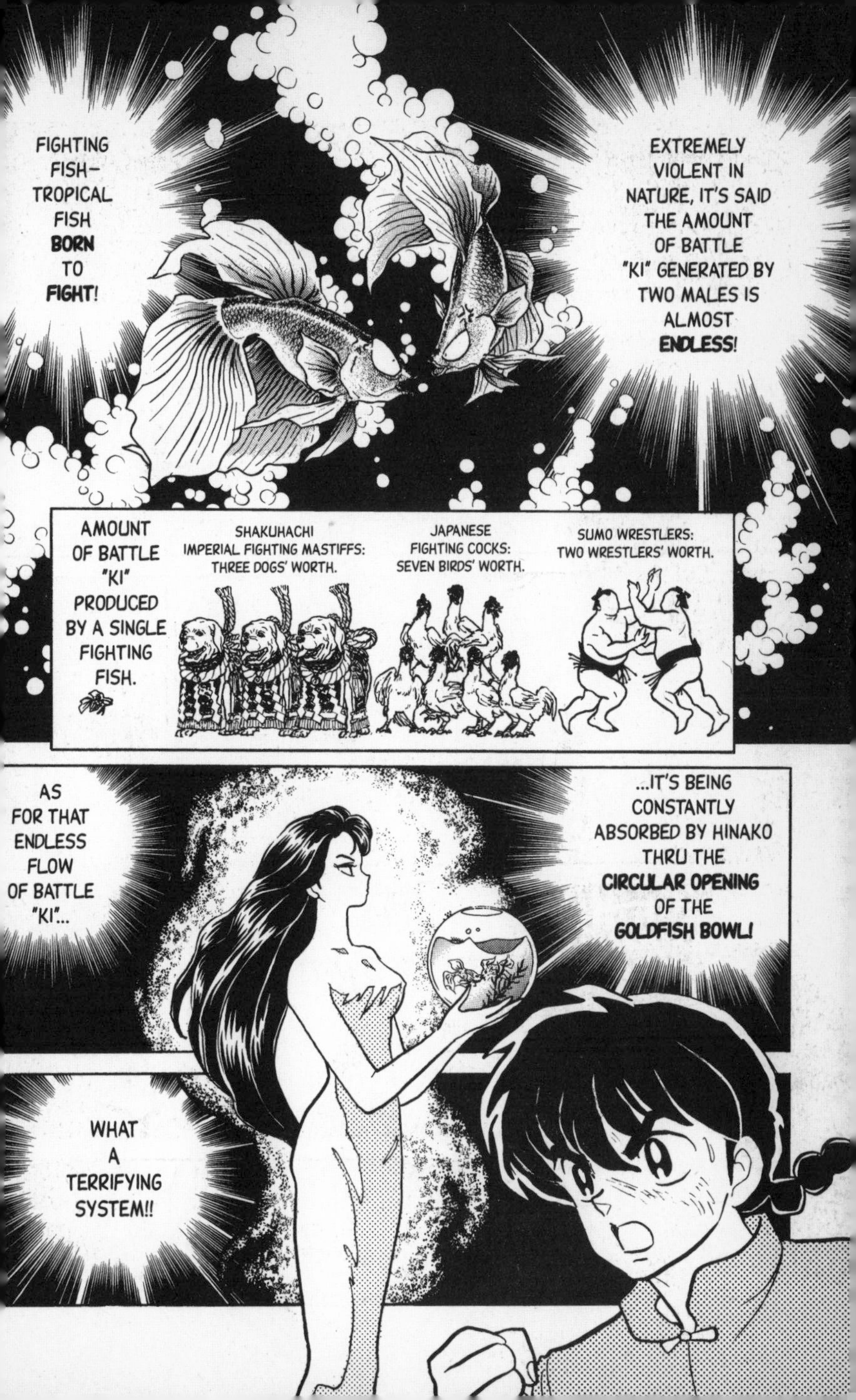
FIGHTING FISH— TROPICAL FISH **BORN** TO **FIGHT**!
EXTREMELY VIOLENT IN NATURE, IT'S SAID THE AMOUNT OF BATTLE "KI" GENERATED BY TWO MALES IS ALMOST **ENDLESS**!
AMOUNT OF BATTLE "KI" PRODUCED BY A SINGLE FIGHTING FISH.
SHAKUHACHI IMPERIAL FIGHTING MASTIFFS: THREE DOGS' WORTH.
JAPANESE FIGHTING COCKS: SEVEN BIRDS' WORTH.
SUMO WRESTLERS: TWO WRESTLERS' WORTH.
AS FOR THAT ENDLESS FLOW OF BATTLE "KI"...
...IT'S BEING CONSTANTLY ABSORBED BY HINAKO THRU THE **CIRCULAR OPENING** OF THE **GOLDFISH BOWL**!
WHAT A TERRIFYING SYSTEM!!

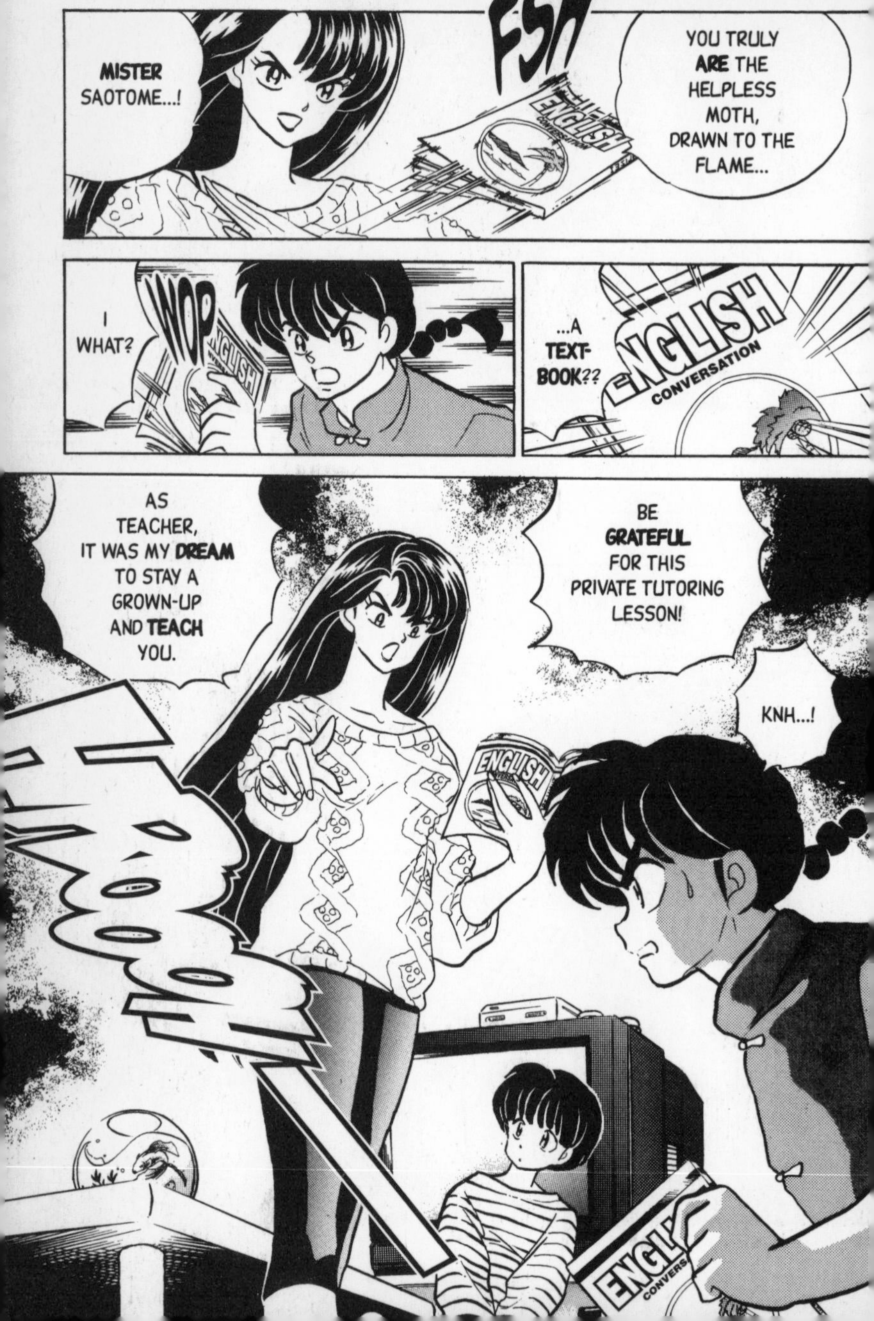
MISTER SAOTOME...!
FSH
ENGLISH CONVERSATION
YOU TRULY ARE THE HELPLESS MOTH, DRAWN TO THE FLAME...
WOP
I WHAT?
...A TEXT-BOOK??
ENGLISH CONVERSATION
AS TEACHER, IT WAS MY DREAM TO STAY A GROWN-UP AND TEACH YOU.
BE GRATEFUL FOR THIS PRIVATE TUTORING LESSON!
KNH...!
ENGLISH

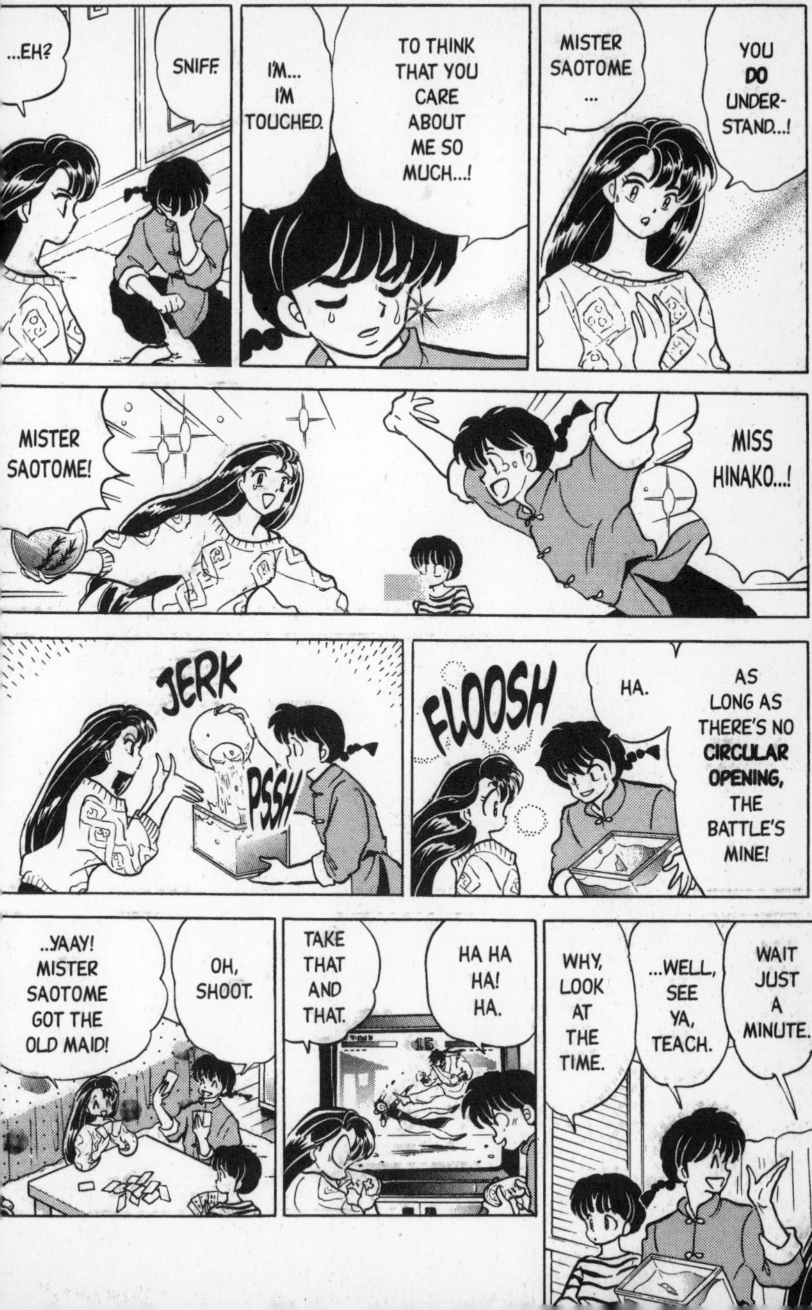
...EH?
SNIFF.
I'M... I'M TOUCHED.
TO THINK THAT YOU CARE ABOUT ME SO MUCH...!
MISTER SAOTOME ...
YOU **DO** UNDER-STAND...!
MISTER SAOTOME!
MISS HINAKO...!
JERK
PSSH
FLOOSH
HA.
AS LONG AS THERE'S NO **CIRCULAR OPENING,** THE BATTLE'S MINE!
...YAAY! MISTER SAOTOME GOT THE OLD MAID!
OH, SHOOT.
TAKE THAT AND THAT.
HA HA HA! HA.
WHY, LOOK AT THE TIME.
...WELL, SEE YA, TEACH.
WAIT JUST A MINUTE.

STUDYING! WHAT HAPPENED TO **STUDYING?!**

HAPPO 50-YEN ATTACK...!

UH-OH.

HA. I'VE SEALED THE **HOLES** OF ALL THE **COINS** IN THE ROOM!

EEEEK-

YOU **MEANIE!** I **TRUSTED** YOU!!

GAH?! A .SCOOP..?

HAH! I HAD THIS READY JUST IN CASE SOMETHING LIKE THIS HAPPENED!

YOU DIDN'T TRUST ME AT **ALL**...!

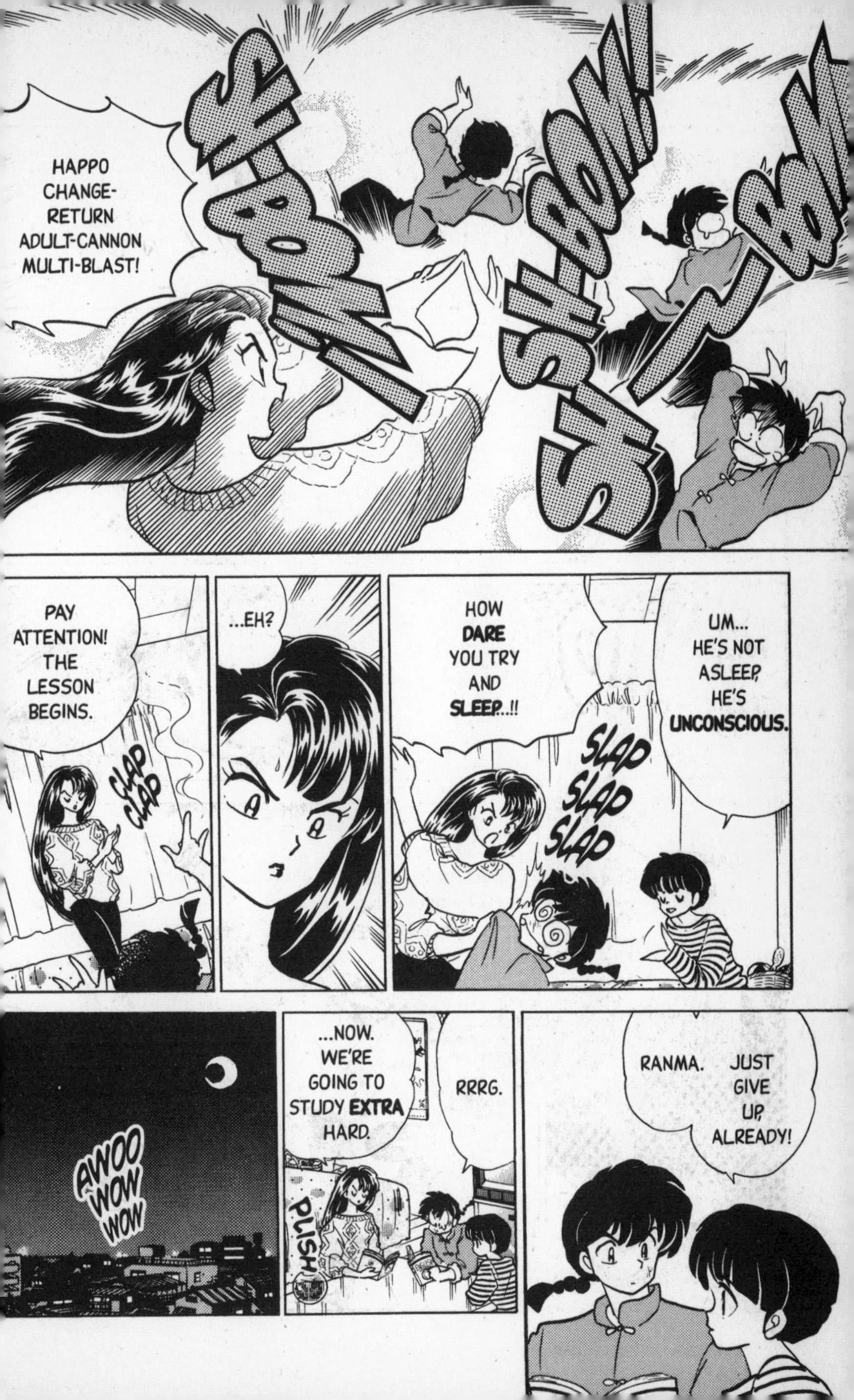
HAPPO CHANGE-RETURN ADULT-CANNON MULTI-BLAST!
PAY ATTENTION! THE LESSON BEGINS.
CLAP CLAP
...EH?
HOW DARE YOU TRY AND SLEEP...!!
SLAP SLAP SLAP
UM... HE'S NOT ASLEEP, HE'S UNCONSCIOUS.
AWOO WOW WOW
...NOW. WE'RE GOING TO STUDY EXTRA HARD.
PLISH
RRRG.
RANMA.
JUST GIVE UP, ALREADY!

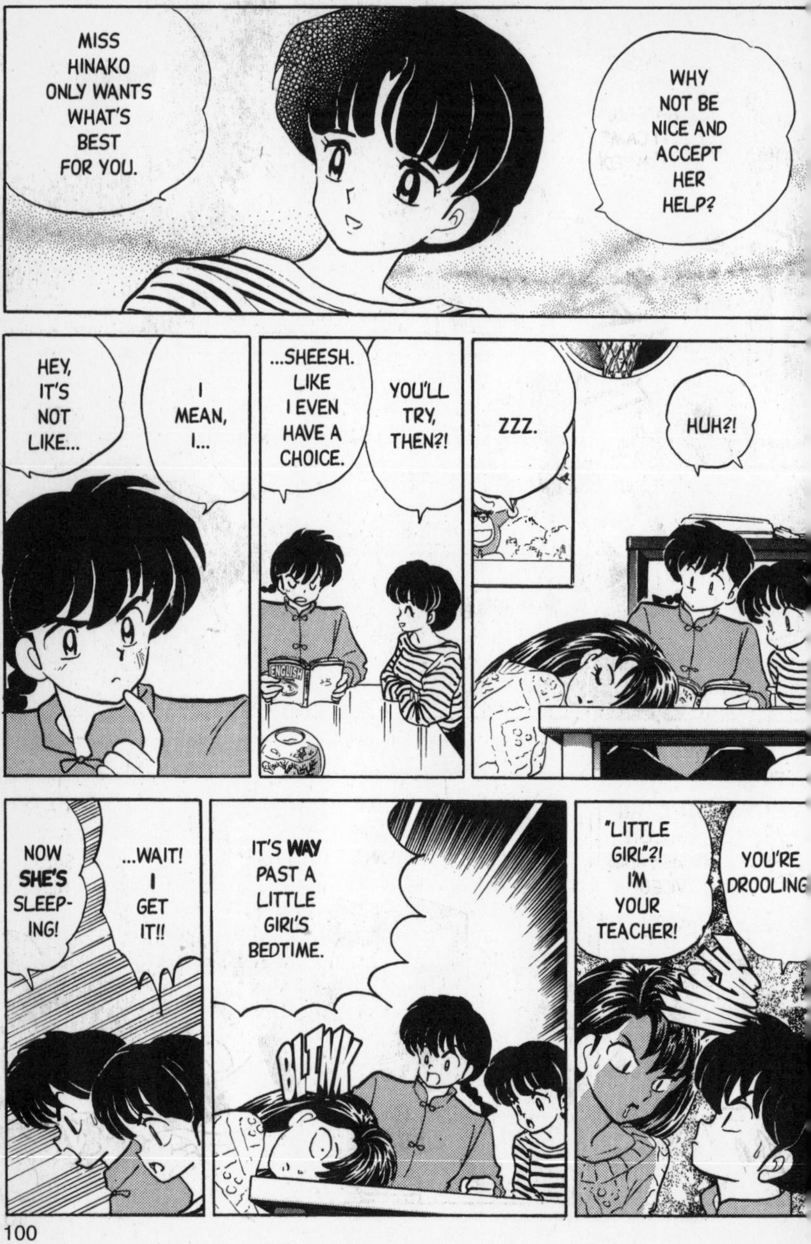
MISS HINAKO ONLY WANTS WHAT'S BEST FOR YOU.
WHY NOT BE NICE AND ACCEPT HER HELP?
HEY, IT'S NOT LIKE...
I MEAN, I...
...SHEESH. LIKE I EVEN HAVE A CHOICE.
YOU'LL TRY, THEN?!
ZZZ.
HUH?!
NOW SHE'S SLEEP-ING!
...WAIT! I GET IT!!
IT'S WAY PAST A LITTLE GIRL'S BEDTIME.
BLINK
"LITTLE GIRL"?! I'M YOUR TEACHER!
YOU'RE DROOLING

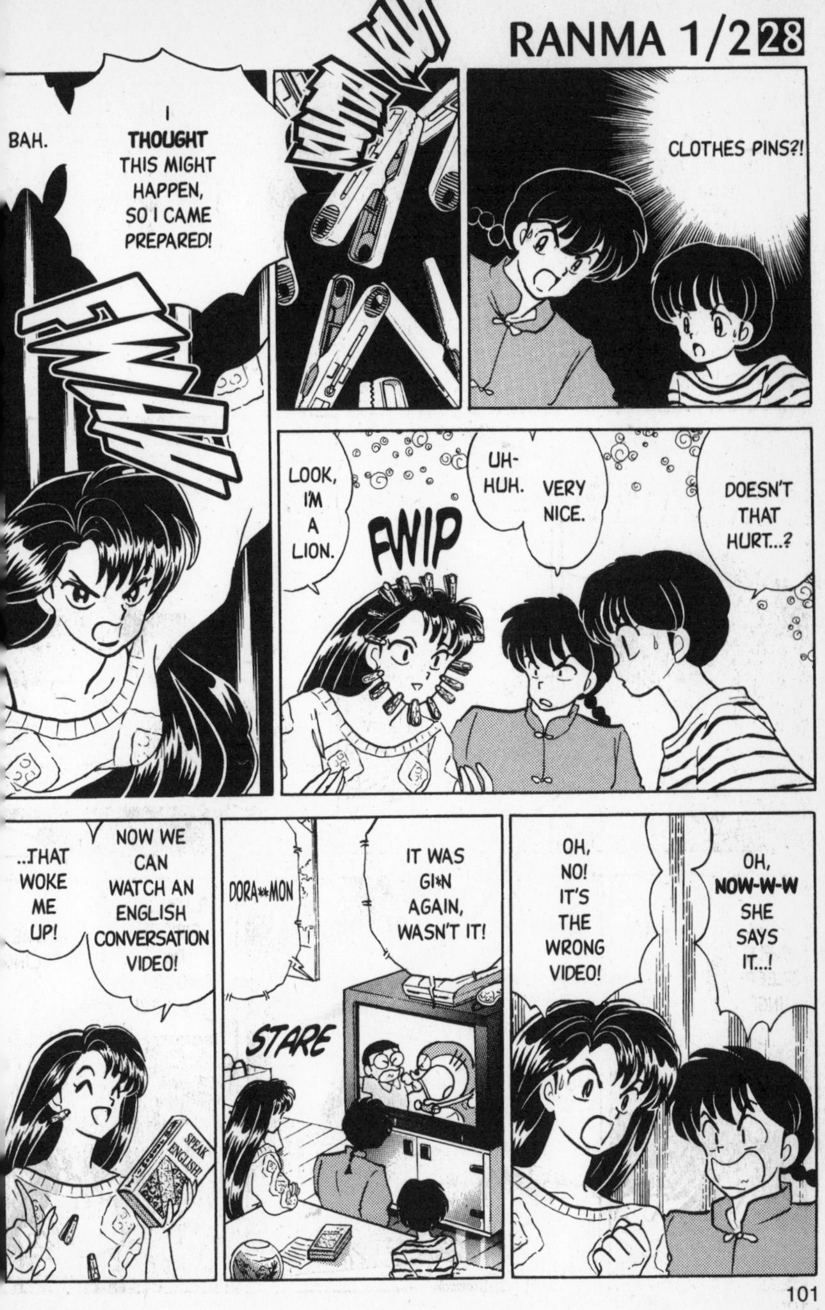
BAH.
I THOUGHT THIS MIGHT HAPPEN, SO I CAME PREPARED!
CLOTHES PINS?!
LOOK, I'M A LION.
FWIP
UH-HUH.
VERY NICE.
DOESN'T THAT HURT...?
...THAT WOKE ME UP!
NOW WE CAN WATCH AN ENGLISH CONVERSATION VIDEO!
SPEAK ENGLISH!
DORA**MON
IT WAS GI*N AGAIN, WASN'T IT!
STARE
OH, NO! IT'S THE WRONG VIDEO!
OH, NOW-W-W SHE SAYS IT...!

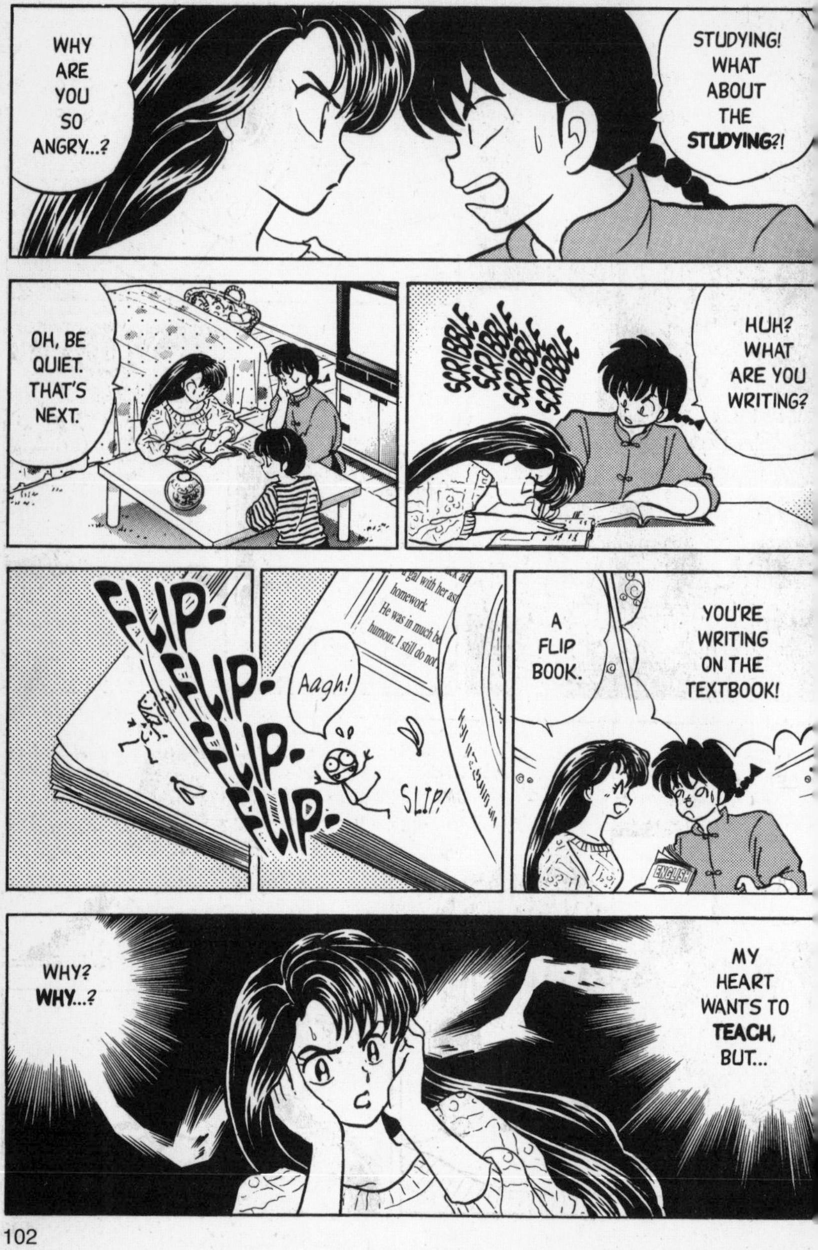

WHY ARE YOU SO ANGRY...?
STUDYING! WHAT ABOUT THE **STUDYING**?!
OH, BE QUIET. THAT'S NEXT.
SCRIBBLE SCRIBBLE SCRIBBLE SCRIBBLE
HUH? WHAT ARE YOU WRITING?
FLIP-FLIP-FLIP-FLIP-
Aagh!
SLIP!
A FLIP BOOK.
YOU'RE WRITING ON THE TEXTBOOK!
ENGLISH
WHY? **WHY...?**
MY HEART WANTS TO **TEACH,** BUT...

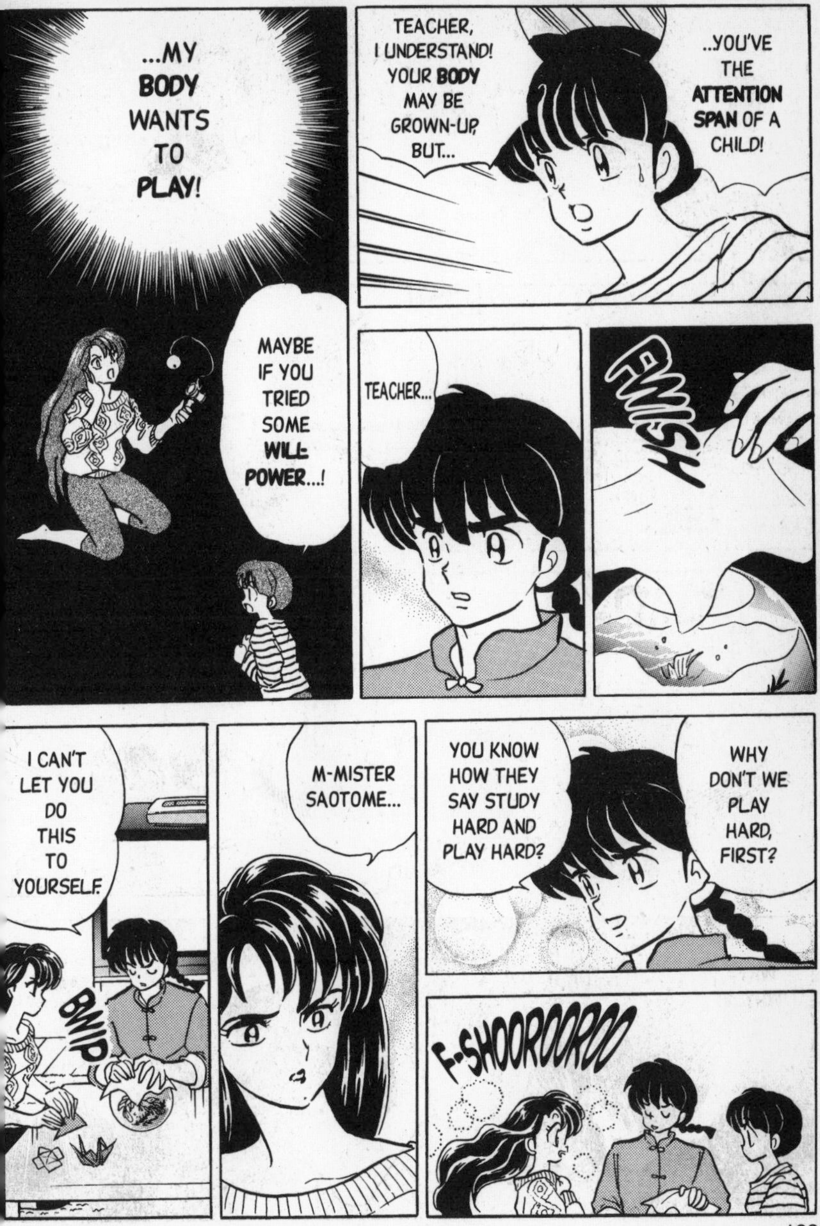
...MY BODY WANTS TO PLAY!
MAYBE IF YOU TRIED SOME WILL POWER...!
TEACHER, I UNDERSTAND! YOUR BODY MAY BE GROWN-UP, BUT...
...YOU'VE THE ATTENTION SPAN OF A CHILD!
TEACHER...
FWISH
I CAN'T LET YOU DO THIS TO YOURSELF.
BWIP
M-MISTER SAOTOME...
YOU KNOW HOW THEY SAY STUDY HARD AND PLAY HARD?
WHY DON'T WE PLAY HARD, FIRST?
F-SHOOROOROO

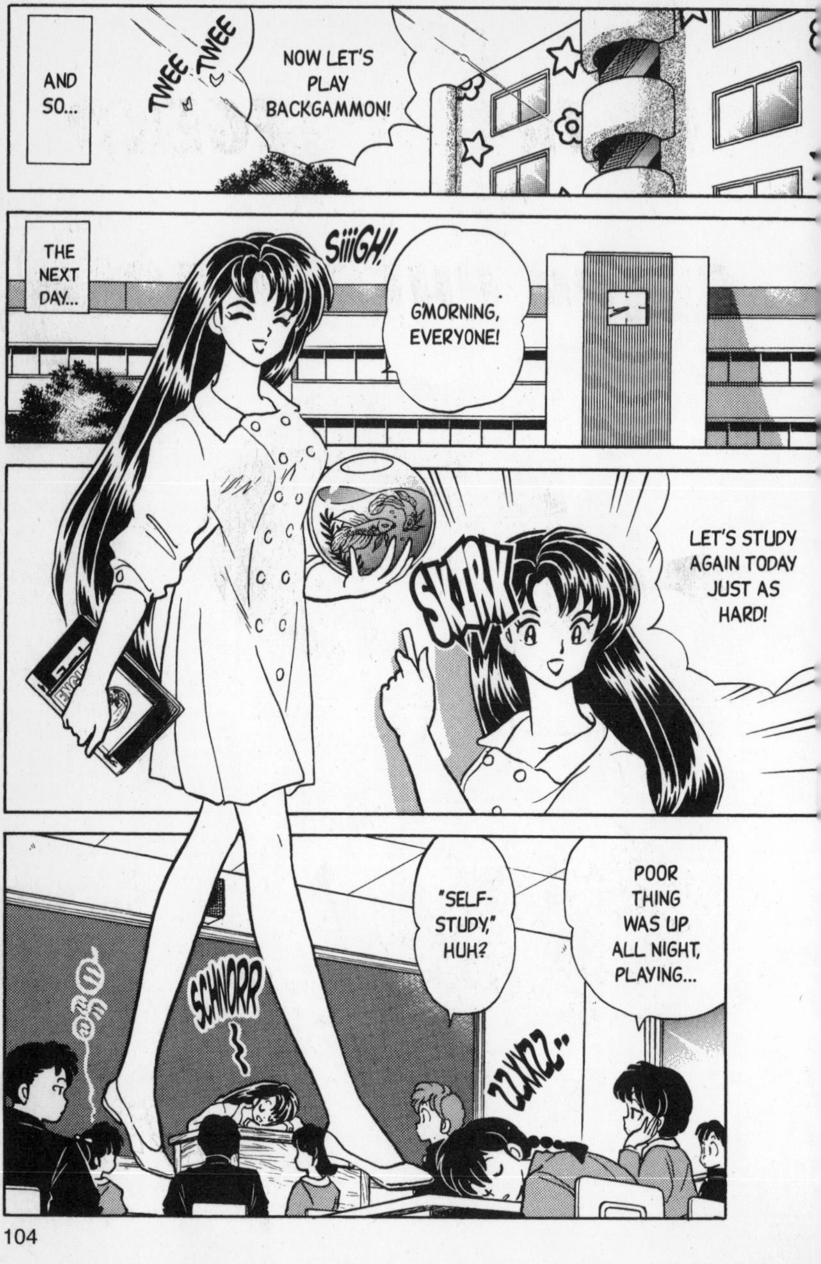
AND SO...
TWEE TWEE
NOW LET'S PLAY BACKGAMMON!
THE NEXT DAY...
SIiiGH!
G'MORNING, EVERYONE!
SKRRK
LET'S STUDY AGAIN TODAY JUST AS HARD!
"SELF-STUDY," HUH?
POOR THING WAS UP ALL NIGHT, PLAYING...
SCHNORR
ZZXYZZ..

PART 7

THE TRAGIC LEGEND OF THE BLACK CHERRY TREE

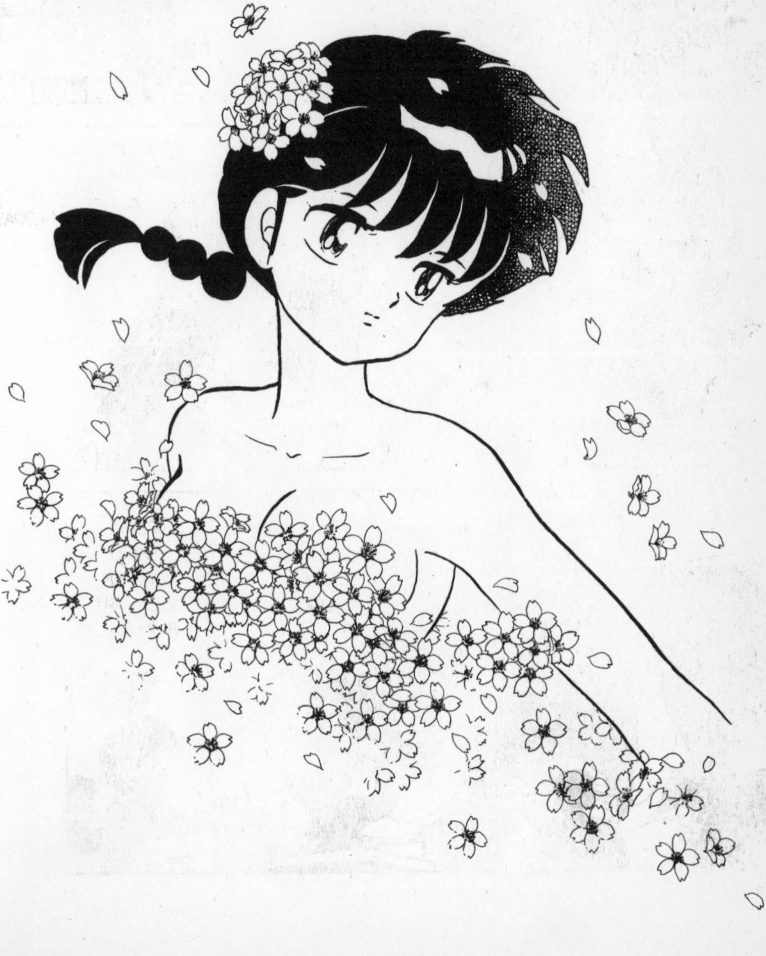

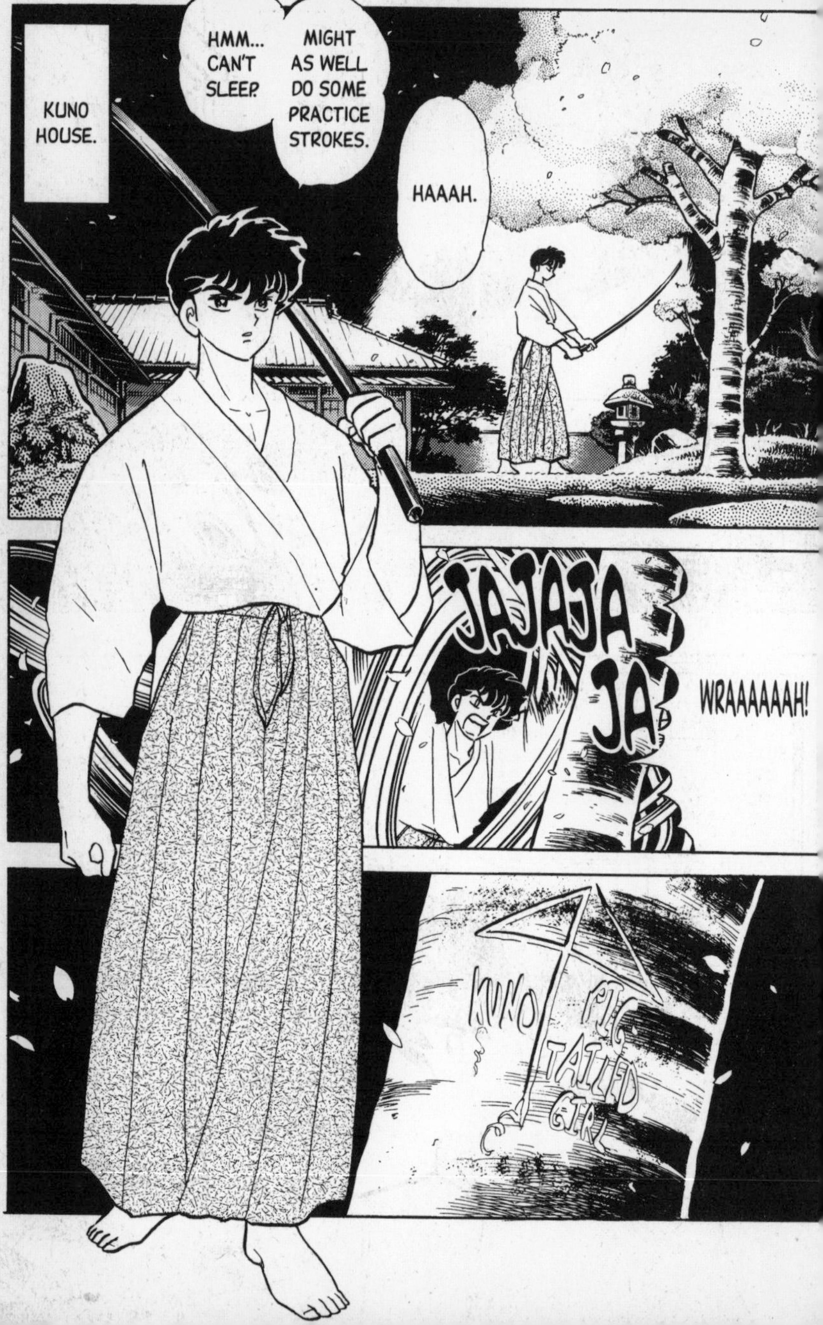
KUNO HOUSE.
HMM... CAN'T SLEEP.
MIGHT AS WELL DO SOME PRACTICE STROKES.
HAAAH.
JAJAJA JA!
WRAAAAAAH!
KUNO
PIG TAILED GIRL

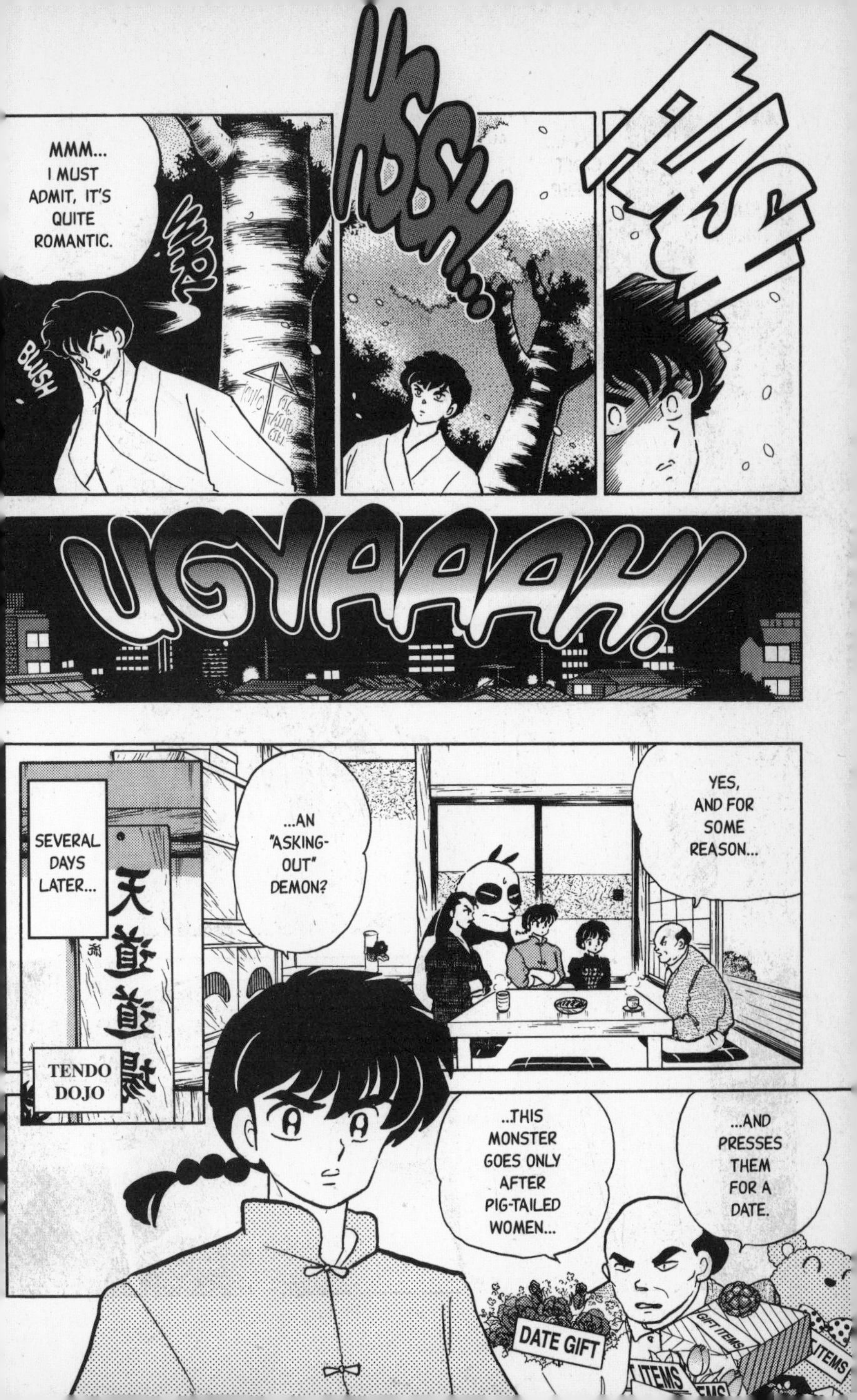
MMM... I MUST ADMIT, IT'S QUITE ROMANTIC.
BLUSH
UGYAAAH!
SEVERAL DAYS LATER...
TENDO DOJO
...AN "ASKING-OUT" DEMON?
YES, AND FOR SOME REASON...
...THIS MONSTER GOES ONLY AFTER PIG-TAILED WOMEN...
...AND PRESSES THEM FOR A DATE.
DATE GIFT
GIFT ITEMS

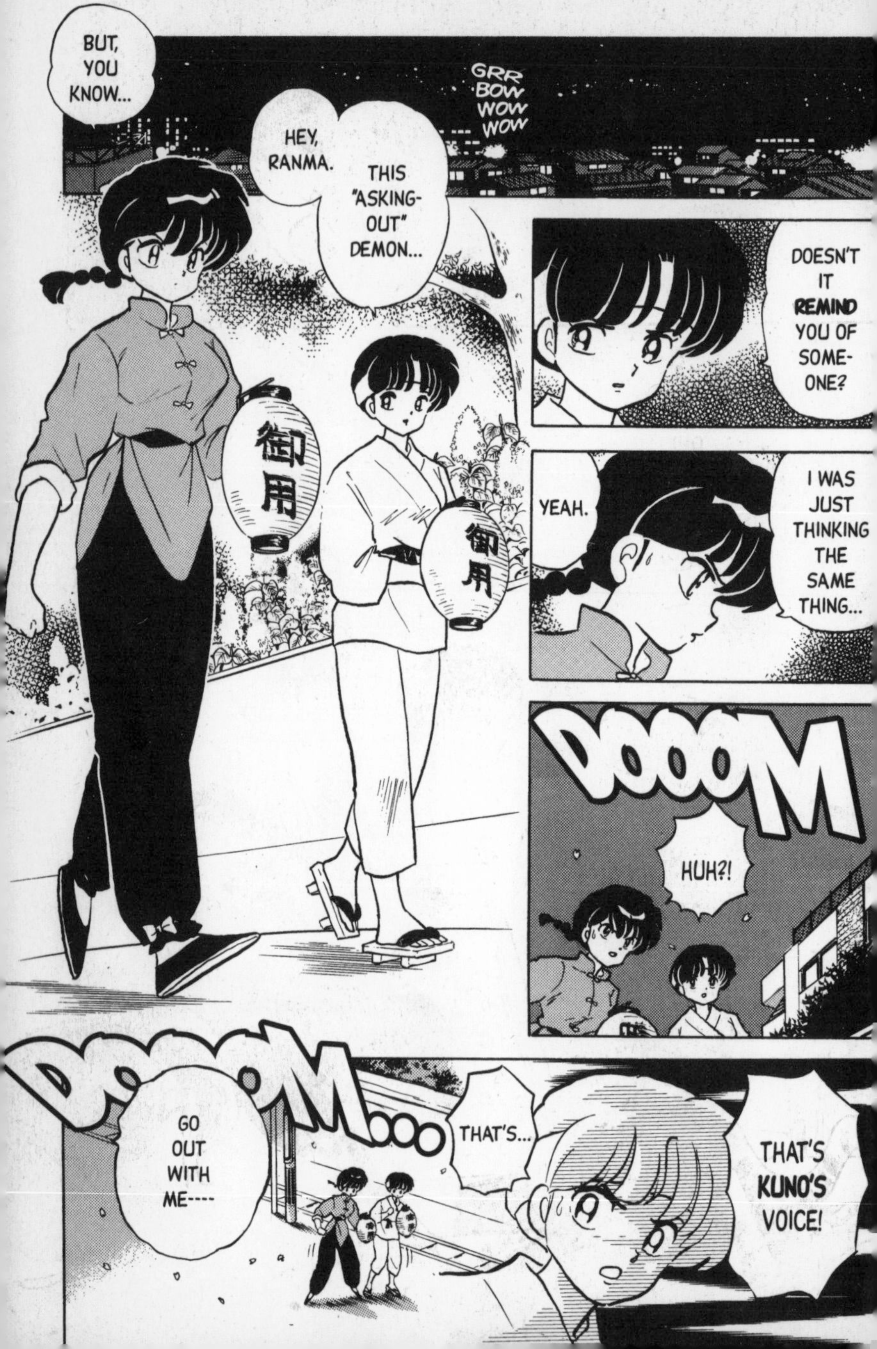

BUT, YOU KNOW...
HEY, RANMA.
THIS "ASKING-OUT" DEMON...
GRR BOW WOW WOW
御用
御用
DOESN'T IT **REMIND** YOU OF SOME-ONE?
YEAH.
I WAS JUST THINKING THE SAME THING...
DOOOM
HUH?!
DOOOM...
GO OUT WITH ME----
THAT'S...
THAT'S **KUNO'S** VOICE!

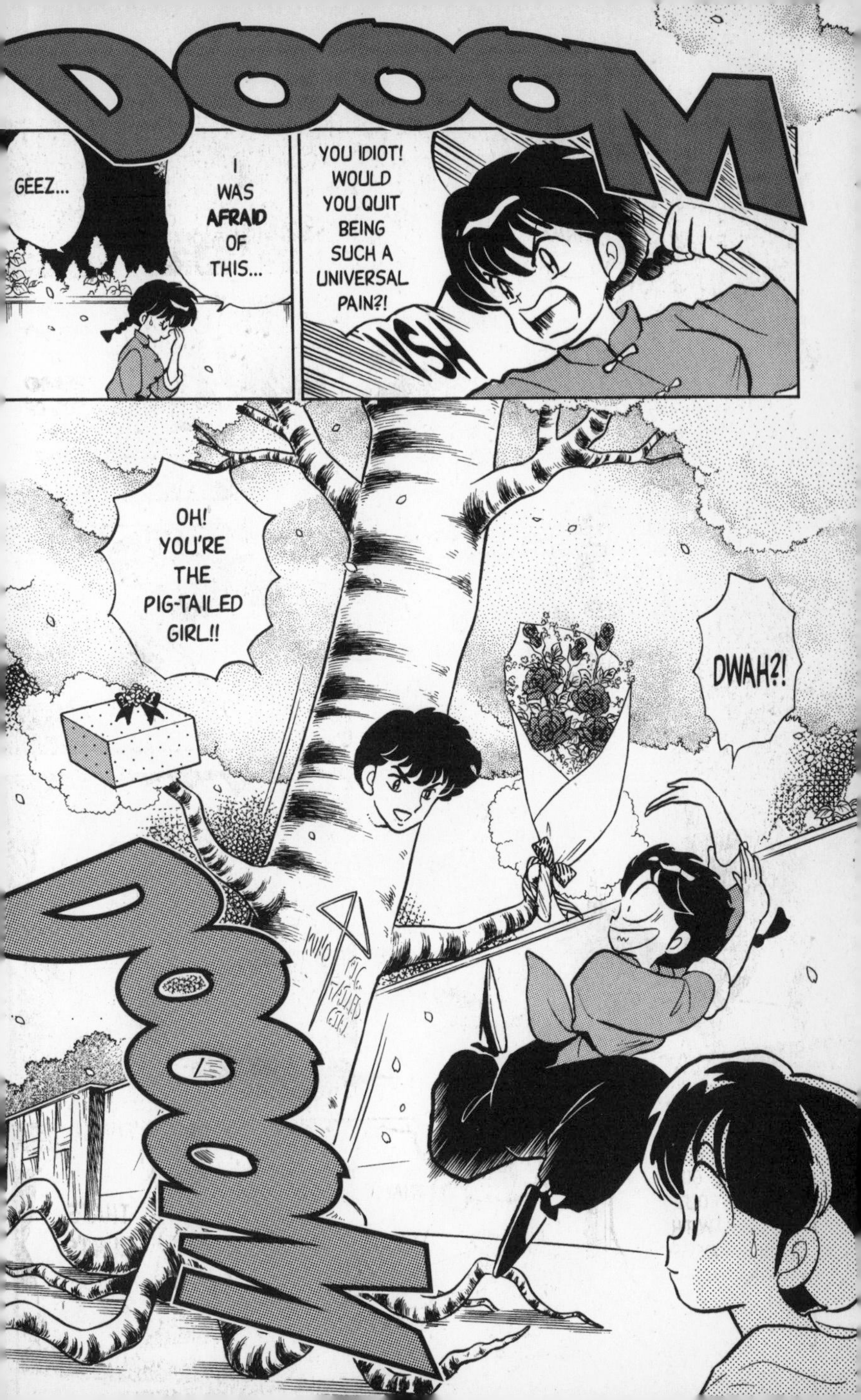
DOOOM
GEEZ...
I WAS AFRAID OF THIS...
YOU IDIOT! WOULD YOU QUIT BEING SUCH A UNIVERSAL PAIN?!
OH! YOU'RE THE PIG-TAILED GIRL!!
DWAH?!
KUNO
PIG-TAILED GIRL
DOOOM

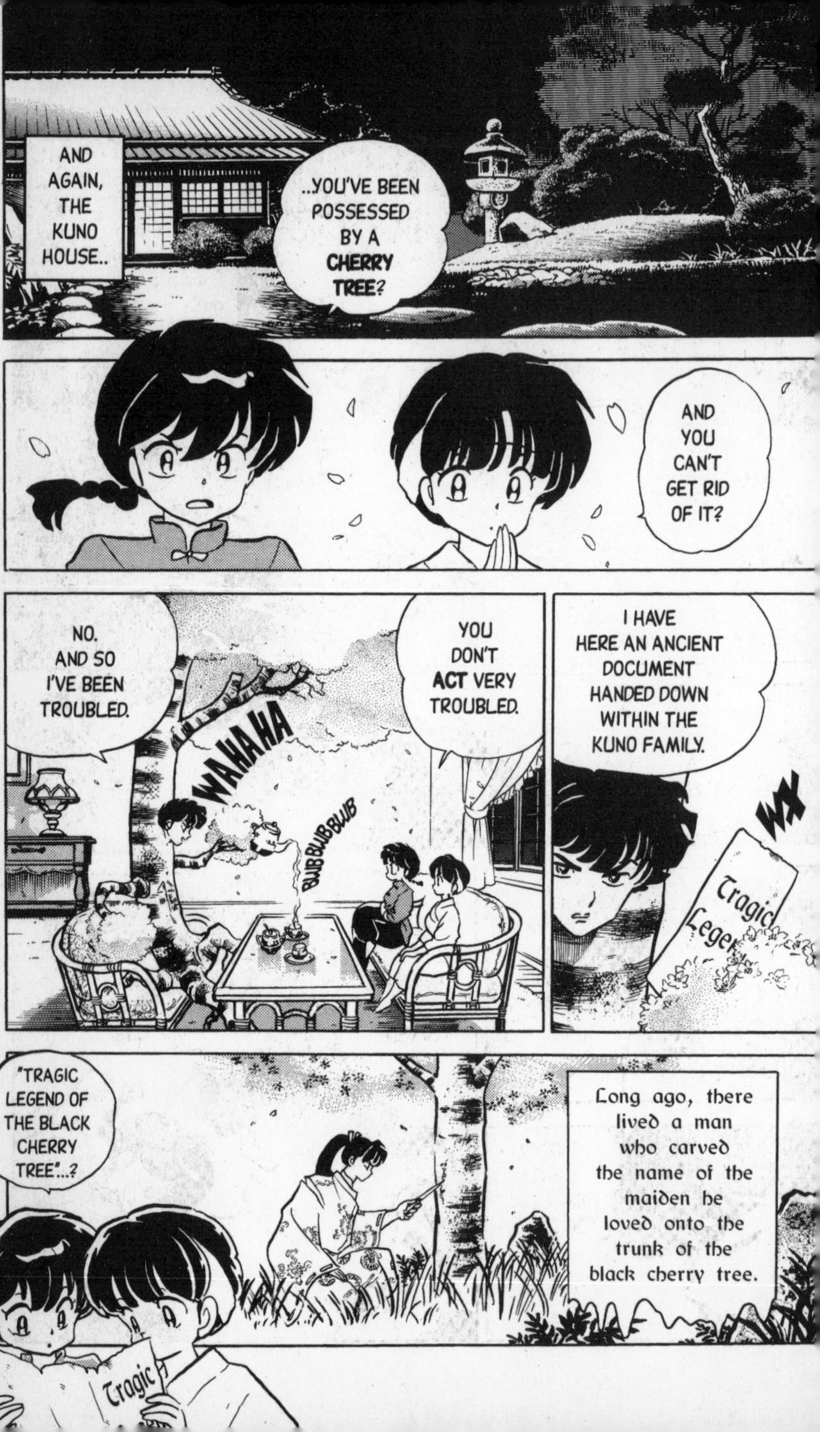
AND AGAIN, THE KUNO HOUSE..
...YOU'VE BEEN POSSESSED BY A CHERRY TREE?
AND YOU CAN'T GET RID OF IT?
NO. AND SO I'VE BEEN TROUBLED.
WAHAHA
BLUBBLUBBLUB
YOU DON'T ACT VERY TROUBLED.
I HAVE HERE AN ANCIENT DOCUMENT HANDED DOWN WITHIN THE KUNO FAMILY.
Tragic
"TRAGIC LEGEND OF THE BLACK CHERRY TREE"...?
Long ago, there lived a man who carved the name of the maiden he loved onto the trunk of the black cherry tree.
Tragic

The black cherry tree, greatly angered, possessed the man...

...and sacrificed the maiden whose name was carved onto its trunk.

HMM... A SACRIFICE.

SO...

...IF YOU BECOME THE SACRIFICE, I'LL BE SAVED.

BONK

INDEED. AND BECAUSE OF THIS...

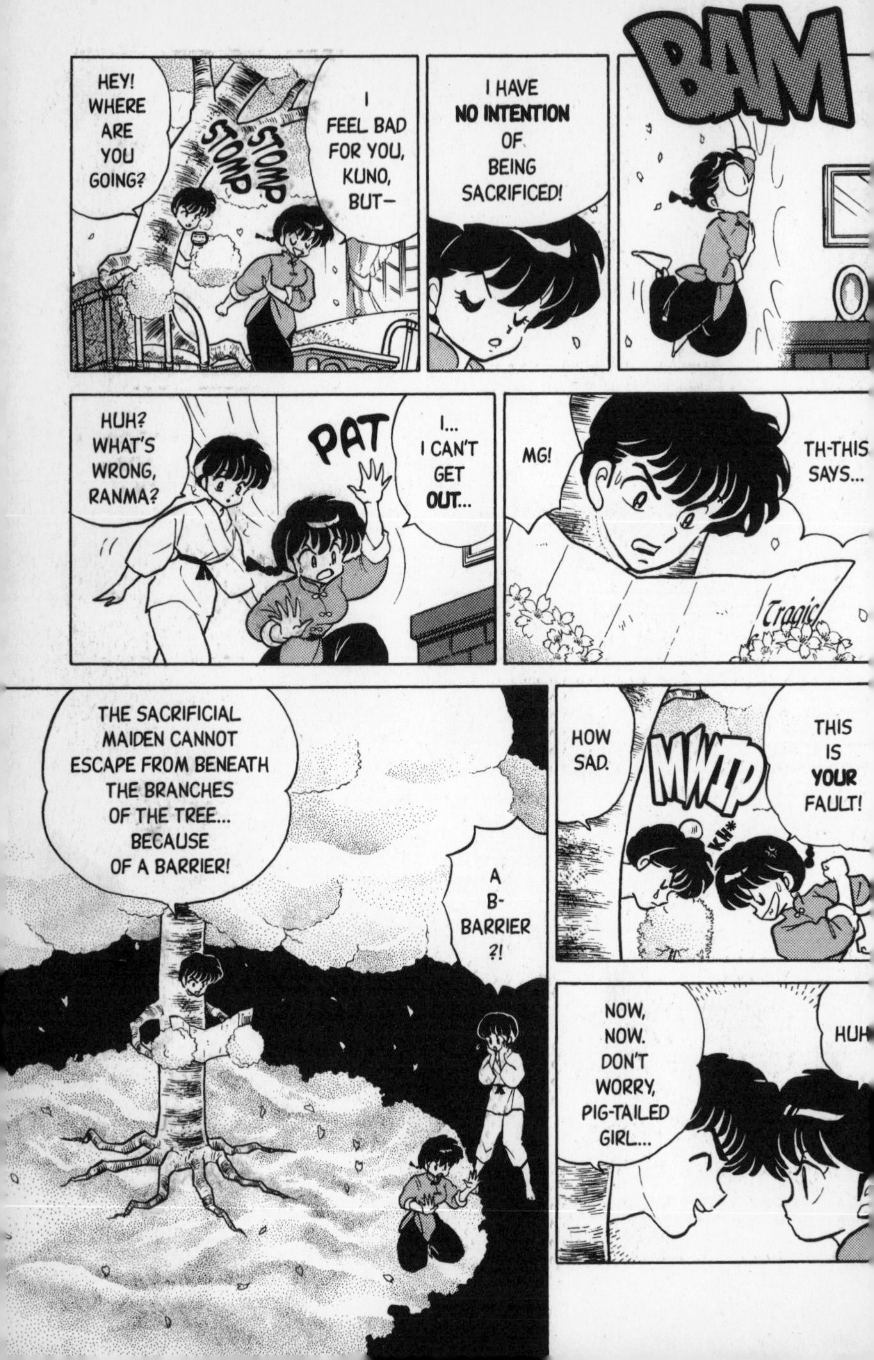
HEY! WHERE ARE YOU GOING?
STOMP STOMP
I FEEL BAD FOR YOU, KUNO, BUT—
I HAVE **NO INTENTION** OF BEING SACRIFICED!
BAM
HUH? WHAT'S WRONG, RANMA?
PAT
I... I CAN'T GET **OUT**...
MG!
TH-THIS SAYS...
Tragic
THE SACRIFICIAL MAIDEN CANNOT ESCAPE FROM BENEATH THE BRANCHES OF THE TREE... BECAUSE OF A BARRIER!
A B-BARRIER?!
HOW SAD.
MWIP
KH*
THIS IS **YOUR** FAULT!
NOW, NOW. DON'T WORRY, PIG-TAILED GIRL...
HUH

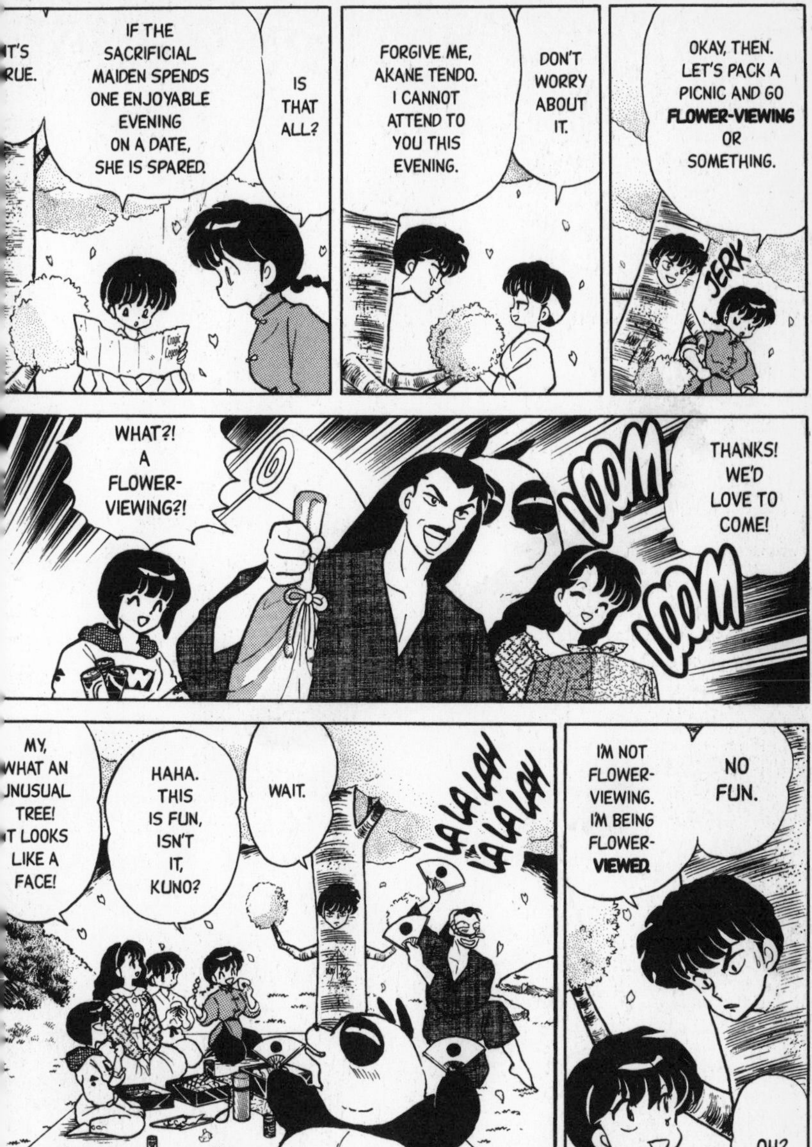
T'S RUE.
IF THE SACRIFICIAL MAIDEN SPENDS ONE ENJOYABLE EVENING ON A DATE, SHE IS SPARED.
IS THAT ALL?
FORGIVE ME, AKANE TENDO. I CANNOT ATTEND TO YOU THIS EVENING.
DON'T WORRY ABOUT IT.
OKAY, THEN. LET'S PACK A PICNIC AND GO FLOWER-VIEWING OR SOMETHING.
JERK
WHAT?! A FLOWER-VIEWING?!
VOOM
THANKS! WE'D LOVE TO COME!
VOOM
MY, WHAT AN JNUSUAL TREE! T LOOKS LIKE A FACE!
HAHA. THIS IS FUN, ISN'T IT, KUNO?
WAIT.
LA LA LAH LA LA LAH
I'M NOT FLOWER-VIEWING. I'M BEING FLOWER-VIEWED.
NO FUN.
OH?

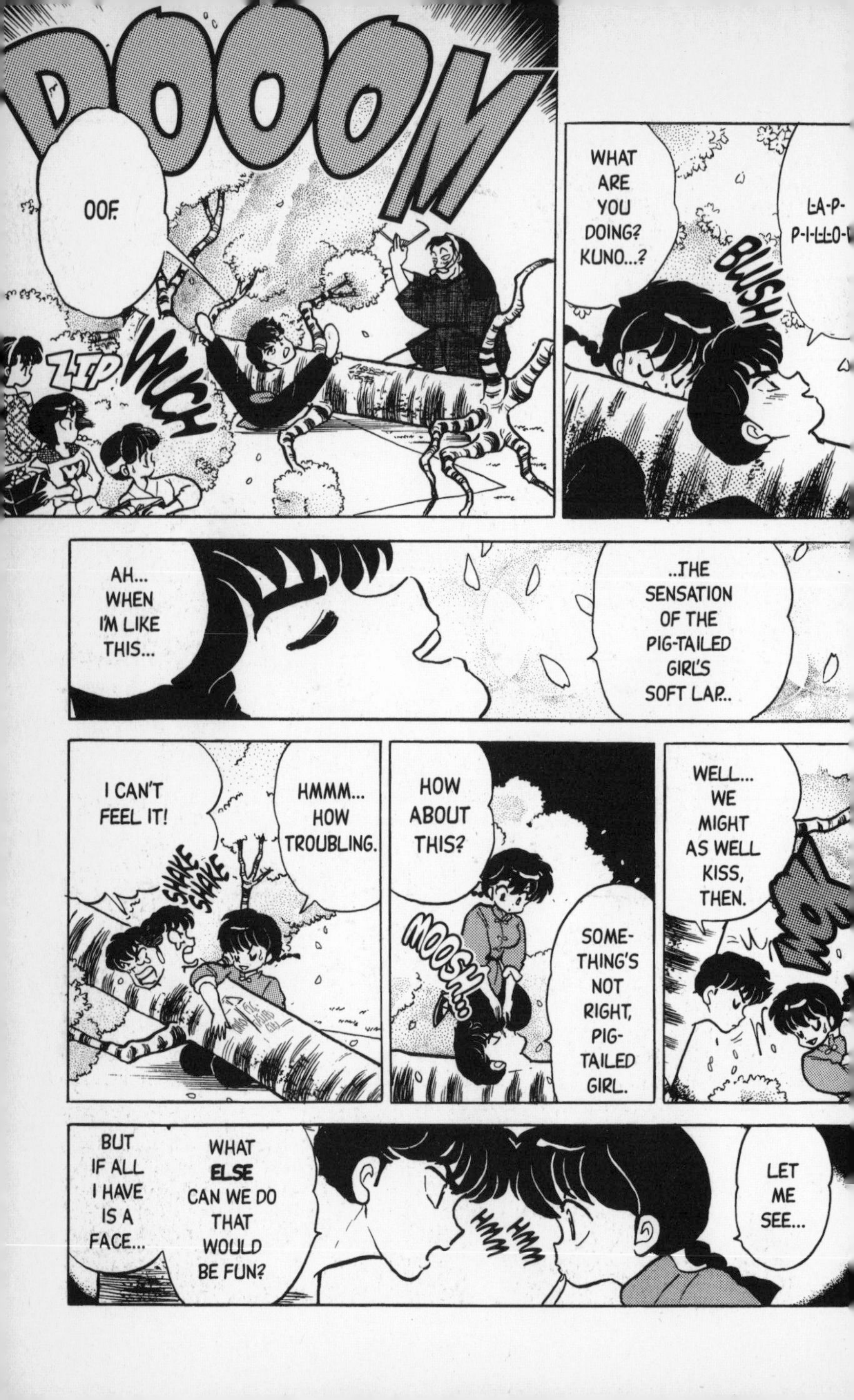
DOOOM
OOF.
ZIP
WUCH
WHAT ARE YOU DOING? KUNO...?
BLUSH
L-A-P-P-I-L-L-O-
AH... WHEN I'M LIKE THIS...
...THE SENSATION OF THE PIG-TAILED GIRL'S SOFT LAP...
I CAN'T FEEL IT!
SHAKE SHAKE
HMMM... HOW TROUBLING.
HOW ABOUT THIS?
MOOSH...
SOME-THING'S NOT RIGHT, PIG-TAILED GIRL.
WELL... WE MIGHT AS WELL KISS, THEN.
BUT IF ALL I HAVE IS A FACE...
WHAT **ELSE** CAN WE DO THAT WOULD BE FUN?
HMM HMM
LET ME SEE...

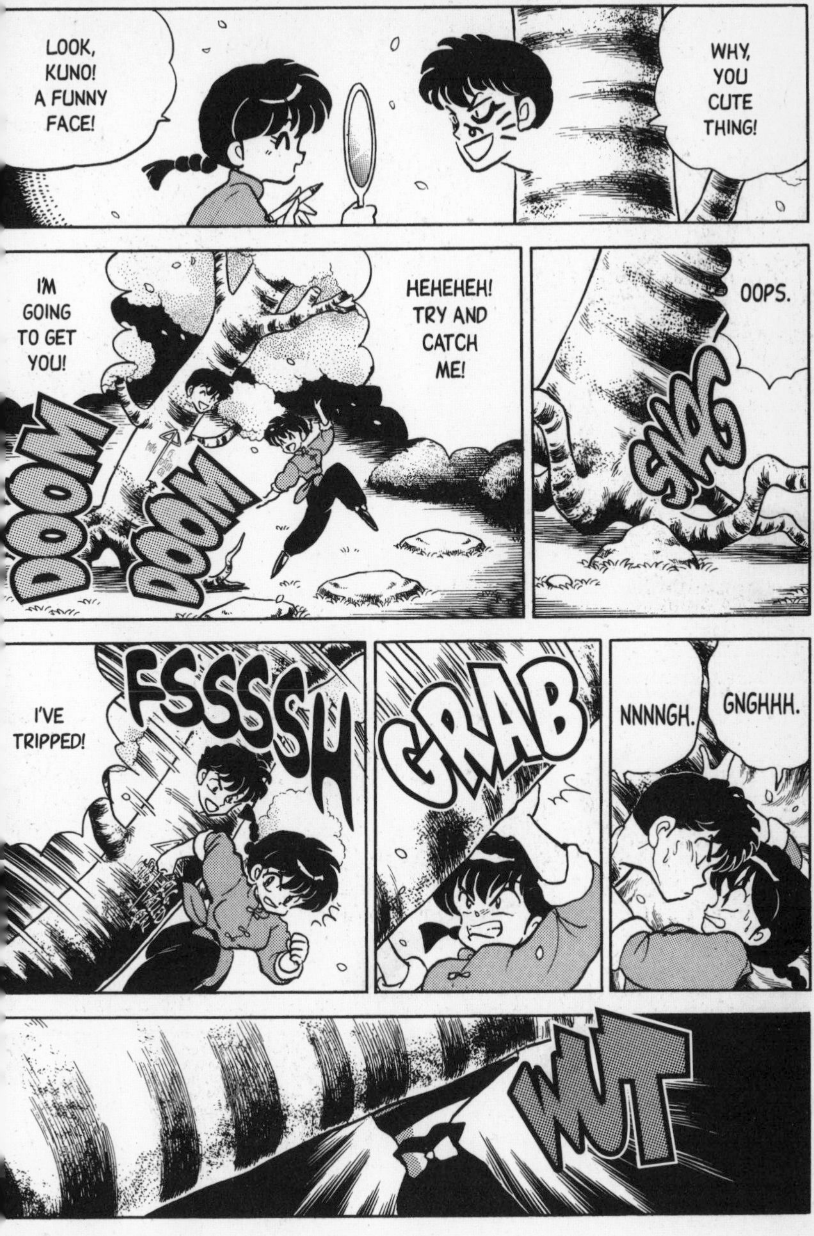
LOOK, KUNO! A FUNNY FACE!
WHY, YOU CUTE THING!
I'M GOING TO GET YOU!
HEHEHEH! TRY AND CATCH ME!
DOOOM
DOOOM
OOPS.
SNAG
I'VE TRIPPED!
FSSSSH
GRAB
NNNNGH.
GNGHHH.
WHUMP

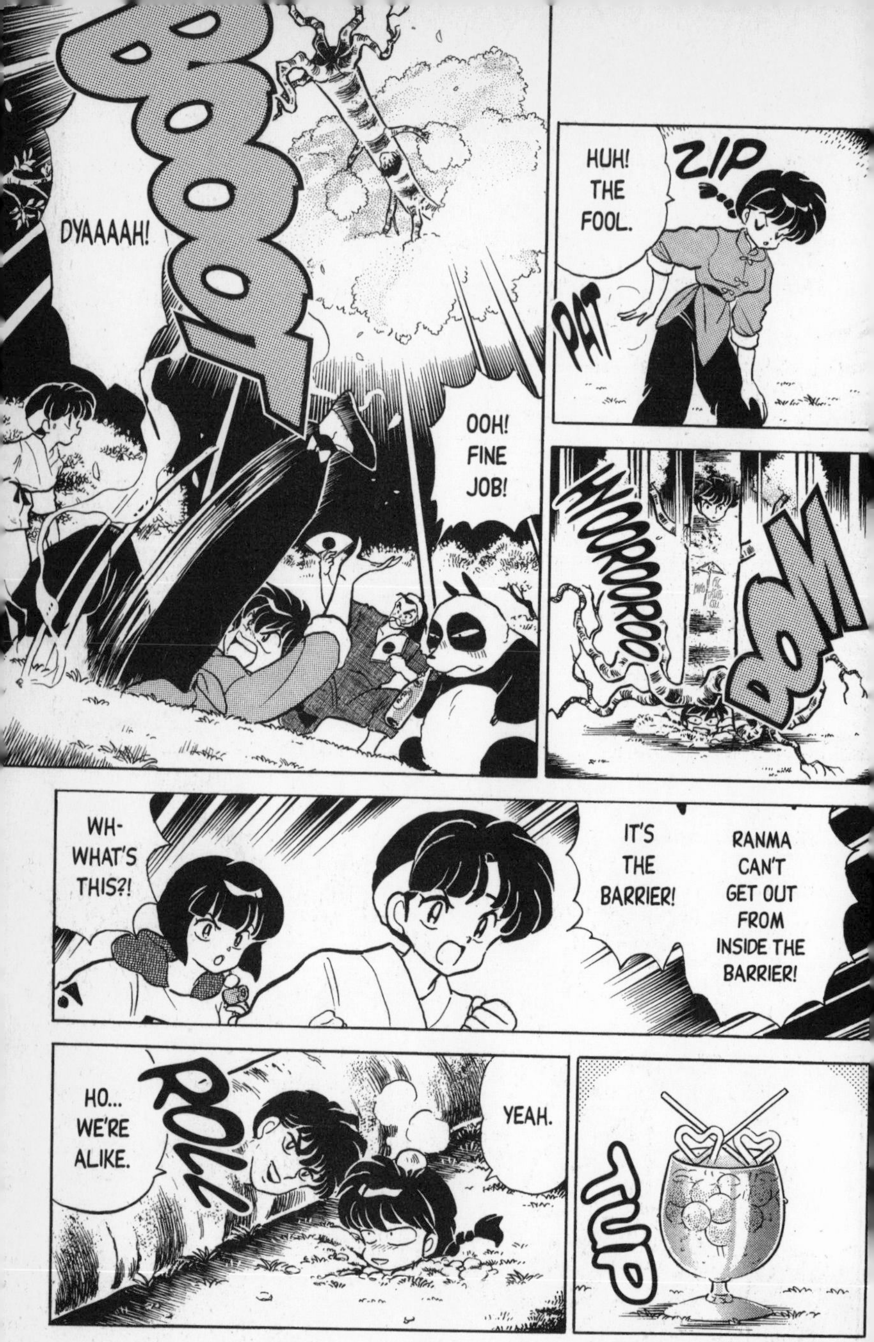
BOOOOM!
DYAAAAH!
OOH! FINE JOB!
HUH! THE FOOL.
ZIP
PAT
HYOOROOROO
BOOM
WH- WHAT'S THIS?!
IT'S THE BARRIER!
RANMA CAN'T GET OUT FROM INSIDE THE BARRIER!
HO... WE'RE ALIKE.
ROLL
YEAH.
TUP

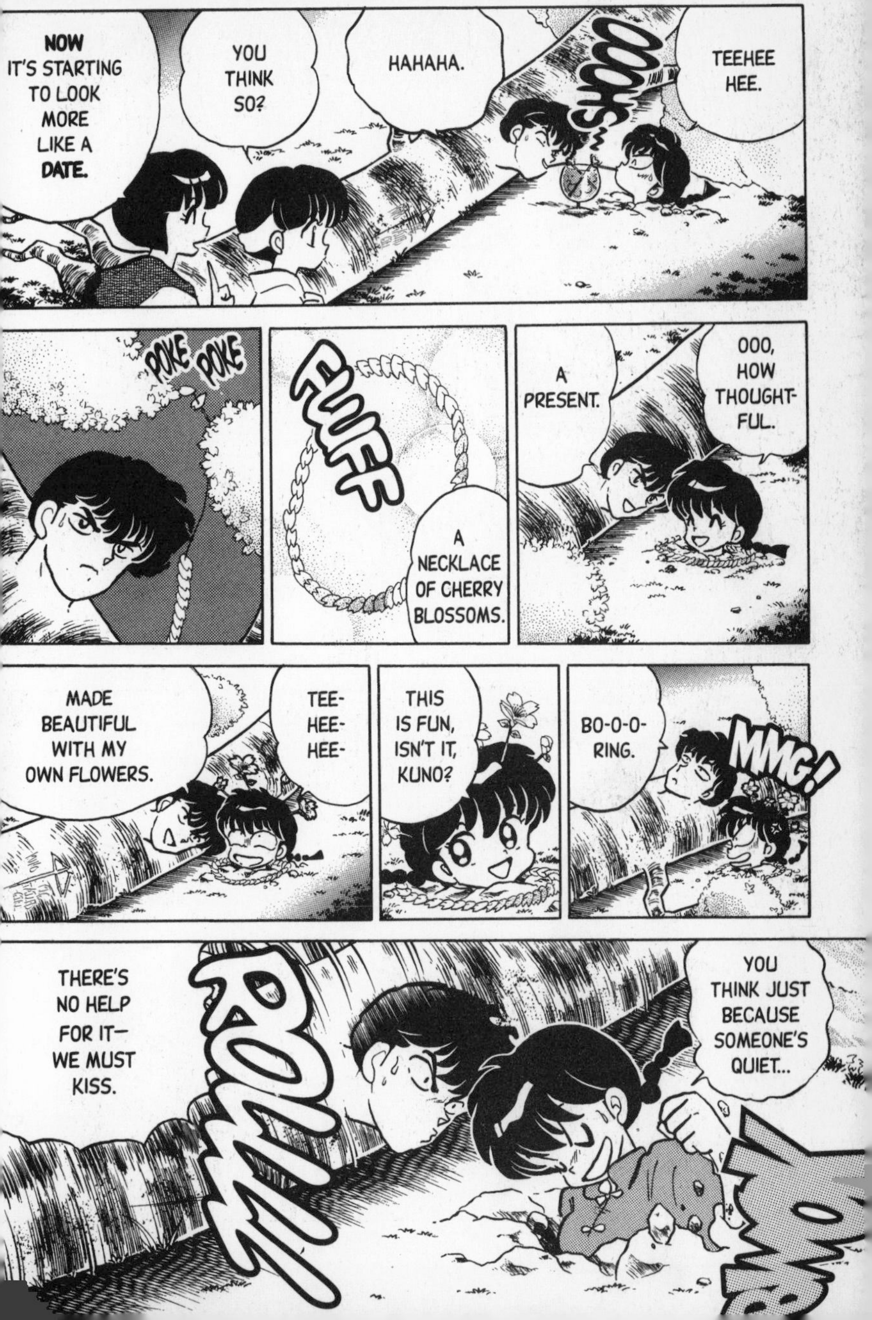
NOW IT'S STARTING TO LOOK MORE LIKE A DATE.
YOU THINK SO?
HAHAHA.
SHOOO
TEEHEE HEE.
POKE POKE
FLUFF
A NECKLACE OF CHERRY BLOSSOMS.
A PRESENT.
OOO, HOW THOUGHTFUL.
MADE BEAUTIFUL WITH MY OWN FLOWERS.
TEE-HEE-HEE-
THIS IS FUN, ISN'T IT, KUNO?
BO-O-O-RING.
MMG!
THERE'S NO HELP FOR IT— WE MUST KISS.
ROWL
YOU THINK JUST BECAUSE SOMEONE'S QUIET...

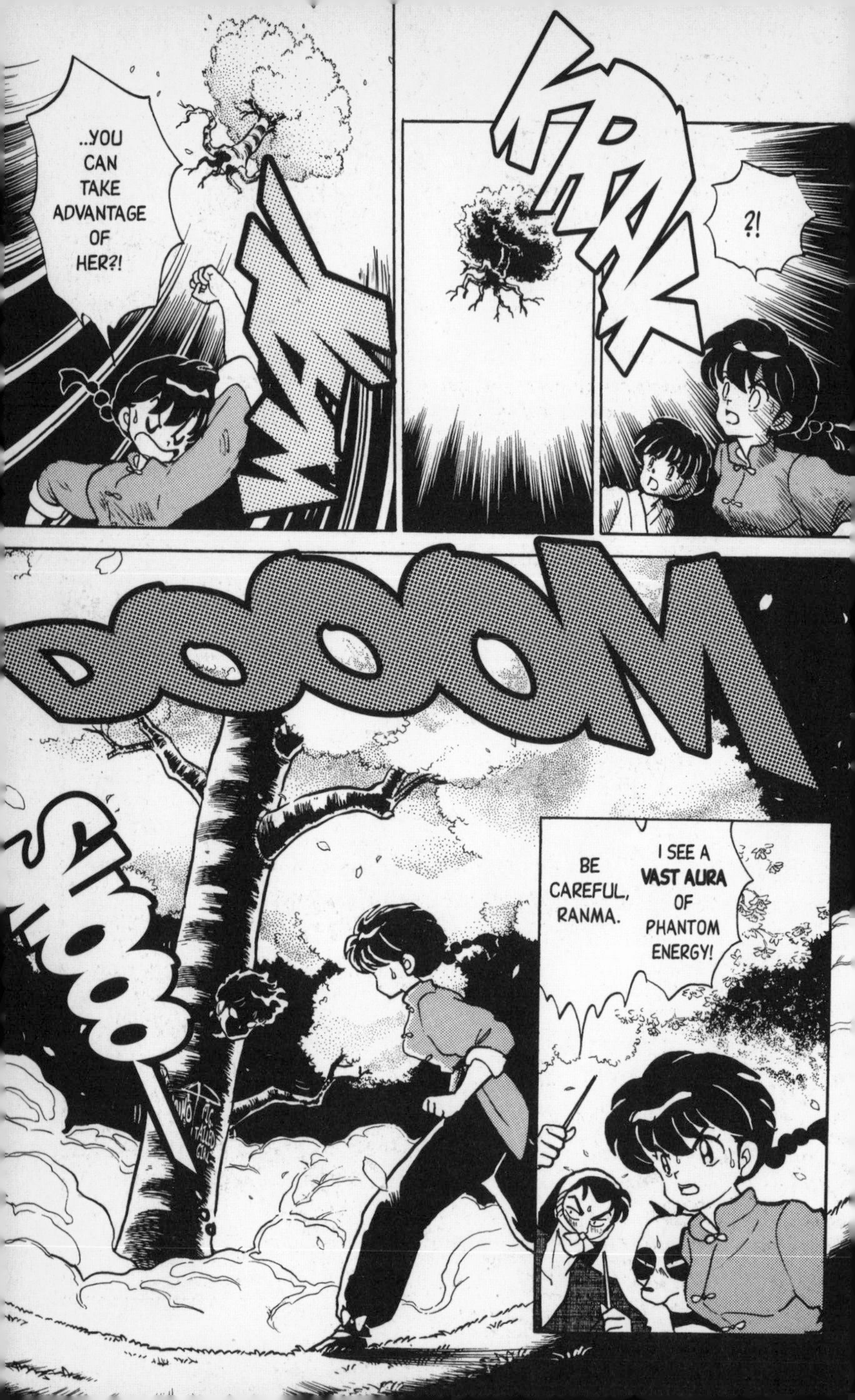
..YOU CAN TAKE ADVANTAGE OF HER?!
KRAK
?!
DOOOM
SHOOO
BE CAREFUL, RANMA.
I SEE A **VAST AURA** OF PHANTOM ENERGY!

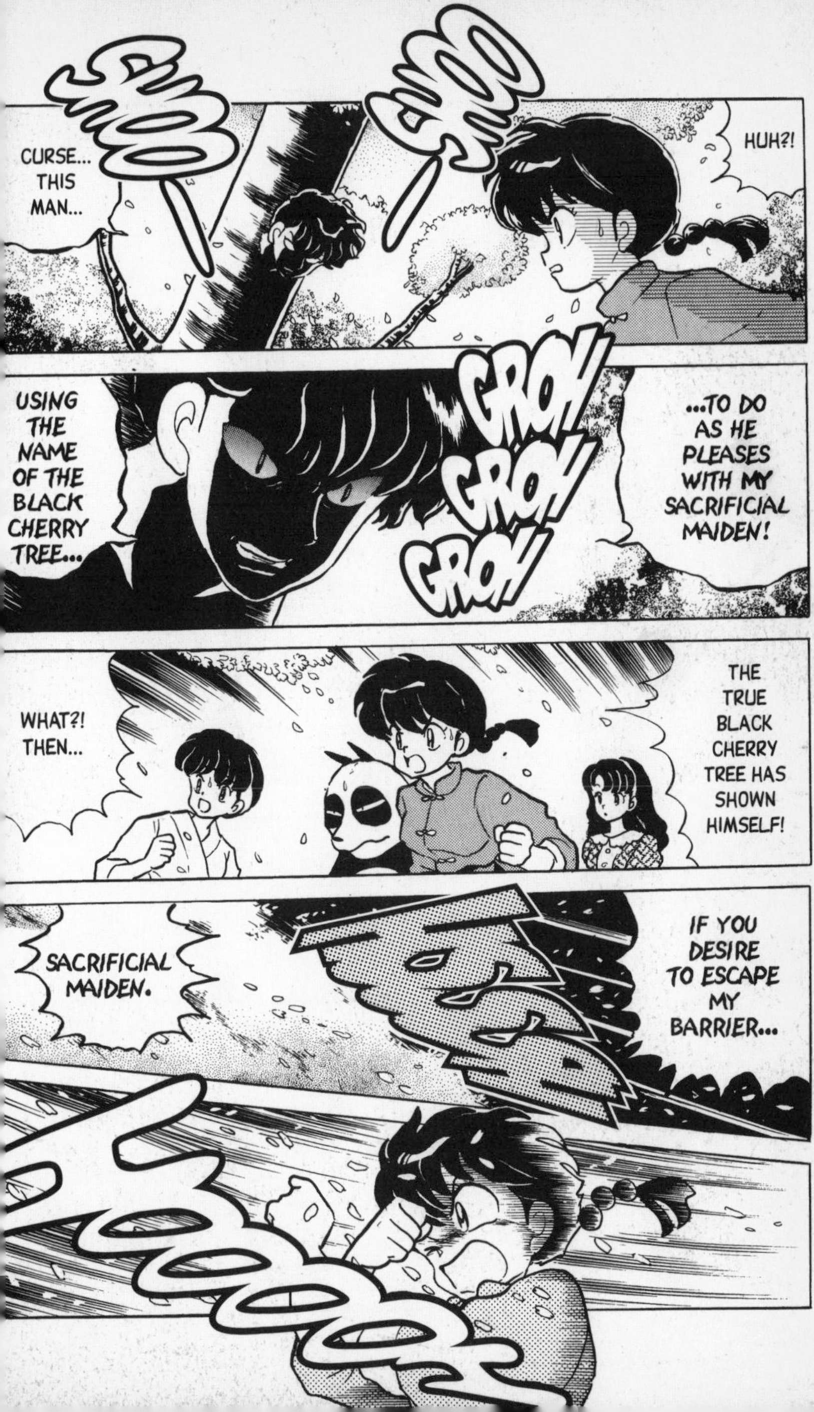
CURSE... THIS MAN...
HUH?!
USING THE NAME OF THE BLACK CHERRY TREE...
GROH GROH GROH
...TO DO AS HE PLEASES WITH MY SACRIFICIAL MAIDEN!
WHAT?! THEN...
THE TRUE BLACK CHERRY TREE HAS SHOWN HIMSELF!
SACRIFICIAL MAIDEN.
IF YOU DESIRE TO ESCAPE MY BARRIER...

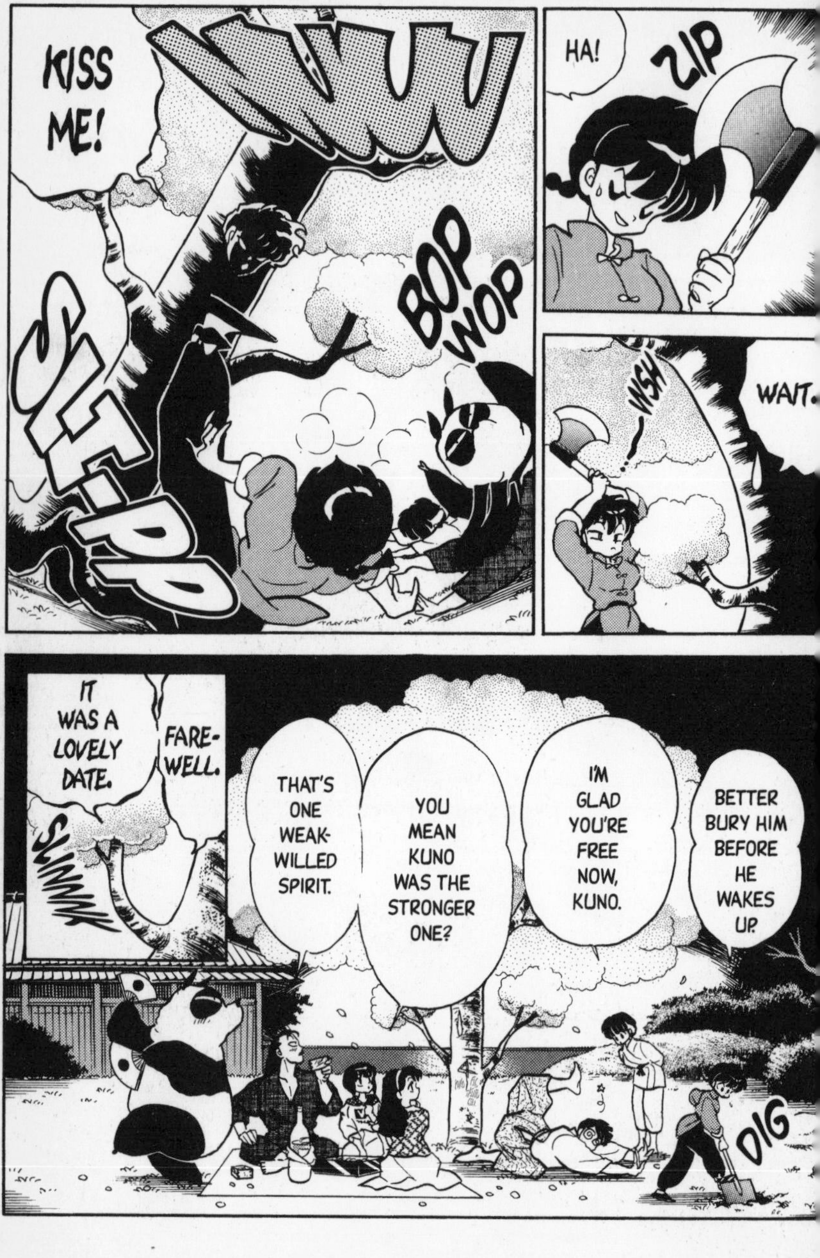
KISS ME!
BOP WOP
HA!
ZIP
WSH
WAIT.
IT WAS A LOVELY DATE.
FARE-WELL.
THAT'S ONE WEAK-WILLED SPIRIT.
YOU MEAN KUNO WAS THE STRONGER ONE?
I'M GLAD YOU'RE FREE NOW, KUNO.
BETTER BURY HIM BEFORE HE WAKES UP.
DIG

PART 8

RANMA CATCHES A COLD

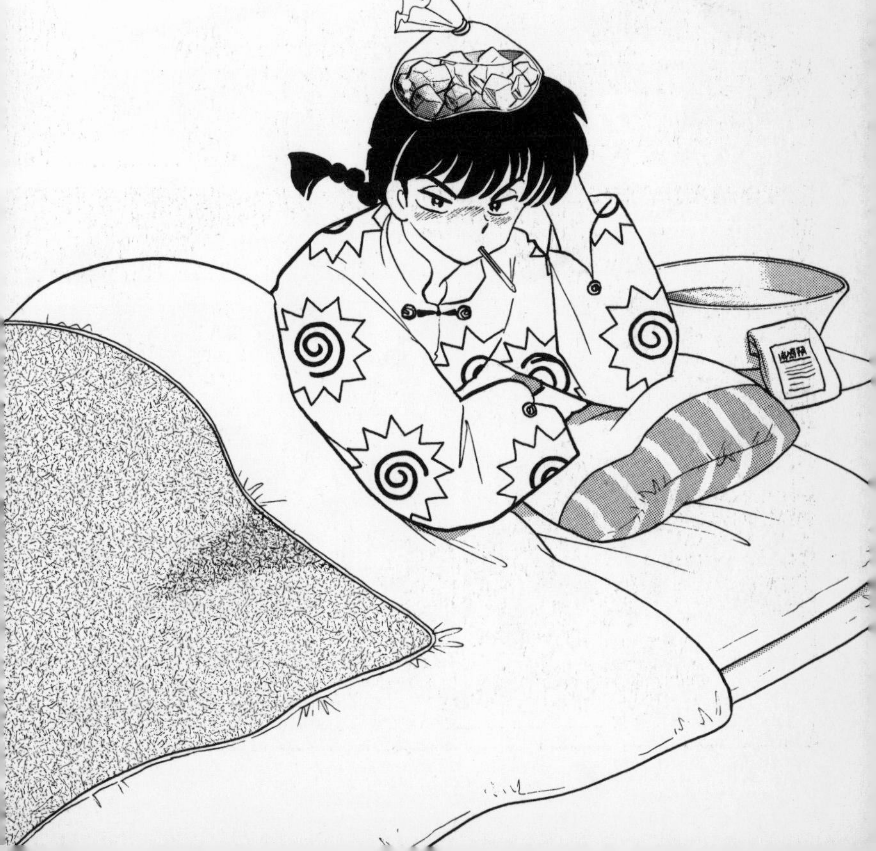

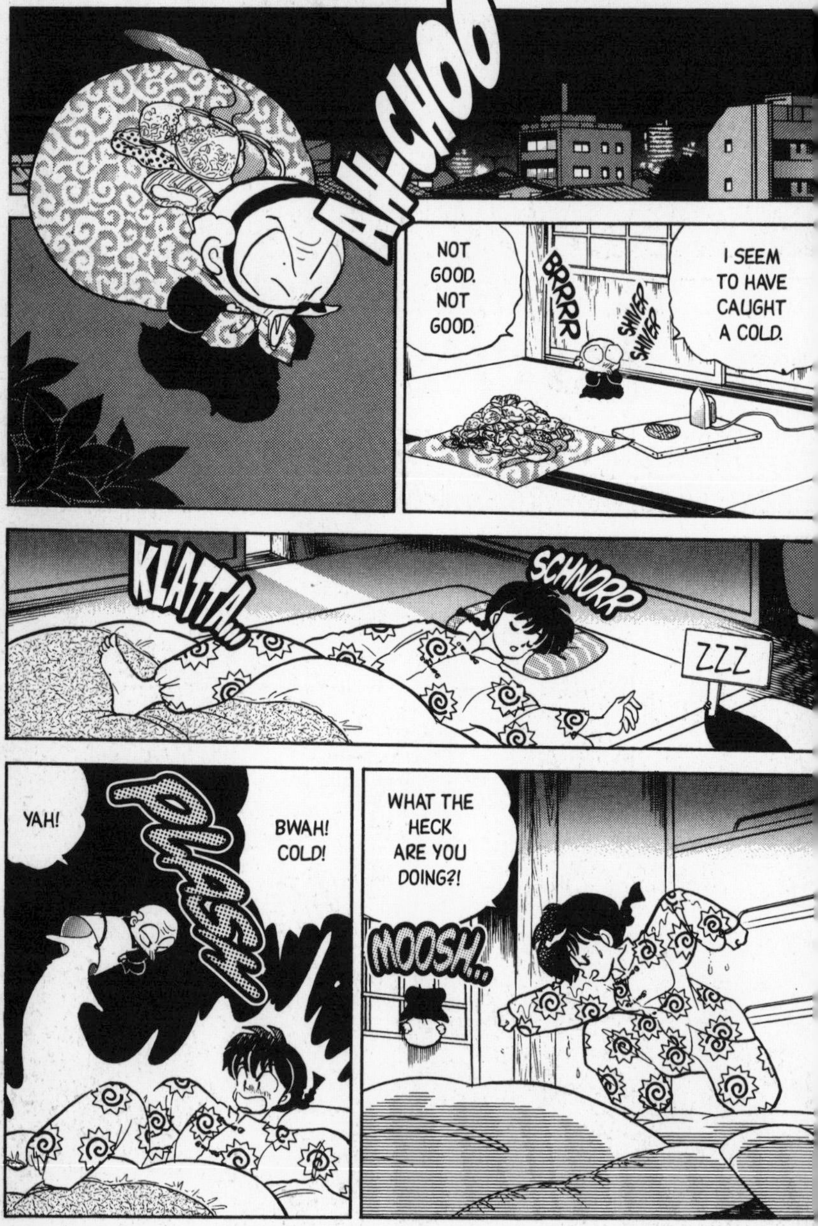
AH-CHOO
NOT GOOD. NOT GOOD.
BRRRR
SHIVER SHIVER
I SEEM TO HAVE CAUGHT A COLD.
KLATTA...
SCHNORR
ZZZ
YAH!
BWAH! COLD!
WHAT THE HECK ARE YOU DOING?!
MOOSH...

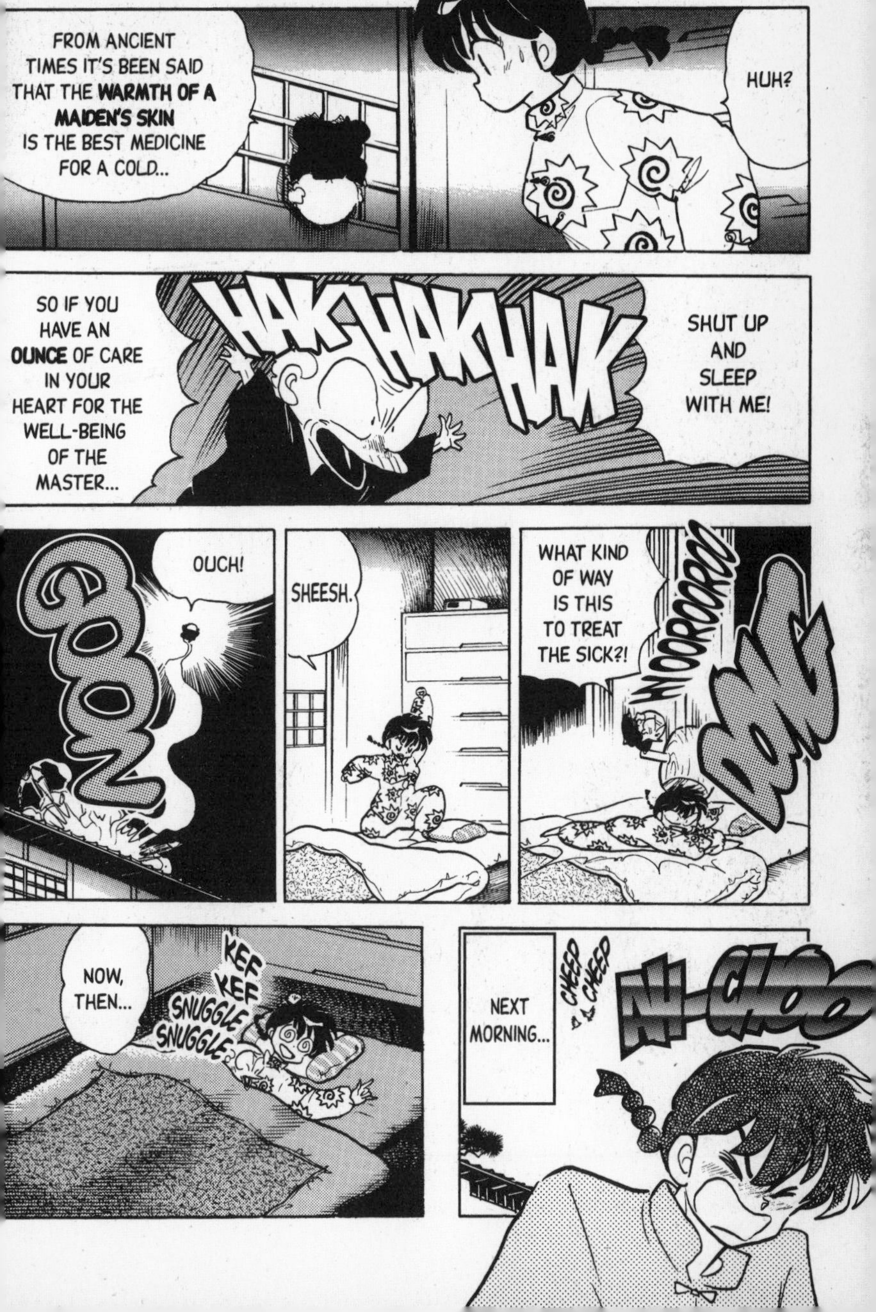
FROM ANCIENT TIMES IT'S BEEN SAID THAT THE **WARMTH OF A MAIDEN'S SKIN** IS THE BEST MEDICINE FOR A COLD...
HUH?
SO IF YOU HAVE AN **OUNCE** OF CARE IN YOUR HEART FOR THE WELL-BEING OF THE MASTER...
HAK HAK HAK HAK
SHUT UP AND SLEEP WITH ME!
GOON
OUCH!
SHEESH.
WHAT KIND OF WAY IS THIS TO TREAT THE SICK?!
WOOROOROO
BOING
NOW, THEN...
KEF KEF
SNUGGLE SNUGGLE
NEXT MORNING...
CHEEP CHEEP
AH-CHOO

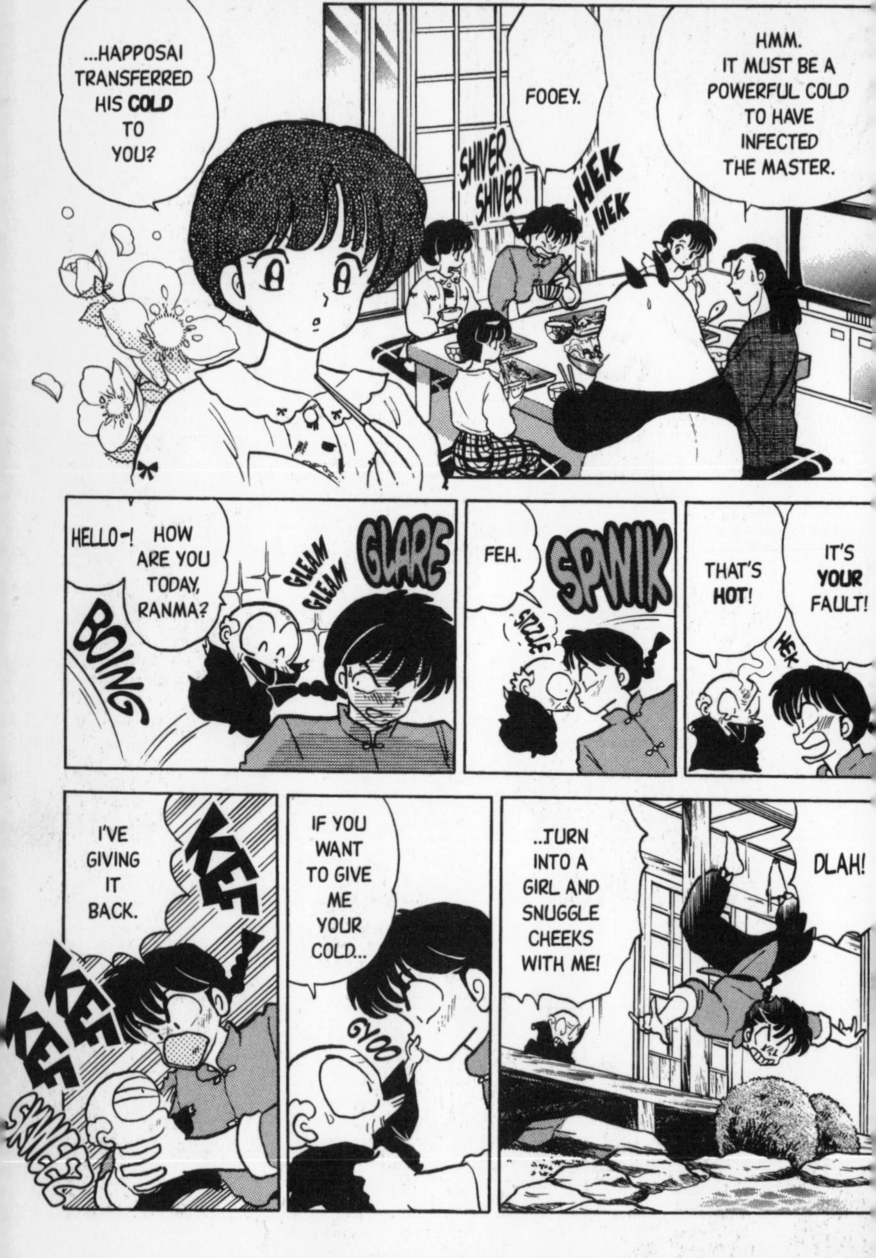
...HAPPOSAI TRANSFERRED HIS **COLD** TO YOU?
SHIVER SHIVER
FOOEY.
HEK HEK
HMM. IT MUST BE A POWERFUL COLD TO HAVE INFECTED THE MASTER.
HELLO-! HOW ARE YOU TODAY, RANMA?
BOING
GLEAM GLEAM
GLARE
FEH.
SPNIK
SIZZLE
THAT'S **HOT**!
IT'S **YOUR** FAULT!
HEK
I'VE GIVING IT BACK.
KEF KEF KEF
SKWEEZ
IF YOU WANT TO GIVE ME YOUR COLD...
GYOO
...TURN INTO A GIRL AND SNUGGLE CHEEKS WITH ME!
DLAH!

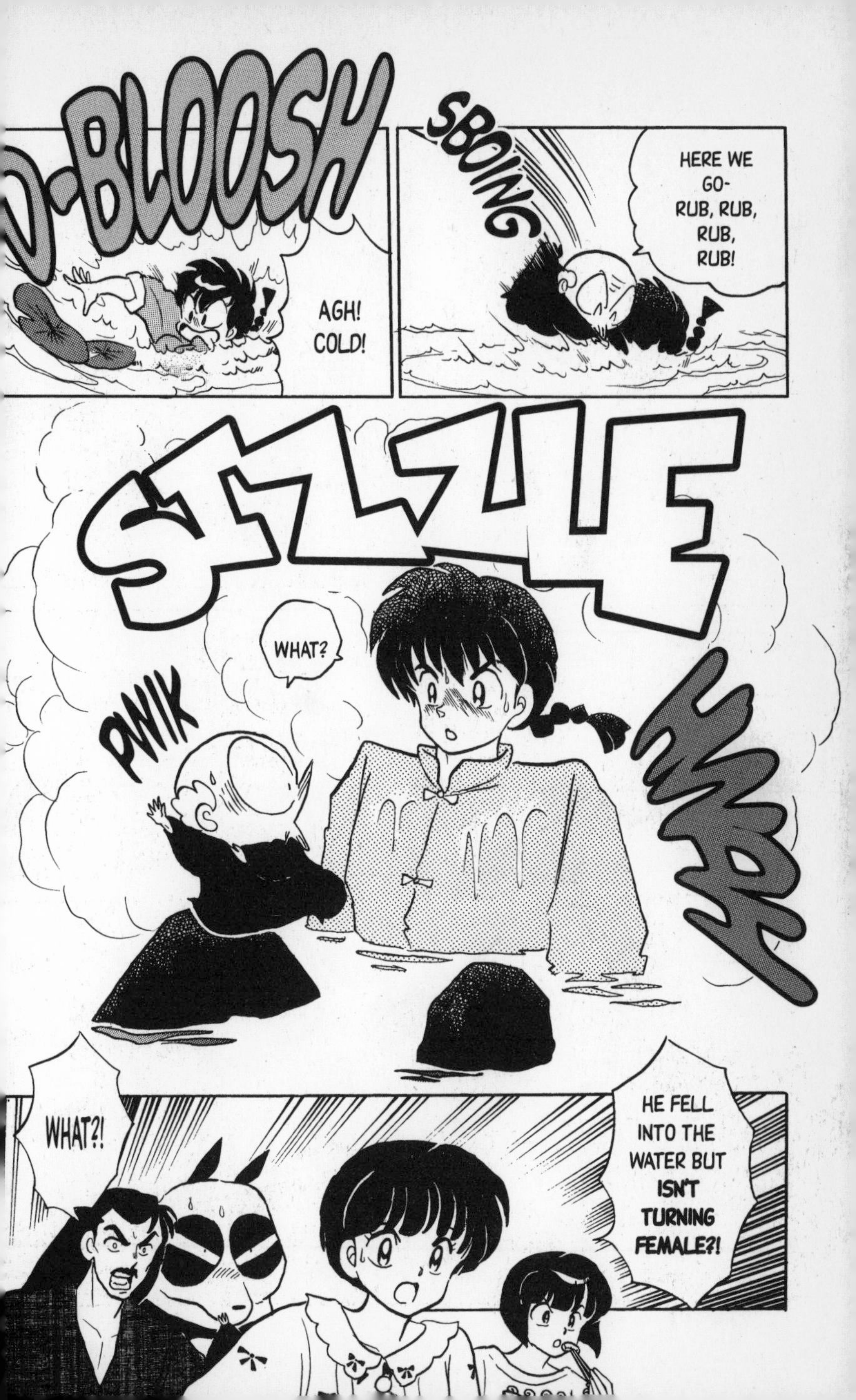

D-BLOOSH
AGH! COLD!
SBOING
HERE WE GO- RUB, RUB, RUB, RUB!
SIZZLE
WHAT?
PWIK
HMPH
WHAT?!
HE FELL INTO THE WATER BUT ISN'T TURNING FEMALE?!

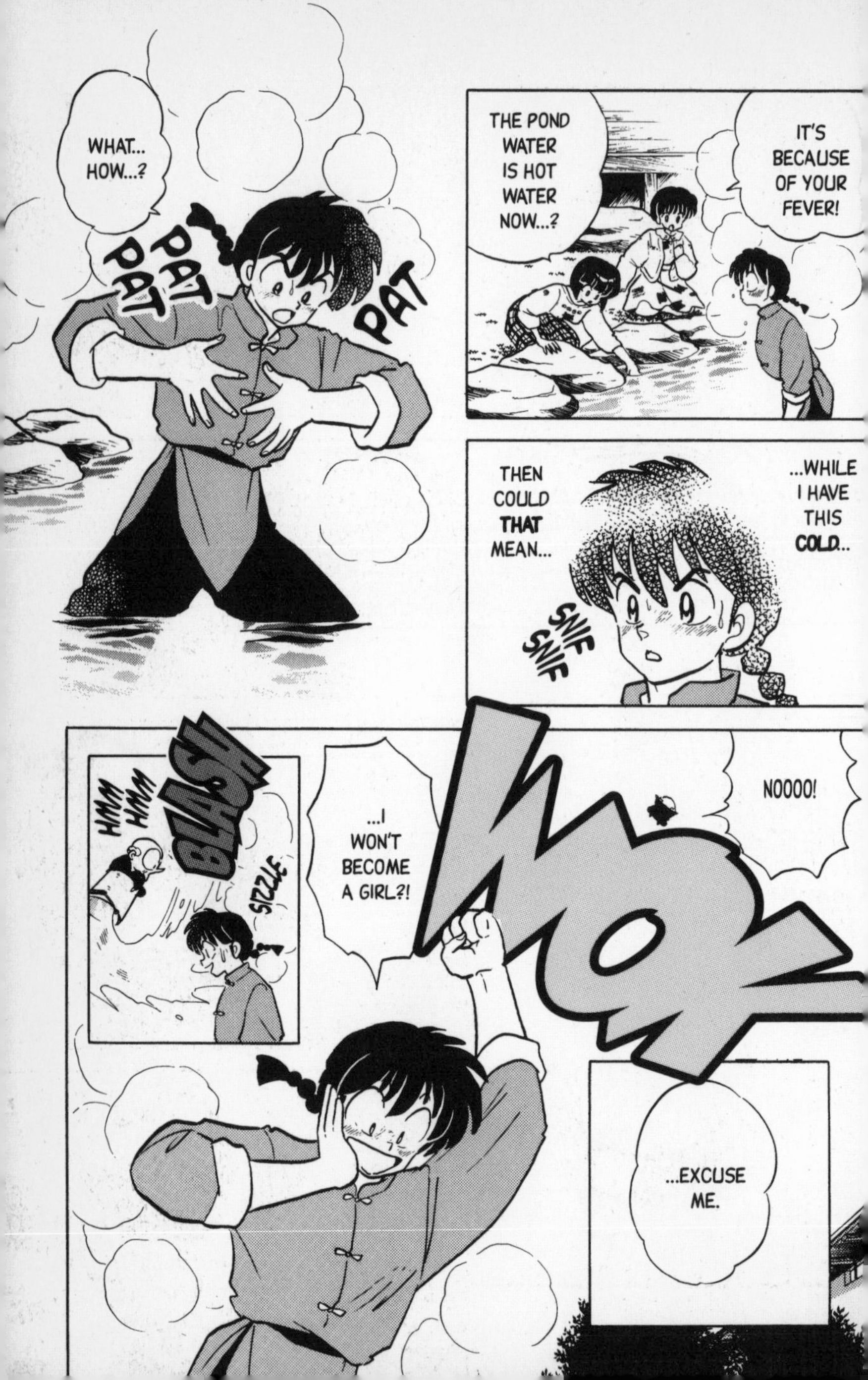
WHAT... HOW...?
PAT PAT
PAT
THE POND WATER IS HOT WATER NOW...?
IT'S BECAUSE OF YOUR FEVER!
THEN COULD **THAT** MEAN...
...WHILE I HAVE THIS **COLD**...
SNIF SNIF
HWAH HWAH
SIZZLE
...I WON'T BECOME A GIRL?!
WOW
NOOOO!
...EXCUSE ME.

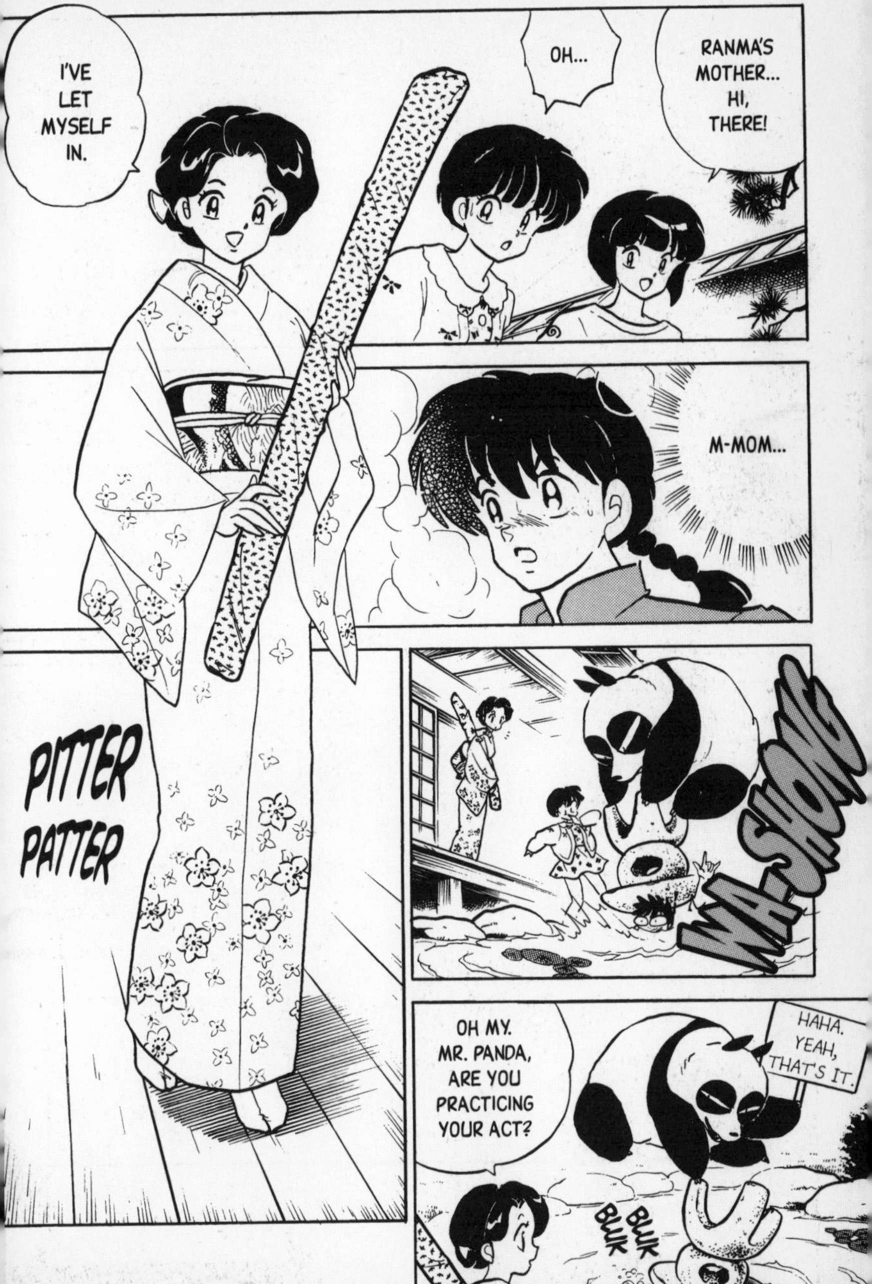
I'VE LET MYSELF IN.
PITTER PATTER
OH...
RANMA'S MOTHER... HI, THERE!
M-MOM...
WA-SHOW
OH MY. MR. PANDA, ARE YOU PRACTICING YOUR ACT?
HAHA. YEAH, THAT'S IT.
BUK BUK

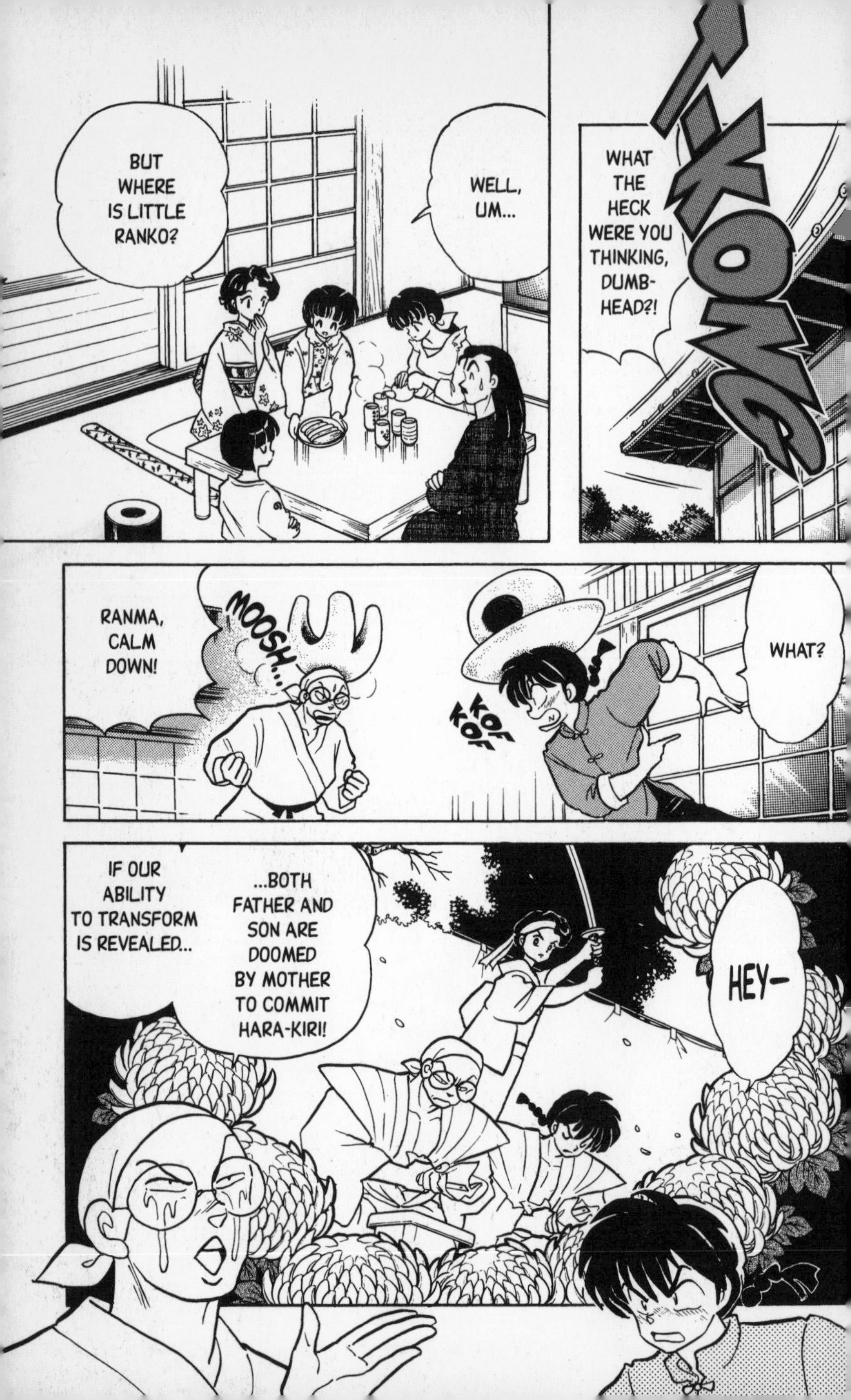

BUT WHERE IS LITTLE RANKO?
WELL, UM...
WHAT THE HECK WERE YOU THINKING, DUMB-HEAD?!
T-KONG
RANMA, CALM DOWN!
MOOSH...
KOF KOF
WHAT?
IF OUR ABILITY TO TRANSFORM IS REVEALED...
...BOTH FATHER AND SON ARE DOOMED BY MOTHER TO COMMIT HARA-KIRI!
HEY-

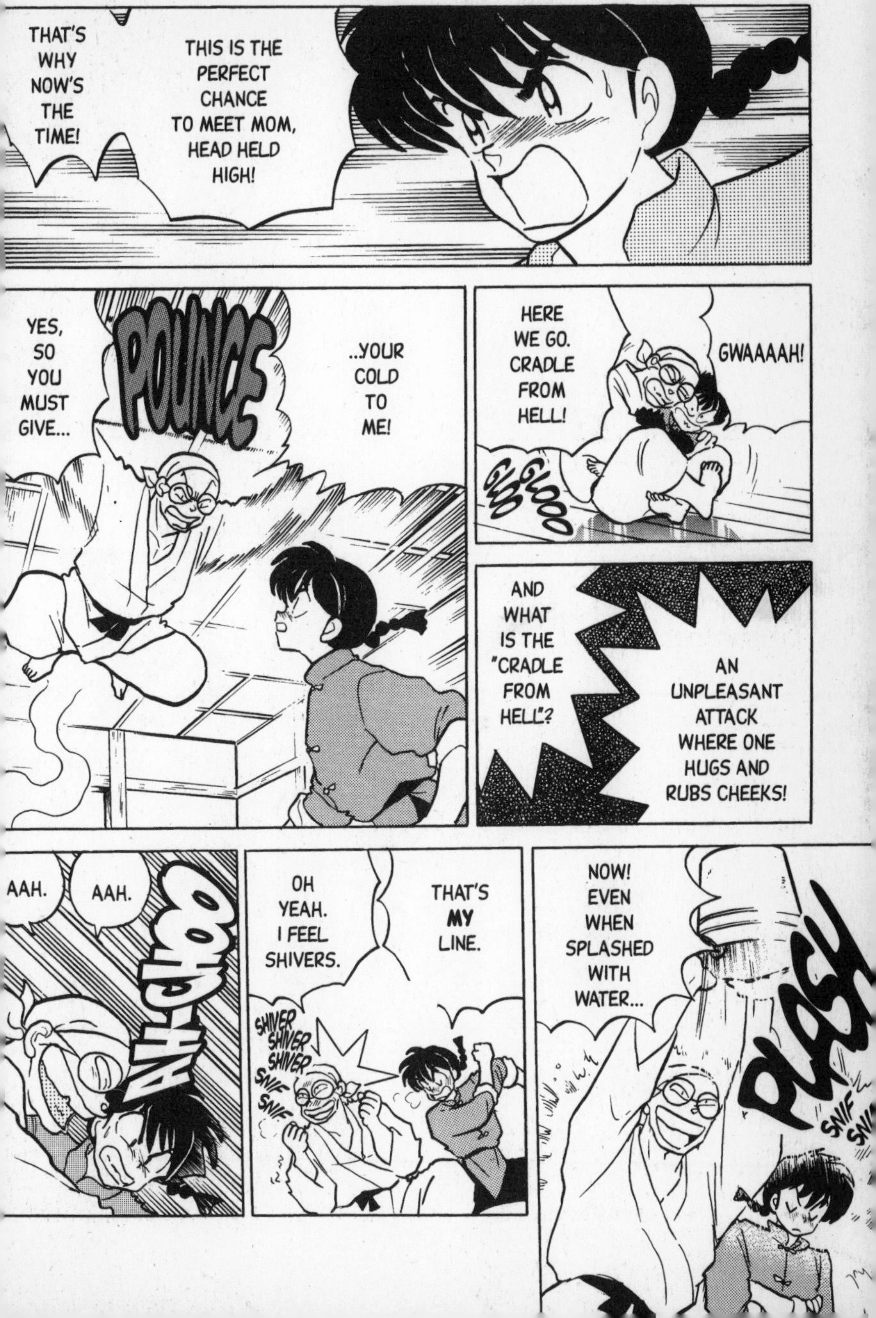
THAT'S WHY NOW'S THE TIME!
THIS IS THE PERFECT CHANCE TO MEET MOM, HEAD HELD HIGH!
YES, SO YOU MUST GIVE...
POUNCE
...YOUR COLD TO ME!
HERE WE GO. CRADLE FROM HELL!
GWAAAAH!
GLOOO GLOO
AND WHAT IS THE "CRADLE FROM HELL"?
AN UNPLEASANT ATTACK WHERE ONE HUGS AND RUBS CHEEKS!
AAH.
AAH.
AH-CHOO
OH YEAH. I FEEL SHIVERS.
THAT'S **MY** LINE.
SHIVER SHIVER SHIVER
SNIF SNIF SNIF
NOW! EVEN WHEN SPLASHED WITH WATER...
PLASH
SNIF SNIF

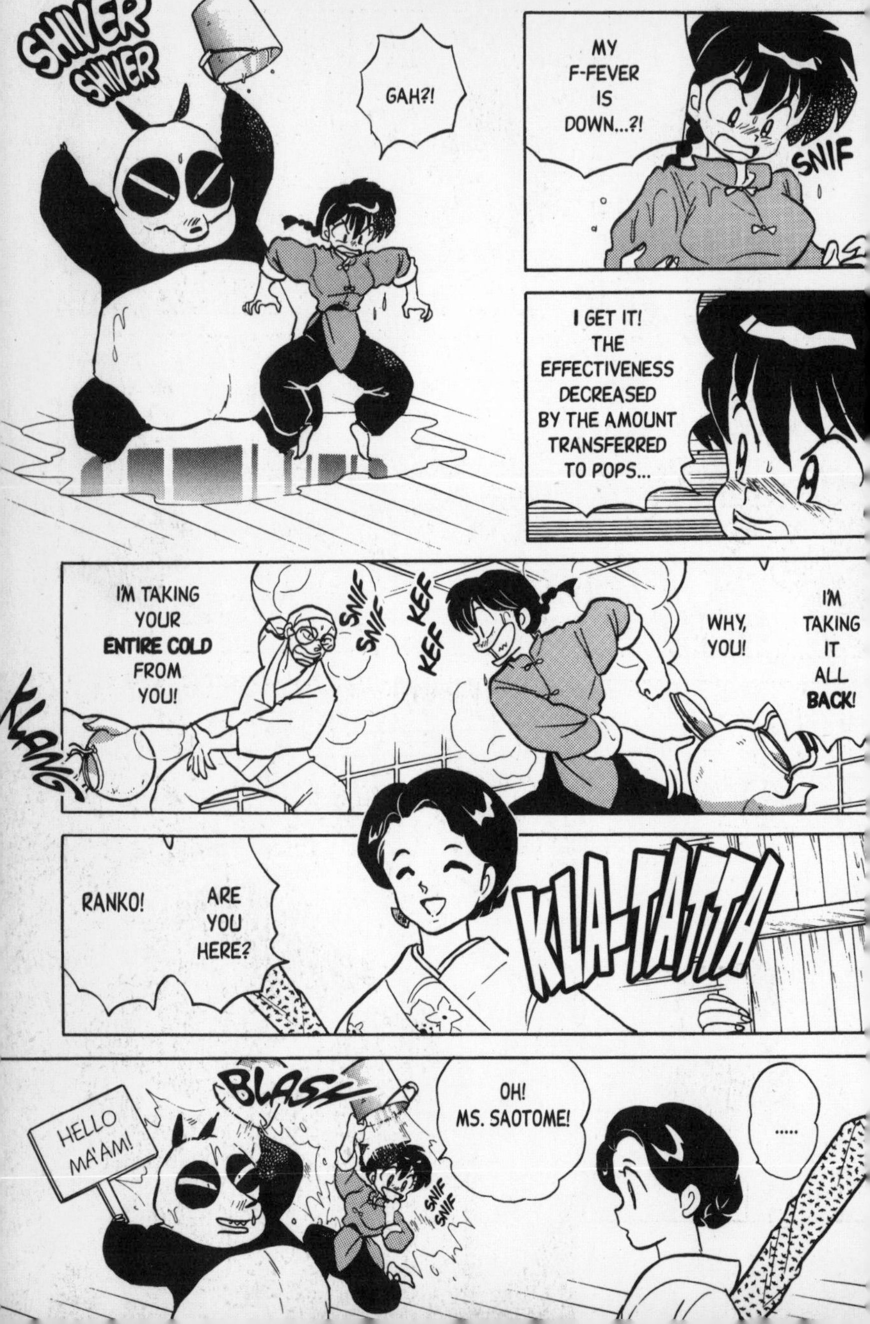
SHIVER SHIVER
GAH?!
MY F-FEVER IS DOWN...?!
SNIF
I GET IT! THE EFFECTIVENESS DECREASED BY THE AMOUNT TRANSFERRED TO POPS...
KLANG
I'M TAKING YOUR ENTIRE COLD FROM YOU!
SNIF SNIF
KEF KEF
WHY, YOU!
I'M TAKING IT ALL BACK!
RANKO!
ARE YOU HERE?
KLA-TATTA
HELLO MA'AM!
BLASH
SNIF SNIF
OH! MS. SAOTOME!
.....

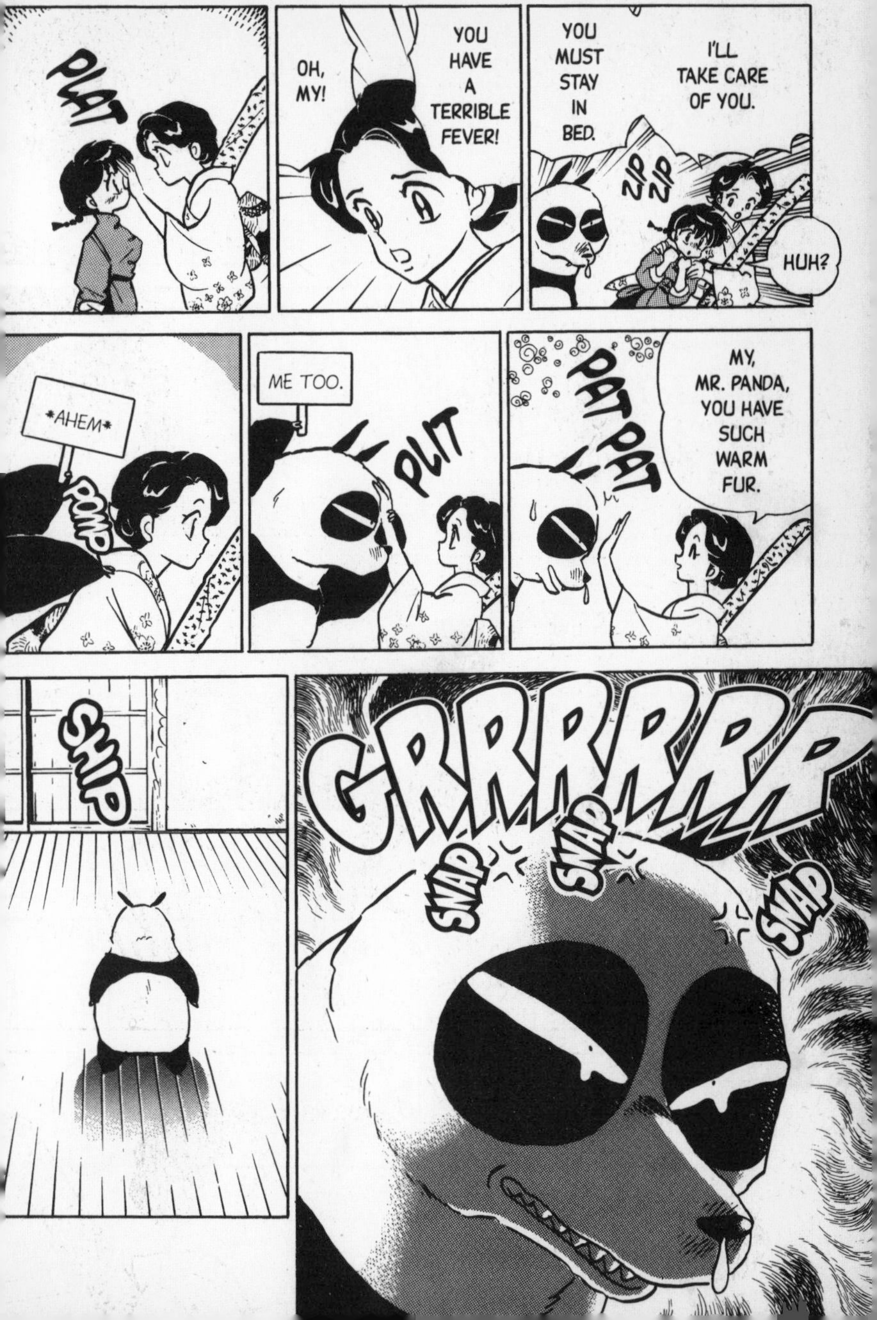
PLAT
OH, MY!
YOU HAVE A TERRIBLE FEVER!
YOU MUST STAY IN BED.
I'LL TAKE CARE OF YOU.
ZIP ZIP
HUH?
AHEM
POMP
ME TOO.
PLIT
PAT PAT
MY, MR. PANDA, YOU HAVE SUCH WARM FUR.
SHNP
GRRRRRP
SNAP
SNAP
SNAP

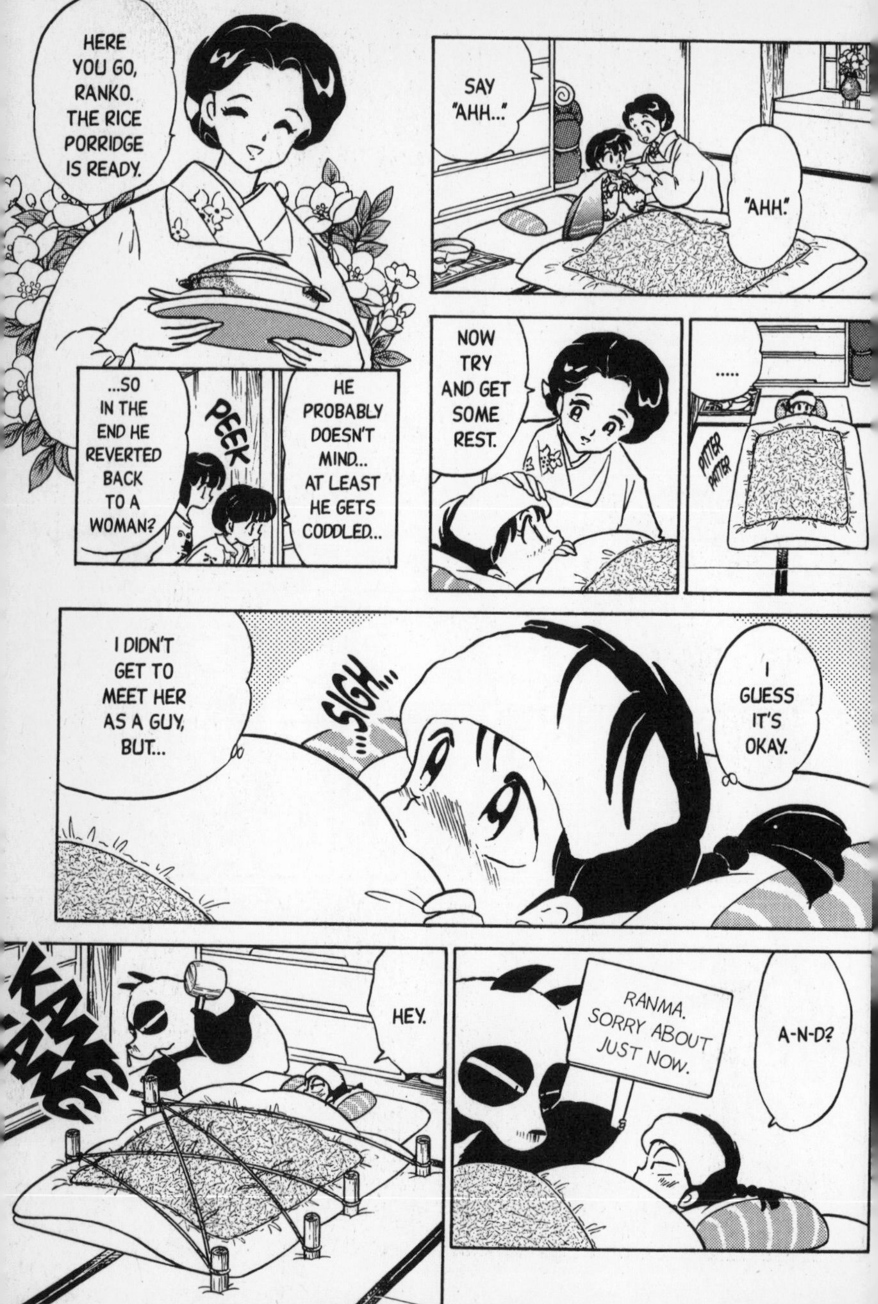
HERE YOU GO, RANKO. THE RICE PORRIDGE IS READY.
SAY "AHH..."
"AHH."
...SO IN THE END HE REVERTED BACK TO A WOMAN?
PEEK
HE PROBABLY DOESN'T MIND... AT LEAST HE GETS CODDLED...
NOW TRY AND GET SOME REST.
.....
PITTER PATTER
I DIDN'T GET TO MEET HER AS A GUY, BUT...
...SIGH...
I GUESS IT'S OKAY.
KANG-ANG
HEY.
RANMA. SORRY ABOUT JUST NOW.
A-N-D?

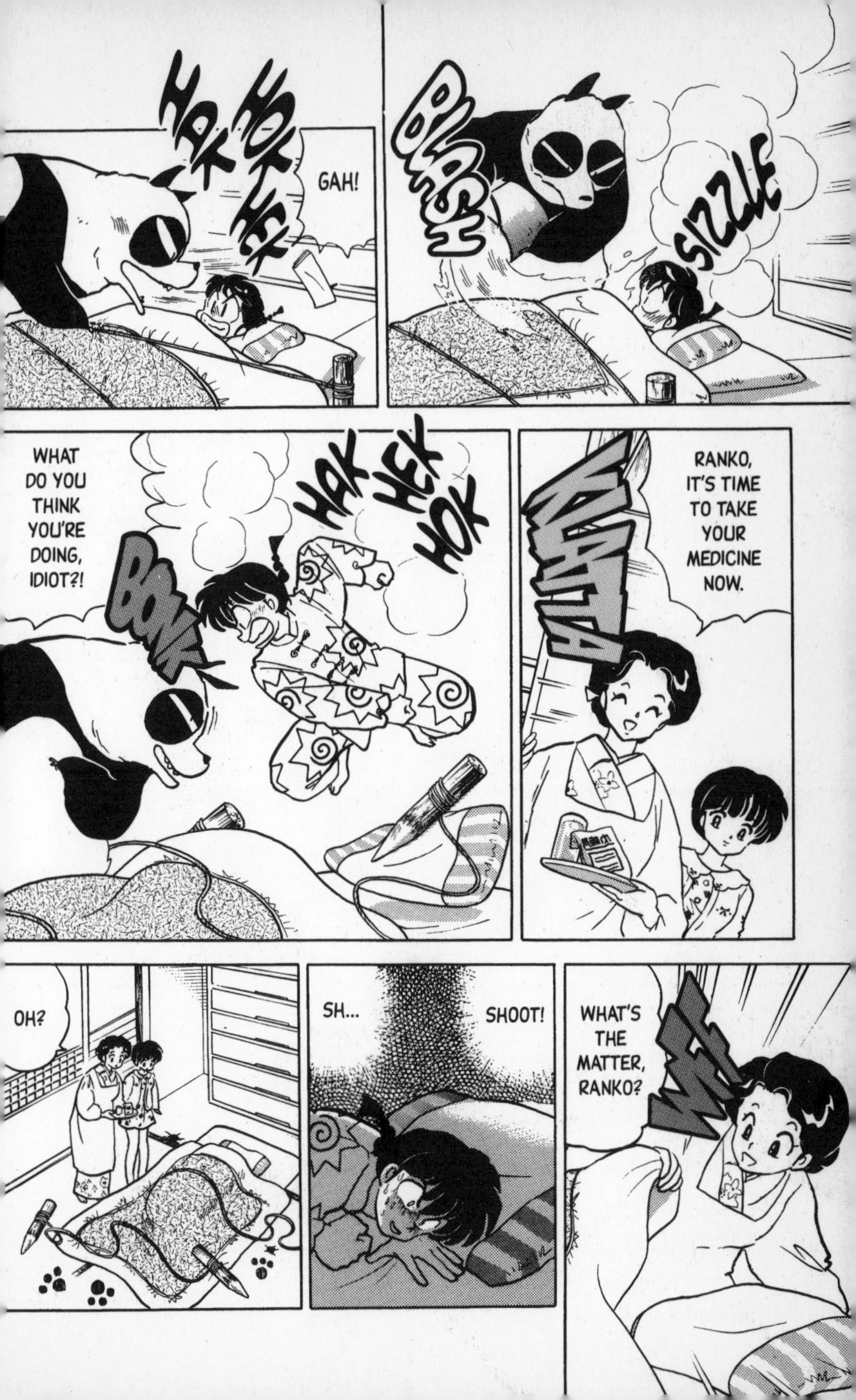
HAK
HOK HEK
GAH!
BLASH
SIZZLE
WHAT DO YOU THINK YOU'RE DOING, IDIOT?!
BONK
HAK HEK HOK
RANKO, IT'S TIME TO TAKE YOUR MEDICINE NOW.
OH?
SH...
SHOOT!
WHAT'S THE MATTER, RANKO?

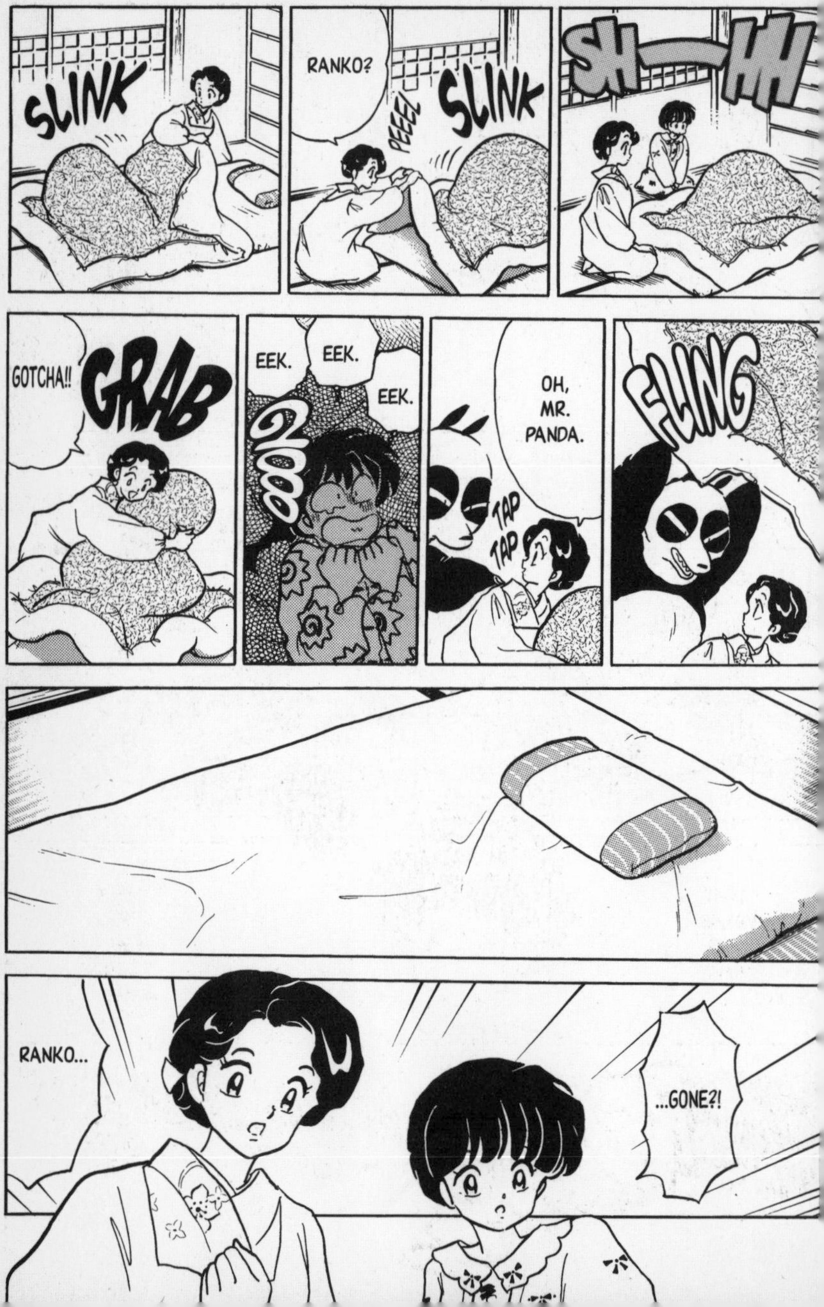
SLINK
RANKO?
PEEEL
SLINK
SH—HH
GOTCHA!!
GRAB
EEK.
EEK.
EEK.
ZOOO
OH, MR. PANDA.
TAP TAP
FLING
RANKO...
...GONE?!

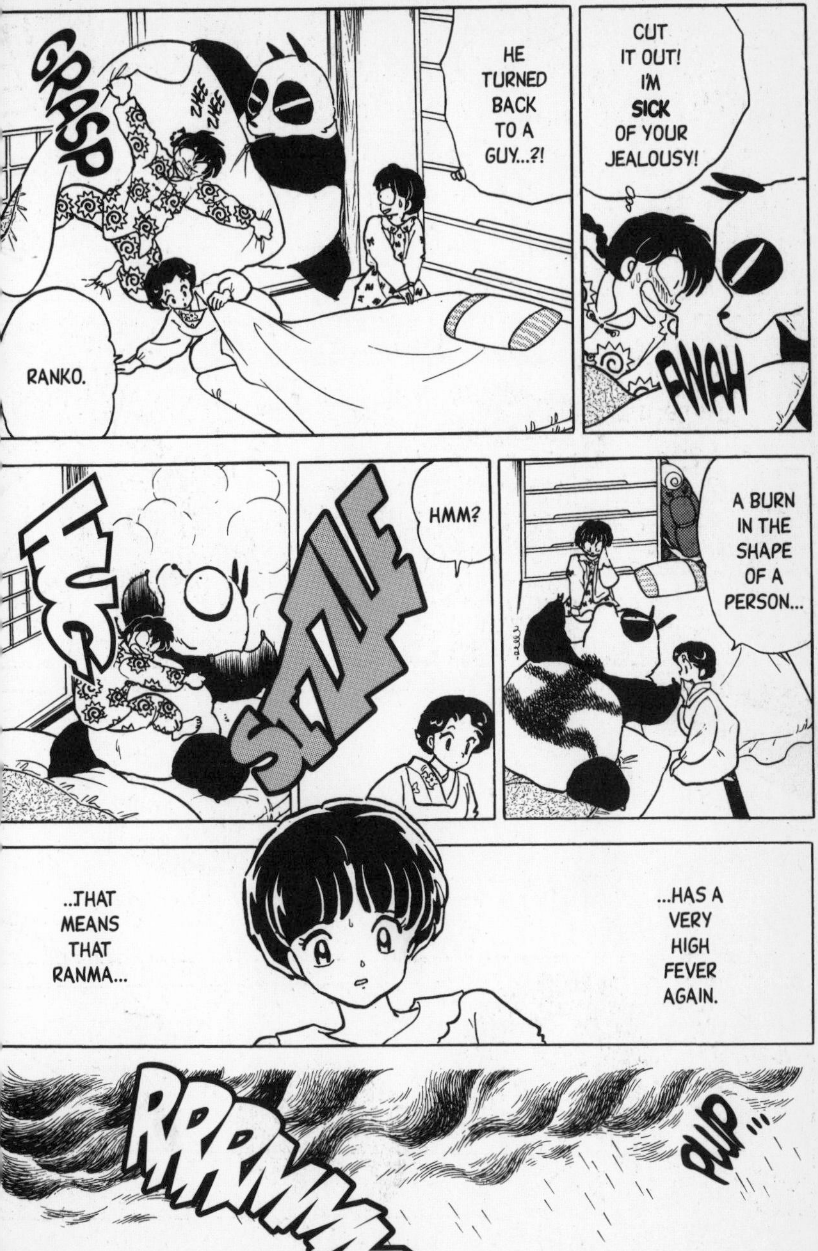
GRASP
ZHEE ZHEE
HE TURNED BACK TO A GUY...?!
RANKO.
CUT IT OUT! I'M **SICK** OF YOUR JEALOUSY!
AWAH
HUG
HMM?
SIZZLE
A BURN IN THE SHAPE OF A PERSON...
...THAT MEANS THAT RANMA...
...HAS A VERY HIGH FEVER AGAIN.
RRRMMM
PLIP...

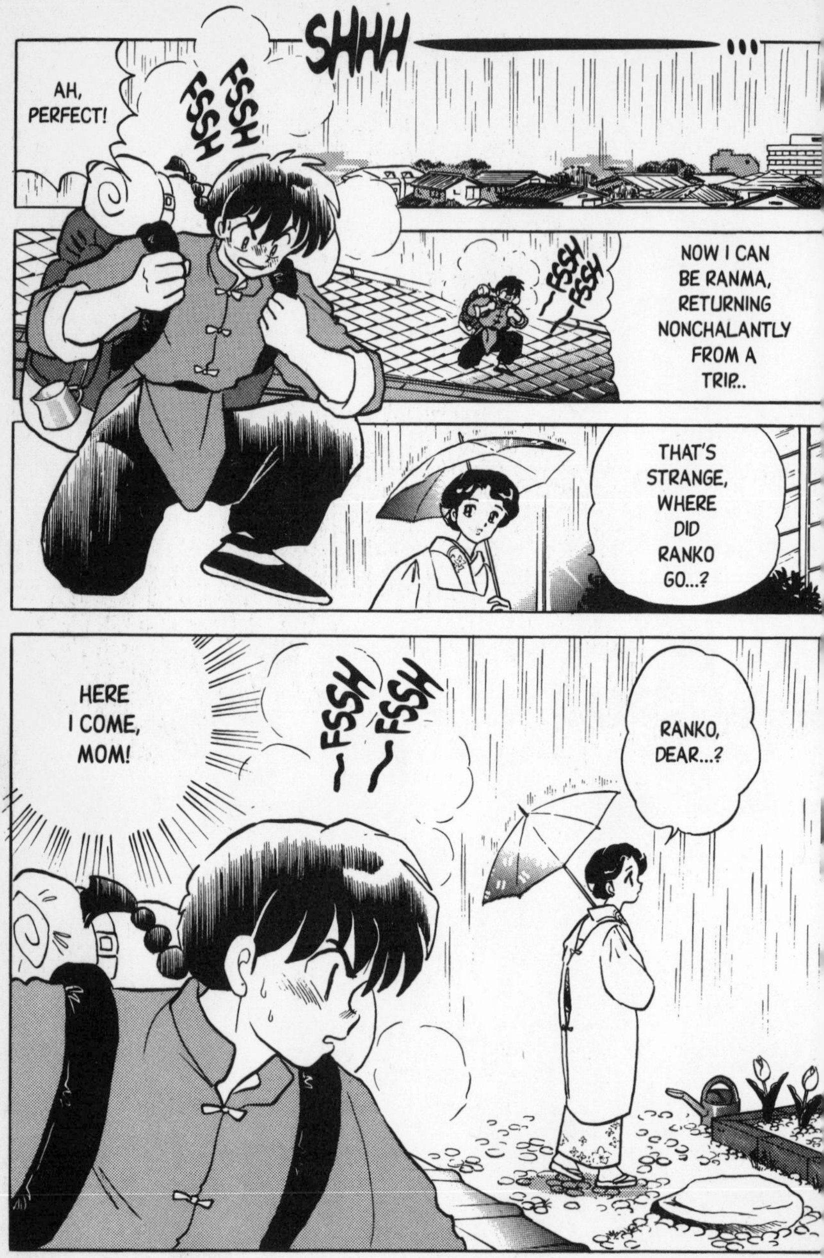
AH, PERFECT!
FSSH FSSH
SHHH...
~FSSH ~FSSH
NOW I CAN BE RANMA, RETURNING NONCHALANTLY FROM A TRIP..
THAT'S STRANGE, WHERE DID RANKO GO...?
HERE I COME, MOM!
~FSSH ~FSSH
RANKO, DEAR...?

PART 9

A HOT REUNION?!

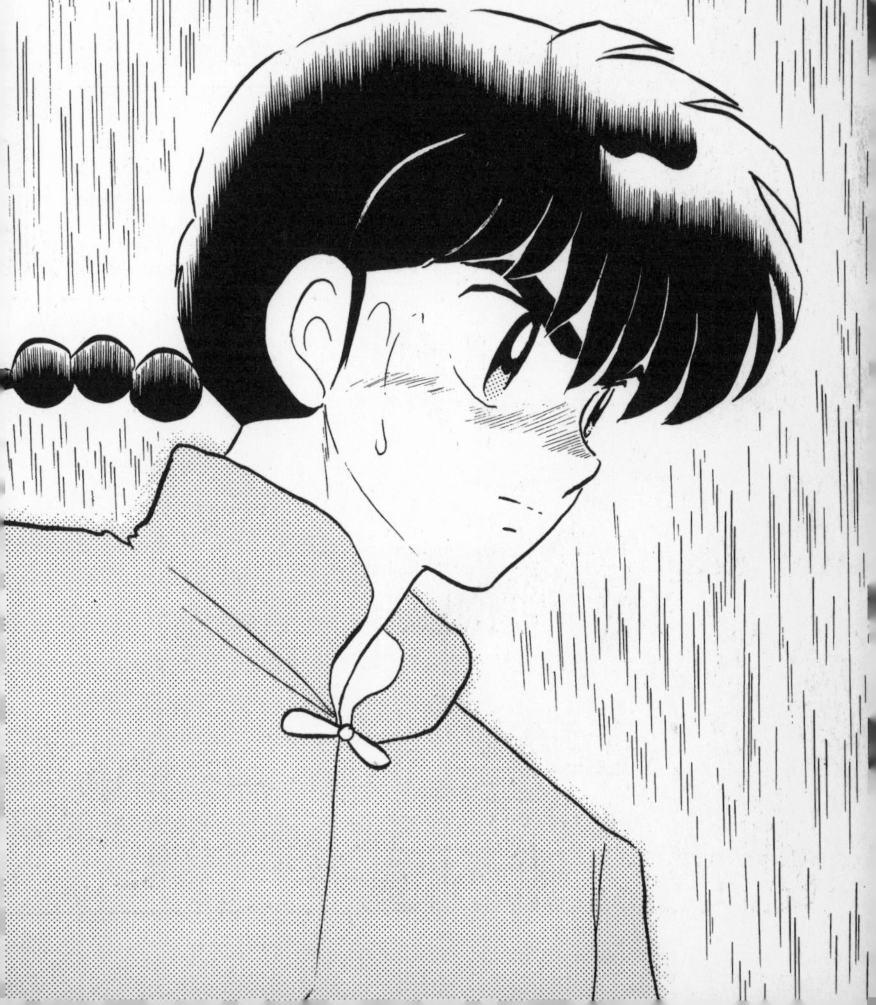

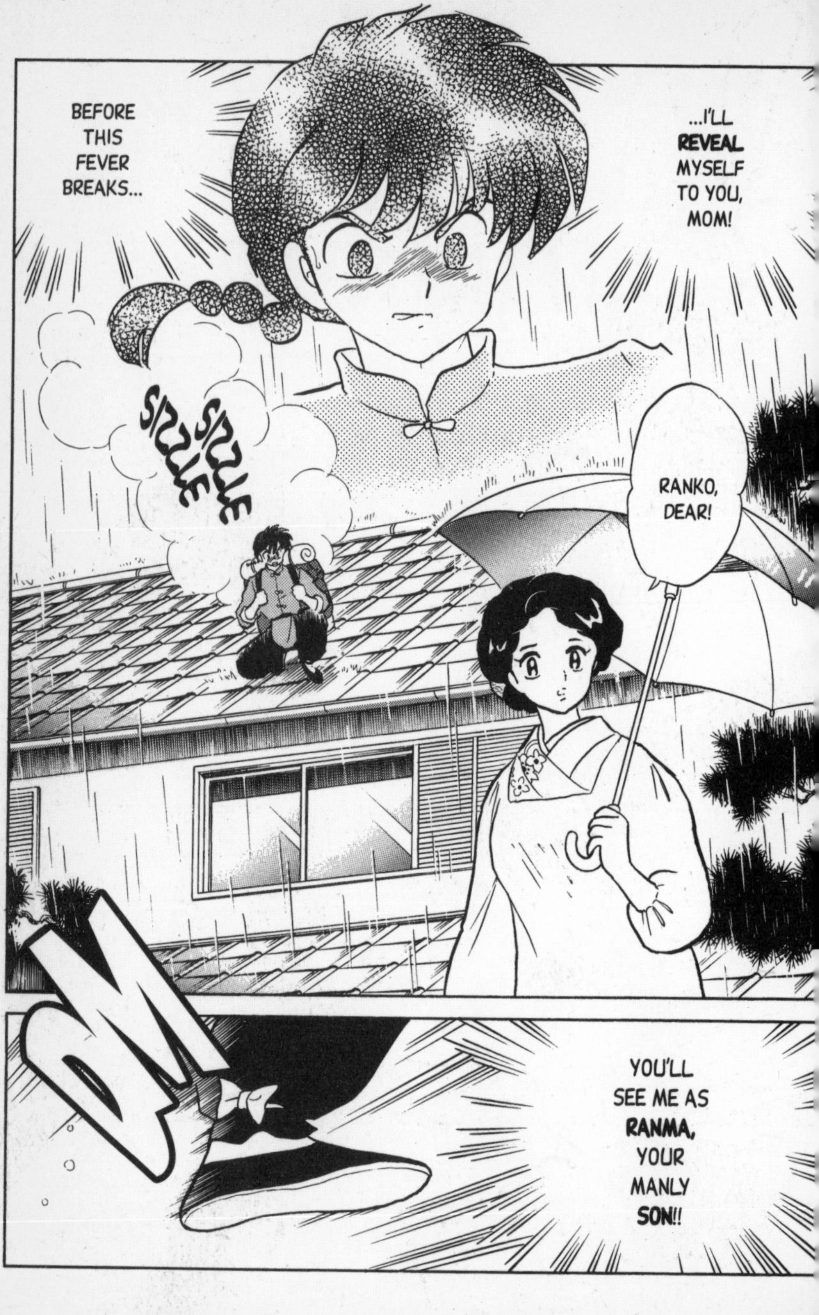

BEFORE THIS FEVER BREAKS...
...I'LL **REVEAL** MYSELF TO YOU, MOM!
SIZZLE SIZZLE
RANKO, DEAR!
YOU'LL SEE ME AS **RANMA,** YOUR MANLY **SON!!**

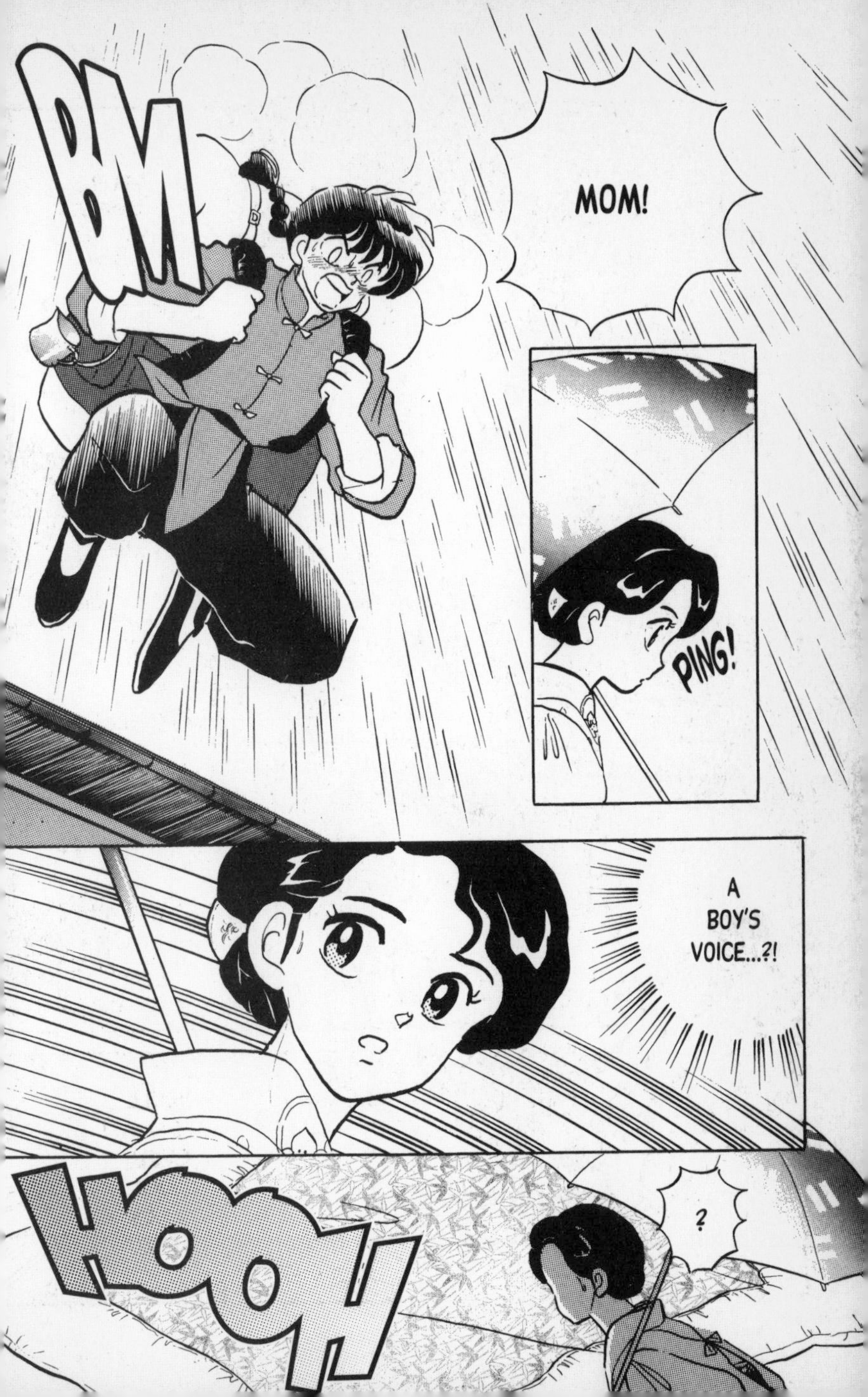
BM
MOM!
PING!
A BOY'S VOICE...?!
HOOSH
?

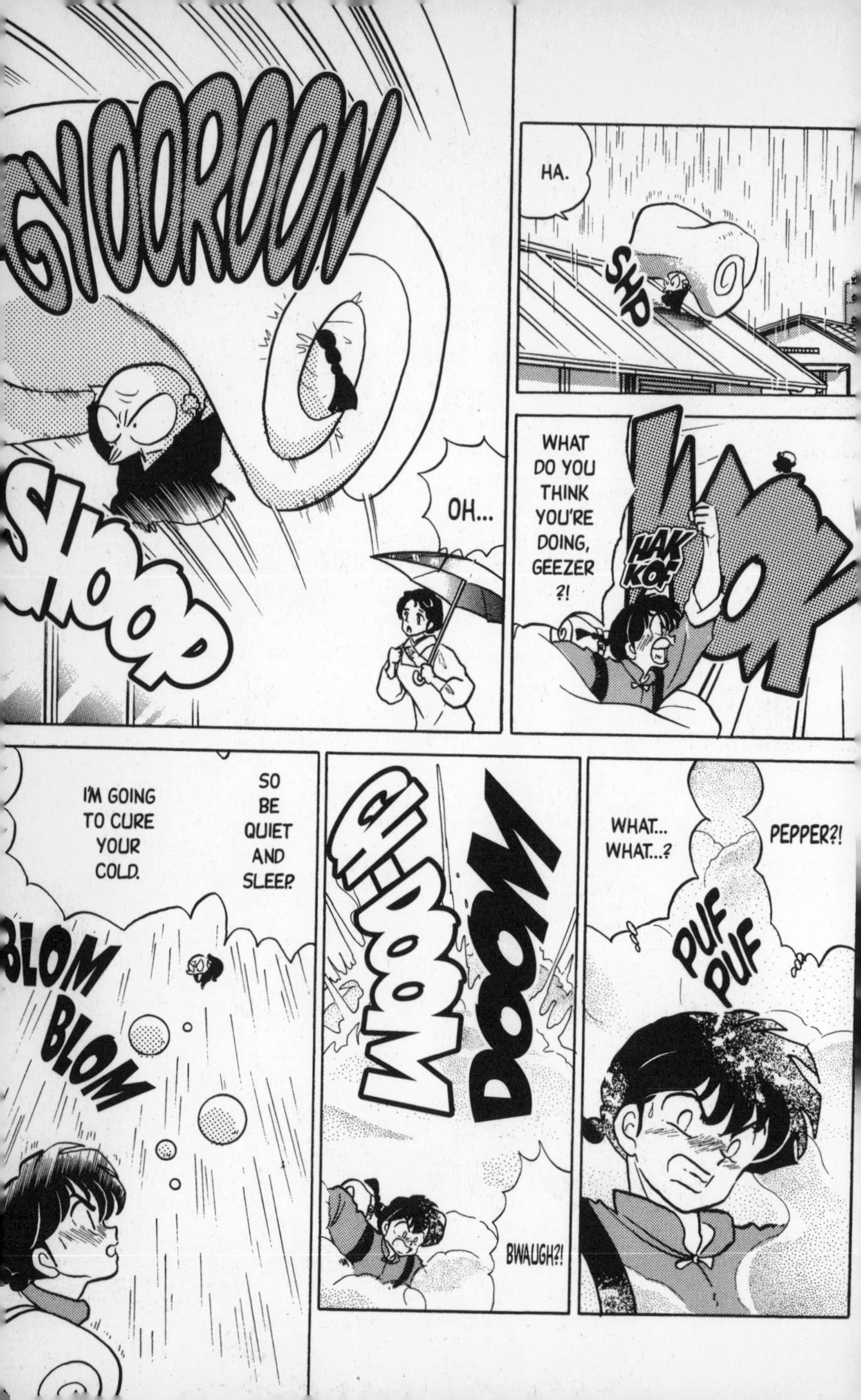
GYOOROON
SHOOP
OH...
HA.
SHP
WHAT DO YOU THINK YOU'RE DOING, GEEZER ?!
HAK KOF
I'M GOING TO CURE YOUR COLD.
SO BE QUIET AND SLEEP.
BLOM BLOM BLOM
DOOM DOOM
BWAUGH?!
WHAT... WHAT...?
PEPPER?!
PUF PUF

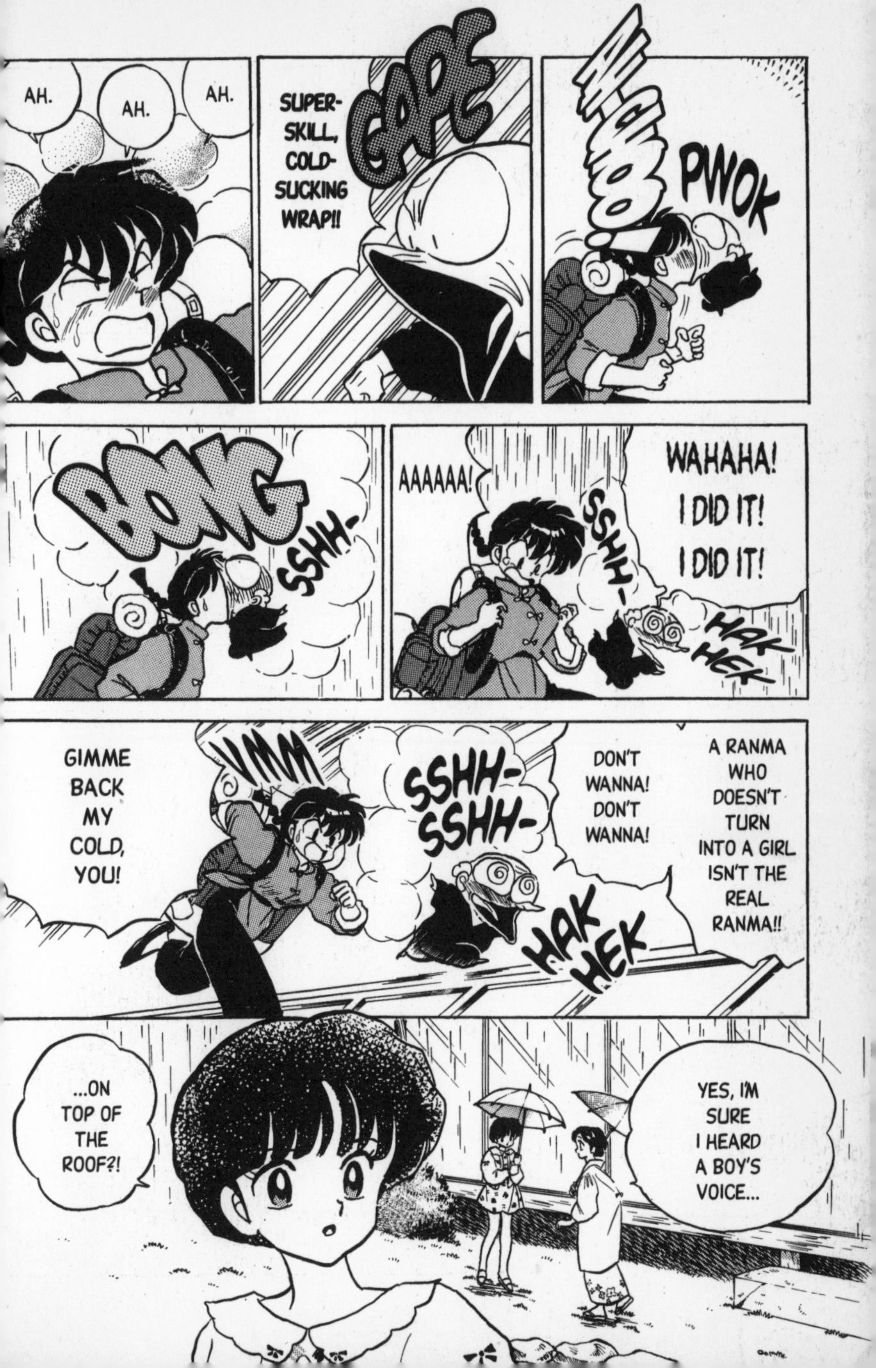
AH.
AH.
AH.
SUPER-SKILL, COLD-SUCKING WRAP!!
GAPE
PWOK
BOING
SSHH-
AAAAAA!
SSHH-
WAHAHA! I DID IT! I DID IT!
HAK HEK
GIMME BACK MY COLD, YOU!
VMM
SSHH- SSHH-
HAK HEK
DON'T WANNA! DON'T WANNA!
A RANMA WHO DOESN'T TURN INTO A GIRL ISN'T THE REAL RANMA!!
...ON TOP OF THE ROOF?!
YES, I'M SURE I HEARD A BOY'S VOICE...

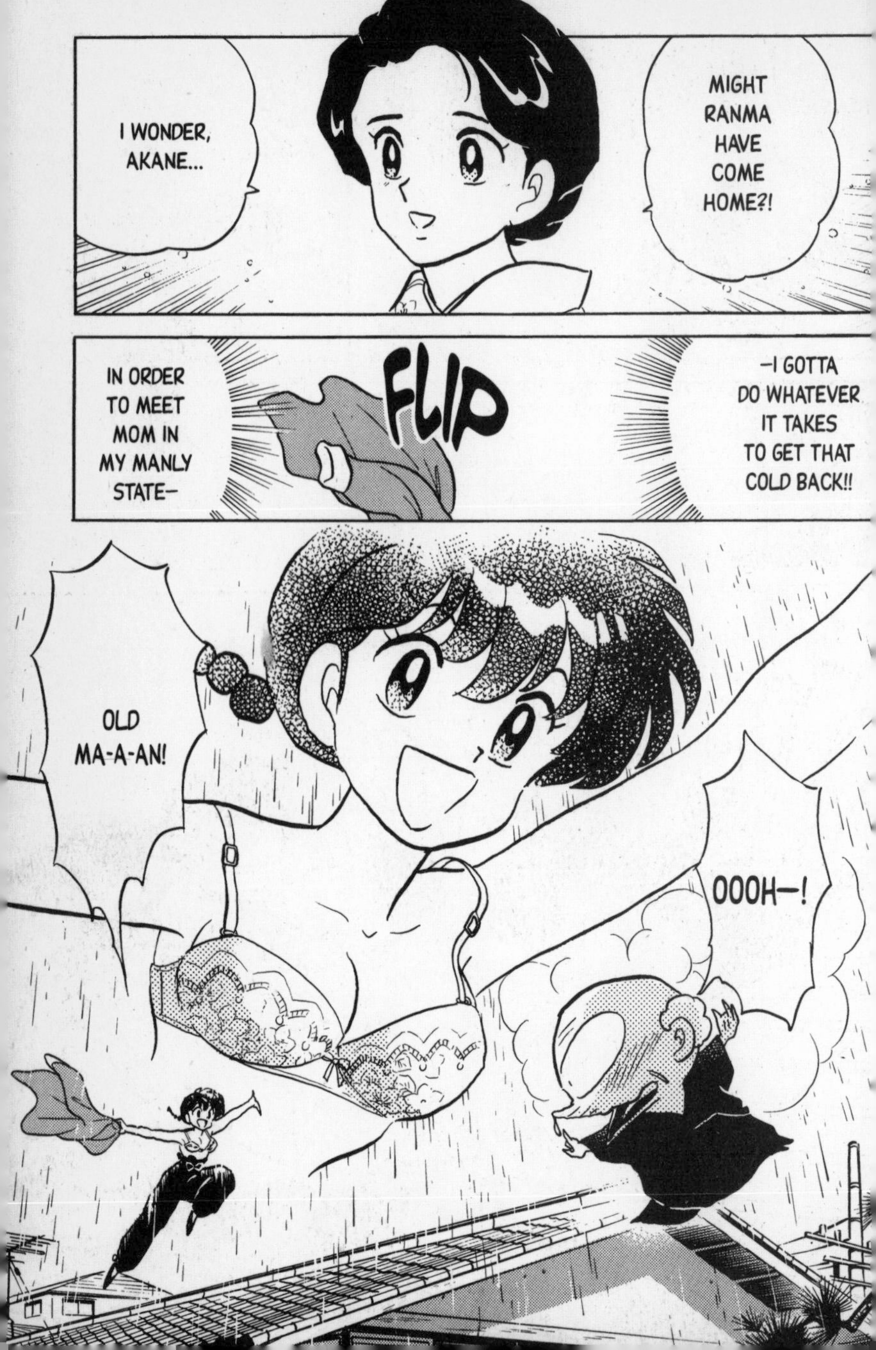
I WONDER, AKANE...
MIGHT RANMA HAVE COME HOME?!
IN ORDER TO MEET MOM IN MY MANLY STATE—
FLIP
—I GOTTA DO WHATEVER IT TAKES TO GET THAT COLD BACK!!
OLD MA-A-AN!
OOOH—!

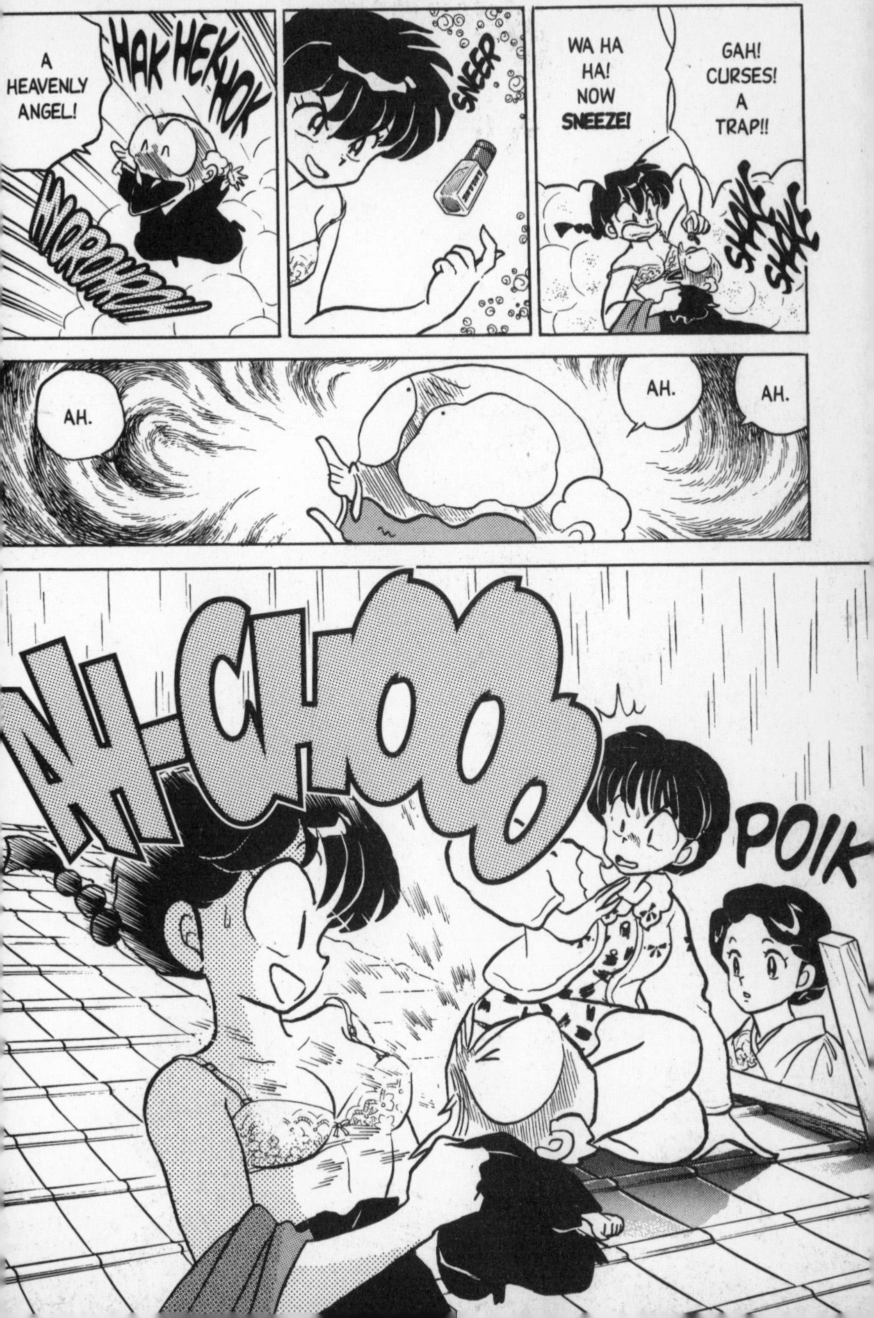
A HEAVENLY ANGEL!
HAK HEK HOK
SNEER
WA HA HA! NOW SNEEZE!
GAH! CURSES! A TRAP!!
SHAKE SHAKE
AH.
AH.
AH.
AH-CHOOO
POIK

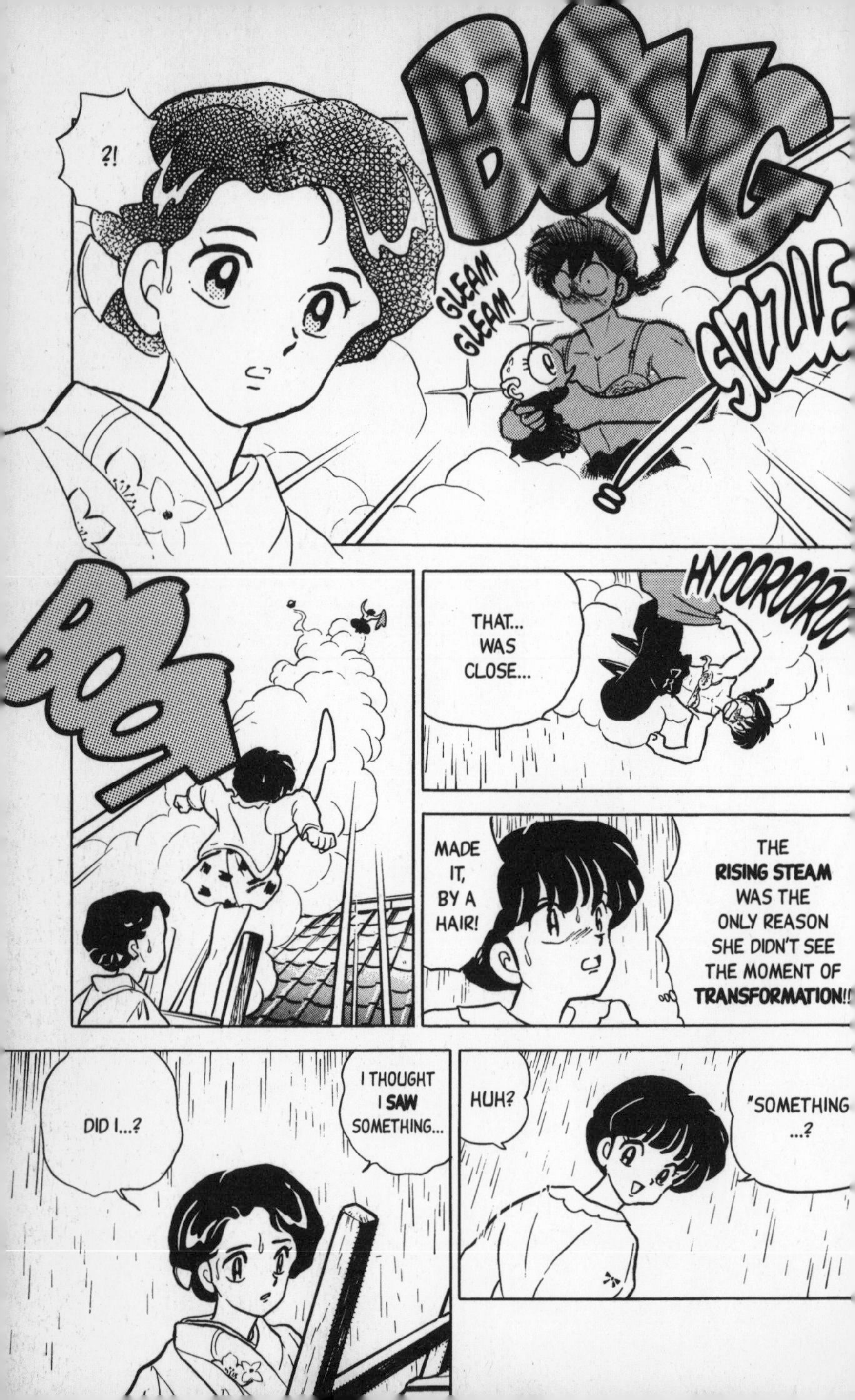
?!
BONG
GLEAM GLEAM
SIZZLE
BOOM
THAT... WAS CLOSE...
HYOORORORU
MADE IT, BY A HAIR!
THE RISING STEAM WAS THE ONLY REASON SHE DIDN'T SEE THE MOMENT OF TRANSFORMATION!!
DID I...?
I THOUGHT I SAW SOMETHING...
HUH?
"SOMETHING ...?

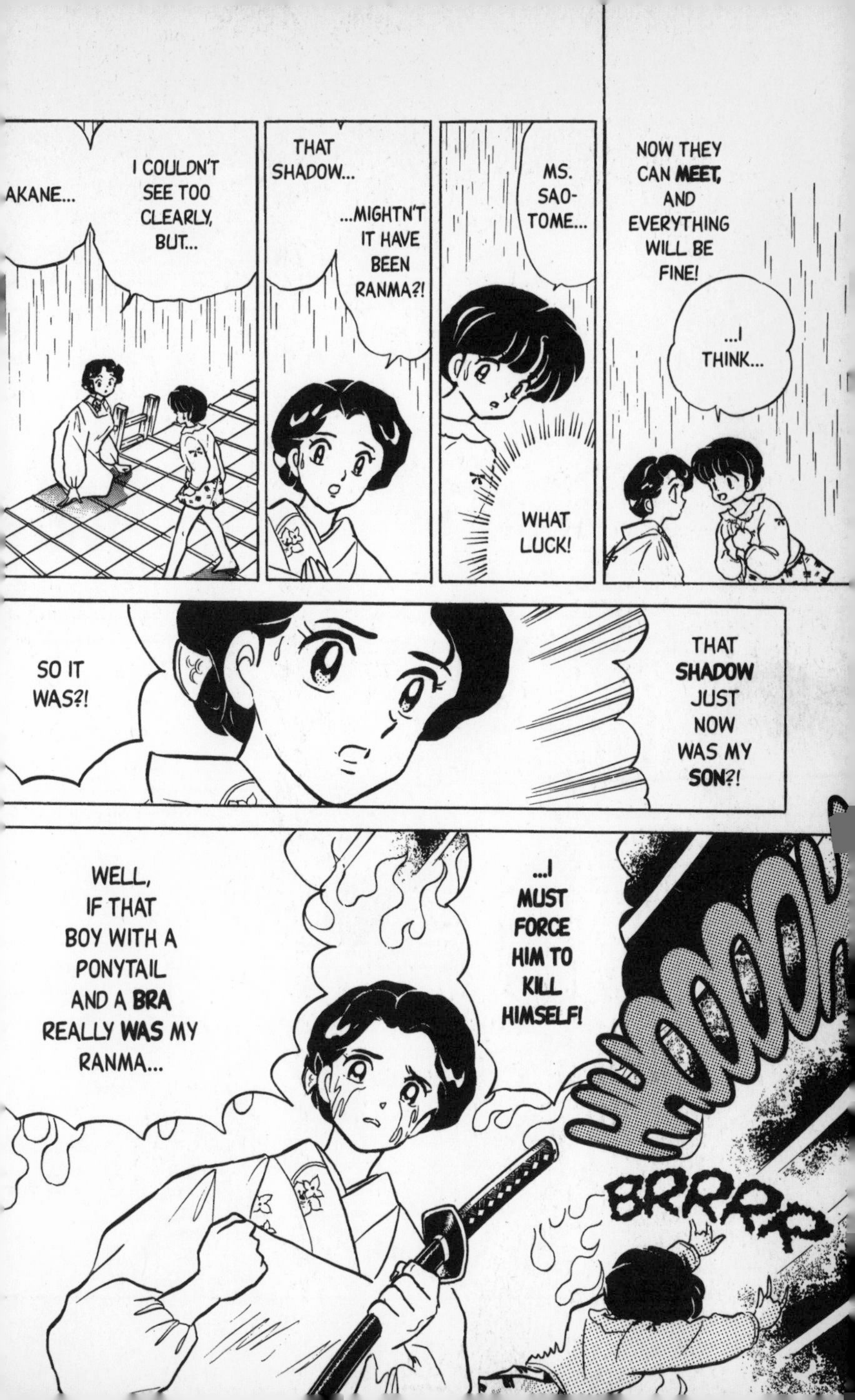
AKANE...
I COULDN'T SEE TOO CLEARLY, BUT...
THAT SHADOW...
...MIGHTN'T IT HAVE BEEN RANMA?!
MS. SAO-TOME...
WHAT LUCK!
NOW THEY CAN MEET, AND EVERYTHING WILL BE FINE!
...I THINK...
SO IT WAS?!
THAT SHADOW JUST NOW WAS MY SON?!
WELL, IF THAT BOY WITH A PONYTAIL AND A BRA REALLY WAS MY RANMA...
...I MUST FORCE HIM TO KILL HIMSELF!
BRRRR

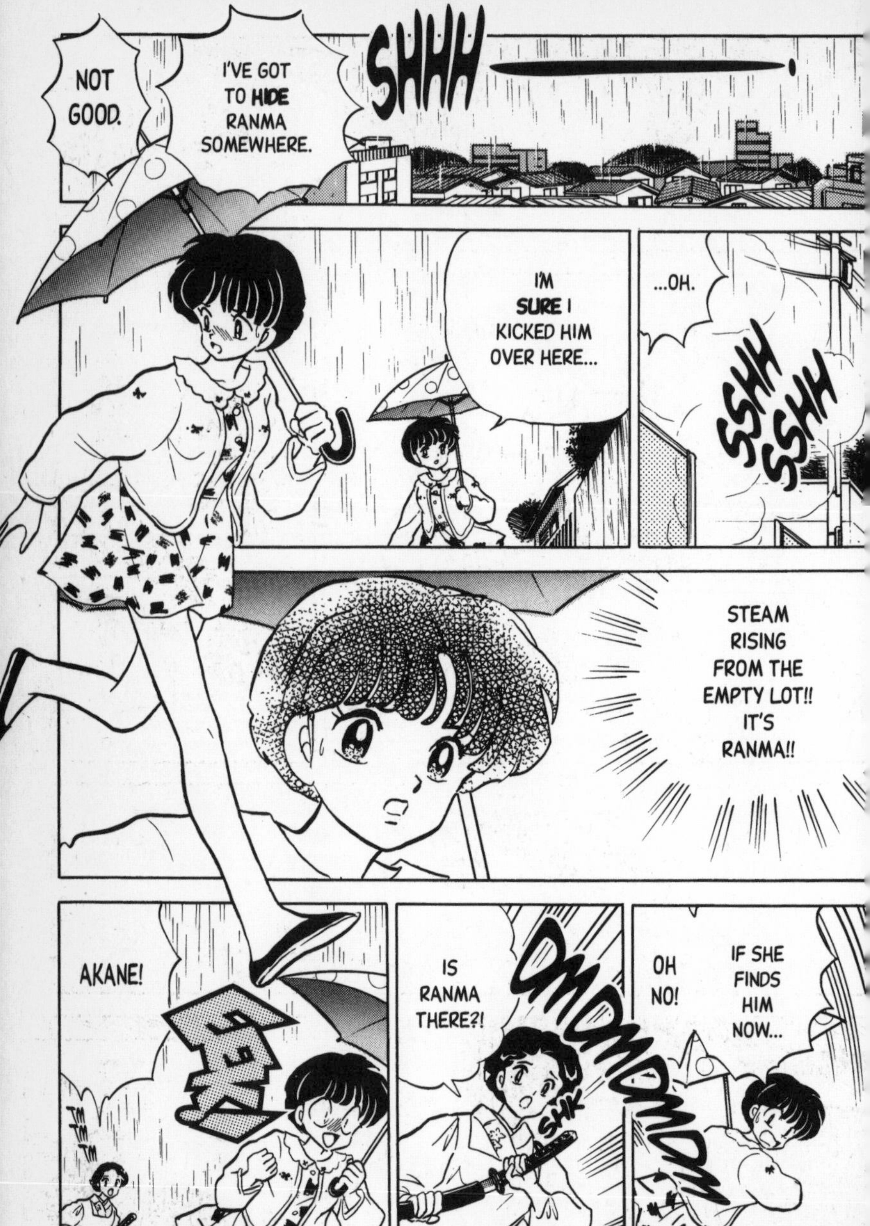
NOT GOOD.
I'VE GOT TO HIDE RANMA SOMEWHERE.
SHHH
I'M SURE I KICKED HIM OVER HERE...
...OH.
SSHH SSHH
STEAM RISING FROM THE EMPTY LOT!! IT'S RANMA!!
AKANE!
TM TM TM
IS RANMA THERE?!
SHK
OH NO!
IF SHE FINDS HIM NOW...

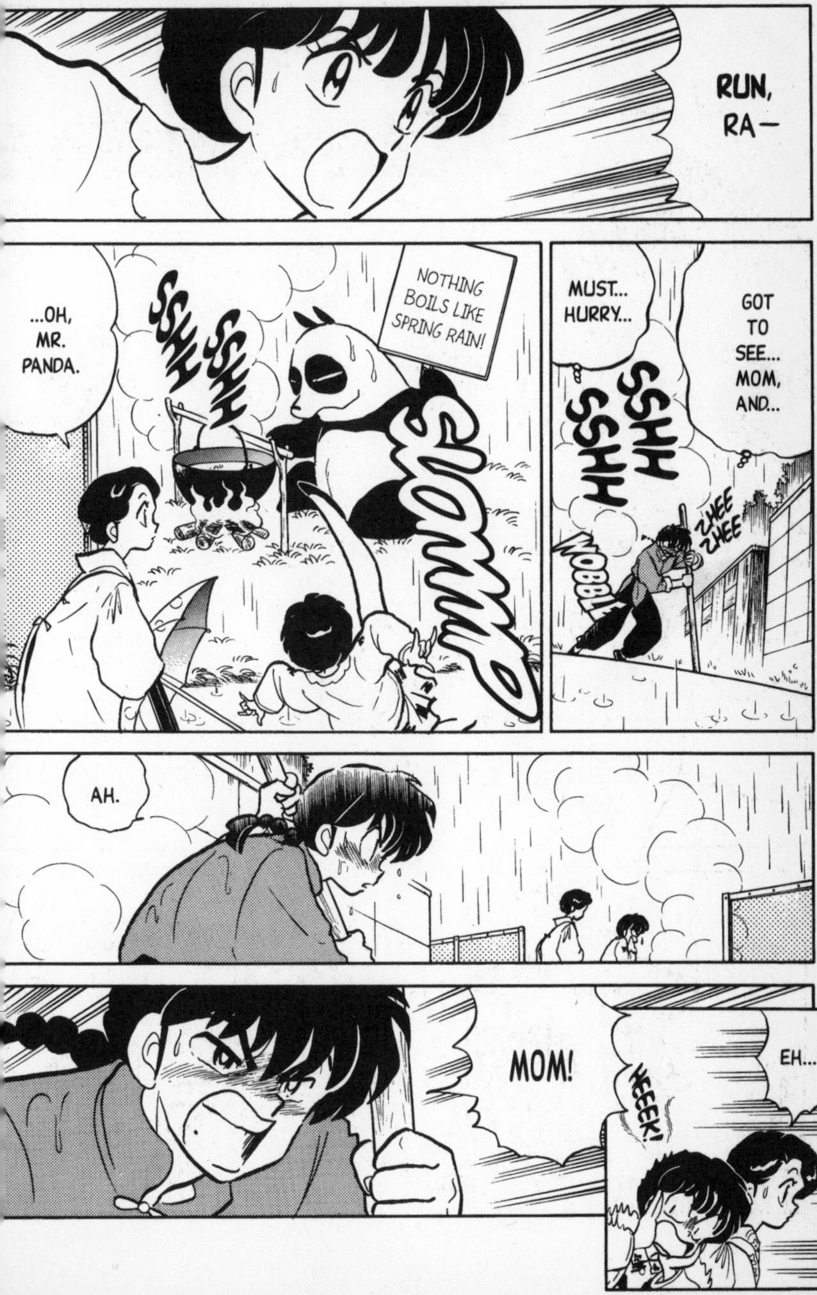
RUN, RA—
...OH, MR. PANDA.
SSHH
SSHH
NOTHING BOILS LIKE SPRING RAIN!
MUST... HURRY...
GOT TO SEE... MOM, AND...
SSHH
SSHH
ZHEE ZHEE
WOBBL
AH.
MOM!
HEEEK!
EH...?

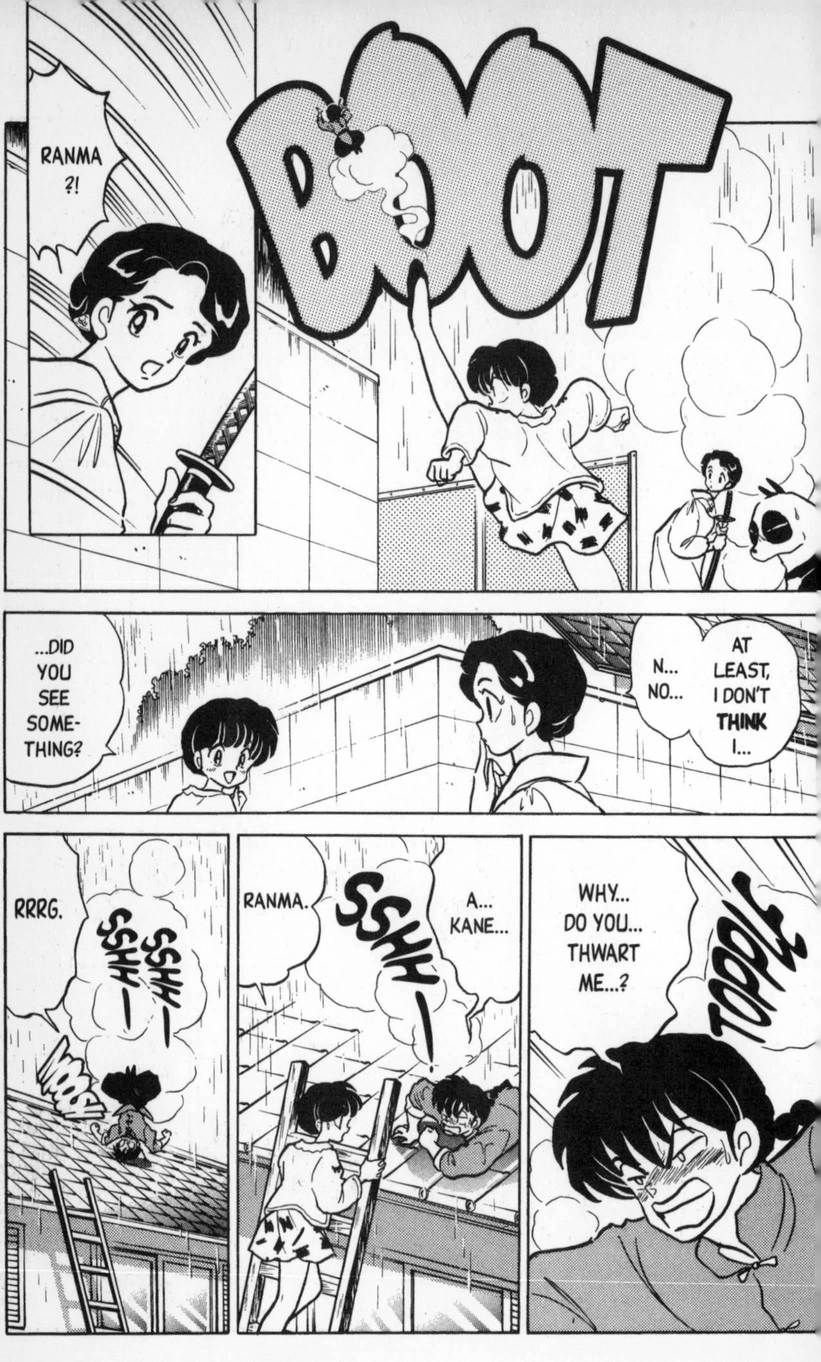
RANMA ?!
BOOT
...DID YOU SEE SOME-THING?
N... NO...
AT LEAST, I DON'T THINK I...
RRRG.
SSHH— SSHH—
WOOSH
RANMA.
SSHH—!
A... KANE...
WHY... DO YOU... THWART ME...?
TOPPLE

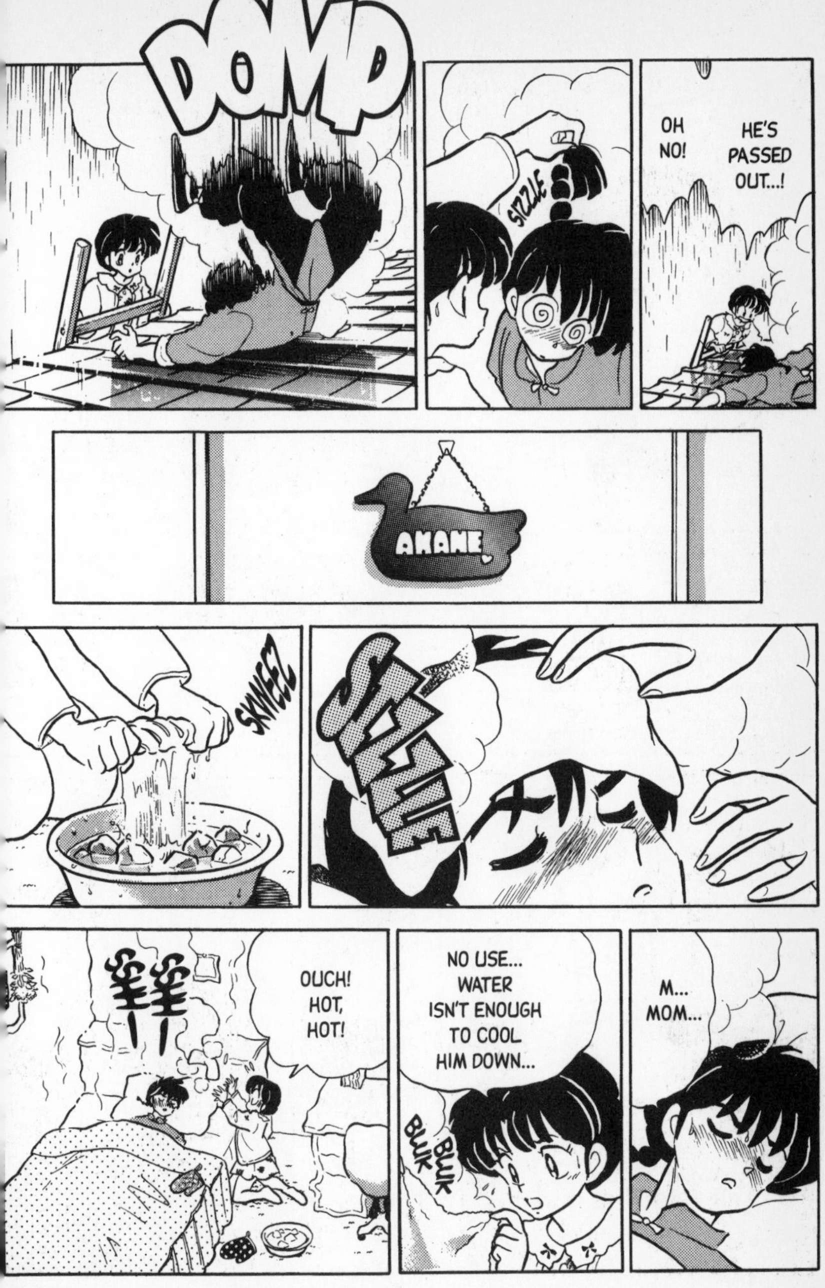
DOMP
SIZZLE
OH NO!
HE'S PASSED OUT...!
AKANE
SKWEEZ
SIZZLE
OUCH! HOT, HOT!
NO USE... WATER ISN'T ENOUGH TO COOL HIM DOWN...
BLUK BLUK
M... MOM...

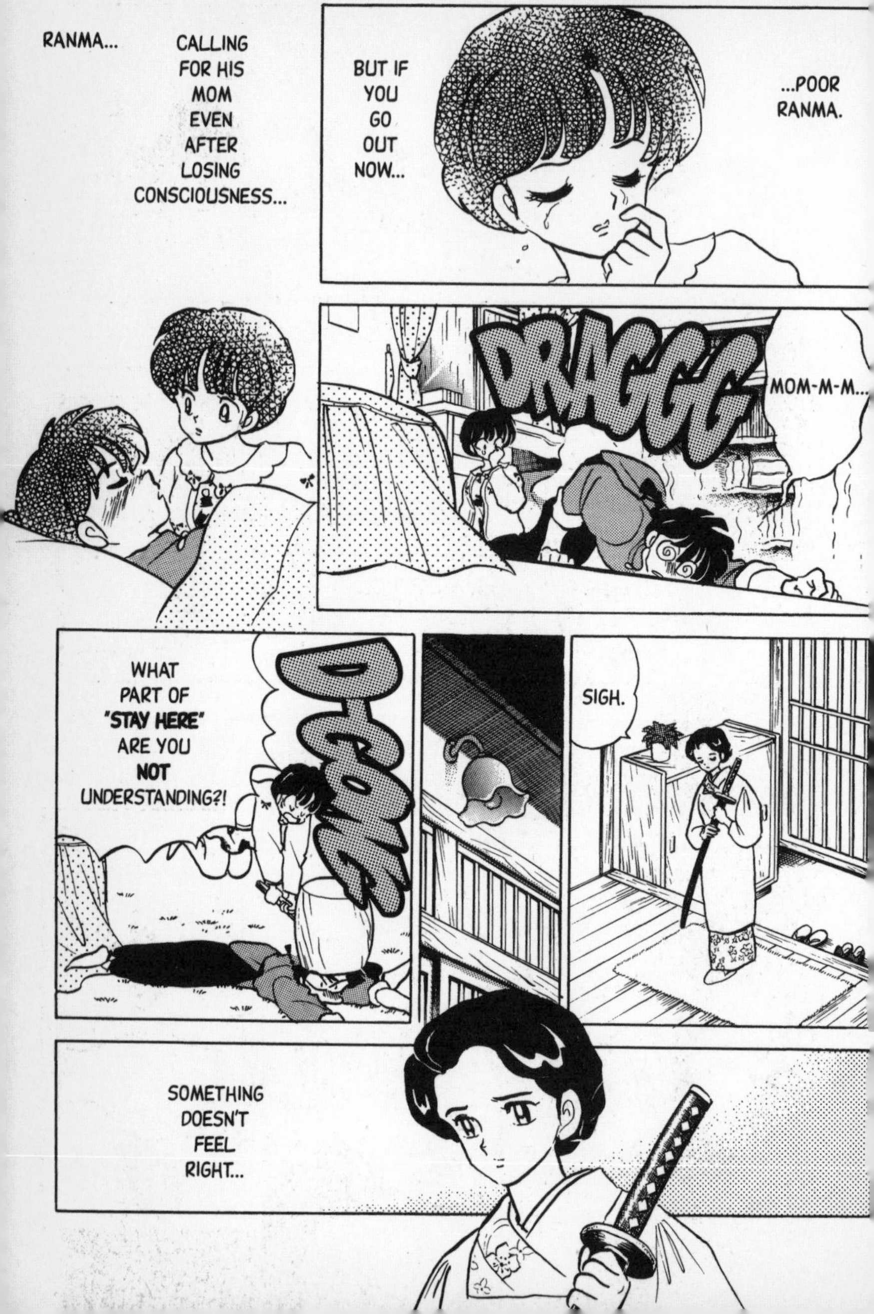
RANMA...
CALLING FOR HIS MOM EVEN AFTER LOSING CONSCIOUSNESS...
BUT IF YOU GO OUT NOW...
...POOR RANMA.
DRAGGG
MOM-M-M...
WHAT PART OF "STAY HERE" ARE YOU NOT UNDERSTANDING?!
SIGH.
SOMETHING DOESN'T FEEL RIGHT...

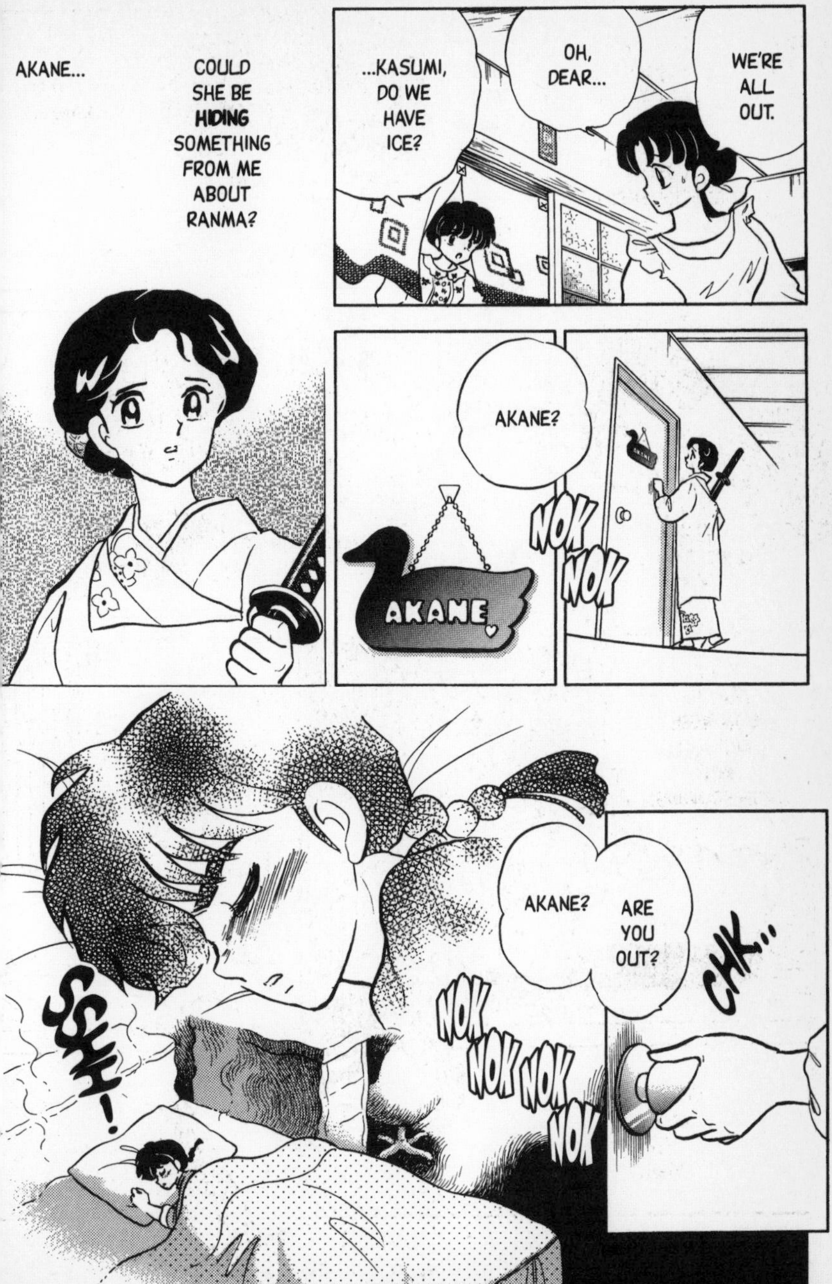
AKANE...
COULD SHE BE HIDING SOMETHING FROM ME ABOUT RANMA?
...KASUMI, DO WE HAVE ICE?
OH, DEAR...
WE'RE ALL OUT.
AKANE
AKANE?
NOK NOK
AKANE?
ARE YOU OUT?
SSH!
NOK NOK NOK NOK
CHK...

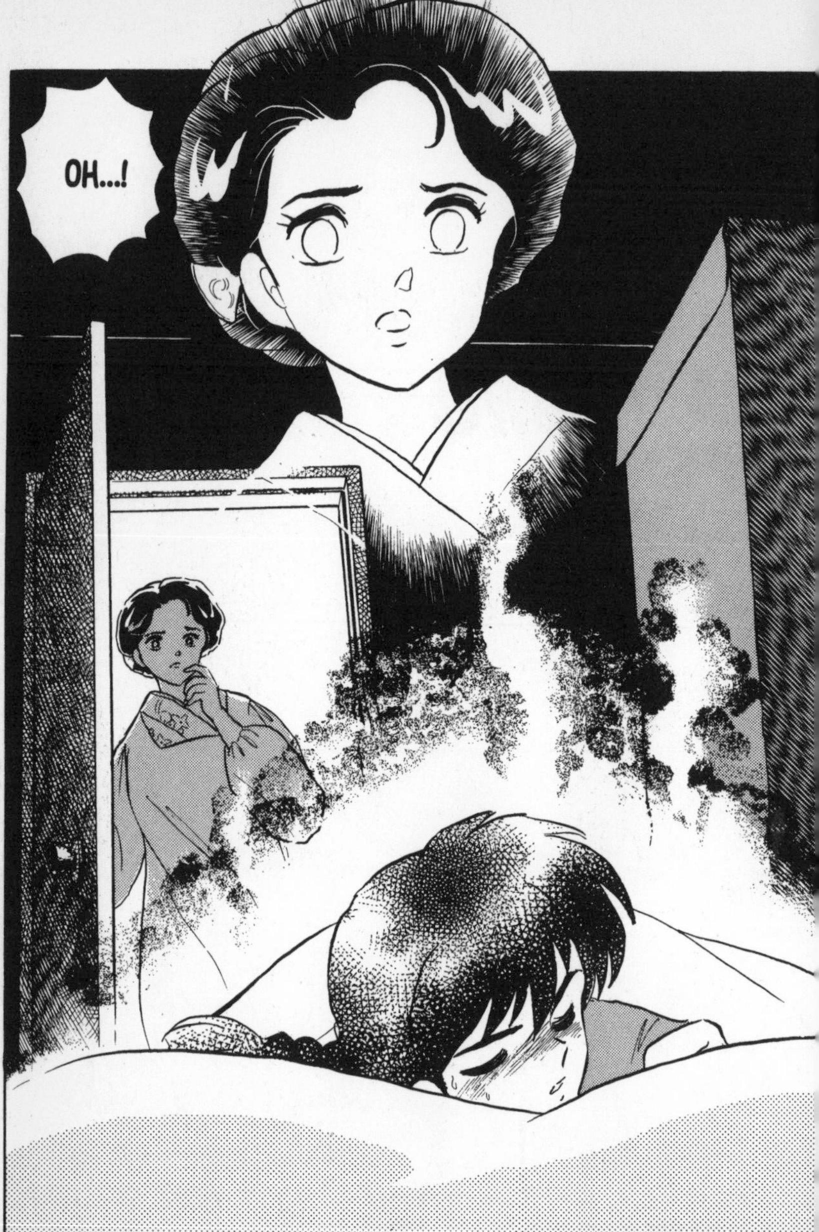
OH...!

PART 10

RANMA TILL MORNING

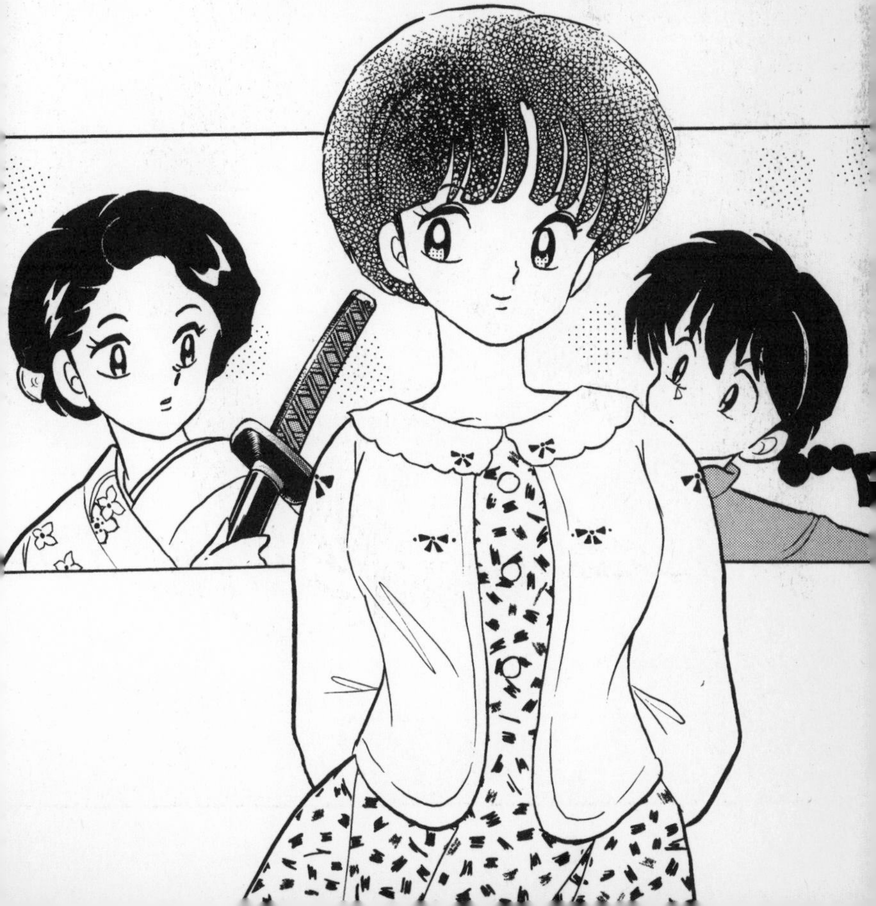

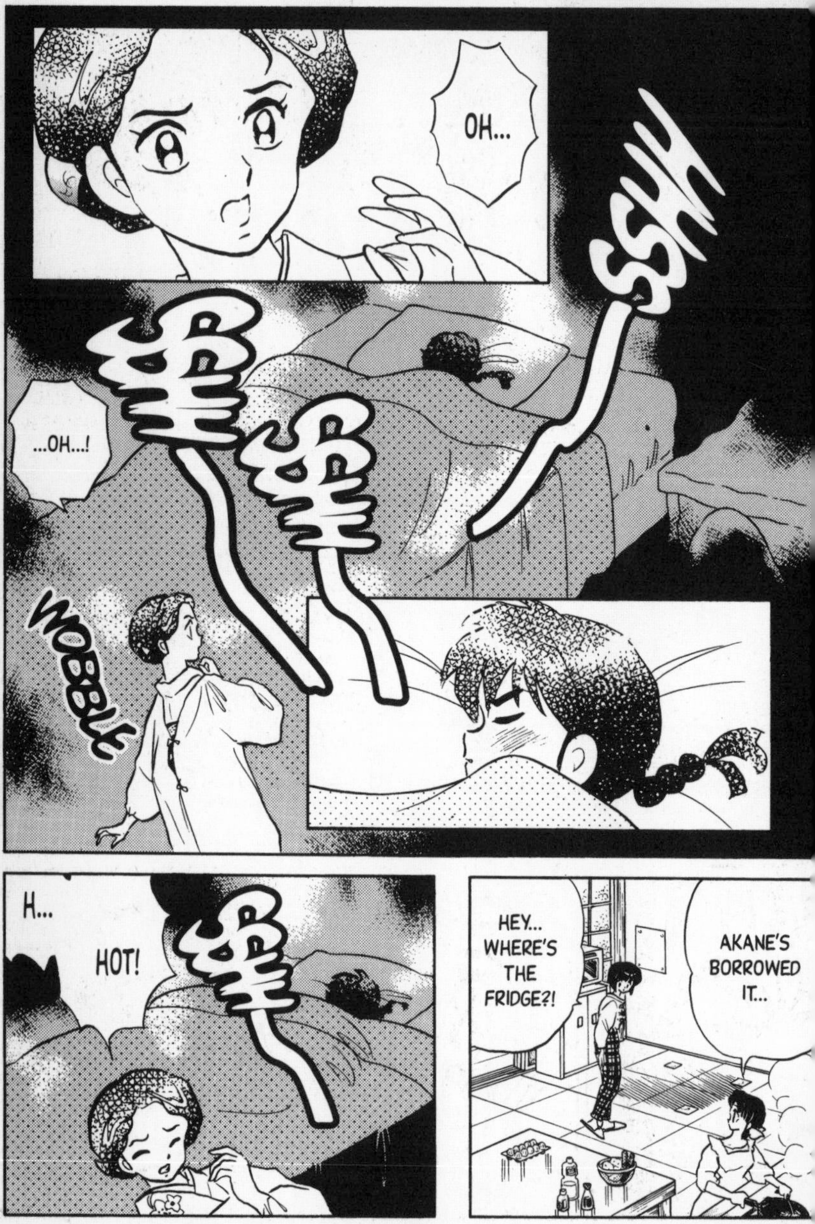
OH...
SSHH
...OH...!
WOBBLE
H...
HOT!
HEY... WHERE'S THE FRIDGE?!
AKANE'S BORROWED IT...

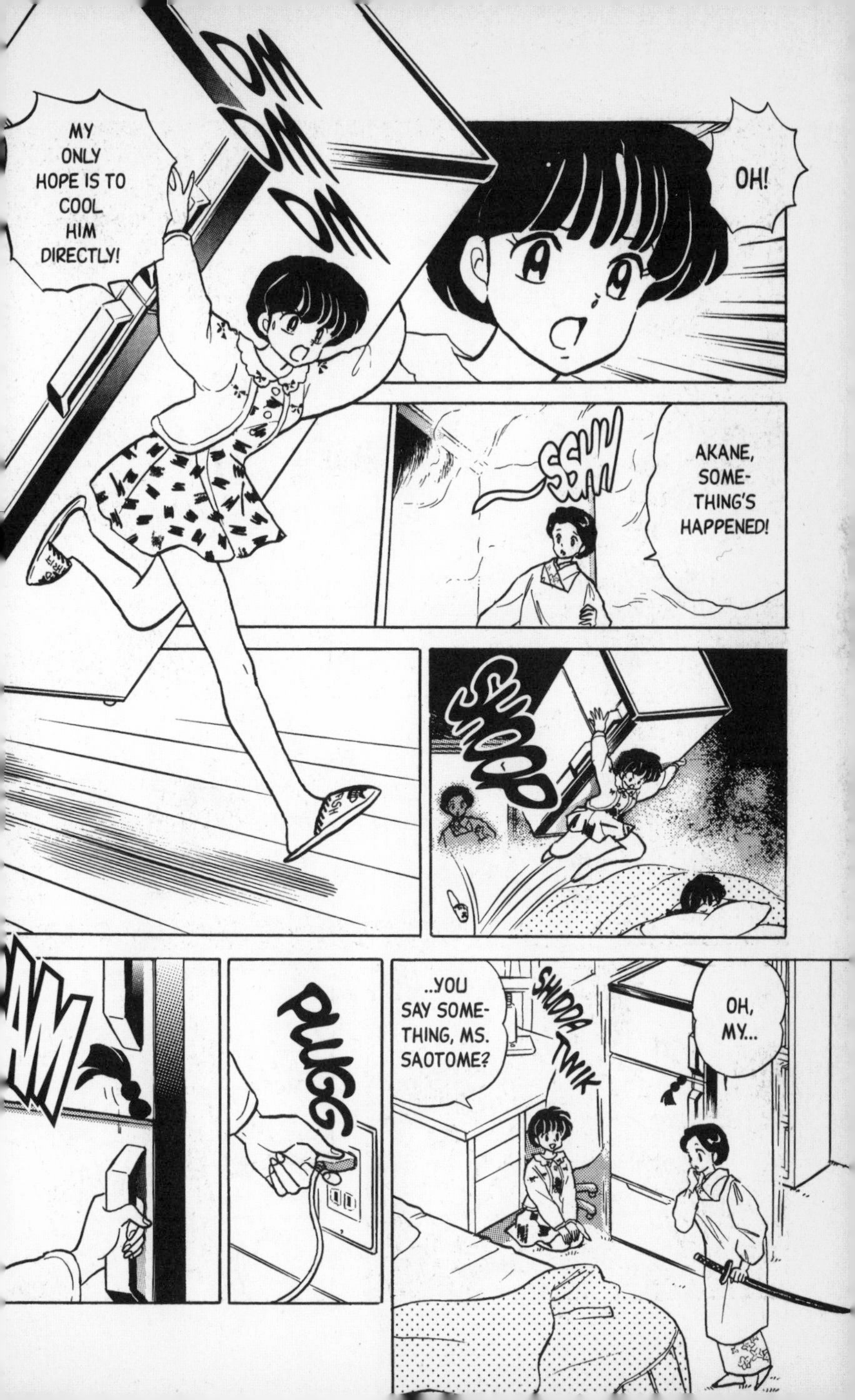

MY ONLY HOPE IS TO COOL HIM DIRECTLY!
DM DM DM
OH!
SSHH
AKANE, SOME-THING'S HAPPENED!
SWOOP
AM
PLUGG
...YOU SAY SOME-THING, MS. SAOTOME?
SHUDDA TWIK
OH, MY...

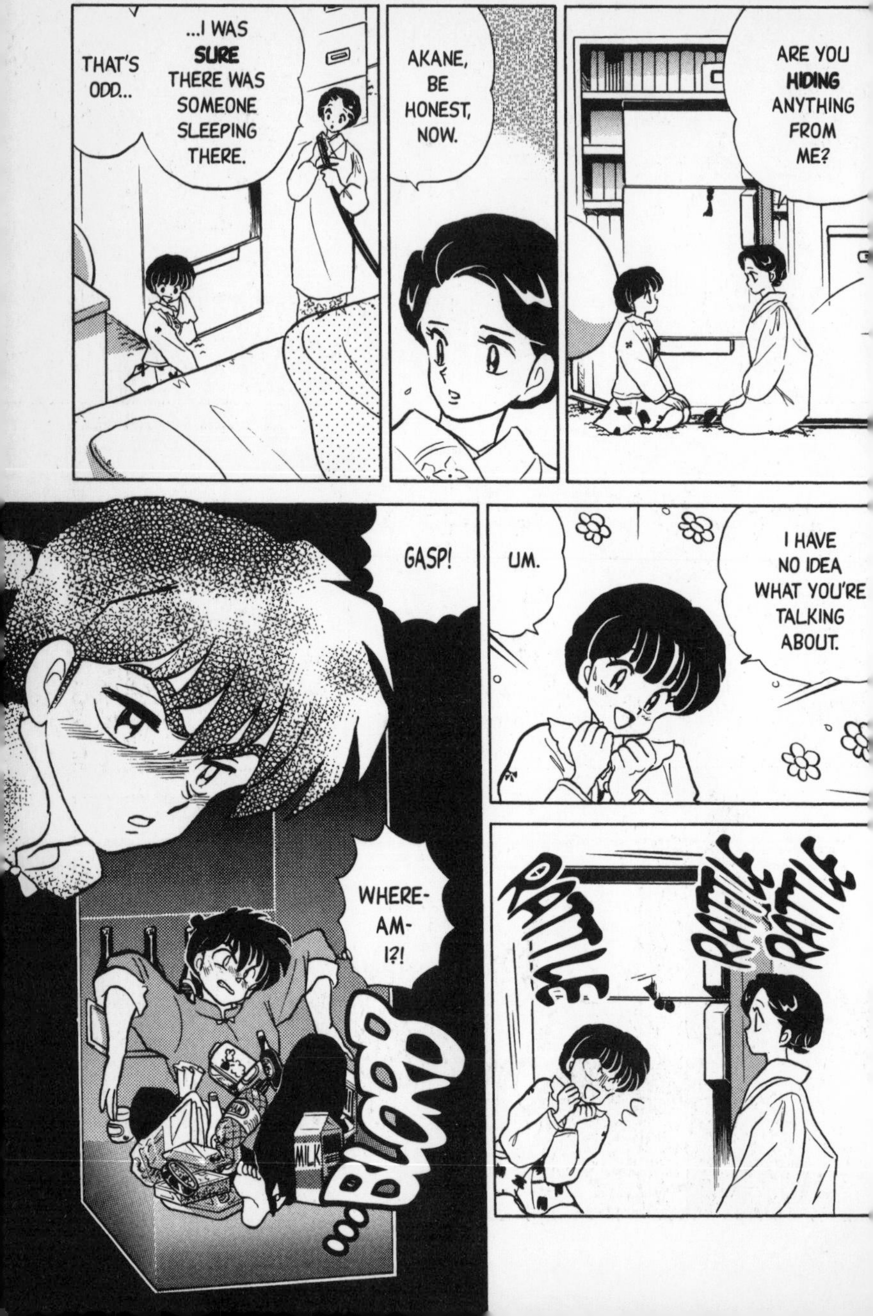
THAT'S ODD...
...I WAS **SURE** THERE WAS SOMEONE SLEEPING THERE.
AKANE, BE HONEST, NOW.
ARE YOU **HIDING** ANYTHING FROM ME?
GASP!
WHERE-AM-I?!
MILK
...BLORB
UM.
I HAVE NO IDEA WHAT YOU'RE TALKING ABOUT.
RATTLE RATTLE RATTLE

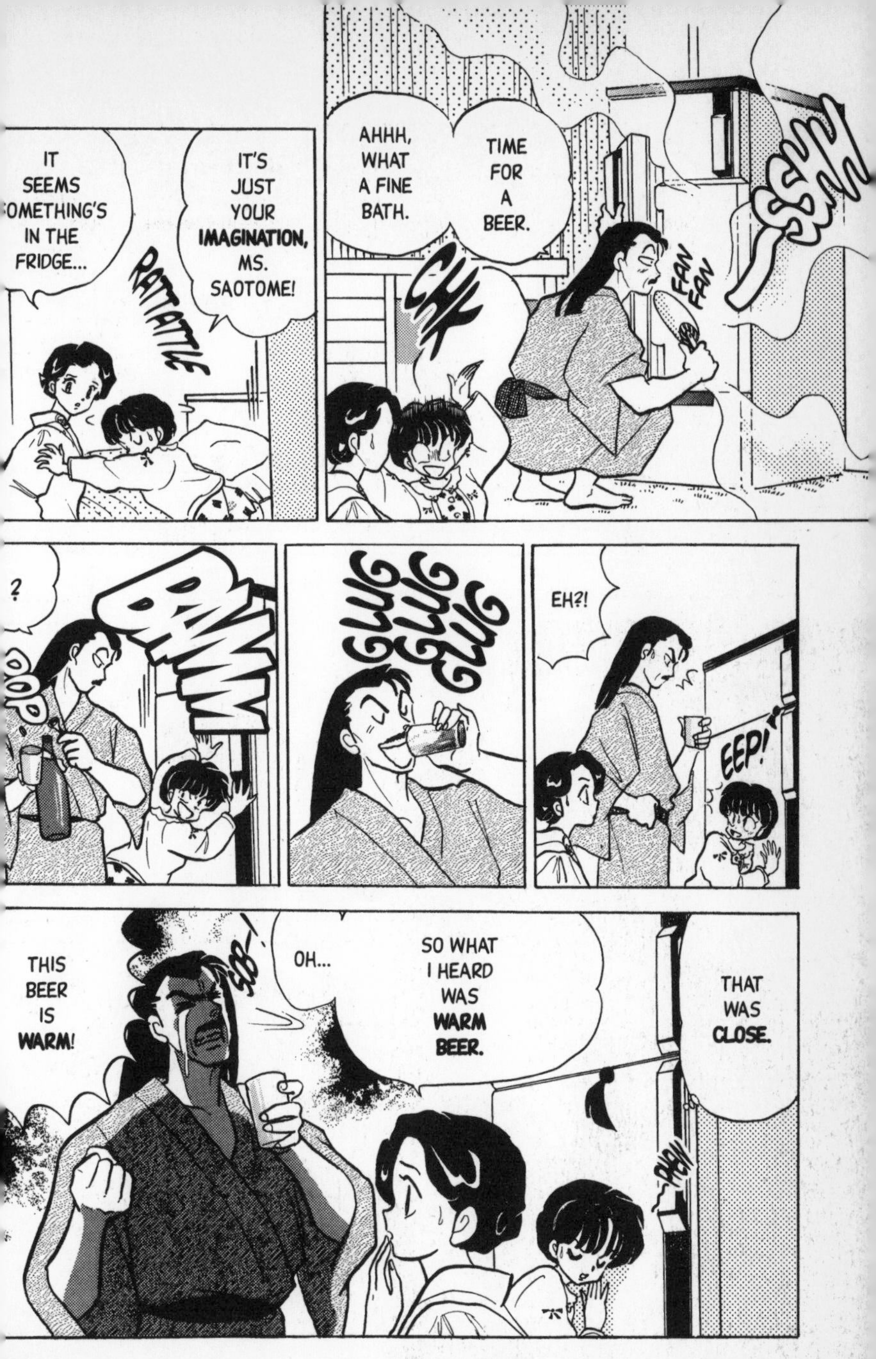

IT SEEMS SOMETHING'S IN THE FRIDGE...
IT'S JUST YOUR IMAGINATION, MS. SAOTOME!
RATTATTLE
AHHH, WHAT A FINE BATH.
TIME FOR A BEER.
CHK
FAN FAN
SSSH
?
BAMM
POP
GLUG GLUG GLUG
EH?!
EEP!
THIS BEER IS WARM!
SOB
OH...
SO WHAT I HEARD WAS WARM BEER.
THAT WAS CLOSE.
PHEW

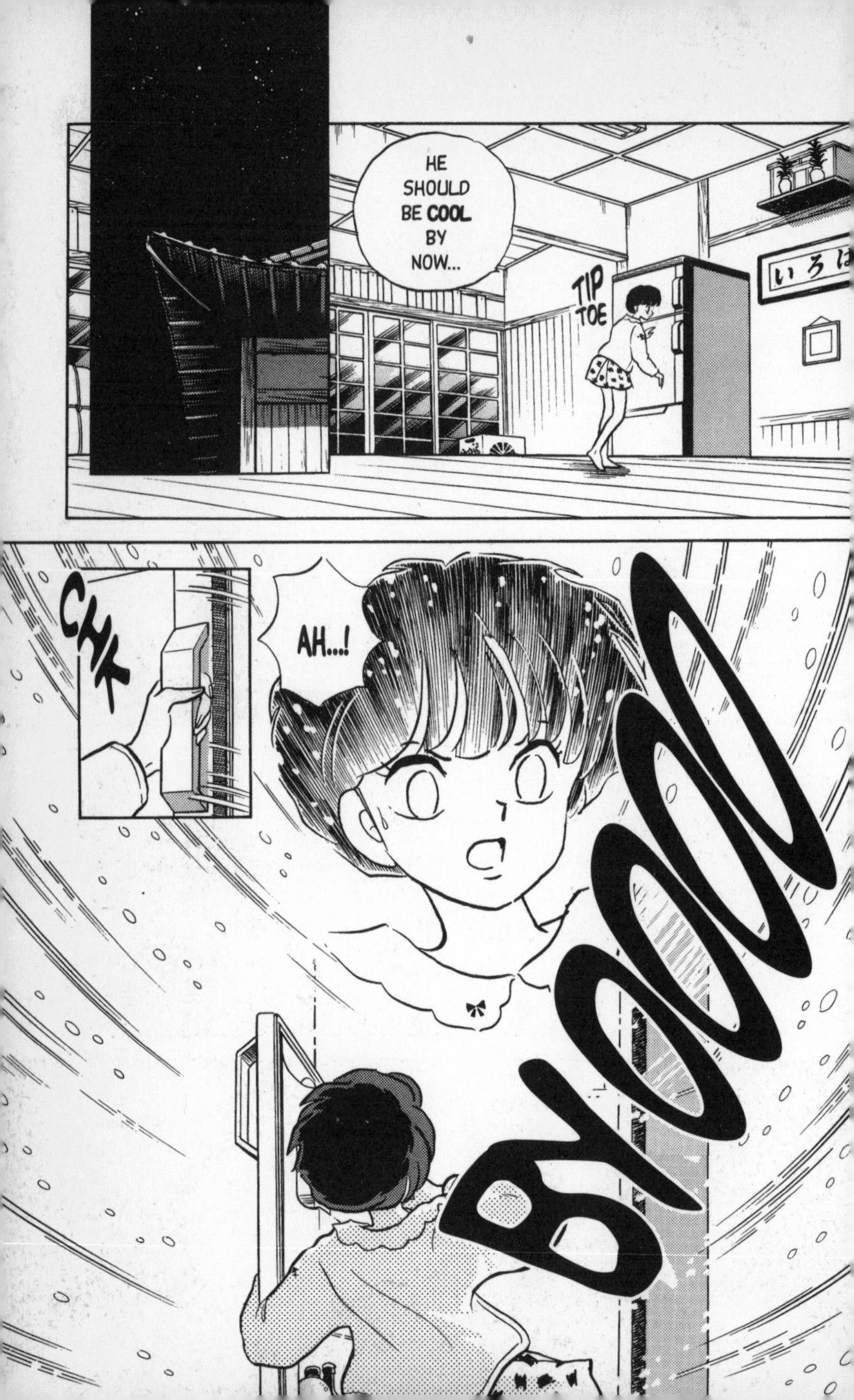

HE SHOULD BE COOL BY NOW...
TIP TOE
いろは
CHK
AH...!
BYOOO

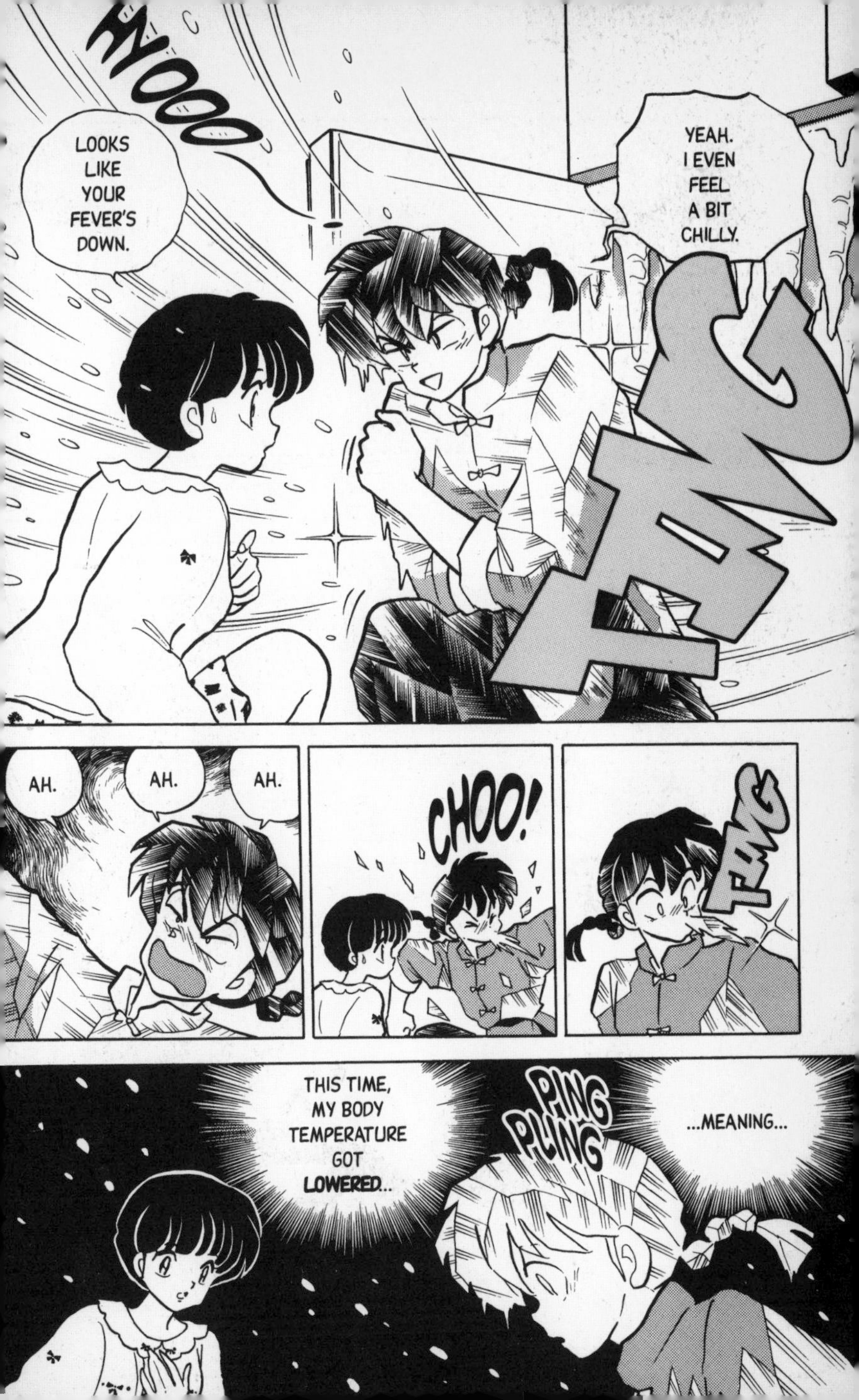
HYOOO
LOOKS LIKE YOUR FEVER'S DOWN.
YEAH. I EVEN FEEL A BIT CHILLY.
FZING
AH.
AH.
AH.
CHOO!
FZING
THIS TIME, MY BODY TEMPERATURE GOT LOWERED...
PING PLING
...MEANING...

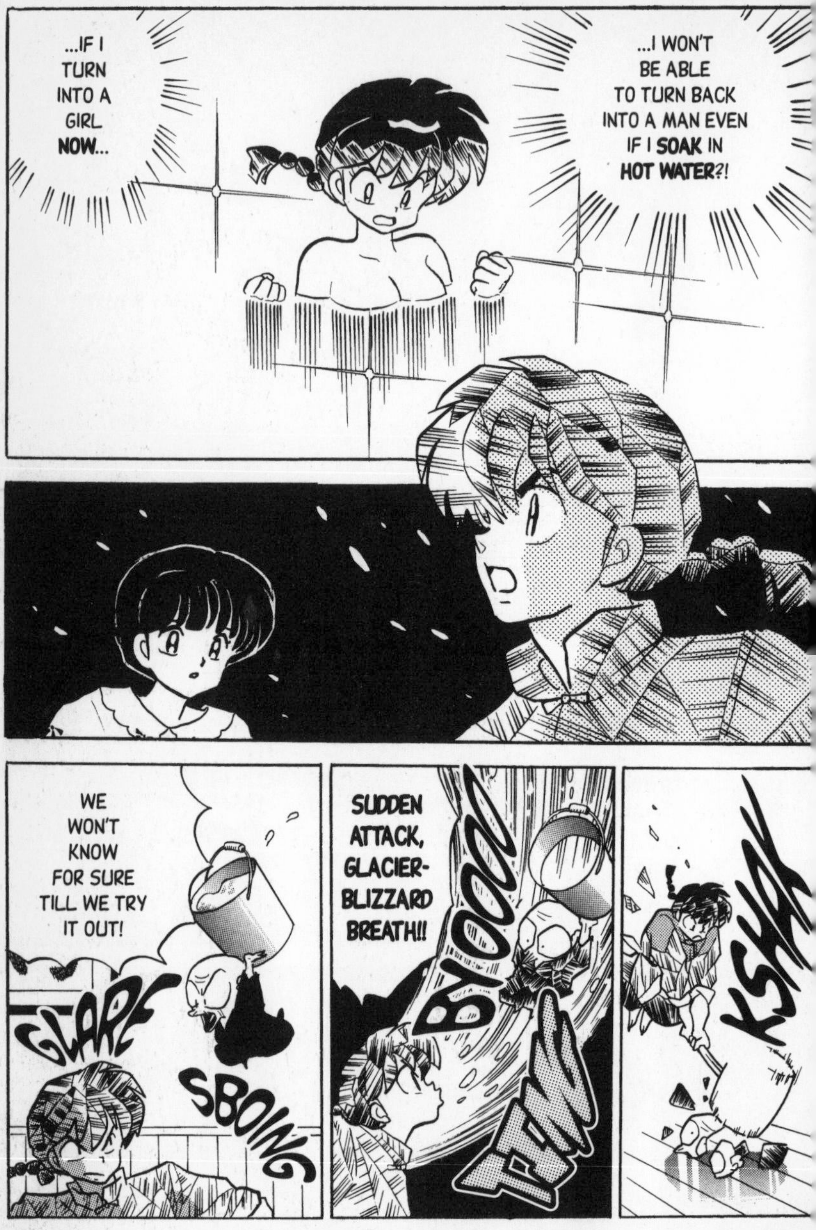
...IF I TURN INTO A GIRL NOW...
...I WON'T BE ABLE TO TURN BACK INTO A MAN EVEN IF I SOAK IN HOT WATER?!
WE WON'T KNOW FOR SURE TILL WE TRY IT OUT!
GLARE
SBOING
SUDDEN ATTACK, GLACIER-BLIZZARD BREATH!!
BYOOOO
KSHAK

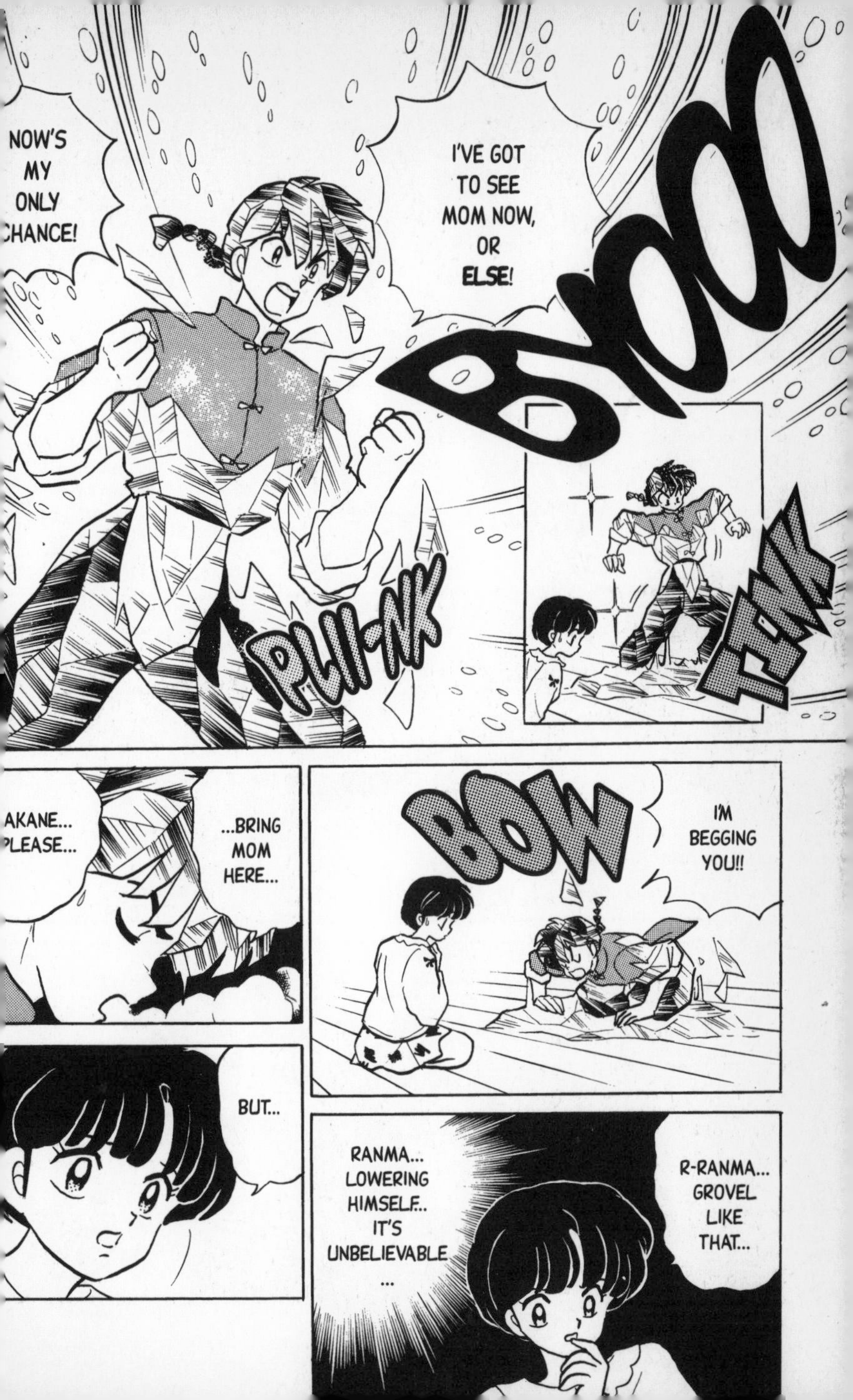
NOW'S MY ONLY CHANCE!
I'VE GOT TO SEE MOM NOW, OR ELSE!
BYOOO
PLII-NK
TINK
AKANE... PLEASE...
...BRING MOM HERE...
BOW
I'M BEGGING YOU!!
BUT...
RANMA... LOWERING HIMSELF.. IT'S UNBELIEVABLE ...
R-RANMA... GROVEL LIKE THAT...

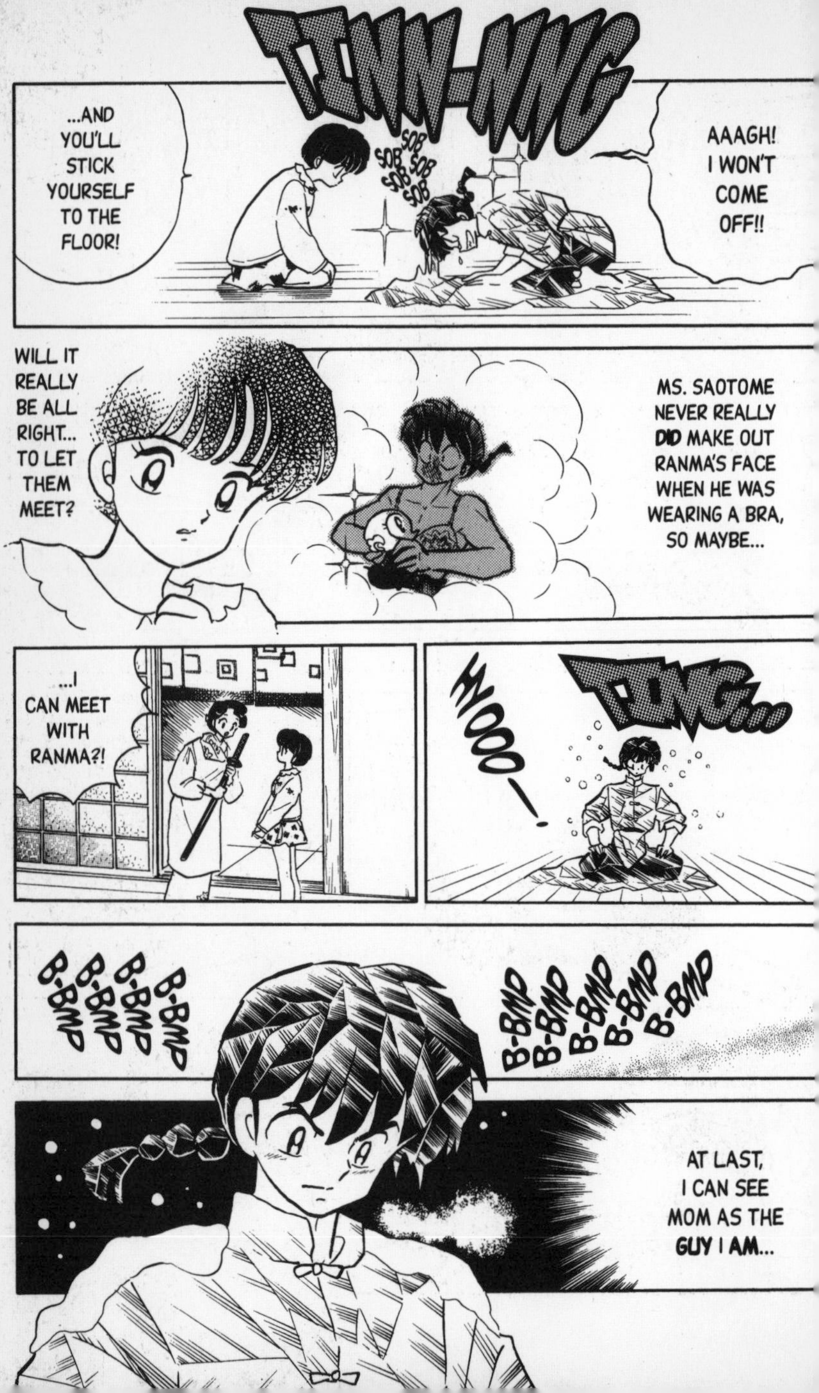
TZINN-NNNG
...AND YOU'LL STICK YOURSELF TO THE FLOOR!
SOB SOB SOB SOB SOB SOB
AAAGH! I WON'T COME OFF!!
WILL IT REALLY BE ALL RIGHT... TO LET THEM MEET?
MS. SAOTOME NEVER REALLY DID MAKE OUT RANMA'S FACE WHEN HE WAS WEARING A BRA, SO MAYBE...
...I CAN MEET WITH RANMA?!
HYOOO—!
TZING...
B-BMP B-BMP B-BMP B-BMP
B-BMP B-BMP B-BMP B-BMP B-BMP
AT LAST, I CAN SEE MOM AS THE GUY I AM...

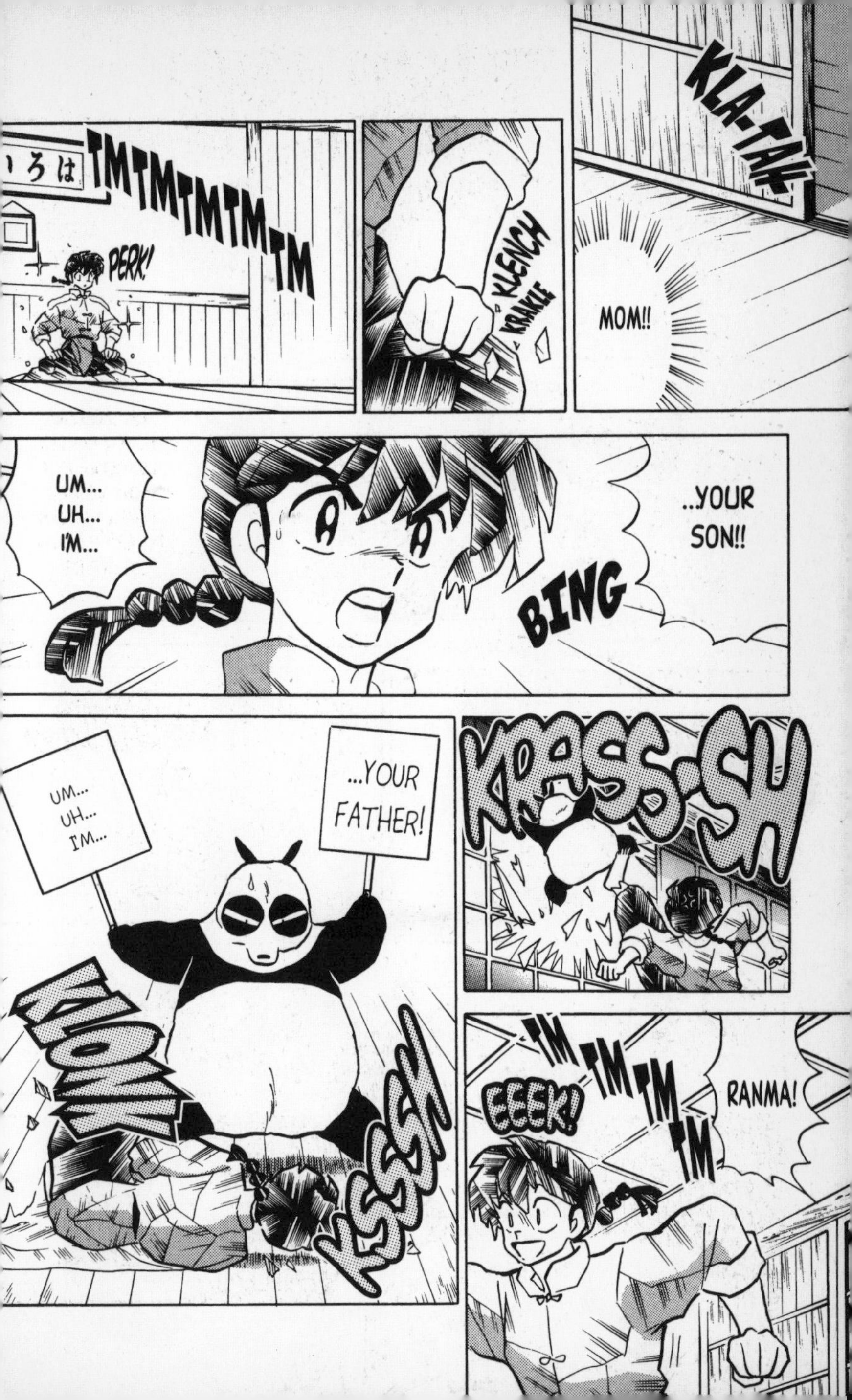
いろは
TMTMTMTMTMTM
PERK!
KLENCH
KRAKLE
KLA-TAK
MOM!!
UM... UH... I'M...
...YOUR SON!!
BING
UM... UH... I'M...
...YOUR FATHER!
KSSSH
KRASS-SH
EEEK!
TM TM TM TM TM
RANMA!

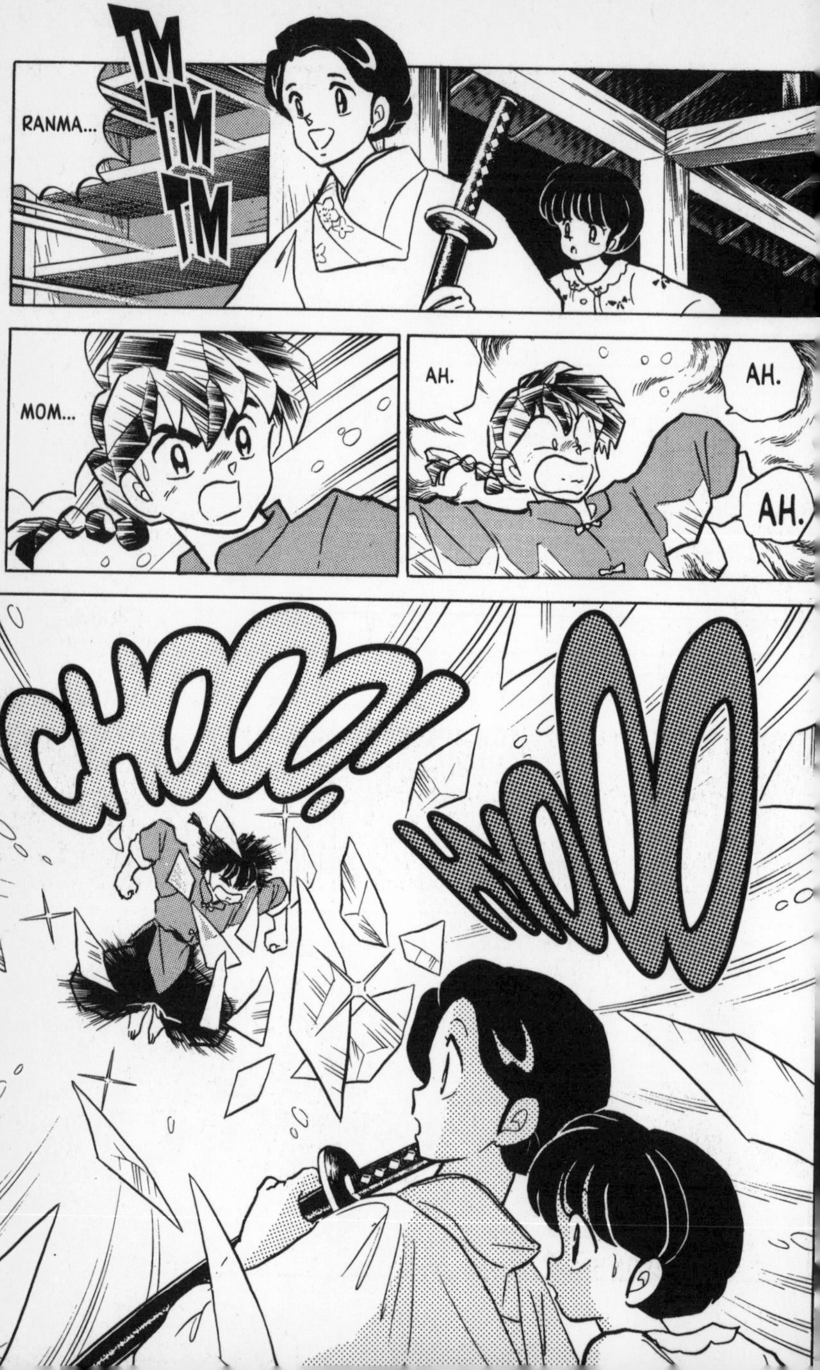
TMTMTMTM
RANMA...
MOM...
AH.
AH.
AH.
CHOOO!
WHOOO

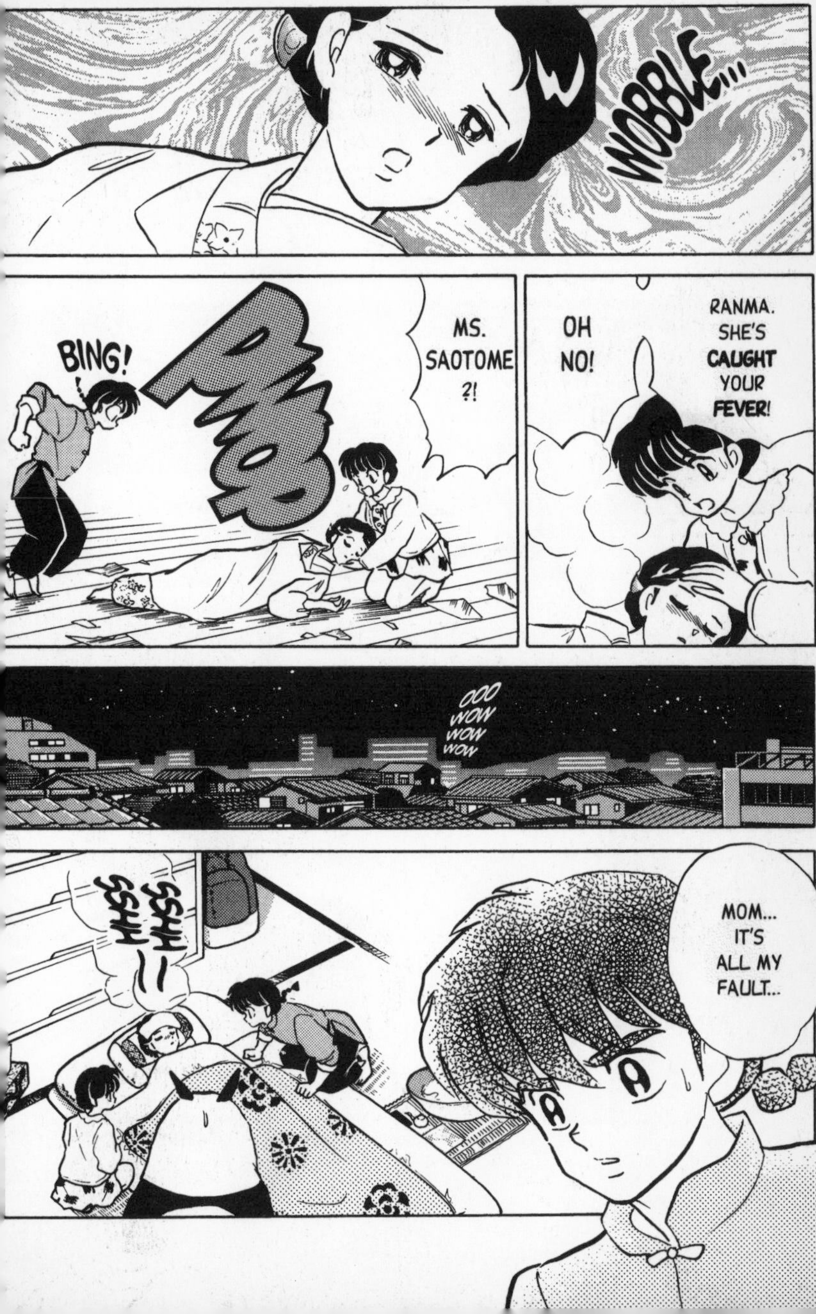
WOBBLE...
BING!
PLOP
MS. SAOTOME ?!
OH NO!
RANMA. SHE'S CAUGHT YOUR FEVER!
OOO WOW WOW WOW
SSHH SSHH
MOM... IT'S ALL MY FAULT...

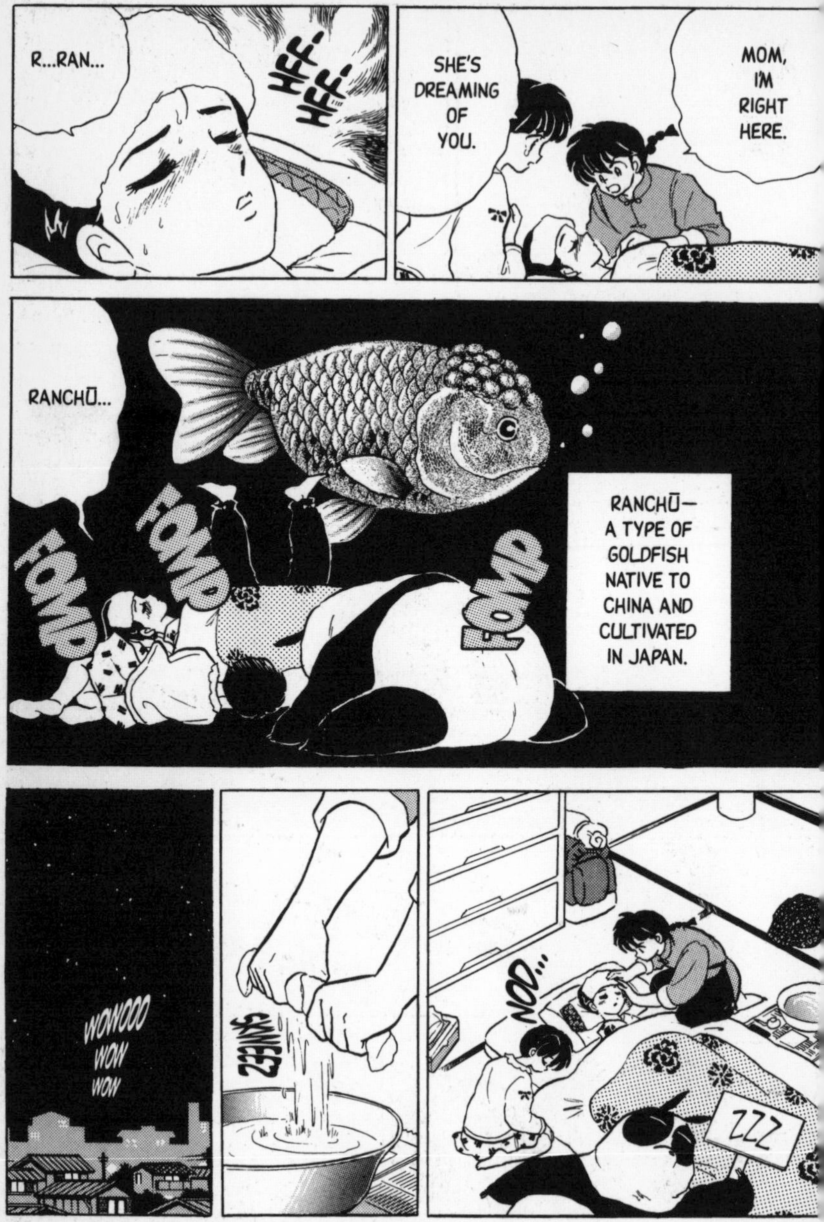
R...RAN...
HEFF HEFF
SHE'S DREAMING OF YOU.
MOM, I'M RIGHT HERE.
RANCHŪ...
FOMP
FOMP
FOMP
RANCHŪ— A TYPE OF GOLDFISH NATIVE TO CHINA AND CULTIVATED IN JAPAN.
WOWOOO WOW WOW
SKWEEZ
NOD...
ZZZ

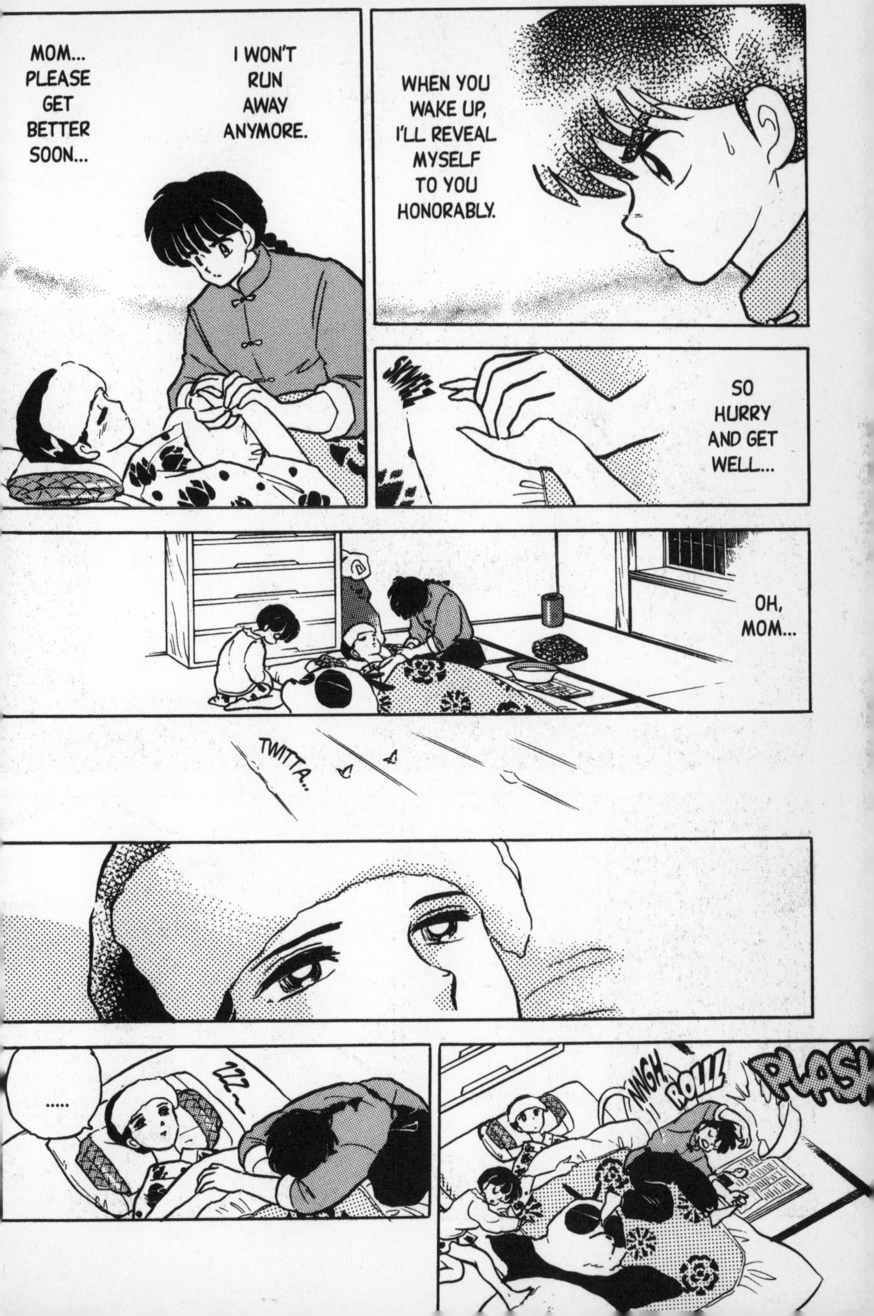
MOM... PLEASE GET BETTER SOON...
I WON'T RUN AWAY ANYMORE.
WHEN YOU WAKE UP, I'LL REVEAL MYSELF TO YOU HONORABLY.
TWINS
SO HURRY AND GET WELL...
OH, MOM...
TWITTA...
.....
ZZZ~
NNGH
ROLLL
PLASH

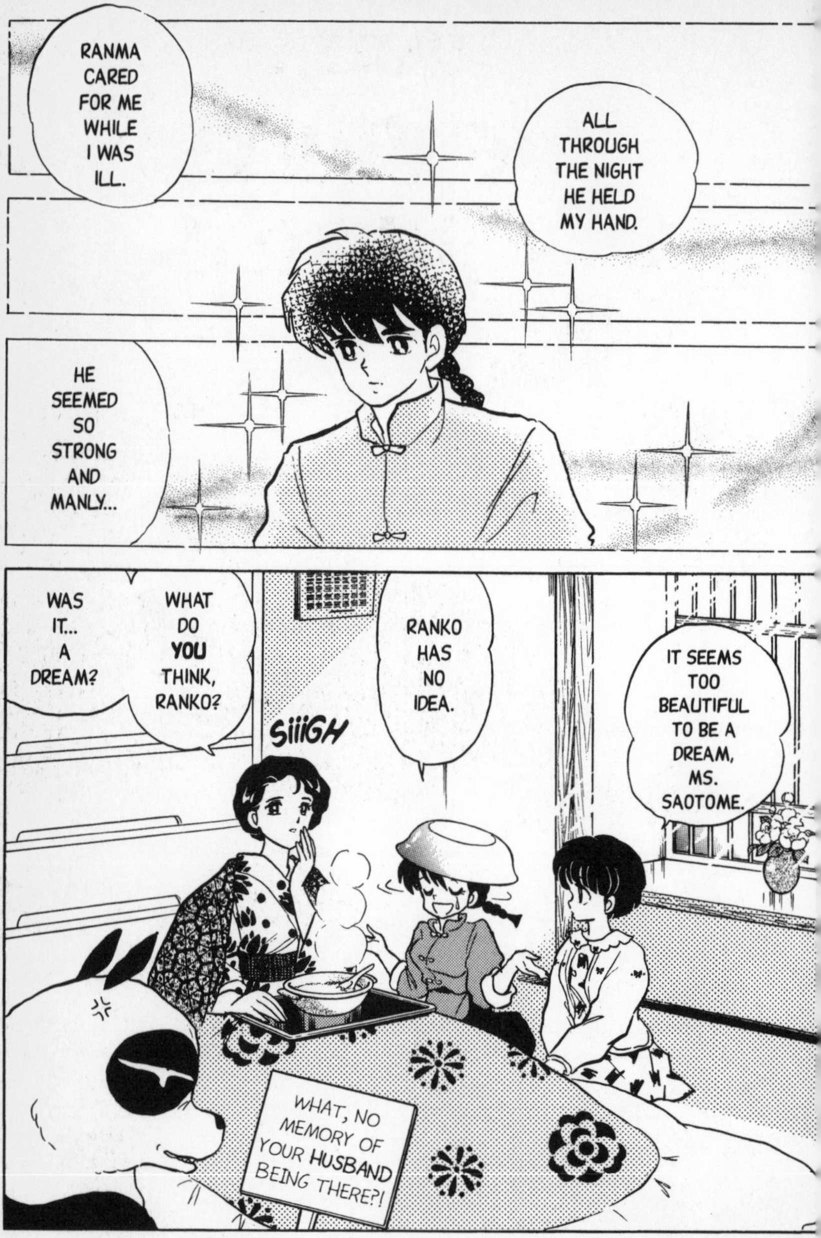
RANMA CARED FOR ME WHILE I WAS ILL.
ALL THROUGH THE NIGHT HE HELD MY HAND.
HE SEEMED SO STRONG AND MANLY...
WAS IT... A DREAM?
WHAT DO **YOU** THINK, RANKO?
SiiiGH
RANKO HAS NO IDEA.
IT SEEMS TOO BEAUTIFUL TO BE A DREAM, MS. SAOTOME.
WHAT, NO MEMORY OF YOUR **HUSBAND** BEING THERE?!

PART 11
THE CURSED SPATULA

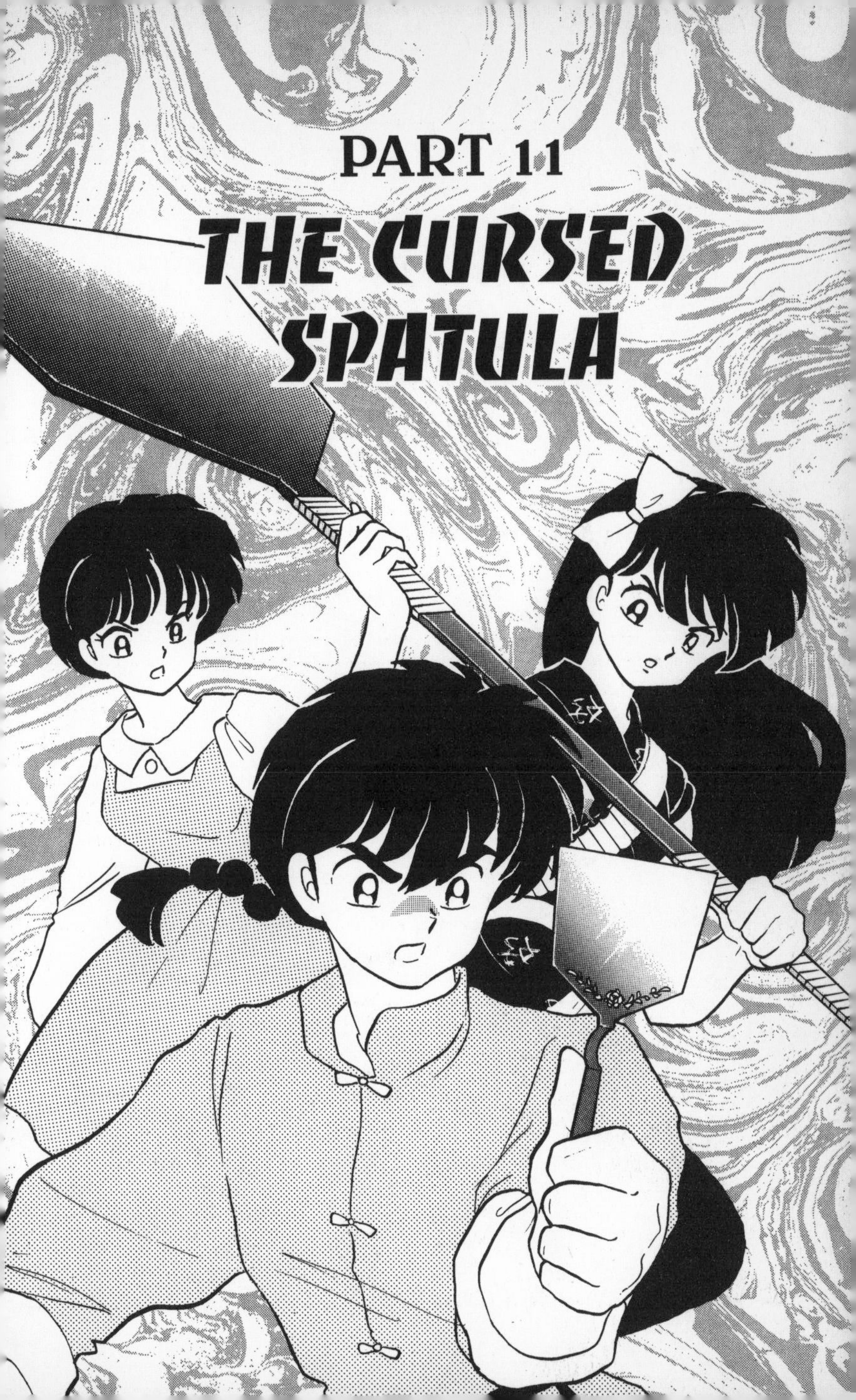

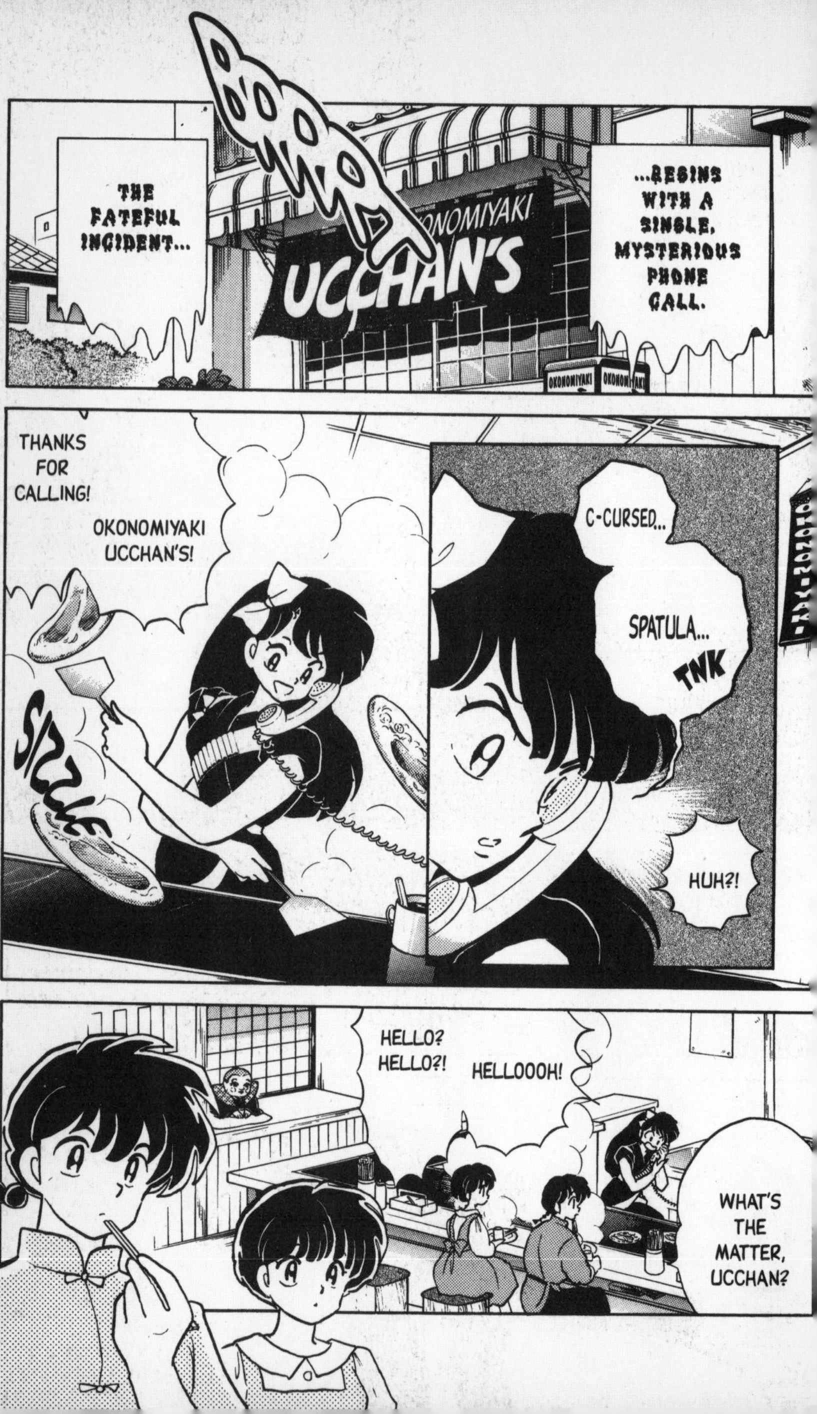
THE FATEFUL INCIDENT...
OKONOMIYAKI UCCHAN'S
...BEGINS WITH A SINGLE, MYSTERIOUS PHONE CALL.
OKONOMIYAKI
OKONOMIYAKI
THANKS FOR CALLING!
OKONOMIYAKI UCCHAN'S!
SIZZLE
C-CURSED...
SPATULA...
TNK
HUH?!
HELLO? HELLO?!
HELLOOOH!
WHAT'S THE MATTER, UCCHAN?

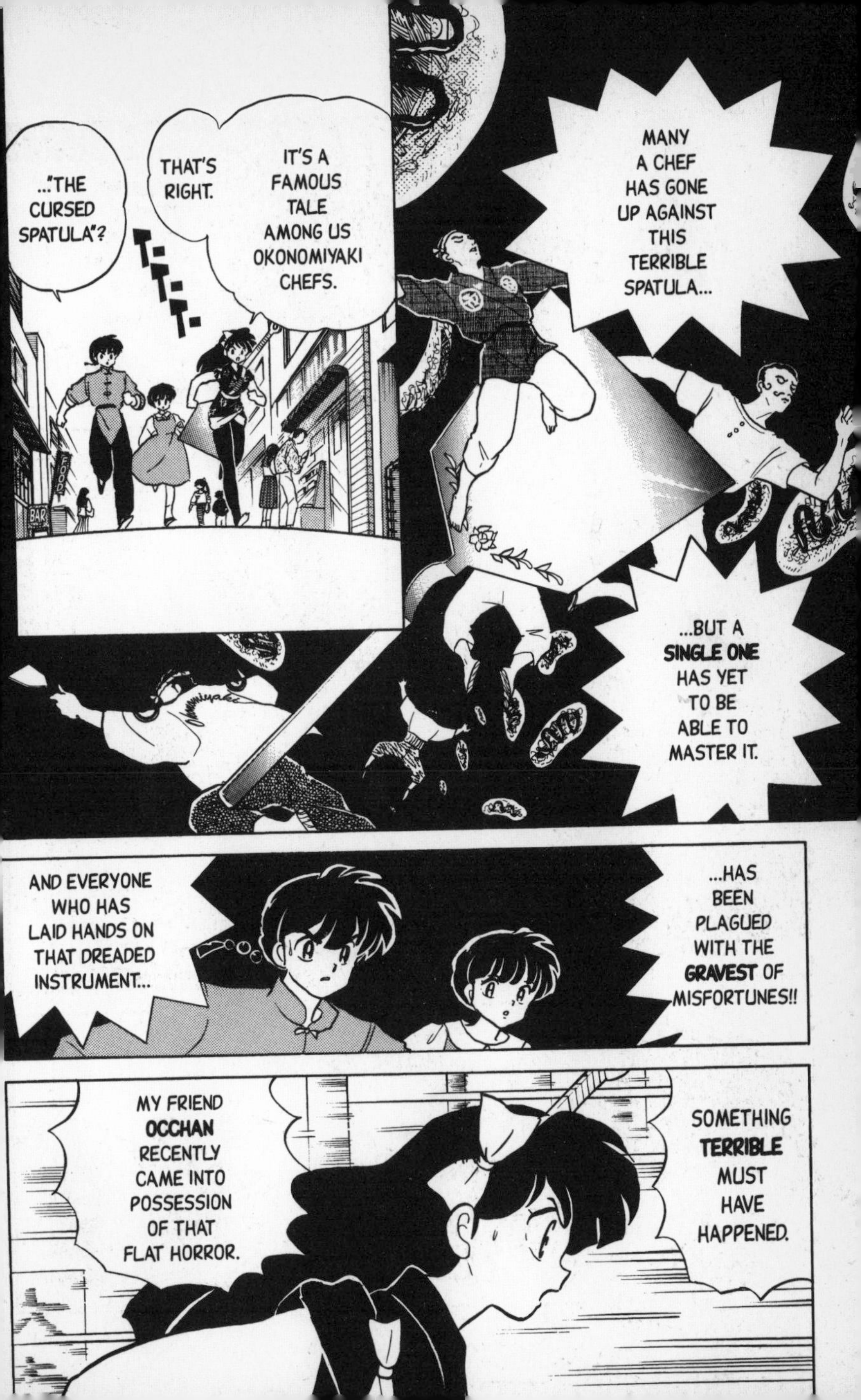

..."THE CURSED SPATULA"?
THAT'S RIGHT.
IT'S A FAMOUS TALE AMONG US OKONOMIYAKI CHEFS.
T-T-T-T-
FOOD
BAR
MANY A CHEF HAS GONE UP AGAINST THIS TERRIBLE SPATULA...
...BUT A **SINGLE ONE** HAS YET TO BE ABLE TO MASTER IT.
AND EVERYONE WHO HAS LAID HANDS ON THAT DREADED INSTRUMENT...
...HAS BEEN PLAGUED WITH THE **GRAVEST** OF MISFORTUNES!!
MY FRIEND **OCCHAN** RECENTLY CAME INTO POSSESSION OF THAT FLAT HORROR.
SOMETHING **TERRIBLE** MUST HAVE HAPPENED.

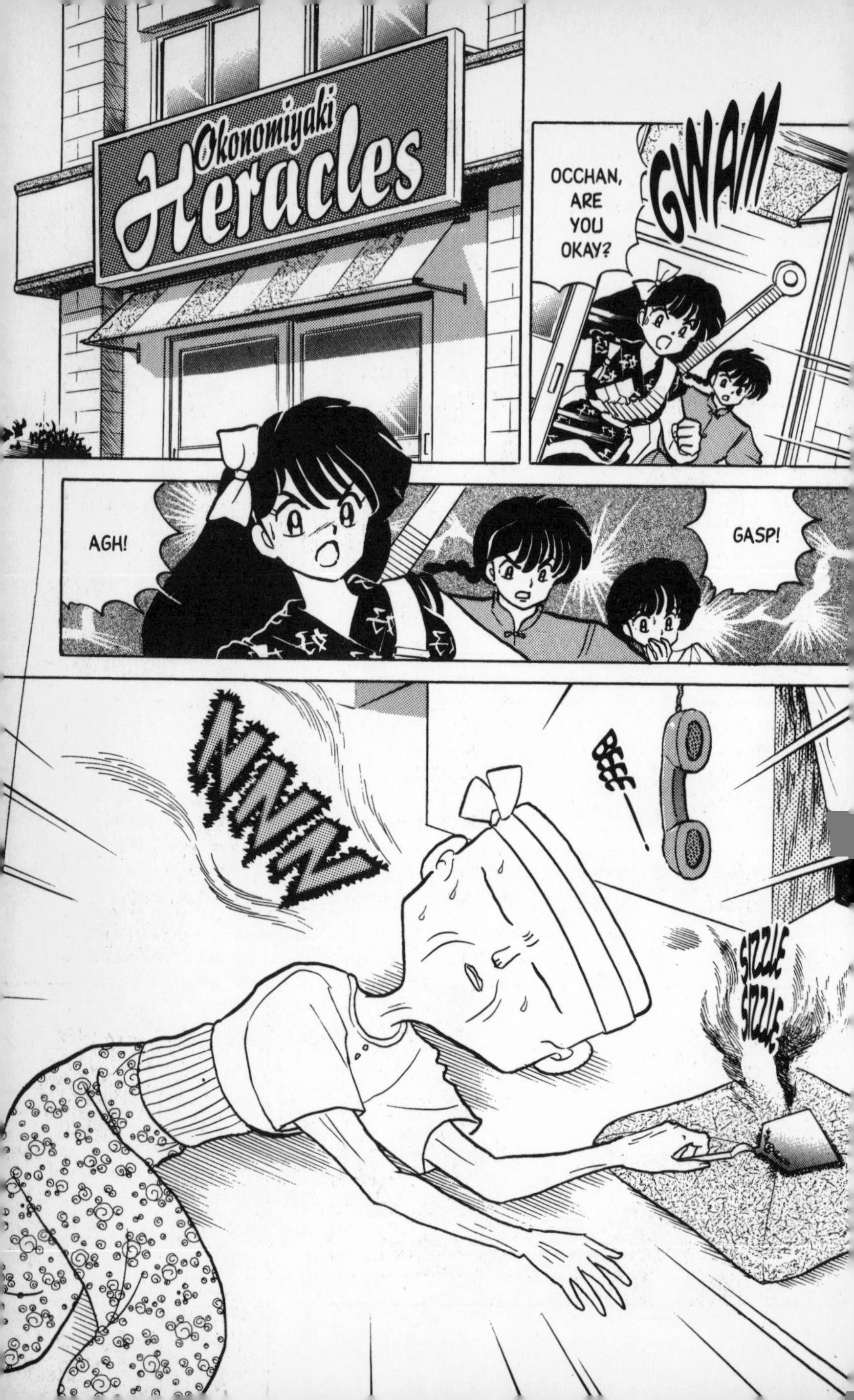

Okonomiyaki
Heracles
OCCHAN, ARE YOU OKAY?
GWAM
AGH!
GASP!
BEEE!
SIZZLE SIZZLE

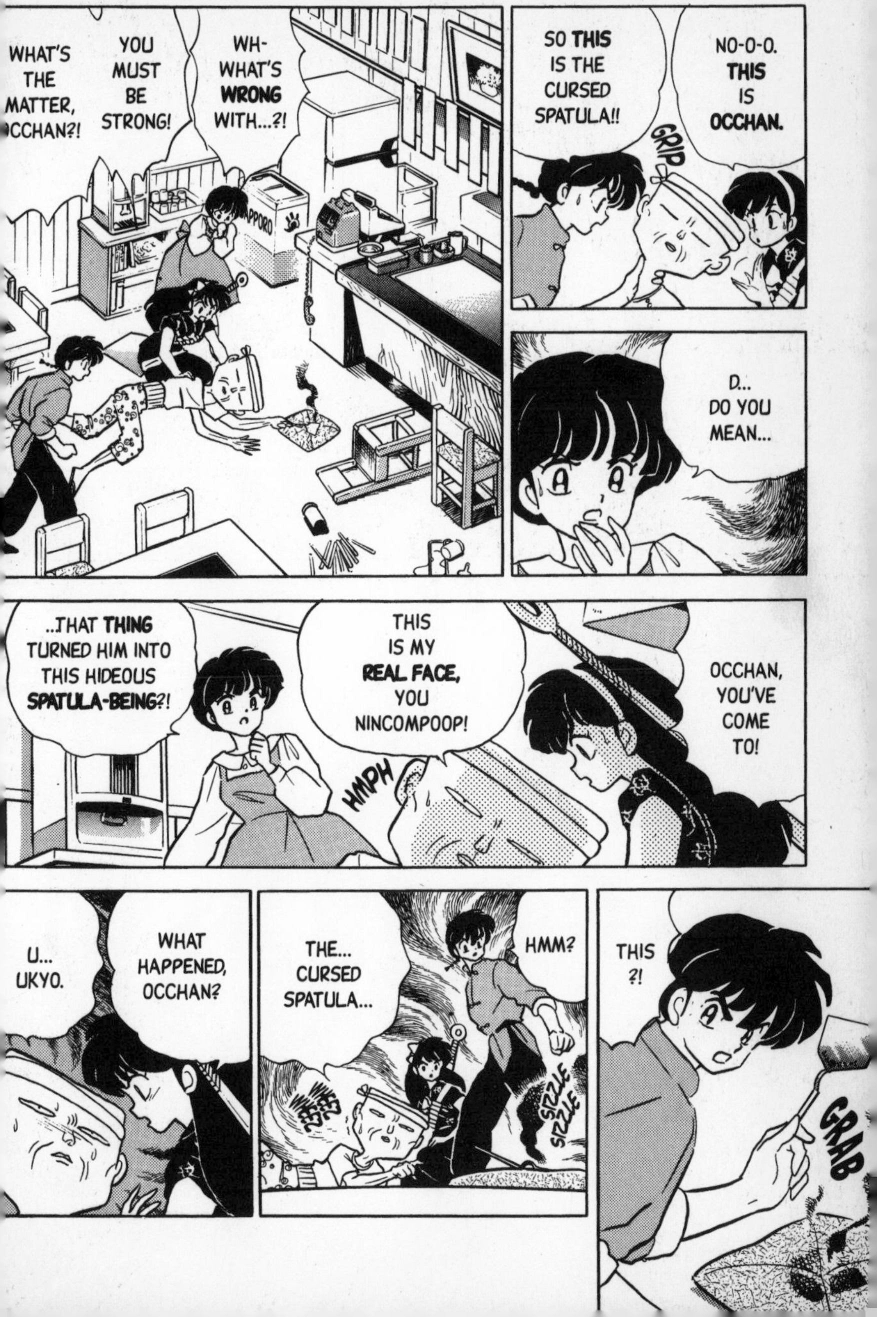
WHAT'S THE MATTER, OCCHAN?!
YOU MUST BE STRONG!
WH- WHAT'S WRONG WITH...?!
APPORO
SO THIS IS THE CURSED SPATULA!!
GRIP
NO-O-O. THIS IS OCCHAN.
D... DO YOU MEAN...
...THAT THING TURNED HIM INTO THIS HIDEOUS SPATULA-BEING?!
THIS IS MY REAL FACE, YOU NINCOMPOOP!
HMPH
OCCHAN, YOU'VE COME TO!
U... UKYO.
WHAT HAPPENED, OCCHAN?
THE... CURSED SPATULA...
HMM?
SIZZLE SIZZLE
THIS ?!
GRAB

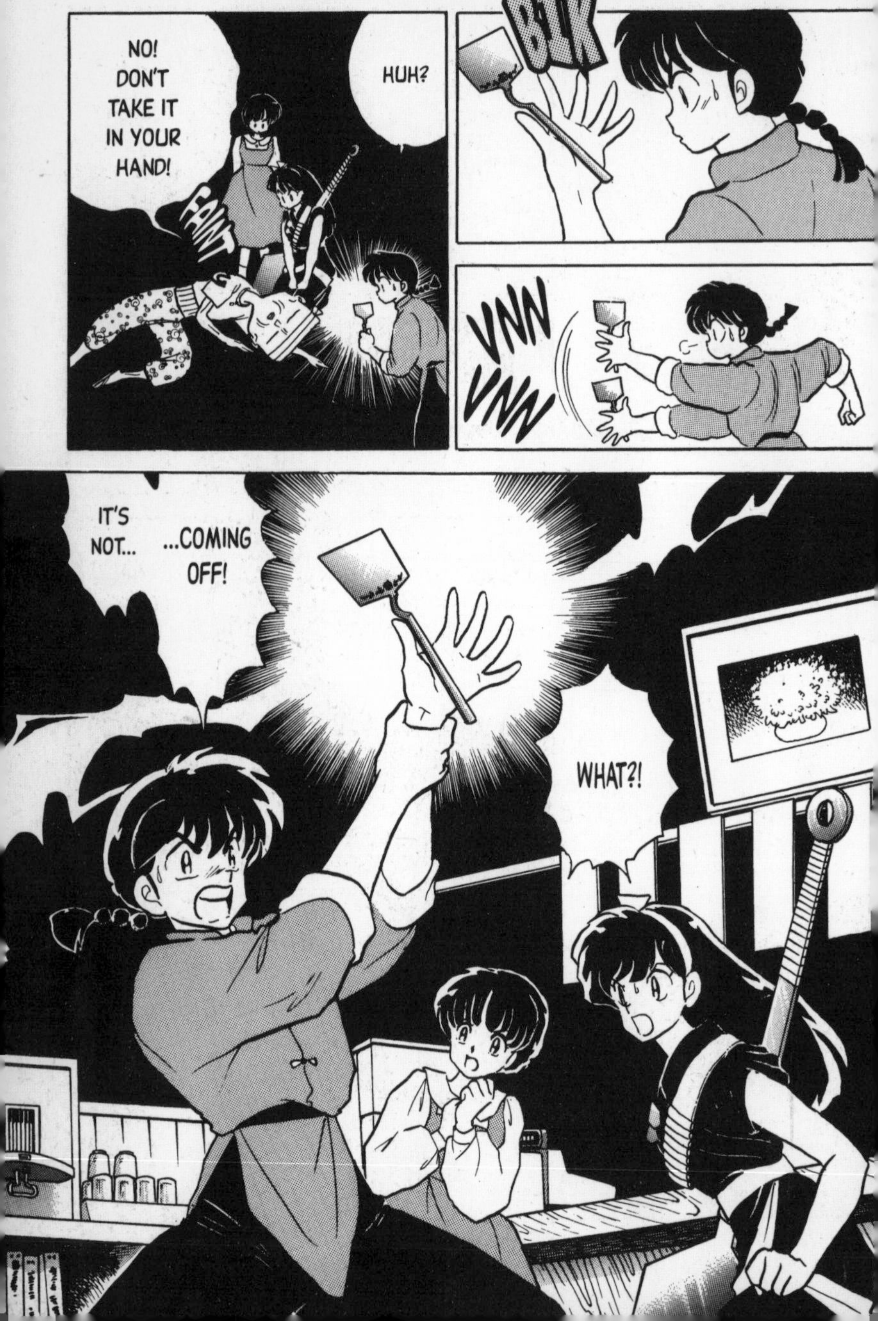
NO! DON'T TAKE IT IN YOUR HAND!
FAINT
HUH?
BLIK
VNN VNN
IT'S NOT...
...COMING OFF!
WHAT?!

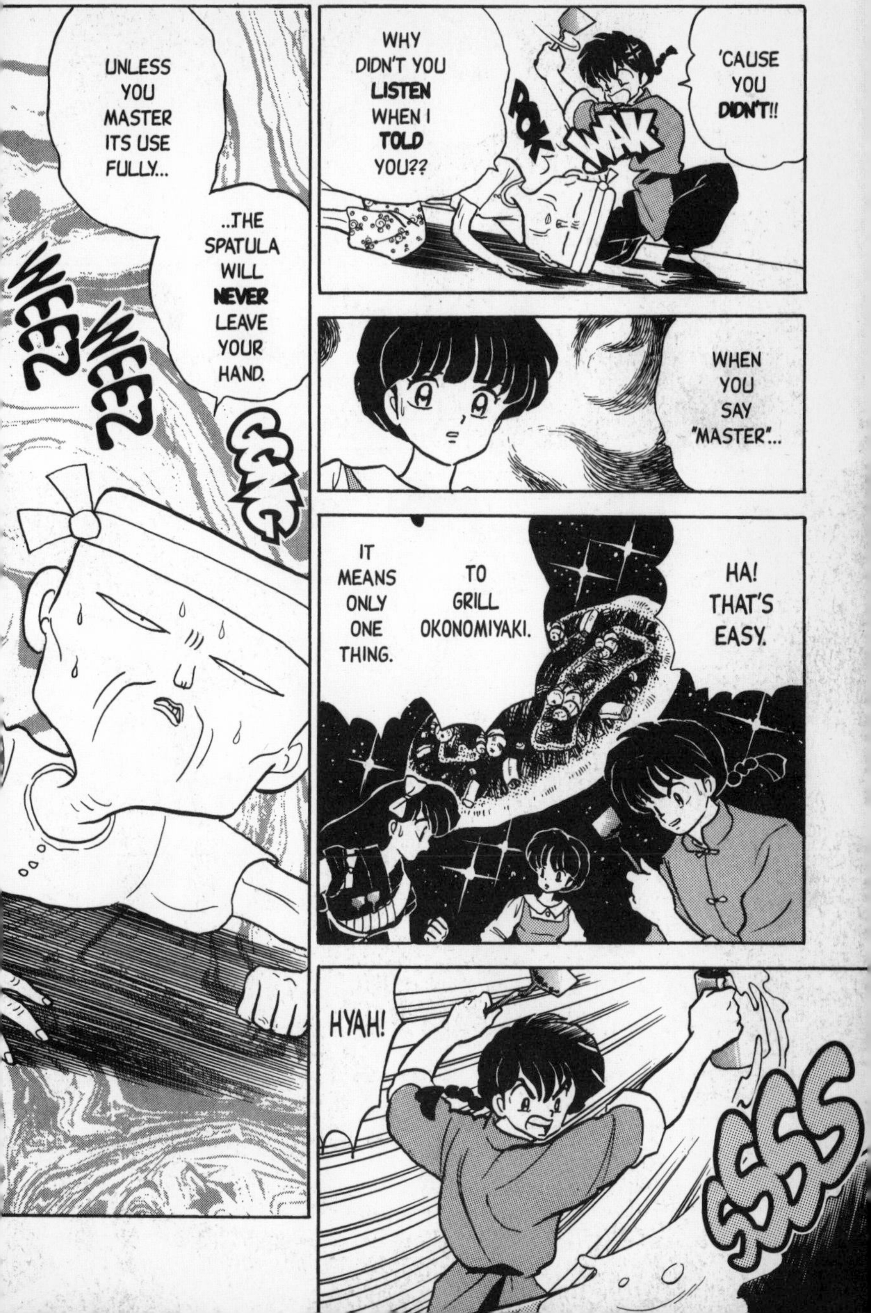
UNLESS YOU MASTER ITS USE FULLY...
..THE SPATULA WILL **NEVER** LEAVE YOUR HAND.
WEEZ
WEEZ
GGNG
WHY DIDN'T YOU **LISTEN** WHEN I **TOLD** YOU??
POK
WAK
'CAUSE YOU **DIDN'T**!!
WHEN YOU SAY "MASTER"...
IT MEANS ONLY ONE THING.
TO GRILL OKONOMIYAKI.
HA! THAT'S EASY.
HYAH!

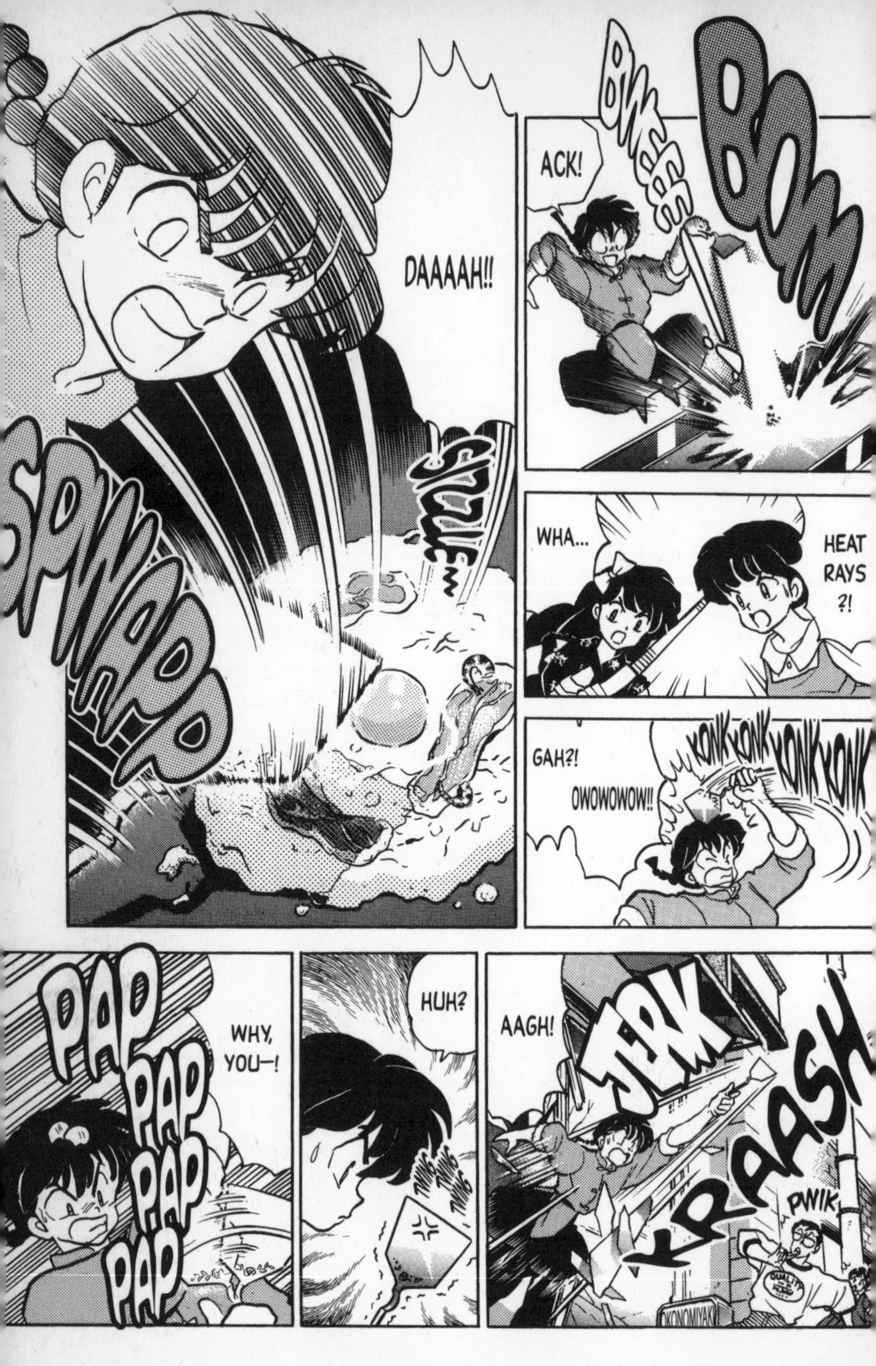
DAAAAH!!
ACK!
BOOM
WHA...
HEAT RAYS ?!
GAH?!
OWOWOWOW!!
KONK KONK KONK KONK
PAP PAP PAP PAP PAP
WHY, YOU—!
HUH?
AAGH!
JERK
KRAASH
PWIK
OKONOMIYAKI

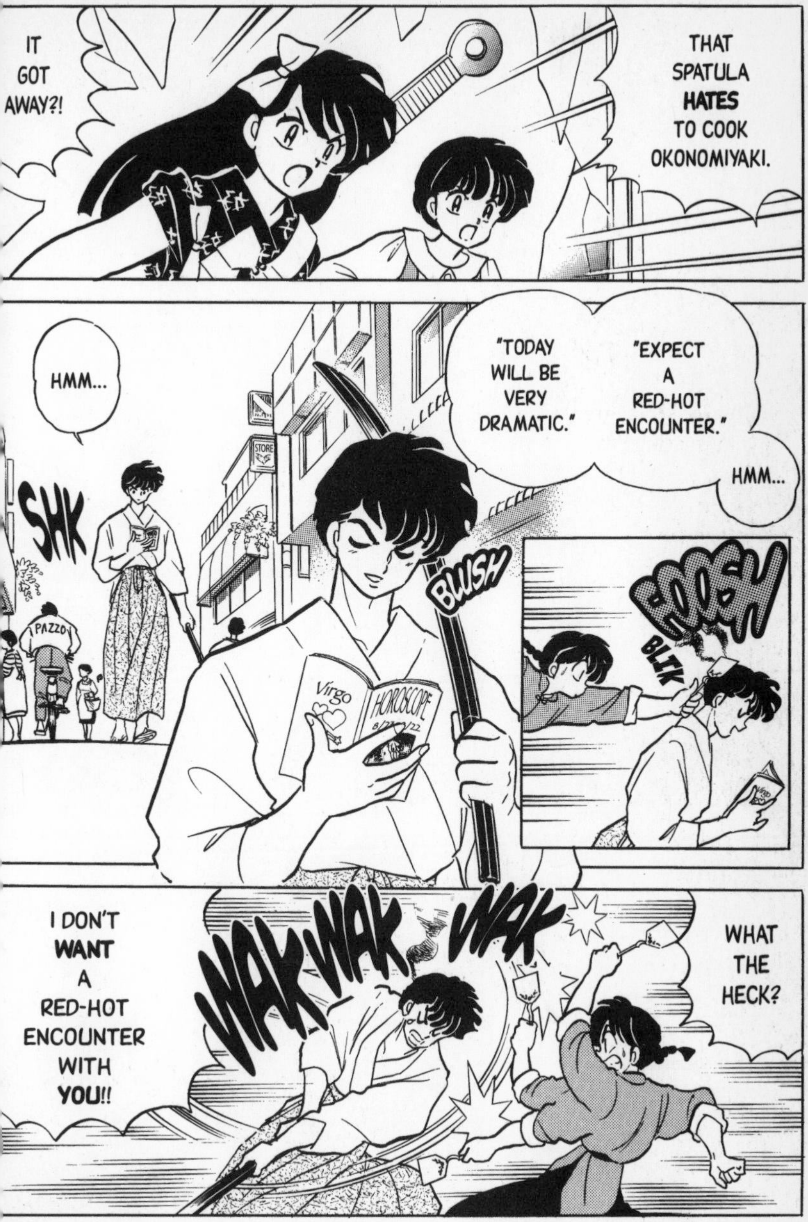
IT GOT AWAY?!
THAT SPATULA HATES TO COOK OKONOMIYAKI.
HMM...
SHK
PAZZO
STORE
"TODAY WILL BE VERY DRAMATIC."
"EXPECT A RED-HOT ENCOUNTER."
HMM...
BLUSH
Virgo
HOROSCOPE
FOOSH
BLIK
I DON'T WANT A RED-HOT ENCOUNTER WITH YOU!!
WAK WAK WAK
WHAT THE HECK?

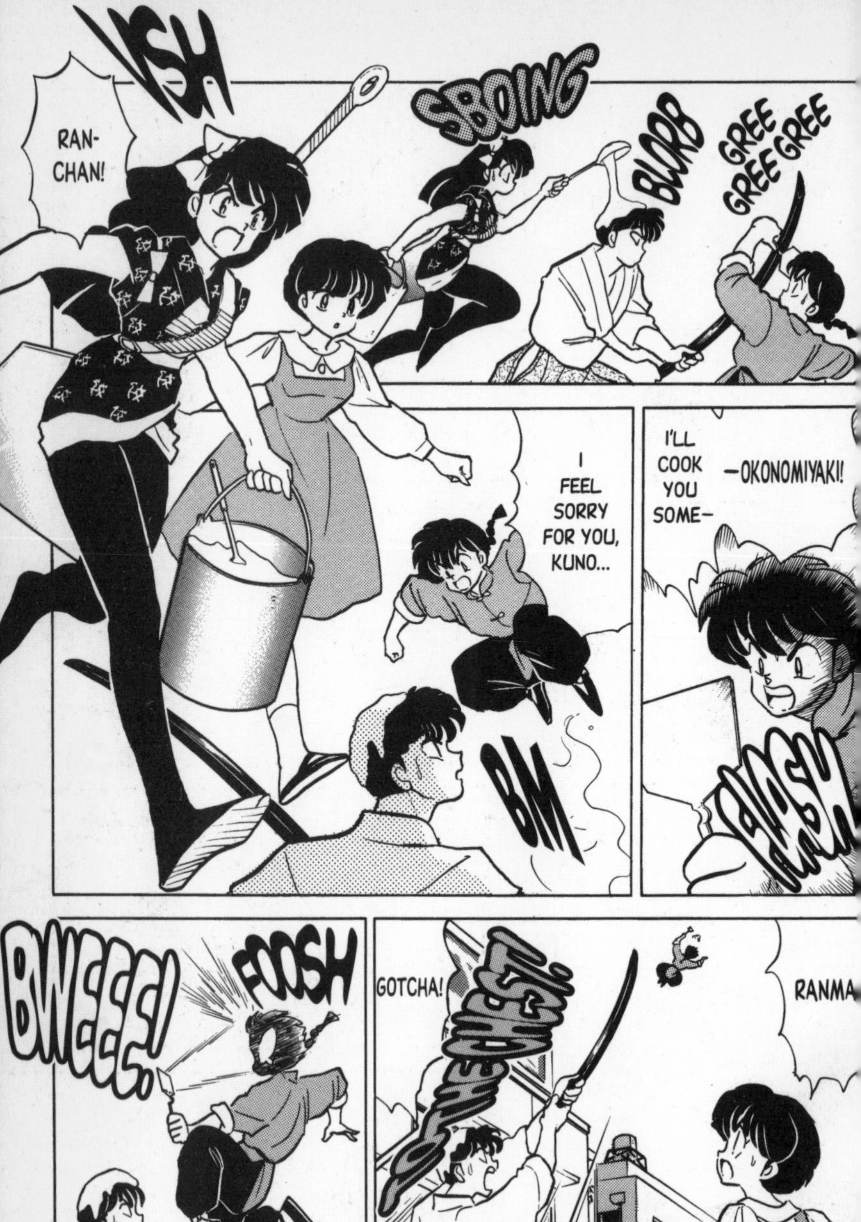
VSH
RAN-CHAN!
SBOING
BLORB
GREE GREE GREE
I FEEL SORRY FOR YOU, KUNO...
BM
I'LL COOK YOU SOME—
—OKONOMIYAKI!
BWEEEE!
FOOSH
GOTCHA!
RANMA

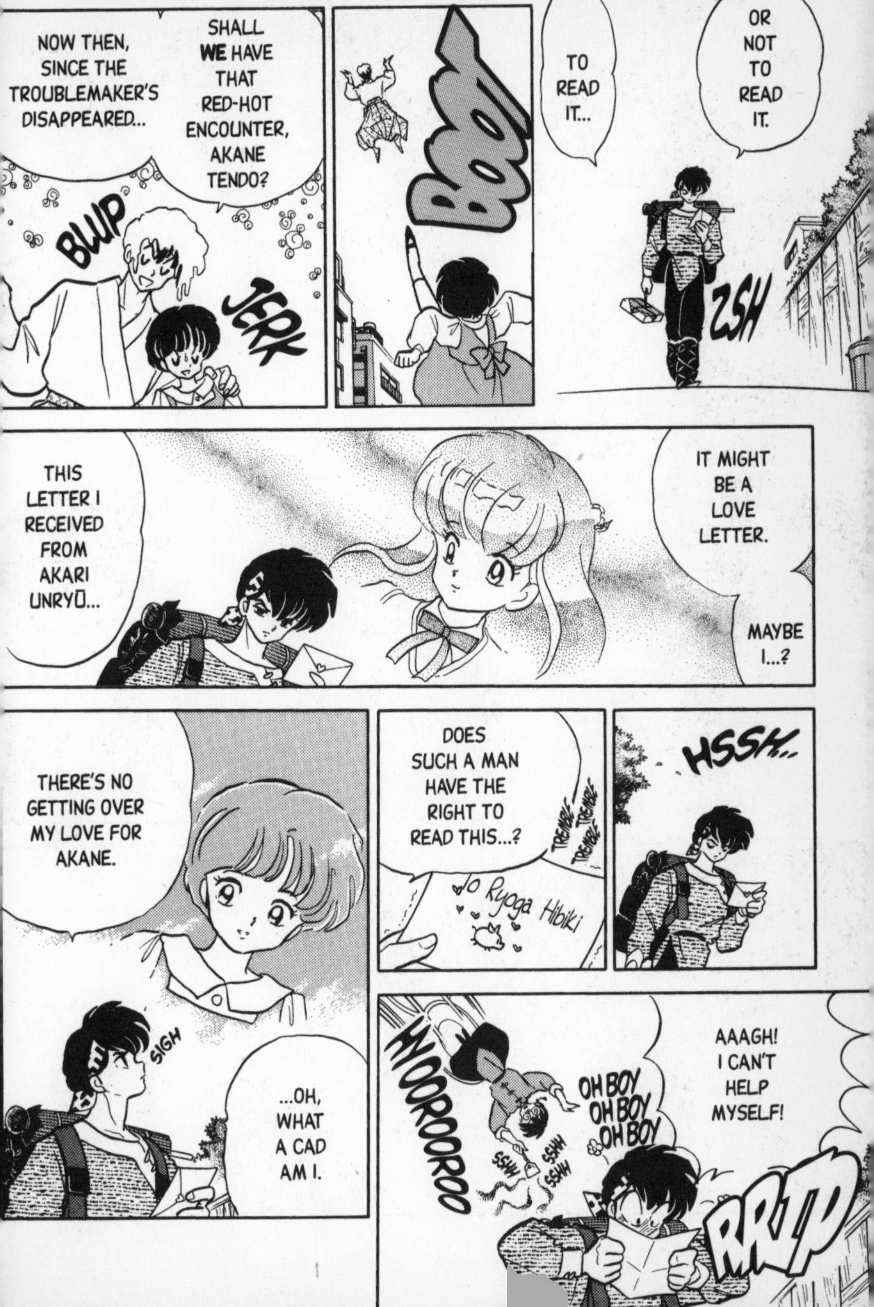
NOW THEN, SINCE THE TROUBLEMAKER'S DISAPPEARED...
SHALL WE HAVE THAT RED-HOT ENCOUNTER, AKANE TENDO?
BLUP
JERK
BOOT
TO READ IT...
OR NOT TO READ IT.
ZSH
THIS LETTER I RECEIVED FROM AKARI UNRYŪ...
IT MIGHT BE A LOVE LETTER.
MAYBE I...?
THERE'S NO GETTING OVER MY LOVE FOR AKANE.
SIGH
...OH, WHAT A CAD AM I.
DOES SUCH A MAN HAVE THE RIGHT TO READ THIS...?
TREMBLE TREMBLE TREMBLE
To Ryoga Hibiki
HSSH...
WOOROOROO
SSHH SSHH SSHH
OH BOY OH BOY OH BOY
AAAGH! I CAN'T HELP MYSELF!
RRIP

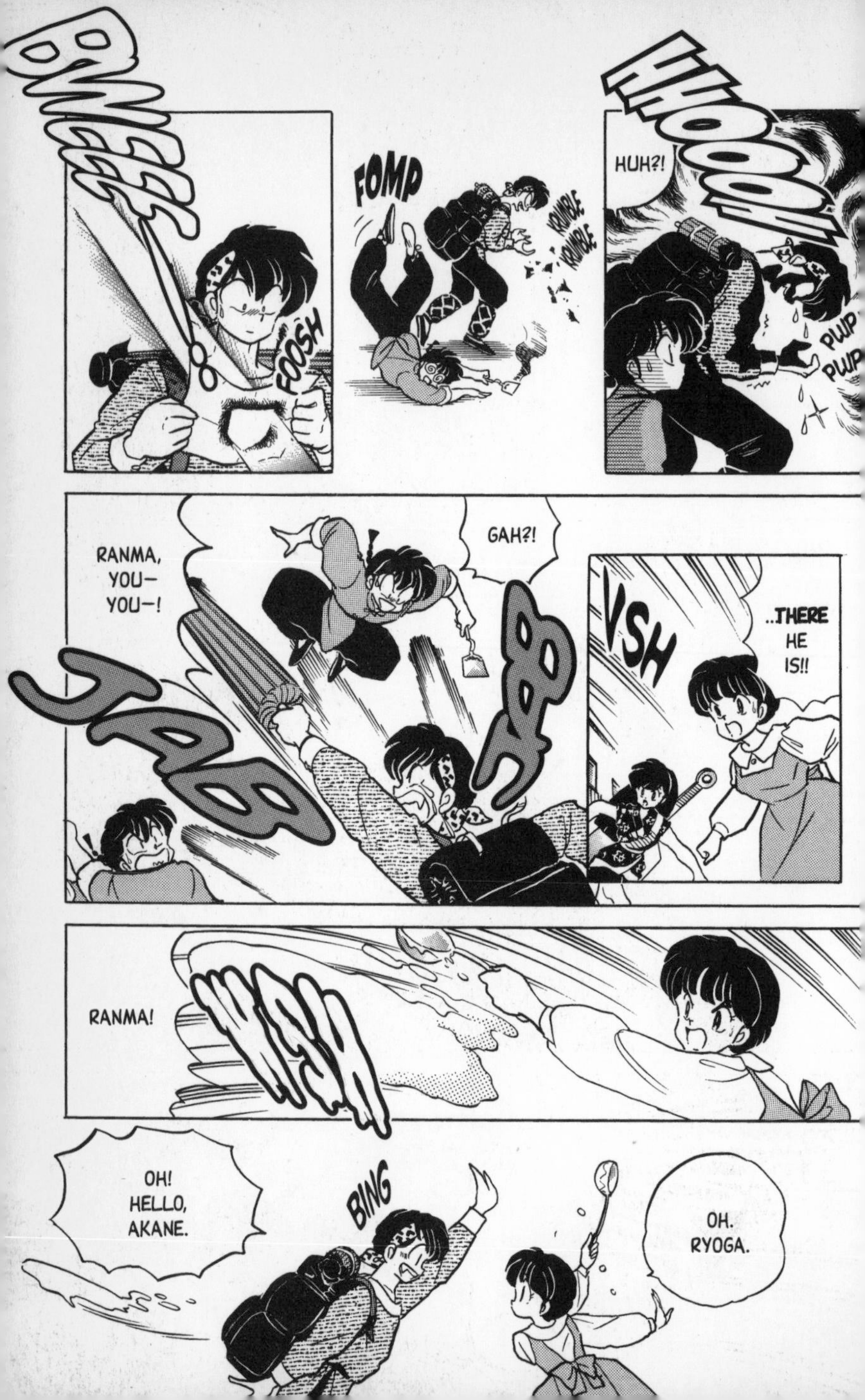

BWEEEE
FOOSH
FOMP
RUMBLE RUMBLE
WHOOOH!!
HUH?!
PWIP PWIP
RANMA, YOU— YOU—!
GAH?!
JAB
VSH
...THERE HE IS!!
RANMA!
OH! HELLO, AKANE.
BING
OH. RYOGA.

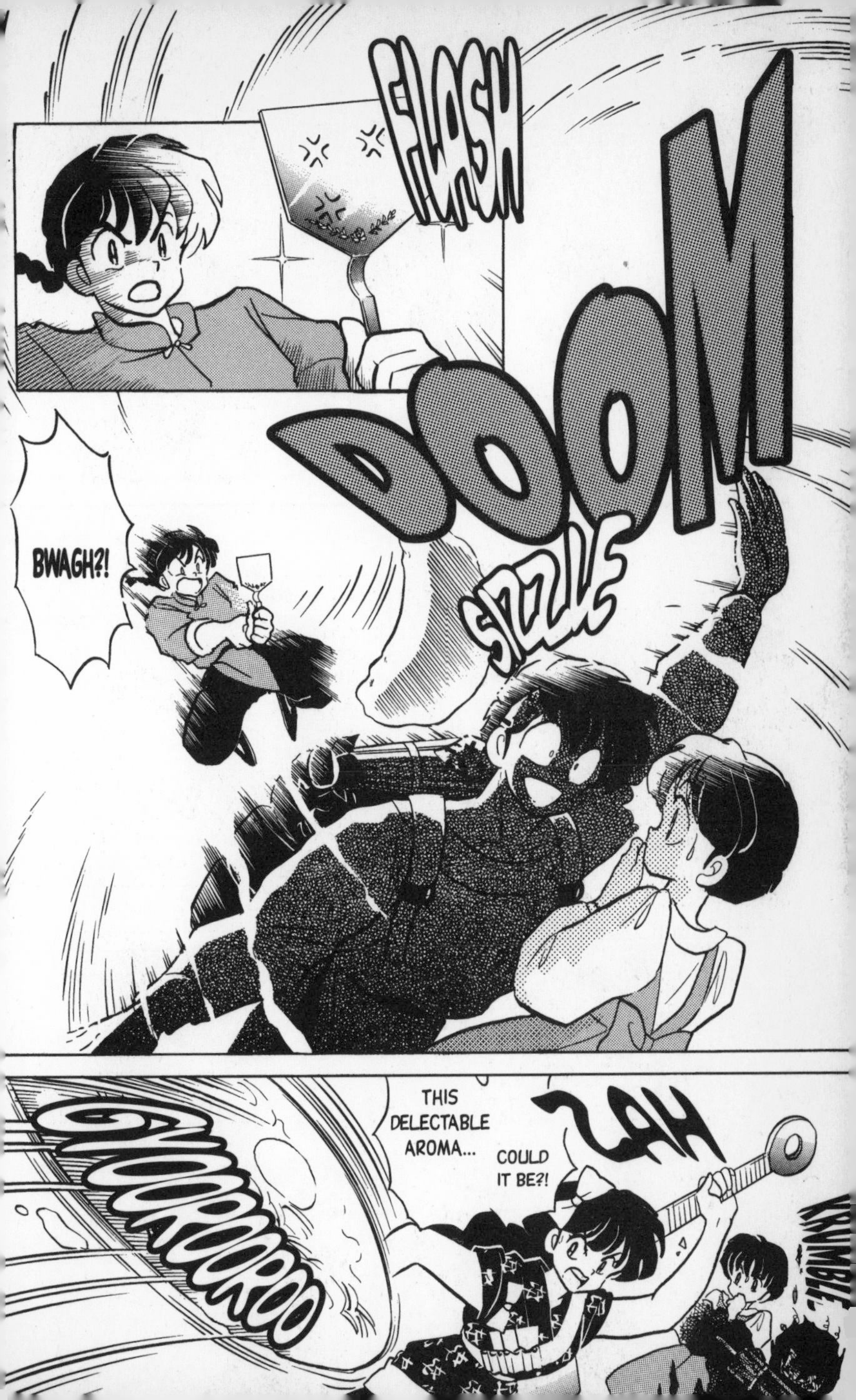
FLASH
DOOM
BWAGH?!
SIZZLE
GYORORORORO
THIS DELECTABLE AROMA...
ZAH
COULD IT BE?!
KRUMBLE

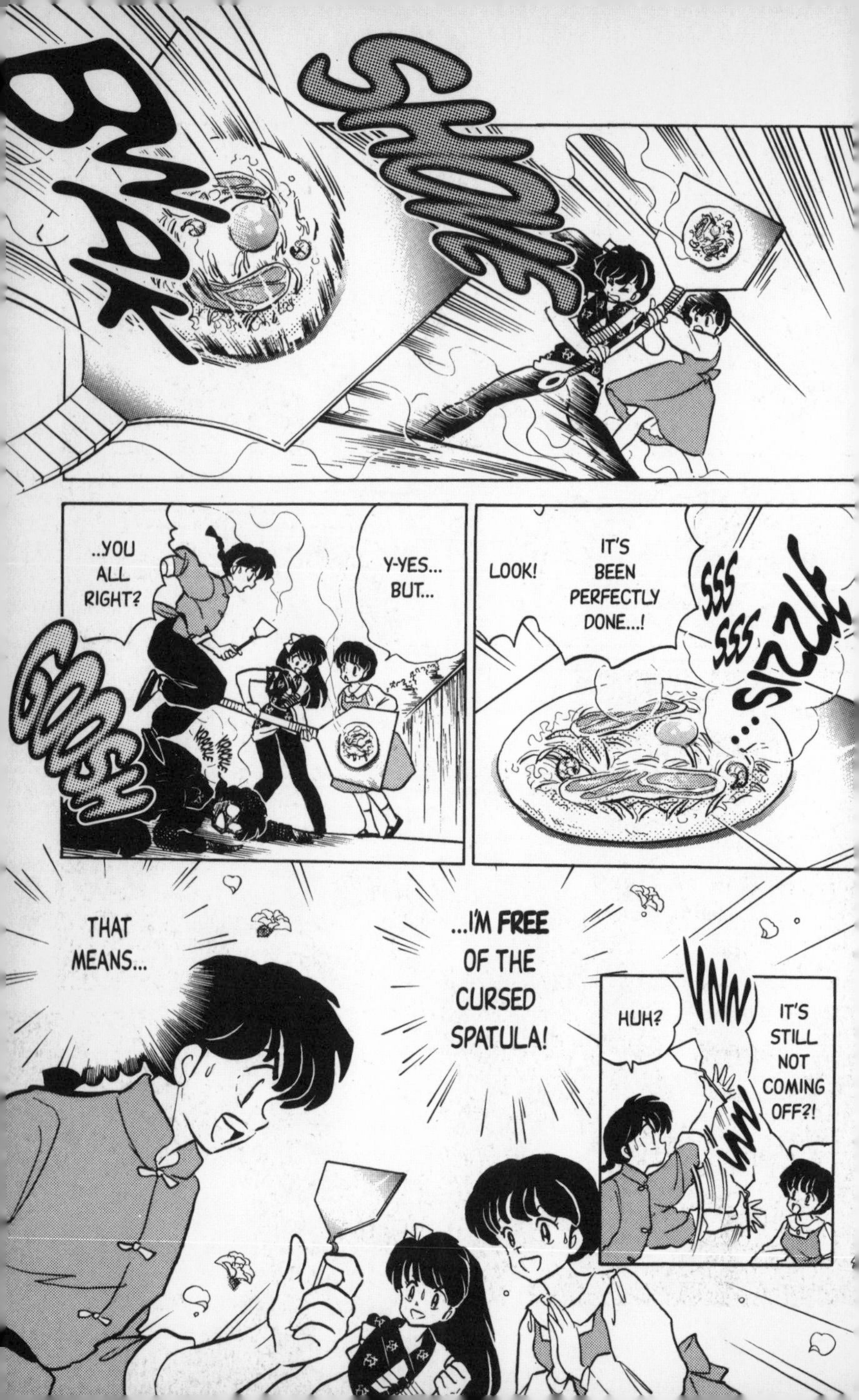
BWAK
SHOVE
..YOU ALL RIGHT?
GOOSH
KRACKLE KRACKLE
Y-YES... BUT...
LOOK!
IT'S BEEN PERFECTLY DONE...!
SSS SSS
...SIZZLE
THAT MEANS...
...I'M FREE OF THE CURSED SPATULA!
HUH?
VNN
IT'S STILL NOT COMING OFF?!
VNN

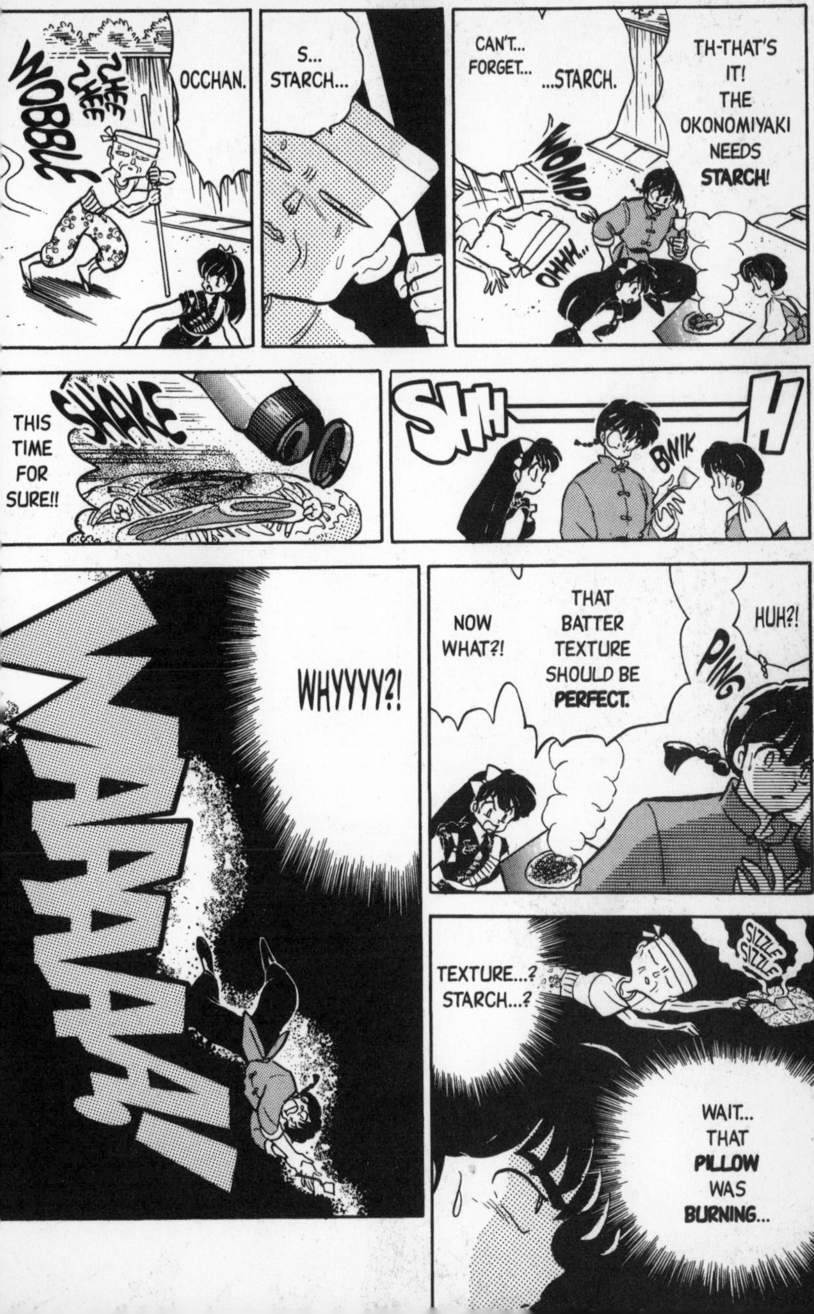

WOBBBLE
THEE THEE
OCCHAN.
S...
STARCH...
CAN'T... FORGET...
...STARCH.
WOMP
OHHH...
TH-THAT'S IT! THE OKONOMIYAKI NEEDS STARCH!
THIS TIME FOR SURE!!
SHAKE
SHHH
BWIK
WAAAAAAH!
WHYYYY?!
NOW WHAT?!
THAT BATTER TEXTURE SHOULD BE PERFECT.
HUH?!
PING
TEXTURE...? STARCH...?
SIZZLE SIZZLE
WAIT... THAT PILLOW WAS BURNING...

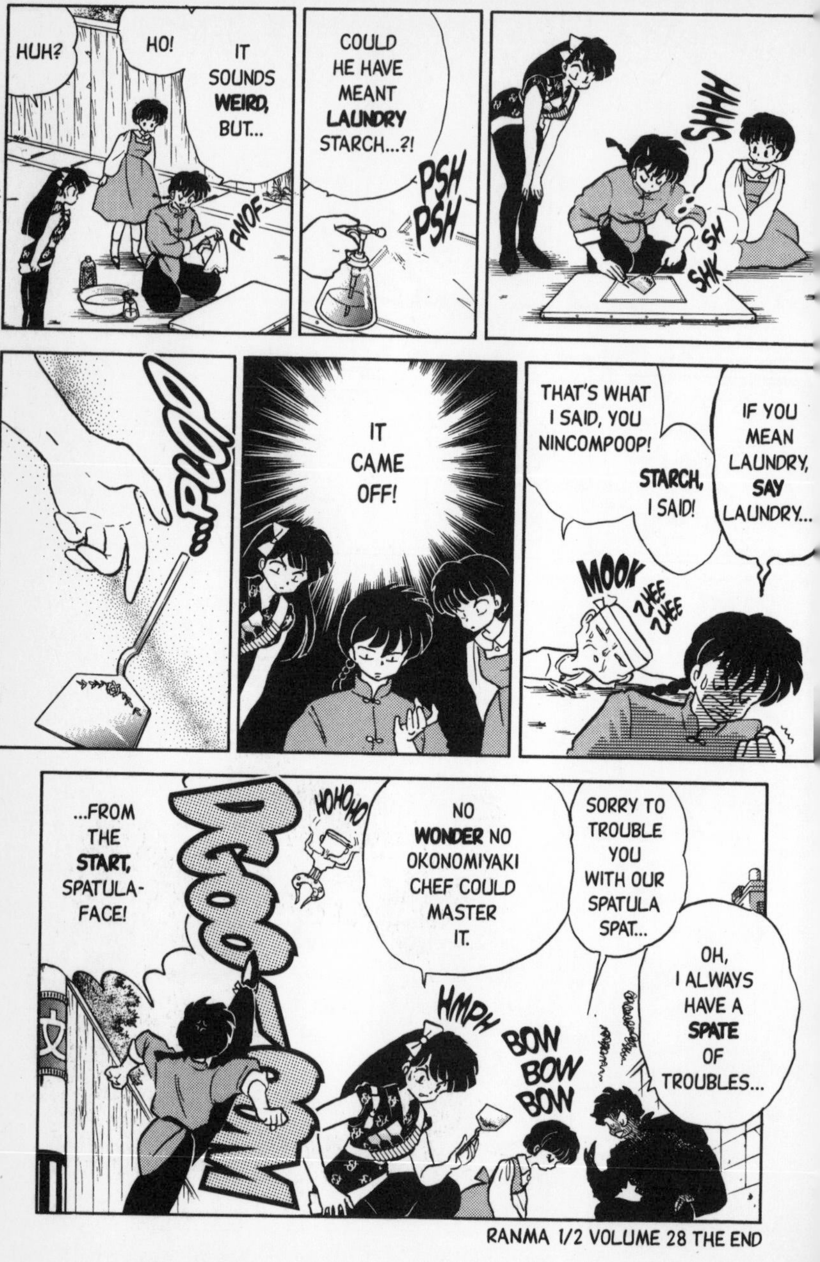
HUH?
HO!
IT SOUNDS WEIRD, BUT...
FWOF
COULD HE HAVE MEANT LAUNDRY STARCH...?!
PSH PSH
SHHH
SH SHK
DOINK...
IT CAME OFF!
THAT'S WHAT I SAID, YOU NINCOMPOOP!
STARCH, I SAID!
IF YOU MEAN LAUNDRY, SAY LAUNDRY...
MOOK
ZHEE ZHEE
...FROM THE START, SPATULA-FACE!
DOOOM
HOHOHO
NO WONDER NO OKONOMIYAKI CHEF COULD MASTER IT.
SORRY TO TROUBLE YOU WITH OUR SPATULA SPAT...
OH, I ALWAYS HAVE A SPATE OF TROUBLES...
HMPH
BOW BOW BOW

RANMA 1/2 VOLUME 28 THE END

About Rumiko Takahashi

Born in 1957 in Niigata, Japan, Rumiko Takahashi attended women's college in Tokyo, where she began studying comics with Kazuo Koike, author of CRYING FREEMAN. She later became an assistant to horror-manga artist Kazuo Umezu (OROCHI). In 1978, she won a prize in Shogakukan's annual "New Comic Artist Contest," and in that same year her boy-meets-alien comedy series URUSEI YATSURA began appearing in the weekly manga magazine SHÔNEN SUNDAY. This phenomenally successful series ran for nine years and sold over 22 million copies. Takahashi's later RANMA 1/2 series enjoyed even greater popularity.

Takahashi is considered by many to be one of the world's most popular manga artists. With the publication of Volume 34 of her RANMA 1/2 series in Japan, Takahashi's total sales passed one hundred million copies of her compiled works.

Takahashi's serial titles include URUSEI YATSURA, RANMA 1/2, ONE-POUND GOSPEL, MAISON IKKOKU and INUYASHA. Additionally, Takahashi has drawn many short stories which have been published in America under the title "Rumic Theater," and several installments of a saga known as her "Mermaid" series. Most of Takahashi's major stories have also been animated, and are widely available in translation worldwide. INUYASHA is her most recent serial story, first published in SHÔNEN SUNDAY in 1996.

EDITOR'S RECOMMENDATIONS

© 2001 Rumiko Takahashi/Shogakukan,
Inc. © Rumiko Takahashi/Shogakukan,
Yomiuri TV, Sunrise 2000
Ani-Manga is a trademark of VIZ, LLC

INU YASHA ANI-MANGA

The story you've come to love using actual frames of film in full color from the TV and video series *Inuyasha!*

©1988 Rumiko Takahashi/Shogakukan, Inc.

MERMAID SAGA

This is the series Rumiko Takahashi created as her "hobby." Unpressured by editors and deadlines, she lets her creativity flow in this romantic-horror epic. Eating the flesh of a mermaid grants eternal life. But living forever can be a blessing or a curse. Immortal lovers Yuta and Mana are relatively lucky...others who partake of the mermaid's flesh are transformed into savage lost souls!

©1997 Rumiko Takahashi/Shogakukan, Inc.

INUYASHA

When high-school student Kagome is transported back in time to Japan's feudal era, she accidentally releases the feral half-demon dog-boy Inu-Yasha from his imprisonment for stealing the "Jewel of Four Souls." But after a battle with fearsome demons, the jewel has been shattered and its countless shards scattered all over Japan. Now, bound together by a spell, Inu-Yasha and Kagome must join forces to reclaim the jewel and its terrifying powers from demons and mortals alike that would use it as a tool of unspeakable evil!

Your Favorite Rumiko Takahashi Titles...Now Available From VIZ!

Complete your collection with these Takahashi anime and manga classics!

Get yours today!

www.viz.com

INUYASHA™

...ted #1 on Cartoon
...twork's Adult
...vim!

In its
original
unedited
form.

DOWN THE WELL
INUYASHA

maison ikkoku™

...e beloved romantic
...medy of errors—a fan
...vorite!

ranma ½™

...e zany, wacky study
...martial arts at its
...st!

COMPLETE OUR SURVEY AND LET US KNOW WHAT YOU THINK!

☐ Please do NOT send me information about VIZ products, news and events, special offers, or other information.

☐ Please do NOT send me information from VIZ's trusted business partners.

Name: _____

Address: _____

City: _____ **State:** _____ **Zip:** _____

E-mail: _____

☐ Male ☐ Female **Date of Birth (mm/dd/yyyy):** __ / __ / __ (Under 13? Parental consent required)

What race/ethnicity do you consider yourself? (please check one)

☐ Asian/Pacific Islander ☐ Black/African American ☐ Hispanic/Latino

☐ Native American/Alaskan Native ☐ White/Caucasian ☐ Other: _____

What VIZ product did you purchase? (check all that apply and indicate title purchased)

☐ DVD/VHS _____

☐ Graphic Novel _____

☐ Magazines _____

☐ Merchandise _____

Reason for purchase: (check all that apply)

☐ Special offer ☐ Favorite title ☐ Gift

☐ Recommendation ☐ Other _____

Where did you make your purchase? (please check one)

☐ Comic store ☐ Bookstore ☐ Mass/Grocery Store

☐ Newsstand ☐ Video/Video Game Store ☐ Other: _____

☐ Online (site: _____)

What other VIZ properties have you purchased/own? _____

How many anime and/or manga titles have you purchased in the last year? How many were VIZ titles? (please check one from each column)

ANIME	MANGA	VIZ
☐ None	☐ None	☐ None
☐ 1-4	☐ 1-4	☐ 1-4
☐ 5-10	☐ 5-10	☐ 5-10
☐ 11+	☐ 11+	☐ 11+

I find the pricing of VIZ products to be: (please check one)

☐ Cheap ☐ Reasonable ☐ Expensive

What genre of manga and anime would you like to see from VIZ? (please check two)

☐ Adventure ☐ Comic Strip ☐ Science Fiction ☐ Fighting
☐ Horror ☐ Romance ☐ Fantasy ☐ Sports

What do you think of VIZ's new look?

☐ Love It ☐ It's OK ☐ Hate It ☐ Didn't Notice ☐ No Opinion

Which do you prefer? (please check one)

☐ Reading right-to-left
☐ Reading left-to-right

Which do you prefer? (please check one)

☐ Sound effects in English
☐ Sound effects in Japanese with English captions
☐ Sound effects in Japanese only with a glossary at the back

THANK YOU! Please send the completed form to:

NJW Research
42 Catharine St.
Poughkeepsie, NY 12601

All information provided will be used for internal purposes only. We promise not to sell or otherwise divulge your information.